Hoping that you enjoy
this iconic example of Russia's
Cold War power — it's not quite the
Great European novel, but it should be
an interesting read!

Alan
OCT 2007

TUPOLEV TU-22

TUPOLEV TU-22

RUSSIA'S PIONEERING SUPERSONIC BOMBER

Sergey Burdin and Alan Dawes

Pen & Sword
AVIATION

First published in
Great Britain in 2006
By Pen & Sword Aviation
An imprint of Pen and Sword Books Ltd
47 Church Street
Barnsley
South Yorkshire
S70 2AS
England

ISBN 1 84415 241 3

A CIP record for this book is available from the British Library.

Typeset in the UK by Mac Style, Nafferton, E. Yorkshire.
Printed and bound in Singapore by Koyodo.

Pen & Sword Books Ltd incorporates the imprints of Pen & Sword Aviation, Pen & Sword Maritime, Pen & Sword Military, Wharncliffe Local History, Pen & Sword Select, Pen & Sword Military Classics and Leo Cooper.

For a complete list of Pen & Sword titles please contact
Pen & Sword Books Limited
47 Church Street, Barnsley, South Yorkshire, S70 2AS, England
E-mail: enquiries@pen-and-sword.co.uk
Website: www.pen-and-sword.co.uk

Contents

Acknowledgements

The author, Sergey Burdin, wishes to take this opportunity to express his gratitude to the many friends and colleagues who have helped in the creation of this book. In the first instance, however, I wish to thank the staff of the A.N. Tupolev Design Bureau (www.tupolev.ru) for the great understanding shown towards the aim of this work. Invaluable help was extended to me by Col Sergey Yelisyeyev, a former lecturer in the military faculty of the Moscow Institute for Civil Aviation Engineers, who taught a course there for reserve officers assigned to serve in the Tu-22 fleet. The book would not be so richly illustrated were it not for the generous assistance extended to the author in the 1990s by the Commander of 121 Heavy Bomber Regiment, Col Viktor Podtykalov, who graciously permitted photography of his regiment's aircraft at Machulishchi in that period. At the same time I should like to express sincere gratitude to the pilots and navigators of 121 TBAP for access to their archive material and personal recollections of flying the Tu-22. It is a great pleasure to list them by name: Section Commander (*Komandir Otryada*), Maj Gennady Klepikovskii; Deputy Squadron Commander, Lt-Col Eduard Kozinyets; Squadron Navigator, Major Aleksey Konoryev; Section Commander, Major Sergey Serikov, and Senior Pilot, Major Yuri Fut'yanov. Former air and ground crew of 203 TBAP at Baranovichi played a significant part in providing the historical perspective of operating the Tu-22K missile-carrier. These included the Deputy Regiment Commander, Lt-Col Aleksandr Ignatov; the Deputy Regiment Commander for Engineering Services, Lt-Col Nikolai Rachkov; Head of Second-line Servicing (TEhCh), Major Igor' Kozlov; and the Head of Demolition at 6213 Aviation Disposal Base at Engel's, Aleksandr Kostyetskii.

I also wish to express my gratitude to 'veterans' of 290 ODRAP at Zyabrovka for their archive material and personal recollections, which have enlivened the pages of this book. Particular thanks in this regard are extended to Squadron Commanders, Lt-Col Aleksandr Yerusenko and Lt-Col Mikhail Chernyshev, along with Senior Crew Chief, Major Mikhail Ivashutin. Separately, I also wish to offer special thanks to former Tu-22 airborne operator, Major Ivan Khvorost for his active help over the many years of my research of the aircraft. I have used several photographs in the book provided by my aviation history colleagues, Alfred Matusyevitch, a former Inspector in the Air Army HQ in L'vov in the Ukraine, and Valery Romanenko, a journalist with the Ukrainian magazine *Voysko Ukrainy*. Thanks to their generosity I have been able to include photographs of the Tu-22 in service with 341 TBAP and 199 ODRAP, which were based on Ukrainian territory. Another of my colleagues, aviation historian and photographer Sergey Tsvetkov, provided photographs from his archive, including those depicting the Tu-22R in Soviet Naval Air Force service, for which I am very grateful. To conclude, I wish to acknowledge the great contribution made by all those who created, tested and operated the Tu-22, without whose involvement there would not have been a story to tell about this fascinating aircraft. Finally, translator and co-author Alan Dawes would also like to take this opportunity to thank his friend Stu Clay and his colleagues at BAE Systems at Warton in Lancashire for clarification of certain technical and electronics queries arising during translation.

Translator's Comment

For the benefit of readers who know Russian, the more important abbreviations in the text have been expanded and transliterated to give a better understanding of certain items of equipment, or their function. The transliteration 'system' used has been chosen to enable the reader to read and pronounce the word as accurately as possible, without any pretension to it being a Russian language guide. Wherever possible, given the difficulties of providing a literal equivalent of some Russian (Cyrillic) letters in English, the original 'shape' of the Russian word has been retained, including the use of the apostrophe mark (') to represent the Russian 'soft sign' placed after certain letters. (The effect of this is to soften the sound of the preceding letter, but proper discussion of this feature of Russian is beyond the scope of this book.) I hope that inclusion of these transliterated items within the text will be more useful to the reader than a glossary at the end of the book. Alan Dawes

Map showing locations of Soviet Long-range Air Force Tu-22 bases and their associated weapons ranges. *Sergey Burdin*

Introduction

The subject of this book was once one of the most feared and respected, albeit imperfectly understood, Soviet Air Force adversary facing NATO in the darkest period of the Cold War. In fact, there has perhaps never been a military aircraft in recent history which has given rise to so many 'legends' and so much speculative analysis as Tupolev's formidable Tu-22 *Blinder*. In no small way this was due to the heavy cloak of secrecy which enshrouded everything about Soviet society and its military institutions, making the Tu-22 no less mysterious to the inquisitive outsider than the Egyptian pyramids were to early explorers! This was not helped by the practice at the time for Western defence analysts to attribute greater capability and performance to Russian weapons in a perverse attempt to exaggerate the threat 'from the East' and so encourage 'retaliatory' defence spending. Now, using material accumulated after more than ten years of research, Sergey Burdin provides us with the opportunity to take a more reasoned look at this fascinating aircraft and reassess its true position in the history of military aviation. Much of the material is based on Soviet Ministry of Defence archive material, which was declassified in 1993–4 by the General Staff of the Russian Federation Air Force, augmented by Sergey Burdin's own archive data.

Using this material, we have attempted to examine the Tu-22 objectively, neither embellishing its merits, nor resorting to unjustified criticism of its failings. We hope that after reading the book the reader will be better able to judge the often tenuous comparisons between the Tu-22 and its US counterpart, the Convair B-58 Hustler, frequently found in books and magazine articles over the years. In spite of its shortcomings, the Tu-22 was clearly the more successful of these two pioneering supersonic bombers, outliving its American rival by more than two decades and only being retired from service in the mid-1990s. With a take-off weight similar to that of the Tu-16, its more conventional stablemate, the supersonic Tu-22 exhibited almost fighter-

A Tu-22PD in close formation with the leader, the distance between the two aircraft being no more than 20m (65ft). *S Burdin Archive*

like performance and allowed the Soviet Air Force's long-range aviation branch to develop a number of operational tactics which were, hitherto, the natural province of tactical aviation. Equally importantly, it also gave this vital component of Russia's deterrent force a significant head start in the operation of large supersonic bombers. Today, the benefits of that early experience are still being exploited by the crews flying the Tu-22's descendants – the Tu-22M3 *Backfire-C* and the Tu-160 *Blackjack* supersonic bombers.

In addition to a wealth of new factual information about the Tu-22, the value of the book as a work of reference is enhanced by the personal recollections of the pilots, navigators, airborne operators and engineers who devoted their lives to the aircraft. These provide the English-speaking reader with a unique opportunity to discover at first hand what it was like to fly one of Russia's most prestigious combat aircraft in the psychologically demanding conditions of the Cold War.

By definition, bombers are unglamorous aircraft, usually only possessing a singular destructive purpose, but the Tu-22 openly contradicts this definition by also being one of the most graceful-looking combat aircraft ever built. It is thought provoking to consider, moreover, that it was never called upon to be used 'in anger' by the Soviet Air Force, its purpose as an offensive weapon being fulfilled instead by its value as a deterrent force.

Of the 104 Tu-22s struck off charge and transferred to 6213 Aircraft Disposal Base at Engel's up to the end of 1994, only six remain: one aircraft is displayed in front of the garrison HQ at Engel's, a second was put on display in Saratov, at the request of the city's Governor, while the other four are displayed at the Museum of the Long-range Air Force at Engel's airfield. These are, of course, in addition to the aircraft already exhibited at Monino, just outside Moscow and at Ryazan'. We hope that our book will now give wider access to this historically important aircraft from the comfort of the armchair, and possibly inspire visits to see the few remaining examples in the museums mentioned above.

Sergey Burdin
Minsk, Belarus', November 2004
Alan Dawes MRAeS
Cambridgeshire, England, November 2004

Tu-22 Variants

Tu-22A	Blinder-A	Soviet
Tu-22A Variant B	Blinder-A	Iraq/Libya
Tu-22K	Blinder-B	
Tu-22KD	Blinder-B	
Tu-22KDP	Blinder-B	
Tu-22KPD	Blinder-B (Variant)	
Tu-22P	Blinder-E	
Tu-22P1	Blinder-E1	
Tu-22P2	Blinder-E2	
Tu-22P4	Blinder-E	
Tu-22P6	Blinder-E	
Tu-22P7	Blinder-E	
Tu-22PD	Blinder-E	
Tu-22R	Blinder-C	
Tu-22RD	Blinder-C	
Tu-22RDK	Blinder-C (Variant)	
Tu-22RDM	Blinder-C2	
Tu-22RDM-2	Blinder-C2	
Tu-22RM*	Blinder-C (Variant*)	
Tu-22U	Blinder-D	

All the variants are described in detail in the text, but for convenience a brief explanation is also given here:

The suffix 'K' in Tu-22K stands for *Kompleks*, i.e. the entire system of aircraft, missile and control systems of this specialised missile-carrying *Blinder-B* variant.

The suffix 'D', short for *Dal'nii* (long-range), for all aircraft indicates an air-to-air refuelling capability.

The suffix 'P' in Tu-22KPD stands for *Protivo-radiolokatsionnyi* (literally anti-radar) and was the specialist anti-radiation missile-equipped variant of the *Blinder-B*.

The suffix 'P' in all the Tu-22P variants stands for '*Postanovshchik Pomyekh*' (literally producer of interference), the numbered variants being explained in detail in the text.

The suffix 'R' stands for '*Razvyedchik*' (literally military scout) and describes all the reconnaissance variants of the aircraft.

The suffix 'K' in Tu-22RDK stands for *Kub* (cube), the specialised Elint system fitted to twelve modified Tu-22RD aircraft at Zyabrovka.

The suffix 'M' in Tu-22RDM stands for *Modifitsirovannyi* (modified).

---

* A small number of Tu-22R aircraft were modified as 'strike reconnaissance systems', receiving the designation Tu-22RM, although these aircraft were only ever used in trials and did not enter service with the Soviet Air Force.

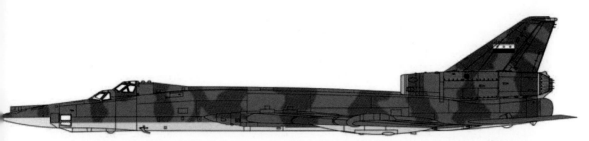

In spite of access to disabled Iraqi Tu-22s by coalition forces after the 2003 war in Iraq, precise information is still not available on the camouflage colours worn by Iraqi Air Force *Blinders*, the green/brown pattern on this Tu-22U being more demonstrative than definitive. Although some Iraqi *Blinders* are known to have carried the air force's triangular symbol on the rear fuselage, without a serial, the national flag on the fin was usually the only sign of identity carried by these bombers. *Sergey Sidorenko*

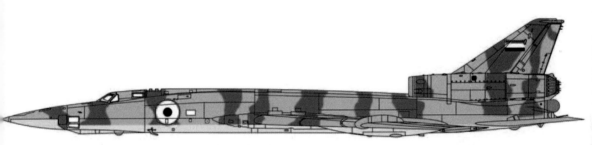

This Libyan Air Force Tu-22A Variant 'B' illustrates the location of the red-white-black roundel valid at the time of delivery in 1975. Serial numbers are not thought to have been assigned to any of the Libyan Tu-22 fleet, at least none that were externally visible. *Sergey Sidorenko*

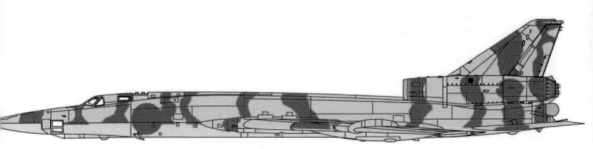

As with Iraqi *Blinders*, details of the actual camouflage colours of the aircraft operated by Libya are not known and those illustrated should be regarded as notional, rather than definitive. In 1977 Libya changed its name to the Socialist Libyan Arab Peoples Jamahiriya and adopted a plain green flag, (signifying devotion to Islam), as its national emblem and used in roundel form to identify Libyan military aircraft and helicopters. The roundel on Libyan Tu-22A Variant 'B' bombers is possibly one of the largest ever worn by a modern military aircraft. *Sergey Sidorenko*

The Tu-22U (*Uchebnyi*) was the training variant, and although later aircraft were modified to carry an in-flight refuelling probe, they were not 'plumbed' to receive fuel and were used solely as procedural trainers. (The designation Tu-22U**D** is, therefore, erroneous.)

Although the original NATO codename *Blinder* is used throughout the text of the book, it is a less effective way of describing the numerous variants of the Tu-22 covered, since many sub-variants were never allocated a designating letter or number. The codenames have only been used in the book to avoid ambiguity or unnecessary repetition of the Russian designation.

CHAPTER ONE

Development History of the Tu-22

Any work dealing with the introduction of the Tu-22 into the Long-range Aviation regiments of the Soviet Air Force must first of all consider the personality of General Designer Andrei Nikolayevich Tupolev himself. Tupolev was considered by many to be a true genius of aeronautics, who commenced his life in aviation in Tsarist times alongside Igor' Sikorsky, another of Russia's famous aircraft designers and a world-renowned helicopter pioneer. Like many geniuses, Tupolev was self-assured, ambitious and possibly even a little authoritarian, but highly respected by friends and colleagues. He was well known before the Second World War for his heavy aircraft designs, but during the war Tupolev became a victim of the widespread Stalinist repression of the time and ended up in prison. [*Stalin's purges of the Soviet Air Force and the Soviet aircraft industry, designed to eliminate all military and political opposition to his dictatorship, are really the subject of a separate study. However, it is relevant to mention here that Andrei Tupolev was arrested on the quite astonishing suspicion of having supplied Germany with information enabling Messerschmitt personnel to design the Bf 109 and Bf 110 fighters! Some sources have suggested that as many as four hundred and fifty aircraft designers, engineers and other specialists were interned under Stalin's orders between 1934 and 1941, of whom around three hundred were set to work in NKVD-supervised design bureaux. It is also thought that about a hundred senior aviation industry personnel died in labour camps and at least fifty were executed. AD*]

It was while he was a prisoner in the Special Technical Department of the People's Committee for Internal Affairs (STO NKVD – *Spetsial'nyi Tekhnicheskii Otdyel Narodnovo Komiteta Vnutrennikh Dyel*) that he designed the well-known and elegant Tu-2 (*Bat*) light bomber. (The NKVD was, of course, the predecessor of the universally feared KGB – *Komitet Gosudarstvennoy*

Andrei Tupolev (1888-1972) in his office in the 1960s. Tupolev was a legendary figure who led his design bureau with great skill and concern for his staff, surrounding himself with a highly talented team to create some of Russia's most important civil and military aircraft of the Soviet era. *OKB Tupolev*

Bezopasnosti, or Committee for State Security). After release from imprisonment he was once again allowed to run his own design bureau, and with the war now ended, the Soviet Union needed new heavy bombers to carry the nuclear weapons which underpinned Russia's post-war defence philosophy. Tupolev was full of bold ideas with which to meet this need, but his ambitious dreams clashed with Stalin's continuing distrust of the designer, and the Communist Party leader instead assigned Tupolev the task of creating a copy of the American Boeing B-29 to spearhead Russia's new bomber force. (*Three B-29s had fallen into Russian hands intact, after making forced landings on Soviet territory in 1944, following bombing raids on Japanese targets*). Tupolev's resulting copy of the B-29 became the Tu-4 *Bull*, and was built in spite of Tupolev's attempts to convince Stalin that he could create a much more modern and advanced aircraft than one based on the US design. The decision was deeply wounding to Tupolev's pride, but the end of the 1940s was a difficult period for many Russian design bureaux, and under Stalin's arbitrary rule many of them were closed down while new ones, acceptable to the dictator's whim of the moment, were opened up.

Thus, at the end of the 1950s, the Sukhoi Design Bureau was also closed down, and the vast majority of Sukhoi designers ended up in OKB-156, led by Andrei Tupolev. Still in these less than ideal conditions, under the continuing shadow of Stalin's interference, OKB-156 carried out work on the development of a truly modern nuclear-capable bomber, the twin-jet Tu-16 *Badger*. However, at the same time, Tupolev's pride was dealt yet another blow. In 1951, by order of the Ministry of Aircraft Production (MAP), a new design bureau, OKB-23, led by Vladimir Myasishchev, was formed specifically to design long-range strategic bombers, hitherto the 'province' of Tupolev himself. In order to staff the new design bureau a large number of designers were transferred by order of the MAP from Tupolev's OKB-156 to the newly created OKB-23. Particularly damaging to Tupolev was the fact that the design teams working exclusively on undercarriages and hydraulic systems were transferred from OKB-156 to OKB-23 in their entirety.

Therefore, the two design bureaux ended up struggling somewhat unequally for the right to design the long-range strategic bomber necessary for the Soviet Union to implement its post-war defence plans for an air-delivered nuclear capability. The first large jet bomber accepted for service was, not surprisingly in the circumstances, the four-engined Myasishchev M-4 *Bison*, and Tupolev had to 'pull out all the stops' to promote his own submissions for this role – the twin-jet Tu-16 *Badger* and the four-engined Tu-95 *Bear* four-turboprop bombers. This was the situation when the Soviet government declared a competition for the design of a supersonic long-range bomber, and Tupolev, probably wishing to exact a certain revenge for his less than honourable treatment, hurriedly set to work on designing the new aircraft. The first direction taken in pursuit of this objective was to develop the basic 'theme' of the Tu-16, in the guise of Aircraft '103', powered either by four VD-7 turbojets developed by V.A. Dobrynin (OKB-36), or AM-13s developed by A. Mikulin.

However, quite early in the preliminary design stage, it became obvious that it would not be feasible to develop a supersonic bomber based on the general layout of the Tu-16, so the OKB-156 design team set to work on an entirely new aircraft. The designers were possibly encouraged by the example of Myasishchev's team, which had designed 'quite a good bomber' (the M-4 *Bison*) in a relatively short time frame and practically from a 'blank sheet of paper'. After examination of a range of preliminary projects within the OKB-156 design offices, a design offered by a team under the leadership of Sergey Mikhailovitch

Yeger (1914–87) was accepted for development. Yeger, a future corresponding member of the Academy of Sciences of the USSR, a Doctor of Technical Sciences and Hero of Socialist Labour, had commenced his aerospace career in 1932 at the world-renowned Central Hydro-dynamics Institute (*Tsentral'nyi Aero-gidrodinamicheskii Institut – TsAGI*) at Zhukovskii. Then, from 1933, he worked at Factory 39 as a designer and then as head of a general design team, and completed his aeronautical studies in 1936 at MAI (Moscow Aeronautical Institute). In 1938 he was arrested by the NKVD and was forced to work in the NKVD's special technical office (TsKB-29) with A.N. Tupolev in a general design team engaged in the design of the Tu-2 (PB – *Pikiruyushchii Bombardirovshchik*) dive-bomber and its derivatives. In 1943 Yeger was appointed Head of the Department of Technical Projects of the Tupolev OKB, and from that moment practically all aircraft carrying the 'Tu-' designation resulted from the creative inspiration at Yeger's desk and drawing-board. It was he and his department colleagues who decided, in the initial stages of the existence of any project for a new Tupolev aircraft, how it should look and perform. Sergey Yeger was the 'author' of all of Tupolev's post-war aircraft designs and, in

Sergey Mikhailovitch Yeger (1914–1987), principal designer of the Tu-22 and 'architect' of the successful introduction to service of this, the Soviet Union's first supersonic medium bomber. Alongside Tupolev himself, Yeger was the inspirational force behind most of Tupolev's post-war heavy aircraft projects. *OKB Tupolev*

addition, devoted much time to questions regarding the operational use of Tupolev aircraft by the Soviet Air Force. It was thanks largely to Yeger that it was possible for the OKB to resolve many problems relating to the effective operation of Tupolev's integrated aircraft and missile systems, and much credit goes to him for the creation of the Tu-22 family and its development into the Tu-22M *Backfire* (Tu-106).

Sergey Yeger's project for Aircraft '105' (the prototype of the Tu-22 *Blinder*) was adopted as the Tupolev candidate to be the Soviet Union's first supersonic long-range bomber, although the '105' had been preceded by Aircraft '98', an earlier unsuccessful supersonic tactical bomber project. In spite of not going into operational service, Aircraft '98' served as a very useful exemplar for the resolution of design problems relating to the larger supersonic bomber. Aircraft '105' was unique at the time in the history of aviation in the former USSR, and indeed in the rest of the world. 'On paper' the design was rather undistinguished, described in typically understated Soviet terms as being 'a cantilevered mid-set swept-wing aircraft, with a tailplane of normal configuration, a tricycle undercarriage and two afterburning turbojets'. However, what did distinguish the '105' from all other preceding bomber designs was that huge improvements in on-board electronics systems had enabled the designers to reduce the crew complement to three men – pilot, navigator and radar operator. The entire crew was housed in a single common pressurised cabin, where all essential conditions for normal flight operations were controlled automatically (i.e. temperature and pressure, etc.). Reduction of the crew size, by dispensing with the need for a second pilot, had both a political impact and an aerodynamic benefit in that the fuselage cross-section could be reduced, which greatly simplified the problem of pressurising the cockpit section. The same route was followed by OKB-23 in the design of the (unsuccessful) M-50 *Bounder* delta-winged strategic bomber. The State Committee for Aviation Technology (*Gosudarstvennyi Komitet po Aviatsionnoy Tekhniki* – GKAT), forerunner of the Ministry for Aircraft Production, approved the design of the '105', allowing work to start without delay.

The '105' was created in extremely difficult circumstances. Three years earlier in 1954, a document entitled 'General Technical Requirements of the Air Force' (*Obshchiye Tekhnicheskiye Trebovaniya Voenno-vozdushnykh Sil* – OTT VVS) had been drawn up for the Tu-16. The OTT VVS for the Tu-16 contained observations and recommendations relating to the aircraft's introduction to service, which would be embodied subsequently in the aircraft's flight operations and servicing manuals. However, no such document existed for a newly built aircraft, still in the early flight test stage, which led to long discussions between the customer (a Soviet-era euphemism for the Soviet military) and the developer, concerning the appearance and layout of the future supersonic bomber. These discussions dwelt particularly on the question of defensive cannon armament, the Tu-16's four such weapons perhaps being seen as the baseline standard for self-defence. The most weighty problem for consideration, however, turned out to be the achievement of supersonic speed. Even the Soviet jet fighter force was still only at the threshold of the supersonic era, and the TsAGI and LII (*Lyotno-Ispytatyel'nyi Institut* – Flight Test Institute) personnel had only just started to study the behaviour of fighter aircraft at transonic and supersonic speeds. This little-researched area of aerodynamics was still shrouded in mystery and hid many puzzles from researchers. Yet another huge problem at this time was the provision of a suitable powerplant. Three types of engine were proposed for the new aircraft, two of which, the VD-5 and the VD-7, were close to entering series production under the supervision of V.A. Dobrynin's OKB-36, albeit only the VD-7 had actually demonstrated the level of thrust required. The third engine, the Kuznetsov NK-6, exhibited the best potential performance, but was only at the preliminary development stage. As a consequence of the possible shortfall in available engine power for the '105' it was decided to exploit all existing possibilities to achieve supersonic performance.

In the first instance, it was decided to use a thin 'clean' wing, with a sweep angle at the quarter chord line of 52°–55° and main undercarriage bogies which retracted into the fuselage, only the main legs retracting into the wings in order to preserve aerodynamic 'cleanliness'. Research conducted at this time on the Lavochkin La-160 by engineers and designers at the LII at Zhukovskii revealed that an aircraft with a swept wing and tailplane showed a tendency to 'pitch up' at speeds around Mach 1. Evidently, the Tupolev design team decided to mount the engines above the fuselage in order to compensate for this pitching moment at transonic and supersonic speeds. Apart from this, such an engine location resulted in the achievement of a lower overall drag coefficient, and the short intake ducts of the engine nacelles permitted internal pressure losses to be reduced to a minimum. Unfortunately, this particular airframe layout was unlikely to impart very good take-off and landing performance, and as a consequence it was decided to base the aircraft only at 'first-class' airfields. (This is usually taken to mean airfields with a concrete runway of at least 3,000m/9,840ft length). At the time it was the inevitable price to pay for the achievement of the performance demanded by the Soviet government for the new generation of supersonic bombers. The other important features of the new bomber, the integral pressure cabin, crew life support systems and new emergency escape systems, were all developed jointly, with OKB-156 working closely with industry and the Scientific Research Institutes of the Soviet Air Force. At the time, the majority of Soviet Air Force bomber regiments were still equipped with the piston-engined Tu-4 *Bull*, and yet the same design bureau was now preparing to introduce a supersonic bomber to the Long-range Air Force. In August 1957, the first prototype of Aircraft '105' was handed over to the Flight Test and Development Base (*Lyotno-Ispytatyel'naya I Dovodochnaya Baza*) of OKB-156 at Zhukovskii, although it was almost a further year before OKB-156 test pilot Yuri Alasheyev was able to complete its maiden flight, on 21 June 1958.

Flight testing of the first prototype revealed that it was not going to be possible to achieve the required speed performance with the aircraft as configured, and the 'struggle for speed' and, therefore, for the large State order for the new bomber, continued. It was unthinkable to fall behind in any way. So, at the same time as carrying out flight tests of the first prototype, OKB-156 engineers continued to work on the design and construction of a second prototype – Aircraft '105A', which embodied a number of significant design changes. These changes affected the pressure cabin, the tail and central fuselage areas, the wing and the tailplane. The main objective of all the changes was to increase the attainable speed by any means possible. Thus, in order to reduce drag at transonic and supersonic speed, the aircraft was built in accordance with the principles of the then recently described 'area rule', a concept originally elaborated by Richard Whitcomb of NACA (more widely known by its later redesignation as NASA). (*The 'area rule' is a rather complex mathematically-derived engineering procedure, albeit with the simple objective of reducing an aircraft's drag at transonic speeds. In essence, this requires the aircraft's cross-sectional shape, including wings and fuselage, to change shape as 'slowly' as possible in order to reduce the number and power of locally generated supersonic shock waves*). The wing root of the '105' was too deep to exploit adequately the requirements of the 'area rule', so it was reduced on the '105A' by adopting a different design for the undercarriage. The main undercarriage was now made to retract fully into cigar-shaped fairings 'set' into the wing trailing edge, similar to those used on the Tu-16, and the tail section was changed to accommodate defensive armament consisting of:

• A trainable 23mm cannon installation comprising a 261P cannon, controlled by a PRS-3 gun-laying radar, with an associated TP-1A television sight (camera) for rear hemisphere protection
• An SPO-3 (Sirena-3) 360-degree radar warning receiver to inform the crew that they were being illuminated by enemy fighter radars.

The wing and tailplane were selected from high-speed profiles of low thickness–chord ratio (6%) with a wing loading of 602kg/m^2 (123lb/sq ft), and along with other measures resulted in the achievement of a drag coefficient of 0.040. The wing was given a relatively high aspect ratio (for a swept wing) of 3.7 in order to obtain good long-range performance, its aerodynamic efficiency being improved by the adoption of –4° of conical twist. The chosen wing design of the '105A' led to the achievement of a very respectable lift–drag ratio in cruising flight of 11.5. Slotted flaps were employed as the wing's principal high-lift devices, the inner flaps deflecting to 35° and the outer sections deflecting to 20° for take-off and landing. Wind tunnel tests revealed that the angle of attack at which stall would occur with flaps down was 14° 30′ and the maximum angle of attack to which the aircraft could be taken on take-off or landing was 12° 33′ (limited by the tail skid contacting the runway), giving a 2° margin in these conditions.

The maiden flight of the newly modified '105A' took place on 7 September 1959, enabling flight tests to be carried out simultaneously with two aircraft – '105' and '105A'. Nevertheless, the first stage of State tests of Aircraft '105' probably confirmed in Tupolev the belief that the development path of these supersonic aircraft was leading to a 'dead end'. Using the chosen aerodynamic layout and engines, it seemed that the maximum potential of the aircraft had already been reached and little else could be done to improve it. 'I do not think (*Sergey Burdin's comment*) that it is correct to say, as some would have it, that Tupolev regarded the "105A" project rather like an unwanted child.' Nevertheless, it was evident that Andrei Tupolev intuitively understood, after the first few test flights of the '105', that neither a scientific nor a technological knowledge base yet existed in the Soviet Union for the creation of this class of aircraft. The era of new technologies and extensive knowledge and understanding of the dynamics and aerodynamics of supersonic flight had not yet arrived, but the General Designer continued work on this 'theme' (i.e. the supersonic bomber project), while devoting much of his attention to other programmes. These were the more promising programmes for the creation of large strategic bombers (i.e. the Tu-95 family) and civil aircraft for Aeroflot – the civil air fleet of the USSR. This was a perfectly reasoned view to take, since these projects would be guaranteed considerable financial backing by the Soviet government and promises of long-running State orders. Tupolev would only return to the subject of producing a new supersonic long-range bomber in earnest after a further seven or eight years.

In the first half of the 1950s, the LII at Zhukovskii had been conducting research into the stability and control of swept-wing aircraft at supersonic speeds. The flight tests involved the use of the MiG-17 *Fresco* fighter (capable of Mach 1.17) in 1952, a MiG-17NBU with hydraulically boosted elevators and ailerons in 1954 and a MiG-19V *Farmer-B* (capable of Mach 1.46) in 1956. Among the LII test pilots involved in this research was Yuri Alasheyev, and his experience in supersonic flight was one of the main reasons for his being invited to join the Tupolev team at OKB-156. However, in spite of the high-speed research programmes being performed by the LII, design of the control systems of Aircraft '105' was being carried out virtually blindfold. At that time the behaviour of lightweight fighters at supersonic speeds was insufficiently well understood, and research into the performance of supersonic bombers had certainly not been planned. The error of such an approach to the design of a large supersonic aircraft was exacerbated by the fact that the heads of the design teams at OKB-156 did not have access 'to the outside world'. In this case the 'outside world' was not what lay beyond the Soviet Union, but simply the Scientific Research Institutes of the Soviet Air Force and other Soviet aircraft design bureaux! Consequently, the Tupolev team had to go through the exercise of 'reinventing the wheel', and everything that had been discovered in designing supersonic fighters had to be 'rediscovered' by the Tupolev designers – a costly and wasteful process. As a consequence of this lack of shared knowledge between the fighter design community and Tupolev as a bomber specialist, the Tupolev designers ended up using an adjustable tailplane with elevators for pitch control, when it had already been established that this combination was inadequate for supersonic flight. The entire pitch control system of the new aircraft was virtually analogous to that used on the subsonic Tu-16, but after the destruction of the first prototype (Aircraft '105') on 21 December 1959, killing test pilot Yuri Alasheyev and navigator I Gavrilenko, significant changes were made to the flight control system of the remaining prototype.

Tests had shown that during the transition to supersonic flight the effectiveness of all flying controls was greatly reduced, while the hinge moment was significantly increased. So the '105A' was fitted with an all-moving tailplane in place of the ineffective tailplane and elevators used on the first prototype. It was decided, therefore, that all channels of the flight control system (pitch, roll and yaw) should be modified to incorporate non-reversible hydraulic actuators, although it was not easy to find a suitable actuator for the tailplane. At the time, there were only two types readily available, the first being the unit installed on the Myasishchev M-4 *Bison*, which satisfied the requirement in terms of power, but was too big and too heavy. The second type was the actuator used at the time on fighter aircraft, which was smaller and lighter, but insufficiently powerful for a large supersonic bomber. It would have been impossible to wait for the development of an entirely new actuator since it would have taken too long and could have led to the cancellation of the programme. An eventual solution to the problem came quite unexpectedly, and its originality was absolutely typical of the style of Andrei Tupolev. He decided to use an actuator from the dive-vane controls of one of the Soviet Navy's diesel submarines, which experienced the same type of hinge moment as that of the tailplane of the '105A'! After some small changes the RP-21 actuator was installed in the second prototype.

Also in 1959, Dmitryi Sergeyevitch Markov (1905–92) was appointed leading designer of the Aircraft '105A' project. Markov began his aviation career in 1928, and while still a student at the Moscow Higher Technical University (MVTU) was sent to work in Factory N1 as a design engineer, completing his aviation studies at MVTU in 1930. From 1931 he worked as head of the design department at Factory N1, and then from 1932 as Chief Designer. During his employment at Factory N1 he was involved in the design and introduction to service of the Polikarpov I-7 (licence-built Heinkel He-37) and R-5 series of aircraft and their various derivatives. In 1938 he was arrested by the NKVD and sent to work at the OTB NKVD, where he worked on the design of the '100', '102' and '103' series of aircraft, and from 1941 worked with Andrei Tupolev

Dmitri Sergeyevitch Markov (1905–92) was Tupolev's chief designer closely involved with the introduction of the Tu-4 *Bull*, design of the Tu-16 *Badger* and Tu-98 *Backfin* and leading designer of the '105' project leading to the Tu-22 and, ultimately, the Tu-22M *Backfire. OKB Tupolev*

The first prototype of 'Aircraft 105', showing its resemblance to the eventual Tu-22, but differing in the nose area and more significantly, in the inward-retracting main undercarriage. *OKB Tupolev*

as Deputy Chief Designer, participating in the development and introduction to service of the Tu-2 (*Bat*). In 1947 Markov was appointed Deputy Chief Designer responsible for the service introduction of heavy aircraft (bombers), and led the work on development and release to service of the Tu-4 *Bull* and its eventual operation by the Soviet Air Force. From 1949, as Chief Designer, he led the programme which resulted in the construction of the Tu-16 and its derivatives, and then later led the design work on the Tupolev OKB's first supersonic aircraft, the Tu-98 *Backfin*. (Later still, he was to lead the design project which resulted in the creation of the Tu-22M *Backfire* variable-geometry supersonic bomber, but that was much later....) The Soviet government was heavily involved at the time in internal discussions about the future of its defence policy, believing that this lay more in the realm of missile defences than in the deployment of large bombers. Since it was the Soviet leader Nikita Khrushchev who had put forward these ideas, rumours about possible reductions in the size and composition of the Soviet Air Force were very real and could not be ignored.

However, in spite of the rumours, the test period for the '105A' was extended, and it was decided to proceed to the second stage of State tests (i.e. in-service trials) as soon as possible. The State Committee for Aviation Technology (GKAT) and the Soviet Air Force understood that introducing such a complex aircraft would be fraught with difficulties, and even before the completion of the first stage of State trials it was decided to lay down the first batch of twenty 'series-production standard' aircraft at Factory 22 at Kazan' in the present-day Tatarstan Republic. This procedure was quite common for Soviet Air Force procurement programmes and had been adopted for the introduction of the Tu-4 and the Tu-16. It was around this time that confusion arose about the naming of the new aircraft, since like the Tu-16, which had been given the 'private' (*zakrytyi*) designation of Tu-16A, the new bomber received the 'private' designation of Tu-22A. ('Private' in this context is a category akin to secret, but probably meaning something like 'for internal eyes only'.) However, in the established rule of the Soviet era, the aircraft was also given the 'open' (*otkrytyi*) designation of 'Article Yu', which could be used in non-classified (i.e. non-secret) documents. [*Evidently, the letter Yu was a purely arbitrary choice and did not signify anything in particular. AD*]. Nevertheless, this first variant of the bomber was often referred to as 'the Tu-22 variant B' (i.e. B for *Bombardirovshchik*, or bomber), which led to the appearance of the incorrect designation of this variant as Tu-22B in some reference sources. [*This was the second use of the designation Tu-22 and was clearly unrelated to the Type '82' (Tu-22 2VK-1) experimental tactical bomber, the first Russian 'heavy' bomber with a swept wing, which made its maiden flight on 24 March 1949. SB*]

Everything relating to the new bomber project then followed the established routine, but in the same year (1959), an event was to occur which would have a profound influence on the future of the Soviet Air Force and on the ultimate 'destiny' of the Tu-22A. In that year, a new branch of the Armed Forces was created, namely the Strategic Rocket Forces (*Raketniye Voiska Strategicheskovo Naznacheniya* – RVSN), equipped with long-range ballistic missiles, comprising twenty-nine 'aviation' regiments, subordinated to three Air Armies. Tupolev understood very well that in these newly emerging circumstances, the Soviet government would probably not provide the Soviet Air Force with finance for the purchase of a new bomber, however much the service wanted it. Indeed, all interested parties backing the procurement of the Tu-22A also understood that the government, promoting the development of the new force, would be unwilling to expend valuable resources on such 'outdated and unpromising means of delivery of nuclear weapons' as aircraft. A rather subtle subterfuge was adopted by OKB-156 and the Soviet Air Force in order to rescue the Tu-22 from potential oblivion. The OKB-156 design team decided to offer the Air Force not just a bomber, but also a long-range supersonic reconnaissance platform which could be re-roled as a bomber by ordinary squadron personnel. Looked at from the sidelines this seemed to be a very reasonable, and indeed reasoned, proposition. A long-range supersonic reconnaissance aircraft was actually needed at that time, and the government was, evidently, ready to allocate procurement funds. Tupolev's solution fully satisfied the 'customer' (i.e. the Soviet Air Force) since the service would then receive a dual-role aircraft. The same approach had been adopted in the procurement of the Tu-16 and had been found acceptable, with a number of sub-variants providing the Soviet Air Force with a very useful multi-role platform.

However, in the case of the Tu-22, designed from the outset purely as a supersonic bomber, it would have had to undergo significant design changes and new flight tests, already behind schedule, in order to satisfy the proposed dual-role criterion. The main problem which had been encountered during flight testing of the Tu-22 was not the aircraft's equipment, but its performance and inadequate engine power. In terms of performance, the first problem related to the aircraft's complex aerodynamics, particularly affecting its behaviour at transonic and supersonic speeds, and the second was the VD-7M engine, which still exhibited a number of design deficiencies and, like the aircraft itself, was still under development. Added to all of this was the problem of guaranteeing that Soviet Air Force crews could quickly master operation of the Tu-22 in the regiments. At that time, even Soviet Frontal Aviation (i.e. tactical) fighter units had only just entered the supersonic era, and for the bomber crews of the Long-range Air Force the aircraft was truly revolutionary! Therefore, with the joint efforts of the 'customer', in the form of the Soviet Air Force itself, GKAT and OKB-156, it was decided to commence the second phase of State flight testing of the aircraft, with Tu-22As which were already being built in Factory 22 at Kazan'.

At this point it is perhaps appropriate to mention briefly the system used in the former Soviet Union in the procurement and formal acceptance for service of military aircraft and helicopters. Before an aircraft could be accepted for service, it had to undergo two stages of State flight testing. The first stage, which was carried out by the design bureau concerned, under the auspices of the Ministry for Aircraft Production (MAP), involved a series of general tests designed to evaluate the aircraft's performance and whether it corresponded to the 'customer's' stated requirements and specifications. These tests were conducted at the design bureau's own Flight Test and Development Base, the majority of which was located at the LII airfield at Zhukovskii on the southern outskirts of Moscow. Part of the testing could thus involve LII and TsAGI personnel, if required. After the aircraft had demonstrated performance close to that specified by the Soviet Air Force, it would then be transferred to an operational regiment where it would undergo pre-service acceptance trials (*Voiskoviye Ispytaniya* – literally 'troop trials'). These would constitute the second stage of State trials, with one or two regiments being selected as the first recipients of the new aircraft and the units involved being described as 'Leader Regiments'.

For this phase of testing, support teams and specialists from the design bureau and the relevant manufacturing plants would be permanently assigned to the 'Leader Regiment' to assist the air and ground crews to convert onto the new aircraft. While seconded to the air force regiment, the OKB and factory specialists would maintain contact with designers and engineers 'back at base' so that they could eliminate, in the shortest possible time and with expert advice, any defects noted during the operational trials. Simultaneously with the regimental trials, the aircraft's weapons would be evaluated in trials conducted by the State Scientific Research Institute (*Gosurdastvennyi Nauchno-ispytatyel'nyi Institut* – GNII) at Vladimirovka airfield, near Akhtubinsk, at the mouth of the River Volga. The Soviet Air Force Combat Application Centres (*Tsentr Boyevovo Primenyeniya* – TsBP), operated by the Long-range Air Force, Frontal Aviation and Naval Aviation as operational conversion units (OCU), would also participate in the 'troop trials'. After passing this stage of testing, the aircraft was usually accepted for service, with appropriate modifications where necessary, and the authorising Certificate (of Airworthiness) was signed. Under this system, by the time an aircraft had been formally accepted for service, it could well have been operated by the Air Force for several years. This often surprises aviation enthusiasts and students of Russian military aviation, but to a Russian, there was nothing strange or unusual about the procedure.

Delivery of the first Tu-22As commenced in 1962 to the 203rd Heavy Bomber Aviation Regiment (203 *Tyazholobombardirovochnyi Aviatsionnyi Polk* – 203 TBAP), subordinated to the 6th Independent Heavy Bomber Aviation Corps (6 *Otdyel'nyi Tyazholobombardirovochnyi Aviatsionnyi Korpus* – 6 OTBAK), this regiment being based at Baranovichi in the then Byelorussian Soviet Socialist Republic. (Following the collapse of the Soviet Union, the Byelorussian SSR became the independent Republic of Belarus'.) In the same year a squadron of Tu-22As was transferred from 203 TBAP to the 290 Independent Long-range Reconnaissance Aviation Regiment (290 *Otdyel'nyi Dal'nyerazvyedyvatyel'nyi Aviatsionnyi Polk* – 290 ODRAP), based at Zyabrovka, near Gomel', also in the Byelorussian SSR. These two regiments thus became the 'Leader Regiments' for the Tu-22's pre-service acceptance trials. The second stage of State trials proved very difficult since neither industry nor the Soviet Air Force was anywhere near ready to introduce a heavy supersonic bomber into operational service. Insufficient knowledge of the stability and control problems of the aircraft in the transonic and supersonic flight regimes led to service personnel having a very negative approach to the Tu-22. Moreover, to issue this aircraft to an ordinary squadron pilot was fraught with potential danger since he would not have the test pilot's experience to cope with unexpected handling problems in these flight regimes, which were entirely new for the long-range bomber force. The first batch of aircraft lacked the device which was later to become an inseparable part of the flight control systems of all supersonic aircraft. Because the control system was non-reversible, the pilot did not feel any loading from the tailplane, and the absence of such sensations led him to make pitch control inputs which could easily lead to excessively large, even destructive, g-loading of the airframe. In flight at high transonic speeds and other specific flight regimes, the aircraft could begin to develop pitch oscillations (pilot-induced oscillations, or PIO) as a result of delays in the aircraft's response to pitch inputs at the control column, often leading to tragic consequences. Additionally, at certain speeds and altitudes, the phenomenon of aileron reversal also manifested itself, and flying the aircraft was likened to 'treading on a knife edge'!

The control difficulties of the Tu-22 forced OKB-156 to find a way of resolving the problem without delay, which subsequently led to the installation of an artificial feel-and-trim system and pitch damper in the tailplane circuit, and a control-column-movement rate-limiter. The tailplane and aileron circuits were also equipped with dry friction dampers. Later, it was decided to provide the Tu-22 with flaperons (described as aileron-flaps – *ehlerony-zakrylki* – by the designers) to serve as high-speed ailerons in order to overcome aileron reversal, and flexible undercarriage mountings to improve flutter resistance (Described in Chapter 4). However, before coming up with a definite solution to the aircraft's control difficulties, Tupolev took the only really correct decision in the circumstances, and imposed limits on the altitude and speed ranges in which it was permitted to operate the Tu-22. The measure was not popular, but it did allow operational trials of the aircraft to continue on the 'Leader Regiments', and reduced to a minimum the likelihood of a squadron pilot ending up with an in-flight emergency resulting from loss of control of the aircraft. The full modification programme, which would lead to the Tu-22 being considered fully operational, was still some way in the future, and the factory at Kazan' went ahead with completion of the construction of the basic aircraft already laid down on the production line.

Meanwhile, OKB-156 in Moscow, along with its 'branch' at Tupolev's associated manufacturing plant, Factory 22 at Kazan', was actively involved in the development of the reconnaissance variant of the Tu-22. This development programme was given the cover-name 'Sibir'-1' (Siberia-1) and the integrated system (or 'Complex' in Russian

A rare, albeit slightly retouched, colour photo of one of the first Tu-22R reconnaissance variants at a 'test airfield'.

In the early years of operation, the Tu-22R possessed an extremely energetic take-off performance, allowing experienced pilots to make dramatic 'high Alpha' climb-outs such as this, similar to those of the British Avro Vulcan and Handley Page Victor in their heyday. This photo dates back to the early 1960s and shows a Dobrynin VD-7M-powered Tu-22R of 290 ODRAP departing Zyabrovka. *Sergey Tsvetkov Archive*

parlance) included the Tu-22R (Article YuR) aircraft and its related reconnaissance suite. The Tu-22R was designed to carry out tactical reconnaissance (*operativnaya razvyedka*) in support of the strategic objectives of the Long-range Air Force, for which it was equipped with cameras and electronic intelligence (Elint) equipment and capable of conducting reconnaissance missions in all weather conditions, day or night and at high and low altitude. As on the Tu-22A, the crew consisted of three men, comprising a pilot and navigator, with an airborne operator (*vozdushnyi operator*) replacing the specialist radar operator (*radist*) of the pure bomber version. The bulk of the camera equipment was carried in the payload bay (*gruzovoy otsek*) and dependent upon the mission the Tu-22R could be equipped with one of four camera 'fits' – three day 'fits' and one night. The inclusion of a night-photography capability made it expedient to retain the original bombing equipment, since this option required the use of photo-bombs (flares) for target illumination at night. This meant that the Tu-22R could be converted quite quickly for bombing missions by regimental ground crews, only involving the removal of the camera equipment from the payload (weapons) bay. The military doctrine of the USSR always maintained that global military conflict would inevitably degenerate into nuclear war, and the tactics and strategy of the Soviet Air Force and its training programmes were all predicated on this concept. Consequently, the Tu-22R had a special weapons capability, allowing it to carry nuclear bombs (in Soviet times these were known by the common generic term '*spetsial'niye izdeliya*', or 'special articles'). Apart from nuclear bombs, in the bombing role the Tu-22R could carry conventional bombs from 250kg (550lb) to 9,000kg (19,840lb) calibre. Powered by two Dobrynin VD-7M engines, each of 16,000kg (35,273lb) thrust at take-off, the Tu-22R was able to achieve speeds of 1,200–1,300kph (650–700kts) at altitude and 850kph (460kts) at sea level.

Mention must be made of an often overlooked historical fact about the Tu-22R, which is that it was conceived not for a nuclear dash capability (which many have supposed), but for supersonic cruising flight. In consequence of this design condition, the VD-7M engines had two afterburner modes, namely 'cruising' and 'maximum'. The power-to-weight ratio of the aircraft compared with that of the Tu-16, plus its (eventually) improved aerodynamic efficiency, enabled the aircraft to reach altitudes of up to 13,500m (44,290ft) in the area of the target. Introduction of the Tu-22R greatly increased the potential of airborne strike formations and took the Long-range Air Force to an altogether higher (literally and figuratively) level of operational capability. The aircraft's equipment comprised an integrated system of sub-elements which constituted an entire suite of interrelated units, and it was one of the first Soviet Air Force aircraft to have an integrated navigation-bombing suite, plus integrated defensive and radar warning, flight control, navigation and radio systems. Considerable attention had been paid to the achievement of navigational accuracy on the Tu-22R, and the aircraft was equipped with the 'Put'-4' (Route-4) integrated flight and navigation system, at the time the most advanced of its kind in Russian service. This was still a system based on analogue techniques, but working in conjunction with the navigation-bombing system, mission tasking could be carried out effectively by the three-man crew of the Tu-22R. Of course, it was by no means the fully integrated system to be seen on aircraft in the 1970s and 1980s, but it was the first attempt to achieve the maximum functional integration of different components of the flight control, navigation and weapons systems on a Russian military aircraft. Overall, the aircraft's avionics facilitated:

• Navigation in day and night instrument meteorological conditions (IMC) within a defined range of speeds and altitudes

A Tu-22RDM *Blinder-C2* of 290 ODRAP taxiing at Zyabrovka. Clearly visible under the central fuselage area is the flush-fitting pod housing the antenna of the Shompol (Ramrod) sideways-looking radar of this improved variant. *S Burdin Archive*

- Day and night visual reconnaissance, with position and target location fixing with the aid of aerial photography, as well as photography of the radar screen for the same purpose in any weather conditions
- Electronic reconnaissance (Elint) of the deployment and operating parameters of enemy radar transmissions, with recordings of the latter on a special photo-film
- Bombing of land-based and ship-borne fixed and moving targets, either with or without optical or radar sighting of the target
- Self-defence against enemy anti-aircraft missile or fighter attacks
- Two-way communications with command posts from the limits of the normal operating radius of the aircraft, communication between other aircraft in the formation, plus normal intercom for the crew
- Return to the aircraft's operating base and the execution of an approach to land in limited visibility, day or night.

OKB-156 managed to bring the Tu-22R up to the second stage of State flight tests in a fairly short space of time, and the first operational deployments commenced in 1963. Initially these were to 290 ODRAP at Zyabrovka and then to 15 ODRAP of the Baltic Fleet Air Force, based at Chkalovsk in the Kaliningrad Region (*Oblast'*) of the former Russian Soviet Federated Socialist Republic of the Soviet Union. (The Kaliningrad Region is a small enclave sandwiched between Poland and Lithuania and since the break up of the Soviet Union has been a Special Economic Zone of the Russian Federation.) With the arrival on the regiments of the dual-role Tu-22R reconnaissance bomber, the Tu-22A pure bombing variant commenced its withdrawal from the combat strength of the Soviet Air Force. In 1965, another two regiments started to re-equip with the Tu-22R – 199 ODRAP of the 2nd Independent Heavy Bomber Aviation Corps – (2 OTBAK), at Nezhin, near Kiev in the Ukraine, and a second Naval Independent Long-range Reconnaissance Aviation Regiment, this time subordinated to the Black Sea Fleet Air Force at Saki airfield on the Crimean peninsula. Naval Tu-22Rs replaced the Il-28R *Beagle* light reconnaissance bomber in the same role. By the beginning of the 1960s, a number of changes were introduced into the operating tactics of the Soviet Long-range Air Force after it had become clear that it was essential that the main strike units should include in their number specialised ECM (electronic jamming) aircraft. So, from 1962, trials were carried out under the 'Sibir'-2' (Siberia-2) programme, which stipulated that a specialised jamming variant, based on the Tu-22, should be built, this aircraft receiving the 'private' designation Tu-22P (for *Postanovshchik Pomyekh*, or literally 'producer of interference'), and also known by the 'open' name of Article YuP. The Tu-22P was designed to provide escort jamming of its own force of reconnaissance bomber variants, using a variety of jamming systems to suppress enemy anti-aircraft defences. The aircraft was based on the Tu-22R and had the same engines and flight systems, but since it was designed for a totally different role it lacked the following equipment of the reconnaissance-bomber version:

- The camera equipment in the payload bay and its associated control systems
- The SRS-6 Elint system
- Payload bay (weapons bay) doors
- Bomb racks, with the exception of the integral BD6-105A rack.

A Tu-22PD of the third squadron of 121 TBAP at Machulishchi undergoing maintenance. When first introduced, engineering support facilities for the Tu-22 included a wide variety of specialised equipment and protective covers, but eventually only the engine servicing towers (seen here) and crew entry steps (*tribunki*) were used regularly. *S Burdin*

The performance of the Tu-22P was exactly the same as the Tu-22R, with the exception of a range reduction of around 180–200km (100–110nm). This resulted from the need to retain an increased level of unused fuel in order to meet the changed centre-of-gravity requirements of the Tu-22P on landing, occasioned by the location of the heavy ECM crates in the payload compartment. Otherwise, the Tu-22P had the same navigation

An elegant study of a Tu-22PD of the third squadron of 290 ODRAP which exhibits the clean lines of the aircraft to good effect. Although modified with an AAR capability and RD-7M engines, it retains the wing-tip anti-flutter weights and therefore does not incorporate the 'flexible undercarriage mounting' of later aircraft. *S Burdin Archive*

A fine study of a 121 TBAP Tu-22PD *Blinder-E*, with the air-intake for the special-equipment crate just visible under the fuselage. *S Burdin Archive*

systems, radar and defensive systems as the Tu-22R, and was capable of unrestricted day and night operations, including take-off and landing in IMC conditions. Most designers involved in developing aircraft for a similar role to that of the Tu-22P have come up against a range of problems associated with the need to find space for large heavy ECM systems, while still providing easy access for ground servicing personnel. Usually added to this is the need to provide special power supplies and, more importantly, to guarantee electronic compatibility of the ECM jammers with the aircraft's own avionics systems.

In the case of the OKB-156 design team, they were able to take advantage of experience gained in the development of specialised electronic variants of the Tu-16, and it was decided to mount the jamming equipment in a removable equipment crate (*konteiner*) which occupied almost the entire area of the payload bay (*gruzovoy otsek*). The heavy crates, raised and lowered on built-in winches, were suspended from the BD6-105A weapons rack, entirely contained within the contours of the payload bay skin-panels, with only the antenna housing projecting below the fuselage. A special APP-22 (*Avtomat Passivnykh Pomyekh* for the Tu-22 aircraft) chaff-dispensing system was developed for the Tu-22P, to sow chaff 'barriers' and 'clouds' for the group protection of attack formations of escorted bombers, the large APP-22 containers being installed at the rear of the payload bay. The Tu-22P was designed for the suppression of those enemy land-based and ship-borne radars which provided surveillance, fighter direction and targeting of air-defence missile systems, working in the frequency ranges of the aircraft's ECM equipment. From the outset, the Tu-22P was to be offered in two different versions, namely the Tu-22P1, equipped with the P1 ECM crate, and the Tu-22P2 with the P2 crate. The P1 variant employed active jamming of radars over a wide range of frequencies, the ECM system itself determining the actual transmitter frequencies being used (i.e. by scanning the frequency spectrum and analysing and identifying those emitters suspected

A Tu-22PD *Blinder-E* of the third squadron of 121 TBAP taxiing at Machulishchi, with the flattened oval-section intake for equipment-crate cooling just visible under the fuselage. *S Burdin Archive*

of being hostile). By contrast, the P2 system was designed to jam radars whose parameters were already known and held in a 'library' of emitters. The two systems were thus able to cover unknown and known threats in a given area of operation. The Tu-22P1 and Tu-22P2 commenced regimental deployment in around 1963, only a little time after the Tu-22R. [*It is of interest to note that it was only towards the latter stages of the Tu-22's operational life, i.e. in the late 1980s, that NATO acknowledged the specific ECM role of the Tu-22P, assigning the designations Blinder-E1 and Blinder-E2 to two recognisably different variants. Later still, it was revealed that a number of other Tu-22P variants existed, which are described in Chapter Four, but were not, so far as is known, given separate sub-designations. AD*]

By this time, the Tu-22 had already been deployed in the regiments in considerable numbers, in reconnaissance and ECM versions, but a training variant had not yet been developed! One can only speculate as to why this should have been, but it is possible that the Soviet Air Force leadership and OKB-156 had simply failed to realise that a training version of the new bomber would be required. After all, before the introduction of the Tu-22, there had never been any need for a specialised training variant of any of the Long-range Air Force's bombers, and even those regiments operating the Myasishchev 3M and M-4 *Bison* bombers used the Tu-16 *Badger* as a trainer. These were operated by the fourth squadron (i.e. the training squadron) of the *Bison* regiments for the specific purpose of

An effective head-on view of a Tu-22U of the first squadron of 121 TBAP at Machulishchi, showing the extent to which the instructor's seat was raised above that of the trainee, useful for in-flight refuelling practice, but hindering his view on take-off and landing.

familiarising newly qualified pilots in the techniques of handling a heavy bomber. However, the 203 Heavy Bomber Regiment's (203 TBAP) initial experience of operating the Tu-22 revealed that it would be impossible to cope without a special training version of the new bomber. Design of the Tu-22U (*Uchebnyi*) training variant began in 1961, differing principally from the baseline Tu-22R in the provision of a raised cockpit for the instructor, who occupied the area previously housing the radar operator/airborne operator's cockpit. Since the aircraft was not intended to have a combat role it lacked the defensive equipment of the operational variants, and the crew comprised:

- the crew commander (instructor)
- deputy crew commander (pilot under instruction)
- navigator.

As stated above, the instructor's cockpit was raised above the level of the trainee pilot's position, to afford him good all-round vision. In the event that the aircraft was to be

A Tu-22U of the third squadron of 121 TBAP taxies in from a sortie with the translating intake lips fully extended to maintain balanced intake flow at slow speed with a comparatively high power setting. *S Burdin*

used for a ferry flight from one airfield to another, for example, a folding table, Morse key and radio press-to-talk switch could be installed in the instructor's cockpit, which was then occupied by the airborne operator (*vozdushnyi operator*) for such flights. A control panel for the 'Neon' radio transmitter and US-8 receiver was permanently installed in the Tu-22U. Normal control of the Tu-22U was carried out from the trainee pilot's position and the instructor's cockpit. With a take-off weight of 63 tonnes (138,800lb) the Tu-22U could perform four consecutive landings during continuation training (CT) in the circuit with undercarriage extended, or five consecutive circuits with undercarriage retracted, before landing to refuel. When the outside air temperature was very high, and to reduce the turn-round time on CT sorties, the wheels and brakes had to be cooled by water from hydrants installed in the dispersal area. Similarly, an additional brake parachute container was installed on the Tu-22U to reduce the preparation time of the aircraft for another sortie. A new, more powerful TSM-2500-38 ejection seat telescoping mechanism (ejection gun) was installed for the instructor's seat, to take account of the extended length of the seat rails from the top of the canopy to the jettisonable entry-hatch cover. Both pilots had control of the engines and in-flight starts (when necessary), with the exception of the fuel shut-off cocks, which were only installed in the trainee's cockpit.

One of the first Tu-22U trainers to be equipped with an air-to-air refuelling probe and powered by up rated RD-7M engines. Note the wing-tip anti-flutter weight of the aircraft above the cameraman. *S Burdin Archive*

Factory trials of the new training variant were completed in 1963 and the aircraft entered service in the same year. The Tu-22U's performance was virtually identical with that of the Tu-22R and had a maximum take-off weight of 85 tonnes (187,390lb) and a maximum landing weight of 65 tonnes (143,300lb). The aircraft was intended to be used as a trainer at the Long-range Air Force Operational Conversion Centre at Ryazan', and for continuation training in regimental service. The Tu-22U provided the following training modes:

- Training of pilots who had already undergone a course of instruction on the Tu-16, familiarising them with the techniques of flight at high subsonic and supersonic flight (up to Mach 1.33) at altitudes and in flight conditions typical of the Tu-22R, day and night
- Circuit flying (continuation training) at airfields operating the Tu-22R and other combat variants
- Carrying out ferry flights in support of regimental deployments.

During initial operations, the aircraft was often referred to in Soviet Air Force technical documentation as the Tu-22UT (*Uchebno-Trenirovochnyi*), a designation used more often for fighter types than for bombers. [*The two words in Russian mean virtually the same thing, almost like 'training trainer'*. AD.] Eventually the designation Tu-22U became the accepted version.

A Tu-22RD of 30 ODRAP of the Soviet Naval Air Force Black Sea Fleet based at Saki on the Crimean Peninsula. *Sergey Tsvetkov Archive*

Apart from all the other early 'teething problems' of the Tu-22, the OKB-156 designers also had to tackle yet another deficiency which manifested itself in initial operations – lack of range. Consequently, design work started (in 1962) to equip the aircraft with an in-flight refuelling capability, although the thin wing of the Tu-22 precluded the use of the wingtip-to-wingtip method established for the Tu-16, and a hose and drogue system was adopted, based on that used by the Tu-95 *Bear* and 3M *Bison* bombers. Initially, the Myasishchev M-4 *Bison* was used as the tanker, and it was not until the introduction of the Tu-16N in 1966 that the Tu-22 had a suitable tanker aircraft to support extended-range operations. [*Tu-16N is 'probably' a classified designation, which has never been released openly, even in the more relaxed conditions following the demise of the Soviet Union. AD.*] The Myasishchev M-4 was really too big and lacked the manoeuvrability to operate in close formation with the Tu-22, and very few airfields used by the Long-range Air Force medium bomber fleet could support such a large tanker, so the Tu-16N was specially designed to be the Tu-22's dedicated in-flight refuelling tanker. The modified Tu-22R with in-flight refuelling capability was given the new designation Tu-22RD (or Article YuRD), and a number of sources have also referred to it as Article YuZA. The letter D in the designation Tu-22RD can be decoded as either *'Dal'nii'*, meaning 'long-range', or *'Dorabotannyi'*, meaning 'modified to a particular standard', although the authors feel that the first explanation is the correct meaning. The Tu-22RD was equipped with a nose-mounted (cantilevered) telescoping refuelling probe and a number of additional items of equipment to aid the in-flight refuelling process, including:

The AAR probe has already been removed from this 121 TBAP Tu-22U in accordance with strategic arms limitation requirements. Of interest is the fact that unlike the majority of Tu-22 variants, this example exhibits almost none of the white anti-corrosion treatment which characterised the *Blinder* fleet. *S Burdin*

1. RSBN-2SV (*Radio-Sistema Blizhnyei Navigatsii-2SV*, i.e. Short-range Navigation System-2-'*Svod-Vstrecha*', where *Svod* (Arch or Vault) is the cover-name of the system and *Vstrecha* (Meeting) is the air-to-air rendezvous mode. RSBN is the Russian equivalent of TACAN (TACtical Air Navigation)
2. Rubin-1L (Ruby-1L) airborne navigation and surface search radar
3. Pion-B (Peony-B) integrated antenna feed system
4. ARK-U2 Istok (Source) UHF automatic radio compass
5. SOD-57M ATC transponder.

These systems differed from those of the Tu-22R and were intended for both normal flight operations and for intra-formation navigation and rendezvous for in-flight refuelling. The intra-formation navigation mode was designed to facilitate search for and approach to the refuelling tanker. Two FPSh-5 searchlights were mounted on the nose of the Tu-22RD to illuminate the drogue during night refuelling, while a 'READY TO RECEIVE FUEL' signal light was mounted on the fin. Other new external lights were also installed on the modified aircraft, including OPS-57 formation lighting to facilitate station keeping in conditions of poor visibility, or at night, along with three OSS-61 anti-collision beacons. The nose radome was modified as a result of installing the Rubin-1L version of the *Short Horn* navigation radar, although the only external evidence of the change was a straight edge to the radome at Frame 9N. A more significant change to the Tu-22RD was the replacement of the original VD-7M engines by the improved RD-7M2, which conferred beneficial effects on the aircraft's altitude and speed performance. However, during the manufacture of the first series of RD-7M2 engines, changes were introduced virtually every month as a consequence of the Rybinsk engine plant making the transition from building the VD-7M to production of the RD-7M2. Full transition took place from March 1965 to May 1966, by which time the final changes to the new engine had been embodied. The Tu-22RD was also among the first aircraft to receive the new R-832M command radio, along with the R-836 Gyelii (Helium) communications radio (up to aircraft number three of the 19th production series – replaced by the Neon radio from aircraft three of the 19th series). Also included were the R-847 Prizma (Prism) HF radio, the R-876 Kometa (Comet) radio receiver, the R-851 Korall (Coral) stand-by emergency radio and the SP-50 ILS system (from aircraft 1 of the 13th production series). Additionally, some aircraft were equipped with the SPS-3 Roza (Rose) ECM system, while others had the SRS-7 Romb-4B (Rhombus-4B) Elint system installed. The Tu-22RD began to enter service in 1965.

In July 1961, following development of the reconnaissance and ECM versions, attention was turned to the creation of the Tu-22K (Article YuK) strategic missile-carrier. Initial trials were conducted with two aircraft (Constructor's Nos 1204 and 1205 – followed somewhat later by 3202 and 3302, all four aircraft being powered by VD-7M engines). As with many Russian missile-carrying aircraft, development did not simply involve an aircraft in isolation, but rather an integrated system comprising the aircraft, the missile and its associated guidance and control sub-systems. In this case, the Tu-22K was the main component of the K-22 long-range cruise missile system, where K stood for *Kompleks*, or 'integrated system'. The K-22 system was intended to destroy ground-based area targets and naval moving and fixed targets, using the Kh-22 (AS-4 *Kitchen*) air-to-surface missile (ASM) delivered by the Tu-22K *Blinder-B* aircraft. After role-changing the aircraft as a bomber, it could also deliver a nuclear bomb (*Spetsizdeliye*), or a variety of conventional bombs up to 9,000kg (19,840lb) calibre. The Tu-22K could thus operate in groups, either as a missile-carrier armed with a single AS-4 *Kitchen* ASM, or as a

A Tu-22K of the first squadron of 121 TBAP in a wooded dispersal at Machulishchi. *S Burdin*

A fine take-off study of a Tu-22K, emphasising the highly swept wing and showing the wing under-surface white anti-corrosion paint and the translating intake lips to good effect. *S Burdin Archive*

nuclear or conventional bomber, protected by Tu-22P escort jammers, the latter capable of both identifying enemy radars and suppressing them with their own on-board ECM systems. The Tu-22K's high speed and high altitude, in conjunction with its built-in defensive weapons (tail gun) and systems, would have made the aircraft less vulnerable to enemy fighter and surface-to-air missile (SAM) attacks, both en route to the target and during the final approach.

The Tu-22K was first shown publicly on 9 June, 1961 during a flypast at that year's Tushino air display, with a dummy AS-4 under the fuselage. However, tests and refinement of the K-22 system were to last another three years, and it was not until 1964 that series production and deliveries to the Soviet Air Force actually started. Flight testing of the Tu-22K and the Kh-22 missile were carried out at GNIII VVS at Vladimirovka and were beset by a multitude of problems, mainly related to the Kh-22 (AS-4 *Kitchen*) missile. The aircraft itself was powered by the new RD-7M2 engines, producing 16,500kg (36,375lb) of thrust in full reheat, pitch dampers, flexible undercarriage mounting and flaperons (*See Chapter 2 for more details on the flexible undercarriage mountings and flaperons.*) The Tu-22K, with the exception of the four development aircraft (C/n 1204, 1205, 3202 and 3302), was equipped with the in-flight refuelling probe developed for the Tu-22RD, and when it went into production it embodied the very best of what the Soviet aerospace industry had to offer at the time. Small changes were made to some of the avionics equipment of the Tu-22K, including:

- An R-832 command radio in place of two earlier RSIU-5V units
- An R-847 Prizma (Prism) HF communications radio in place of the earlier Neon transmitter and US-8 receiver

A Tu-22PD *Blinder-E* of 121 TBAP undergoing post-flight checks at Machulishchi. The graceful curvature of the fuselage is clearly apparent in this view.

- An R-867 receiver installed on some aircraft and an MS-61 cockpit voice recorder was installed for the first time on the aircraft, to record intra-crew conversations and airground radio transmissions.

The aircraft's lighting system also underwent changes, with red-white cockpit floodlighting (back lighting) replacing the older ultra-violet lighting system of the early Tu-22 variants. The aircraft's PRF-4 taxi lights were also moved to a location at the junction of the wing and fuselage, where they would not affect the pilot's night vision on take-off and landing. However, the biggest change was reserved for the aircraft's

A very clean example of the Tu-22's successor, the Tu-22M3 *Backfire-C*, which only shared the Tu-22 designation for reasons of political expediency, rather than being a progressive development of the original *Blinder* design. *S Burdin*

navigation-bombing system, with a TsNVU-B-1B central navigation computer, working in conjunction with a TsGV-5 central gyro unit, replacing the original system. The analogue-digital TsNVU-B-1B computer facilitated the automatic calculation of the aircraft's position and performed dead-reckoning calculations. This was a significant advance on the capability of the Tu-22R. Later, the TsnVU-B-1B was to spur development of the PNK-45 integrated flight-navigation system installed in the Tu-22M2 *Backfire-B* and Tu-22M3 *Backfire-C* swing-wing 'developments' of the *Blinder*. The first Tu-22K missile-carriers were delivered to 203 Heavy Bomber Regiment (203 *Tyazholyi Bombardirovochnyi Polk* – 203 TBAP) at Baranovichi at the end of 1964, followed by the re-equipment of 121 ORAP (becoming 121 TBAP as a result) at Minsk-Machulishchi in 1965 and deliveries to 341 TBAP at Ozyornoye, near Zhitomir, in the same year. All three regiments were subordinated to the 15th Heavy Bomber Division (15 *Tyazholobombardirovochnyaya Aviadiviziya* – 15 TBAD), headquartered at Bobruisk, which was under the overall control of 6 OTBAK. After 1980, 6 OTBAK was restructured and renamed the 46th Air Army of the Supreme High Command.

Also from 1965, production of an improved Tu-22U commenced, with the original VD-7M engines replaced by the RD-7M2 and equipped to a similar standard as the Tu-22RD, including the installation of flaperons, flexible undercarriage mountings and a 'refuelling' probe. However, this was a dummy installation and was not designed to receive fuel, serving only as a realistic training aid to allow crews to practise the technique of in-flight refuelling. Consequently, the designation Tu-22UD frequently used in many reference sources is not strictly correct, although in some early operating documents the designation Tu-22UD *was* used internally by the Soviet Air Force, probably to indicate simply that the particular aircraft had a dummy probe fitted. In the same year, the Tu-22P was also given an in-flight refuelling capability, re-engined with RD-7M2s and received the designation Tu-22PD (Article YuPD). The modified aircraft were initially delivered to the heavy bomber regiments already equipped with Tu-22K *Blinder-B* missile-carriers.

The Tu-22K, Tu-22RD, Tu-22RD, Tu-22U (with dummy refuelling probe) and the Tu-22PD all had the same basic flight control system, but certain elements of this system had been installed gradually and there was no common standard. For example, in 1965, Factory 22 at Kazan' produced some aircraft that were equipped with in-flight refuelling systems, but without flaperon controls and flexible undercarriage mountings. It was only in 1967, when the aircraft was formally accepted by the Soviet Air Force after five years of operational service, that all the flight control systems developed for it by OKB-156 had been fully embodied. By this time, OKB-156 had set to work on the design of an altogether new aircraft, assisted by huge developments in engine technology and better understanding of supersonic aerodynamics, leading to the drafting of 'Aircraft 145', later to become the Tu-22M *Backfire*. At first, this was planned to be a 'deep modernisation' of the Tu-22K *Blinder-B*, equipped with a variable-geometry wing and an improved weapons system. However, by the time the new aircraft, designated Tu-22M0, made its maiden flight on 30 August 1969, it looked significantly different from the original Tu-22 design and bore little resemblance to Russia's first supersonic bomber. The new aircraft was a true multi-role long-range variable-geometry strategic bomber, and following trials with the so-called zero-series (Tu-22M0) aircraft, another small pre-series batch of Tu-22M1 underwent tests, with both the M0 and M1 variants being used to refine and modify the design. Eventually, in 1975, the Tu-22M2 *Backfire-B* variant commenced full-scale production and entered service in the same year. A considerably improved variant, the Tu-22M3 *Backfire-C*, was fielded in the early 1980s, by both the Soviet Air Force and the Soviet Naval Air Force; and at the end of the decade a dedicated reconnaissance variant, the Tu-22MR was being prepared for service. This variant, which so far as is known was not given a separate NATO designation letter, is believed to be in current service in small numbers with the Russian Air Force. Altogether, some 500 *Backfires* were produced by the early 1990s, although further discussion of this aircraft falls outside the framework of this book.

Completion of production of the Tu-22 towards the end of 1969 did not mean the end of OKB-156's involvement with the *Blinder*, and in the 1960s and 1970s the development of Western airborne missile systems had stimulated the development of appropriate Soviet countermeasures to them. This led to part of the Tu-22K fleet being equipped with SPS-100 individual protective ECM systems to counter enemy radars. At the same time, in accordance with Bulletin 1295 (a joint Tupolev/Soviet Air Force document), some Tu-22PDs were equipped with SPS-151 (SPS-152, SPS-153) active jammers and ASO-2I (i.e. I for India, *not* the number 1) chaff dispensers for individual protection of the rear hemisphere from fighter attacks. Aircraft so modified were those equipping the heavy bomber regiments, and because of the improved electronic and chaff-dispensing protection, the tail-gun position was removed from the Tu-22K and Tu-22PDs at this time.

In the 1970s, a curious situation arose in *Blinder* reconnaissance regiments, where aircraft could differ significantly in their equipment 'standards'. What was worse, they could differ in terms of engine type and flight control systems. Some aircraft, for example, had VD-7M engines, while others had RD-7M2s, and only a part of a regiment's fleet might have the full suite of modified flight controls, i.e. pitch dampers, control-column-movement rate-limiter, etc. All of this compromised the safe operation of what was already a very complex aircraft, and the Soviet Air Force leadership took the reasoned view that *all* Tu-22s should be brought up to a uniform modification standard (*Ehtalon*). The 'Standard' (*Ehtalonnyi*) example selected was a Tu-22R powered by RD-7M2 engines, equipped with flaperons, flexible undercarriage mountings and the fully modified flight control system, incorporating all the features required for safe operation at transonic and supersonic speeds. Modification to the specified 'Standard' was carried out at the Ryazan' Aviation Repair Plant, and over a period of years all regiments eventually had sufficient numbers of 'Standard' aircraft on strength. The new variant was given the internal designation 'Article A' (*Izdeliye A*), the reconnaissance aircraft being designated 'Article AR' and the ECM versions being designated 'Article AP'.

The developing capabilities of ground-based electronics systems and the growth in effectiveness of enemy anti-aircraft missile defences in the 1970s had forced Russian systems designers to develop appropriate countermeasures for the Soviet medium bomber force. Some of this work was carried out by design teams in OKBs involved in the development of long-range cruise missiles, and eventually led to the development of an anti-radiation (ARM) variant of the Kh-22 (AS-4 *Kitchen*) ASM. The new missile was equipped with a PGP anti-radiation seeker head and was given the designation Kh-22MP, while the carrier aircraft was equipped with an integrated search and guidance system for initial targeting of the missile. The aircraft system was designated Kurs-N (Course-N) for the Tu-22K and Kurs-NM (Course-NM) for the later Tu-22M3 *Backfire-C*. The Kh-22MP missile was designed to destroy or disable ground-based and naval (ship-borne) radars, and by the end of the 1970s the Tupolev OKB had developed the aircraft and missile system to a level sufficient for operational deployment, under the designation Tu-22KP

A 121 TBAP Tu-22KP in one of the banked earth dispersal areas (*obvalovanie*) at Machulishchi. *S Burdin*

A ground-level view of a Tu-22KP of the second squadron of 121 TBAP. *S Burdin Archive*

(*Blinder-B Mod*). Between 1982 and 1983, aircraft already in operational service were modified to receive the Kurs-N search and target designation system. During this time *Blinder-Bs* of one of the two combat-ready squadrons of each of three Tu-22K regiments (i.e. a total of three squadrons) were put through the modification programme. The work was carried out on the regiments by a team of specialist electronics engineers from the manufacturing plant. The antenna units for the new equipment were installed inside the nose radome and mounted below the main PN (NATO *Downbeat*) radar antenna, so it was not possible to distinguish the Tu-22KP from the unmodified Tu-22K, since there were no obvious external differences.

The Tu-22KP was not the last of the modified variants of the Tu-22, which was now seen as an ideal platform for some of the newly emerging electronic intelligence (Elint) systems coming into service since the 1970s. One of these systems, the Kub-3 (Cube-3), originally designed for use on the MiG-25RBK *Foxbat-B* tactical reconnaissance bomber, was selected to upgrade the capabilities of some Tu-22RDs. Kub-3 was an Elint system designed to identify and classify enemy radars automatically, its receiving elements being fed from two antennae mounted on either side of the forward fuselage of the Tu-22RD, below the cockpit area. Aircraft modified with the Kub-3 system were redesignated Tu-22RDK, and one squadron of aircraft belonging to 199 ODRAP based at Nezhin in the Ukraine was upgraded to this standard, the work being carried out at the Ryazan' aviation repair facility.

Another direction of development involving the Tu-22R was the application of emerging technologies in photo-reconnaissance techniques, with the aerial reconnaissance laboratory at the Flight Test Institute (LII) at Zhukovskii conducting trials in the mid-1970s of new NA-Ya-7 and NA-Ya-8 night cameras, using searchlights to illuminate the target. These cameras were intended to facilitate photo-reconnaissance from low and extremely low level, hence the use of searchlights for illumination, rather than the more usual flares. The laboratory also conducted trials with frame cameras and the Zona (Zone) panoramic camera, these tests confirming the effectiveness of using

An unusual close-up air-to-air study of a 121 TBAP Tu-22KD, showing the slight downwards twist of the wing-tip and clean mounting of the engine nacelle to the rear fuselage support pylon. *S Burdin Archive*

colour and 'spectrozonal' images to detect camouflaged and decoy targets. [*Spectrozonal photography is a technique whereby the natural spectral emissions of all objects are selectively filtered in order to 'image' only those objects within a particular spectral band or zone and eliminate unwanted 'background' emissions.* AD.] The USSR had also invested much time and money in the study and testing of electro-optical reconnaissance systems, leading to the creation of the first Russian infra-red line scanners. Although equivalent in performance to their Western counterparts, they were larger and heavier, but after the Ministry of Defence put development of such systems onto a competitive basis, Russian designers were forced to re-evaluate their systems and reduce their size and weight. In this way, for example, the Zima (Winter) infra-red line scanner was reduced in weight from 150kg (330lb) to 70kg (154lb), this system and the Osyen' (Autumn) unit eventually undergoing trials at LII as possible contenders to re-equip the Tu-22R.

In the 1980s, LII also conducted trials of high-resolution aerial cameras with improved image formats, which demonstrated great effectiveness, and it was decided to install some of these devices on the Tu-22RD. This coincided with an emerging interest on the part of the Soviet military leadership in the creation of an integrated 'reconnaissance-strike' capability for the medium bomber force. The basis of this capability was to be that a strike aircraft, equipped with a relevant package of reconnaissance equipment, would perform a 'first-pass' reconnaissance of the target, recording all of its parameters on a variety of on-board systems. It would then perform a 'second pass', attacking and destroying the target with an appropriate weapon, followed by bomb damage assessment (BDA) using its own cameras. The concept had particularly interested the Soviet military hierarchy because by that time, the physical size of nuclear weapons had been significantly reduced, while at the same time retaining their destructive power. This meant that it was possible for an aircraft to carry both reconnaissance equipment and weapons in the same weapons bay, or on separate pylons in the case of tactical aircraft. Attempts to create such 'reconnaissance-strike complexes' had involved the Mikoyan and Sukhoi Design Bureaux, and the Tupolev MMZ (as OKB-156 was now called) also took up the cause in the early 1980s with plans for a 'reconnaissance-strike' version of the Tu-22RD. This aircraft was initially designated Tu-22RM, but since it was based on the equipment standard of the Tu-22RD it was sometimes referred to in Soviet Air Force documents as the Tu-22RDM. The modifications were carried out by the Ryazan' repair plant, and the aircraft was intended to be used for photo- and Elint reconnaissance of military targets, airfields, naval bases and ports, plus radar installations, with near-simultaneous bombing of these targets on the same sortie. Armed with a small nuclear bomb, there was still sufficient space for the reconnaissance package, which differed from that of the original Tu-22R and incorporated short-focal-length cameras looking fore and aft along the longitudinal axis of the aircraft.

The reconnaissance equipment was installed in a special crate (*Konteiner 1*), and all operational parameters of the Tu-22RM were practically identical with those of the standard Tu-22RD. The maximum speed of the Tu-22RM at 11,000m (36,090ft) in full reheat, with Crate 1 (*Konteiner 1*) and a take-off weight of 70,000kg (154,320lb), was 1,560kph (842kts). Since the aircraft had a new defensive suite, the tail-gun position was removed. Single examples of the Tu-22RM underwent service trials with Crate 1, but the perceived increase in the mobility of troops on and around the battlefield had already stimulated the need for even more advanced reconnaissance systems than this. It was soon decided to abandon the concept of a 'reconnaissance-strike' version of the Tu-22, and the improved Reconnaissance Crate 2 (*Konteiner 2*) was developed instead.

Comparatively few photographs have ever been published of the Tu-22RDK variant of the *Blinder-C*, this example being a former 199 ODRAP aircraft from Nezhin, seen here already wearing Ukrainian Air Force markings after transfer from Russian ownership. The lateral fairing houses the antenna complex of the Kub-3 Elint system. *Valery Romanenko*

Crate 2 incorporated all the very latest achievements in the field of aerial reconnaissance, including infra-red systems, long-focal-length, short-focal-length and panoramic cameras, capable of 'spectrozonal' colour imaging. For the first time on a Soviet bomber, a sideways-looking radar was also installed, using the Shompol (Ramrod) unit from the MiG-25RBSh *Foxbat-D*, plus the SRS-13 Tangazh (Pitch) Elint system, also 'borrowed' from the MiG-25, this time from the MiG-25RBT *Foxbat-B* variant. Target illumination for the night cameras was provided by special pyrotechnic shells, following unsuccessful trials of the searchlight system mentioned earlier and a decision to move away from traditional photo-flash bombs. All the modifications incorporated in the new reconnaissance package were designed to permit the aircraft to be used at much lower altitudes than hitherto. The Tu-22RDM (RM) with Crate 2 was sometimes referred to as the Tu-22RDM-2, but after Crate 1 was withdrawn from use the need to differentiate between the variants disappeared and the modified aircraft were simply referred to as Tu-22RDM. (*These aircraft should not be confused with the above-mentioned 'recce-strike Tu-22RM', which did not go into service.* AD) A total of twelve aircraft, all belonging to the 1st Squadron* of 290 ODRAP at Zyabrovka, were modified to the RDM standard at

---

* Note: It is perhaps expedient at this point to explain that only Soviet Air Force regiments were numbered in a manner similar to Western air force squadrons. Subordinate squadrons were simply designated first, second, third [and fourth in some cases], with the most experienced crews being assigned to the first squadron, and the third and fourth where appropriate being the regiment training squadron. In the case of the Tu-22, the third squadron was also equipped with the Tu-22P/PD *Blinder-E* specialist jamming variant. Obvious exceptions, of course, were the independent squadrons, which *did* receive names and numbers.

the Ryazan' repair plant. The capabilities of Crate 2 were considered to be so great that after the *Blinders* were withdrawn from service, they were transferred to the *Backfire* fleet and formed the basis of the reconnaissance package of the Tu-22MR.

According to information posted on the official website of the Tupolev OAO (www.tupolev.ru), a total of 313 Tu-22s had been built by the end of 1969. This total comprised two prototypes (Aircraft '105' and '105A') built at the OKB-156 Experimental Factory in Moscow, followed by series production of the remaining 311 at Factory 22 at Kazan' in the present-day Republic of Tatarstan. Of the 311, twenty were Tu-22A freefall bombers, 126 were Tu-22R reconnaissance versions (later converted into the sub-variants described in this chapter), seventy-six were Tu-22K missile-carriers (and variants), forty-seven were Tu-22P ECM variants and forty-two were Tu-22U trainers. By the 1970s, many of the problems which beset the aircraft in its early days of operation had been eradicated, and the hard-won experience of pioneering the introduction of this supersonic bomber could be passed on to crews converting onto its 'namesake' – the Tu-22M *Backfire*. The Tu-22 *Blinder* had made it possible to introduce the Tu-22M and, later, the Tu-160 *Blackjack*, with considerably less difficulty than that experienced by its own pioneering crews, and at the same time it had introduced the Soviet Long-range Air Force to the era of supersonic flight.

CHAPTER TWO

Design of the Tu-22

For all practical comparative purposes the former Soviet Air Force's baseline Tu-22 was the Tu-22R (*Razvedchik*/Reconnaissance) *Blinder-C* variant, combining freefall bombing capability with a reconnaissance function, and the initial design descriptions are made with reference to this variant. The Tu-22 marked the Soviet Long-range Air Force's transition into the supersonic era, and as a consequence, the aircraft embodied a number of specific design features which will be elaborated in this chapter. For convenience, the description of the design of the Tu-22 is broken down into sections on the powerplant, fuselage, wing, tail unit and undercarriage.

Powerplant

The powerplant of the early series Tu-22R comprised:

- Two afterburning Dobrynin VD-7M engines
- Engine nacelles
- Fuel supply and lubrication system
- Automatic fuel control systems
- Fire-suppression systems.

The VD-7M engine was, at the time of its introduction at the end of the 1950s, the most powerful series-produced afterburning jet engine available in the former Soviet Union (developing 16,000kg/35,273lb static thrust in reheat), and its main features included:

- The use of a nine-stage axial compressor with an 11:1 pressure ratio at the first supersonic stage, movable inlet guide vanes and an air bleed taken from the fifth and sixth compressor stages
- An afterburner offering 50% greater thrust in reheat than the maximum dry-thrust setting (under bench-test conditions)
- The use of a variable area exhaust nozzle, enabling economic operation in partial reheat with smooth changes of thrust setting
- Engine power controlled by rpm settings, using a fully variable fuel-flow regulator and a regulator controlling compressor bleed air and compressor-inlet guide vanes.

The VD-7M was equipped with two accessory drive gearboxes serving the lubrication system, electrical supplies and related automated systems (*avtomatiki*), as well as all essential monitoring systems and associated electronic equipment. Engine start-up on the ground was electrical, achieved with the aid of starter-generators.

Up to the mid-1970s the Tu-22R was powered by the Dobrynin VD-7M engine, characterised by shorter afterburner nozzles than those of the later RD-7M2. Here a VD-7M powered Tu-22R of 290 ODRAP is being prepared for flight at Zyabrovka. *Sergey Tsvetkov Archive*

Main characteristics of the VD-7M engine

Type	Turbojet
Direction of rotation (viewed from rear)	Right hand
Compressor	9-stage axial
Combustion chamber	14 flame tubes
Turbine section	2-stage axial
Afterburner	Direct flow, with adjustable nozzle
Time to achieve maximum thrust (non-reheat)	Not more than 23 seconds
Time to achieve maximum thrust (in reheat)	Not more than 32 seconds
Type of fuel (for normal in-flight operation)	T-1 or TS-1 kerosene
Type of fuel (for start-up)	B-70 aviation gasoline
Ignition system	Low-voltage electrical
Engine-driven accessories:	
– SGS-30-8 AC generator	One
– STG-18TBP AC generator	Two
(also used as starter-generator)	
Uninstalled weight of engine	3,750kg (8,267lb)
Overall dimensions:	
– Length including afterburner section	7,300mm (23.95ft)
– Length of afterburner section	4,600mm (15.09ft)
– Maximum diameter (in afterburner section)	1,410mm (4.63ft)

VD-7M operating parameters (in ISA conditions)

Parameter	Engine rpm	Thrust	SFC kg/kg thrust/hour	Maximum TGT
Take-off [V=0]	7,400	16,000kg [35,273lb]	2.0	630°
Max non-reheat thrust, on ground [V=0]	7,400	10,500 kg [23,148lb]	0.82	630°
Nominal, on ground [V=0]	7,100	8,600kg [18,960lb]	0.78	540°
Cruising at sea level [0.815 of nominal]	6,850	7,000kg [15,432lb]	0.78	510°
Max reheat at 11,000m [36,090ft] at 1,500kph [810kts]	Not more than 7,450	9,700kg [21,834lb]	2.1	630°
Cruise reheat at 11,000m [36,090ft] at 1,300–1,400kph [702–756kts]	Not more than 7,450	7,500kg [16,534lb]	1.65	630°
Nominal at 11,000m [36,090ft] at 1,000kph [540kts]	7,150	2,500kg [5,511lb]	1.0	540°
Ground idle	Not more than 3,250	Not more than 450kg [992lb]	Not applicable	410°

Nominal was 92% of maximum power.
Maximum permitted continuous use of cruising afterburner at altitudes above 5,500m (18,044ft) – 120 minutes.
Maximum permitted continuous use of full afterburner at altitudes above 5,500m (18,044ft) – 30 minutes.

The engines were mounted on a substantial vertical pylon mounted on the rear fuselage, which also served as the attachment point for the fin and rudder. Each engine was attached to the pylon by a total of six main supports and one auxiliary support strut. Servicing access to the engine-driven accessories was performed from above and below through easily removable engine panels. Access for removal and mounting of the engines was through the upper removable engine panel, with the afterburner section being removed and/or attached to the installed engine inside the nacelle. Engine control was achieved from the pilot's position by means of a system of cables and rods.

The engine nacelle consisted of a forward section (the air intake), a middle section and a rear section incorporating a tail fairing between the engines. Each air intake was designed as a separate assembly, incorporating a duct supplying air to its own engine, and comprised a forward fairing, a movable intake lip, a main supporting frame and removable panels and covers. The length of the air-intake duct from the edge of the movable intake lip to the front face of the engine was 3,160mm (10.37ft). The air-intake assembly was not controllable in flight and was designed to provide a normal shock wave at supersonic speed. The selected layout of the air intake provided minimal pressure loss into the engine at both subsonic and supersonic speeds up to Mach 1.5.

A view of the rear fuselage, showing the fin, rudder, tailplane and RD-7M engine nacelle. Clearly visible is the separation of the air intake lip from the upper fuselage surface, intended to avoid ingestion of the boundary layer and numerous small, but effective, air intakes for cooling the engine and afterburner sections. The shape of the rear fuselage termination reveals this to be a Tu-22U. *S Burdin*

The location of the air intakes close to the fuselage, as a consequence of the selection of the rear-engined, twin nacelle layout of the Tu-22, created the possibility of interference effects between engine and airframe. In order to alleviate this, the lower edge of the air-intake ducts was placed 250mm (9.75in) above the fuselage, so that the boundary layer created in flight could not enter the air-intake and disturb the engine airflow. Each internal duct of the air intake acted as a diffuser (or expansion duct) with a throat area of 0.84m² (9.04sq ft) and an area at the front face of the engine of 1.038m² (11.17sq ft). The throat area of the duct (the smallest cross-section of the duct) was sized to satisfy the subsonic airflow condition.

The leading edge of the air intake was provided with a small radius of curvature which did not produce growth in drag and at the same time provided better airflow characteristics in 'off-design' flight conditions, while reducing intake pressure losses during take-off and landing. Nevertheless, in order to guarantee stable intake airflow conditions at take-off and landing power settings it was provided with a special translating intake lip. The lip was 300mm (11.7in) long and was able to move forward 188mm (7.3in) along the axis of the intake duct, forming an annular slot through which supplementary airflow was able to feed the engines at low airspeeds, by effectively increasing the intake cross-sectional area. When the engine was running on the ground, as well as during take-off and landing, the movable intake lip was extended, but in flight the lip was fully retracted. In the retracted position the lip formed a clearance gap of 1.5–2.0mm (0.06–0.08in) between the main frame of the intake section and the rear of the lip, with a rubber gasket providing a hermetic seal around its periphery. Extension and retraction of the intake lip was achieved with the use of an MPSh-17M electrical drive unit. Extension of the lip took 38 seconds, while retraction required only 30 seconds. Operation of the lip was automatic and was synchronised with the retraction or extension of the flaps and the main oleo of the starboard undercarriage bogie.

The middle section of the engine nacelle was attached at its upper point to the fin post and at its lower point to the fuselage. The connecting joints for the air intakes and the middle and rear sections of the nacelle were provided with splice strips. Hinged panels were provided on the middle section of the nacelle for access to the engine accessory drives and components. An upper panel on each engine was provided with slotted louvres for the expulsion of air tapped from the compressor stages of the engine. In the upper part of Nacelle Frame 9G (G for *Gondola*, i.e. nacelle) an air vent was mounted on the adjacent panel for the expulsion of engine cooling air in the middle section of the nacelle. An afterburner cooling exhaust vent was mounted on the upper panel between Nacelle Frames 7G and 8G, with a similar cooling vent mounted on the lower panel between Frames 8G and 9G. The rear section of the engine nacelle was designed solely to house the afterburner. A fairing joined both of the nacelles at the rear and was located between the engine mounting and the rudder. Hatches were provided on the right-hand side of the nacelle panels for access by servicing personnel to the electrical wiring looms. The rear section of the fairing in the area of the exhaust nozzles was detachable and contained the TP-1 (*Televizionnyi Pritsel*) television camera of the aircraft's passive warning system, along with the KhS-57 tail light.

Fuel was accommodated in thirty-three internal tanks, situated in the fuselage, the wing centre section and the outer wings. The volume of the tanks permitted a total of 48,580kg (107,100lb) of fuel to be carried, with a specific gravity of 0.83. Tanks 1 and 2 were located in the fuselage between the pressure cabin and the front spar of the wing centre section, Tank 3 was situated over the centre section, Tank 4 was in the wing torsion box, while Tanks 5, 6 and 7 were located in the rear of the fuselage. Fuel Tanks 8 to 19 were mounted in the wing torsion box. Tanks 1, 2, 3 and 4 and the fuel tanks in the port wing were intended to supply the port engine, while Tanks 1, 5, 6 and 7, plus the tanks in the

Diagram of Tu-22R, showing fuel tank locations, camera mounting and photo-flash bomb carriage.

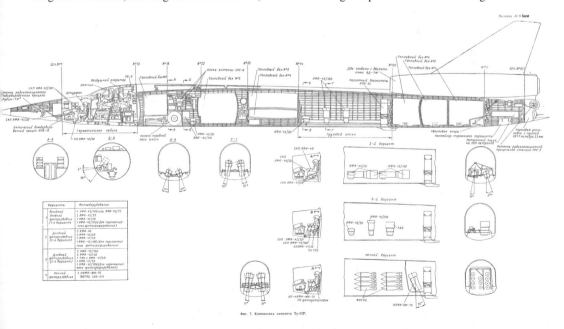

starboard wing, were designed to feed the starboard engine. The relatively thin wing of the Tu-22 permitted the carriage of only 8,460kg (18,650lb) of fuel in the wing tanks, which, in consequence, were not particularly deep. When using the afterburners it was practically impossible to use the fuel from these wing tanks directly, because of the formation of turbulent vortices at the point where the fuel entered the pump. Consequently, this fuel was first pumped into Tanks 3, 4 and 5, from where it could be supplied to the engines in more stable conditions. In consideration of the structural integrity of the aircraft and the need to maintain the centre of gravity within design limits, a strict sequence of fuel consumption (and refuelling), by groups of tanks, was established for the Tu-22, with consumption and centre of gravity controlled by the TATs2-1A (*Toplivomyer s Avtomatom Tsentrovki 2-1*) fuel management system.

The TATs2-1A automatic fuel management system incorporated an electrical fuel-volume-measuring device with an automatic centre-of-gravity calculator, and was designed for the:

• Measurement of fuel remaining in each group of tanks and also for the measurement of the total fuel remaining for each engine separately (the fuel-measuring element of the system)
• Automatic control of the order of fuel consumption in a defined sequence, with warning lights to alert the crew of critical fuel remainders for 30 minutes and 15 minutes of flight respectively (automated fuel-consumption element of the system)
• Automatic maintenance of centre of gravity within design limits in the event of failure of one of the engines, since in this condition the sequence of consumption of fuel from the forward and rear groups of tanks was likely to be disrupted (automated centre-of-gravity calculator)
• Automatic closure of refuelling valves during single-point fuelling (the automated refuelling element of the system).

In the event that fuel had to be jettisoned in flight to bring the aircraft down to a safe landing weight in an emergency, around 28,000kg (61,730lb) of fuel could be dumped in 15 minutes. The Tu-22 had an 'open' fuel drainage system, i.e. the system of turbo-pumps and valves vented to the atmosphere. The Tu-22R was equipped with a single-point fuelling system, with the filler valve installed under the port wing between Ribs 25 and 26. It was possible to replenish all tanks simultaneously, as well as each tank separately, but it was forbidden to replenish Tanks 6 and 7 in isolation, if the forward tanks were empty, since there was a risk of the aircraft tipping backwards onto its tail. The fuel tanks were made of rubber, without self sealing. The refuelling process was controlled on the ground from a portable control panel which plugged into a socket situated in the accessories compartment on the port side of the aircraft near Frame 20.

The aircraft was equipped with a lubrication system which supplied each engine independently from an oil tank and a fuel-oil radiator situated between the engine air-intake ducts. The oil tank was made of soft rubber, without self sealing, and was housed in a glass-cloth laminated container. The oil was cooled in a special radiator using the aircraft's fuel (kerosene) as the coolant medium.

The Tu-22 was equipped with on-board fire protection consisting of:

- A system enabling the fuel tanks to be filled with a neutral gas to hinder the risk of fire in the event that they were penetrated by cannon shells or shrapnel
- A fire-extinguishing system in the engine compartments (nacelles) and in the fuel-tank compartments, enabling a fire to be extinguished when detected.

The neutral gas (carbon dioxide) system for the fuel tanks employed six ballonettes of CO_2 while a total of eight OS-8M fire extinguishers, charged with freon gas, were located in the fuselage, connected by a system of special pipes and incorporating an SSP-2A fire-warning indication system.

Two hand-held OU (CO_2) fire extinguishers were mounted in the crew compartment in order to deal with fires that broke out in that area.

Fuselage
The fuselage of the Tu-22 was of all-metal stressed skin construction, with the skin panels attached to a set of frames and stringers of shaped and extruded profile. The shape of the fuselage was characteristic of supersonic aircraft of the 1950s era, having a sharply pointed nose, an acutely raked leading edge to the cockpit canopy windscreen frame and noticeable 'waisting' at the point where the wing was attached to the fuselage, in conformity with the then 'fashionable' area rule (See Chapter One). Another interesting feature of the design of the fuselage was the use of a robust vertical pylon serving as a base for mounting the engines and the fin and rudder. The fuselage was built around a set of eighty-five transverse frames located at a distance of between 340 and 540 mm (13.25–21.0in) from each other, with a system of forty-eight longitudinal stringers distributed around the frames at approximately every 7–8 degrees of the circumference. Additional stringers were located between the main stringers in those locations which required further strengthening. Apart from this, the fuselage was reinforced with extra beams and longerons where the structure was weakened by cut-outs for access hatches, or at the point of attachment of items such as the nose undercarriage, the weapons bay and tail unit, etc.

The fuselage skin was fabricated from D16A-TV and V95 aluminium and magnesium alloys, with a thickness of between 1.0 and 7.0mm (0.04–0.27in). The skin was reinforced with additional panels on the inside surface in those areas subjected to the greatest loading. The panels were butt-jointed and attached to the frames with flush rivets.

The fuselage comprised:

- Nose section F-1 (i.e. F for *Fyuzelyazhnyi* – Fuselage – first section) situated between the nose cone and Frame 1
- Section F-2, between Frames 1 and 13, enclosing the crew pressure cabin
- Section F-3, between Frames 13 and 33, also described as the forward unpressurised section of the fuselage
- Sections F-4 and F-5, between Frames 33 and 85, described as the middle and tail sections of the fuselage respectively. There was no engineering break between Sections F-4 and F-5.

The fuselage sections were butt-jointed at Frames 1, 13 and 33.

The Nose section. This section consisted of a frame, panels and the radar antenna cover (radome). In the upper part of the panelling of Section F-1 there were two cut-outs, the individual panels of which were covered with fibreglass 'shields' fastened to the inside surface. On aircraft of the 18th production series only one forward cut-out panel was used. An inspection panel was mounted on the left-hand side of the aircraft skin to enable servicing personnel to check the position of the radar antenna prior to removal of the radome. On aircraft of the 22nd production series small hatches were situated on the right-hand side of the nose section for access to the shock-absorbing mountings of the radar installation.

Section F-2 of the fuselage – the crew pressure cabin. This area housed the crew stations, flight instruments and various equipment and control systems of the aircraft. Entry into the cockpit was via access hatches on the underside of Section F-2, which could be jettisoned in the event of emergency egress from the aircraft. The framework of this section also incorporated the duralumin floor of the pilot's cockpit, located between Frames 6 and 10. Aircraft control rods and the engine power-management controls were attached to the floor, while an access 'tunnel' was provided on the right-hand side of the pressure cabin linking the navigator's position with the pilot and radar operator. The floor of this 'tunnel' between Frames 6 and 13 was made of plywood – on aircraft from the 11th production series onwards the plywood was covered with non-slip corrugated rubber.

Folding steps were installed on the right-hand side of the fuselage between Frames 10 and 12 to facilitate access for servicing – on aircraft from the 28th production series an additional folding ladder was provided on the right-hand side of the aircraft under the pilot's cockpit. The glazing of the navigator's station consisted of five single Plexiglas panels, each 20mm (0.78in) thick, while the pilot's canopy consisted of two windscreen panels and a side panel incorporating a sliding direct-vision window, plus an overhead emergency escape hatch. On the outside of the canopy frame, the windscreen was glazed with Plexiglas of 18mm (0.70in) thickness, while on the inside it was reinforced with additional glazing of 3mm (0.12in) thickness. The direct-vision panel slid along a pair of guide rails, and a windscreen wiper was mounted on the left-hand side of the upper canopy frame. The glazing of the radar operator's position consisted of two side panels, each 20mm (0.78in) thick, plus one 14mm (0.55in) thick panel mounted in the emergency escape hatch above his head. All three panels were of Plexiglas and mounted singly in their frames.

The forward unpressurised section F-3. This section itself consisted of three compartments: one housing the nose undercarriage when retracted, one housing Fuel Tanks 1 and 2, and one housing aircraft accessories and equipment, situated under Fuel Tank 1. An easily removable bulkhead was mounted at the rear of the nose undercarriage well, which separated the undercarriage unit when retracted from the equipment bay and cameras. The nose undercarriage doors were situated between Frames 14 and 20, while the compartments housing Fuel Tanks 1 and 2 were located between Frames 14 and 18 and 23 and 31, which acted as the forward and rear bulkheads of the fuel-tank containers.

Fuselage middle section F-4. This section was located between Frames 33 and 60 and housed the wing centre section, Fuel Tank 3, the two halves of Fuel Tank 4 and the weapons bay. [*The latter is referred to in Tu-22 technical documents as the payload or cargo bay* ('gruzovoy otsek'), *since it was not uniquely dedicated to the carriage of weapons per se.* AD]. The skin over the wing centre section between Frames 33 and 44 and in the well of the payload bay between Frames 44 and 53 (as well as the first detachable section of the wing) carried the greatest structural loads and was, therefore, fabricated from panels of varying profile, increasing in thickness towards Frame 44. During the climb and at subsonic speeds, with the aircraft in the normally trimmed condition, the pilot's control column (actually a W-shaped yoke) could deflect spontaneously to the right by 10°. This was due to differential rates of contraction (on cooling) affecting the skin panels and the longitudinal control rods of the ailerons which ran close to the panels inside the fuselage. At supersonic speeds and at high altitude, the effect was reversed, as a result of more intensive (solar) heating of the skin panels than that experienced by the aileron control rods, which expanded at a slower rate, and the control yoke would return to the neutral position and then deflect to the left by up to 6°. In order to try to minimise this phenomenon, it was decided to spray these most heavily loaded panels, made out of D16A-TL duralumin, with a special white paint to protect them from the effects of solar heating and corrosion, as well as to be able to monitor their condition more easily. When so painted, the panels looked like white dielectric antenna covers for electronic equipment and led to a flurry of speculative analysis by NATO 'specialists' regarding their significance, without their true purpose ever being determined. [*Some published sources have referred to these white panels being protective covers for 'special electronic equipment', in spite of a wealth of photography showing them clearly on aircraft in flight and the fact the technique was also applied to the engine nacelles. AD*].

The payload bay was situated between Frames 44 and 60, the main aperture of which was enclosed by two doors. The leading edges of the doors were equipped with aerodynamic spoilers to hinder the flow of air into the bay when the doors were open and reduce vibration when they were opened in flight. A hydraulic system electrically linked to the OPB-15 (*Opticheskii Pritsel Bombomyetaniya-15*) bomb-sight controlled the operation of the bay doors. This allowed the doors of the payload bay to be opened automatically a few seconds before bomb release when the aircraft was being used as a freefall bomber. Each door had three cut-outs serving as windows for the aircraft's camera equipment, which were covered with metal hatches when the aircraft was being used as a bomber. A hot-air manifold was mounted over the central camera port. Between Frames 55 and 58 in the rear of the payload bay there was a special crate for night-photography cameras which protected them from the turbulent air stream when the doors were open. The front wall of the crate acted as a removable protective shield, and on aircraft of the 13th production series the protective shield was mounted on a supporting beam. After removal of two quick-release bolts the assembly could tilt forward in the direction of flight, enabling the cameras to be serviced without removing the shield from the aircraft.

A fine air-to-air study of the Tu-22PD *Blinder-E*, illustrating to good effect the special white corrosion-treated panels which were also used to counter the effects of localised differential heating and cooling of the airframe. Just visible under the fuselage is the combined air intake and antenna housing for the crate-mounted jammers. *S Burdin Archive*

Fuselage tail section F-5. The tail section of the fuselage was located between Frames 60 and 85 and was effectively a continuation of the middle section of the fuselage described above. The fuselage tail section included the vertical fin, the tailplane, the tail skid, brake-parachute housing and the remotely controlled rear gun turret. The vertical fin support was a continuation of the main fuselage structure and was located between Frames 71 and 79. Its upper part, extending from the rear fuselage, formed a pylon onto which the fin, engines and engine nacelles were mounted. A retractable tail skid was mounted under the rear of the tail section between Frames 76 and 79. Also mounted in the tail section were the containers for Fuel Tanks 5, 6 and 7, the container for Tank 5 being located between Frames 60 and 66, Tank 6 between Frames 66 and 71 and Tank 7 between Frames 71 and 79. Between Frames 81 and 83 there was an access hatch for servicing equipment installed in the tail section of the fuselage, the external cover of which served also as the housing for the brake parachutes. On aircraft from the 12th production series a housing was provided between Frames 73 and 74 for an earthing (grounding) cable. A fairing ran along the entire length of the upper fuselage which housed radio antennae and cables. The fairing consisted of a fixed structure and a number of detachable panels. The middle fixed section of the fairing, and all the fibreglass panels, covered the antennae of the aircraft's radio systems. The fairing had a telescopic junction in the region of Frames 52 and 53 to prevent damage to the structure when subjected to 'self-weight deflection' of the fuselage.

Wing

The wing, of P-60 profile at the root and SR-8 profile at the tip, possessed conical twist of –4° and was made up of the centre section, built into the fuselage, two primary detachable sections occupying the region between the centre section and Rib 14 and two secondary detachable sections occupying the area between Rib 14 and the wing-tip.
The primary part of the wing comprised:

The wing of the Tu-22 comprised first and second detachable sections, the entire trailing edge being 'mechanised' with inboard flaps, mid-section flaperons outboard of the undercarriage nacelle and outboard ailerons. This aircraft is equipped with the 'flexible undercarriage mounting' and therefore does not have wing-tip anti-flutter weights. Modification to incorporate the 'flexible undercarriage mounting' can be confirmed by the presence of the small bulges on the upper and lower surface of the nacelle. *S Burdin*

- A torsion box
- Detachable leading edges mounted on the front spar
- A rear section mounted on the rear spar
- Flaps.

The area between the spars was the main load-bearing element of the wing (the torsion box), made up of spar webs and caps and upper and lower panels. The leading edge of the wing was made detachable to facilitate access to the control rods of the ailerons, flaperons, electrical wiring looms and (hydraulic) pipes which were mounted along the length of the front spar. The main undercarriage housings, the undercarriage support structures and the flaps were mounted on the primary detachable part of the wing.

The primary detachable part of the wing extended from the fuselage where Rib 1 was joined to the centre section and terminated at Rib 14, which was the attachment point for the secondary detachable part of the wing. At the wing fuselage juncture there was a leading-edge fillet, cut-outs being provided in this area between Frames 30 and 32 for retractable landing lights under each wing. Fuel tanks were installed between the ribs of the detachable wing-section torsion box.

The beam which carried the supports for the flaps was mounted on a hinged bracket assembly mounted on the rear spar, and on the fuselage (at Frame 51). Consequently, the beam could experience an axial displacement of up to 33mm (1.29in) and up to 7mm (0.27in) on the flaps, which prevented bending of the support beam when the relatively thin wing of the Tu-22 experienced twisting loads in flight. This design eliminated the danger of jamming of the flap drive mechanism. The flaps on the primary detachable section of the wing installed on the aircraft (up to the third aircraft of the 24th production series) were of single slotted design with a movable axis of rotation. The flaps were attached by three support brackets to a beam on the rear section of the wing, between the fuselage side and the undercarriage housing, and were driven by three screw jacks on a common transmission shaft from a gearbox mounted on the rear face of the beam. The flaps deflected to 35° for take-off and landing. With the aim of improving the take-off and landing qualities of the aircraft and elimination of vibration with undercarriage and flaps lowered, the flaps were changed to a double-slotted design from the third aircraft of the 24th production series. The design differed from normal in that the leading edge of the flap in the region of the support bracket was made as a continuous profiled slot.

The secondary detachable part of the wing comprised:

- A torsion box
- Detachable leading edges mounted on the front spar
- A rear section mounted on the rear spar
- Flaps
- Ailerons
- Anti-flutter weights at the wing-tips.

On the upper surface of each secondary (outer) wing panel, in the region of Ribs 15 to 19, an aerodynamic 'fence' was mounted parallel to the longitudinal axis of the aircraft centreline and perpendicular to the wing chord. The wing fence consisted of four separate riveted sections, and a notch was made on the two rear sections of the fence at a distance of 100mm (3.9in) from the surface of the wing. The notches were intended to prevent the

An excellent take-off study of a Tu-22U at Machulishchi showing the main undercarriage bogies articulating into the vertical position before lying horizontally in the middle of the nacelle. *S Burdin Archive*

fences from being damaged or broken when the wing was subjected to twisting and deflection in flight. The maximum height of the wing fences was 423mm (16.5in).

The wing-tip embodied a cigar-shaped fairing which blended smoothly into the profile of the wing from leading edge to trailing edge. The fairing contained a counter-balance weight made out of L40G2 steel weighing 90kg (198lb), selected to improve the wing's anti-flutter characteristics, with the fairing's centre of gravity located ahead of the wing leading edge by 1,000mm (39.0in). Navigation lights were mounted on the outer edge of the anti-flutter weight fairing. The antennae of the SRZO-2 ('Chrome-Nickel') IFF system were mounted in the rear tail cone of the fairing and underneath the removable centre section. The flaps mounted in the outer wing panel were driven by a pair of screw jacks, while the outboard ailerons comprised two sections, incorporating aerodynamic balance and servo trim tabs.

The undercarriage nacelles were mounted on the wings in the region of Ribs 8 to 14, and bolted to the lower and upper surfaces of the torsion box and to the rear spar. An automatic chaff-dispensing unit was installed in the rear part of the undercarriage nacelle, while the extreme tip of the nacelle housed the antennae of the Sirena-3 (Siren) radar warning receiver.

Changes incorporated in the secondary wing panel as a result of introducing flap-ailerons (flaperons) and the so-called 'flexible undercarriage mounting'.

Starting with the fourth aircraft of the 35th production series, the flap section on the secondary (outer) wing panel was changed to permit combined operation as both a flap and an aileron in an attempt to eradicate the phenomenon of 'aileron reversal' (where the aircraft reacts in roll in the opposite sense to the control input, because of structural twisting). The Western convention is to refer to these controls as 'flaperons', and this term will be used throughout the book. The flaperon had exactly the same appearance and construction as the original lift-augmenting flap, but modification to enable it to be used as a high-speed aileron led to the following changes in the design of the outer wing panel:

- Introduction of new flap-control mechanisms and a mechanism to facilitate change-over from flap to aileron and vice versa
- Additional hatches were provided in the wing to facilitate access to and inspection of the new flap-control mechanisms, the flap-aileron change-over unit and control rods
- Control rods and support brackets in the control linkage were strengthened
- The outer wing panel was strengthened in the region of attachment of the flaperon.

Changes incorporated in the design and construction of the undercarriage nacelles as a result of installing the 'flexible undercarriage mounting' and the introduction of flaperons.

On aircraft incorporating the 'flexible undercarriage mounting' and flaperons the undercarriage nacelles themselves underwent a number of small design changes. The essential feature of the 'flexible undercarriage mounting' was that in the retracted position in flight, the undercarriage bogies were able to 'oscillate' within defined limits, helping to relieve the bending moment of the heavy bogies on the wing and airframe structure. The previous design of the nacelles did not allow the essential clearance between the undercarriage bogies and the nacelle itself. The 'flexible undercarriage mounting' provided clearance between the retracted bogie and the rear of the undercarriage door, between the wheels and the rear of the undercarriage door and between the wheels and the retraction jack and the upper part of the inside of the nacelle.

Tail unit
The tail unit of the aircraft incorporated a swept-back tailplane and fin, each with a symmetrical airfoil section, the tailplane being of the all-moving type. On all aircraft up to the 23rd production series (but excluding the first aircraft of the 23rd series), the tailplane could deflect upwards by 1° and down by 18°. The downwards deflection was increased to 19° on aircraft from the 24th production series onwards (and also including the first aircraft of the 23rd series). The slab tailplane comprised two halves mounted on the left and right of the fuselage, on fixed beams, at Frames 76 and 79. Both halves of the tailplane had a common control linkage and could only be deflected synchronously, up or down.

The rudder could deflect to left and right from the neutral position by 25°, while the trim tab could deflect left and right by 5°. After the adoption of the flaperon system of roll control, the rudder was also strengthened to take heavier aerodynamic loads. On aircraft up to the 41st production series, strengthening of the rudder was achieved by the use of a thickened single panel (without a transverse join) at the rear of the surface, which had a reduced number of chemically milled cells. Commencing with aircraft of the 42nd production series, the rudder strength was increased by the insertion of additional ribs in the spaces between the main ribs.

Undercarriage

The undercarriage comprised a twin-wheel nose unit and two four-wheel main bogies, plus a retractable tail skid. The tail skid was an integral part of the undercarriage and was designed to protect the lower part of the rear fuselage from damage in the event of accidental contact with the runway during a hard landing or over-enthusiastic rotation on take-off. All undercarriage elements had oleo-pneumatic shock absorbers. Retraction and extension of the nose and main undercarriage legs involved the use of the primary hydraulic system and, in the event of failure, by the secondary system. In the event that both hydraulic systems failed there was a tertiary back-up system for emergency lowering of the undercarriage. The tertiary system was energised by extension into the airflow of under-wing mounted ATN-15 (*Avariinyi TurboNasos-15*) ram air turbines. Operation of the tail skid was synchronised with the retraction and extension of the nose-wheel leg, and was activated by the MP-250 (*Mekhanizm Privodnoy-250*) drive mechanism. All three undercarriage legs retracted backwards, the nose-wheel retracting into a housing under the crew compartment and the main legs into streamlined nacelles mounted on the wing. The nose-wheel leg was equipped with hydraulic dampers on the shock strut, which also acted as steering cylinders for turning the nose-wheel.

The main undercarriage units were each equipped with a four-wheel bogie, with hydraulic disc brakes and an anti-skid system. The moving elements (*kinematika*) of the bogies were designed so that during retraction the forward pair of wheels moved

downwards and backwards and when fully retracted lay to the rear of the nacelle. This ensured that the undercarriage leg and bogie fitted the contour of the nacelle in the most compact way possible. In the extended position for landing, the forward pair of wheels of the main undercarriage bogies assumed a slightly downward tilted attitude with respect to the rear pair, a characteristic of all of Tupolev's 'big jets'. All undercarriage units were enclosed by doors in the retracted position, while the tail skid aperture was covered by the skid itself in the retracted position. The main undercarriage of the Tu-22 was essentially similar to that developed for its subsonic stablemate, the Tu-16 *Badger*, and was considered suitable for the new aircraft with little modification. A twin-canopy brake-parachute was used to reduce the

The nose-wheel of the Tu-22, flanked by the antennae of the RSIU-5 VHF radio set. *S Burdin*

Main undercarriage of the Tu-22, showing the comparatively simple 'kinematics' of the unit. When information first became available that the aircraft was equipped with a 'flexible undercarriage mounting', at least one reputable British reference source suggested that this allowed the 'main legs to swing rearward for additional cushioning during taxiing and landing on rough runways'! The correct explanation is in the text of this chapter.

landing run, the parachutes being housed in a special container at the rear of the fuselage. The brake-chute was deployed on touchdown and was released at the end of the landing run, usually by a command signal from the pilot, although both the pilot and the navigator had control switches in their individual cockpits. Four dry-powder PRD-63/SPRD-63 (*Startovyi Porokhovoy Raketnyi Dvigatyel'-63*) booster rockets (two on either side) could be mounted underneath the inner wing panels, between the fuselage and the undercarriage nacelles, to reduce the take-off run. The pilot had control of the ignition button, and both the pilot and the navigator had jettison switches for the rockets.

Undercarriage main technical details:

	Main undercarriage	Nose-wheel
Type of wheel	KT-76/4U	KT-100U
Tyre size	1160 × 290V	1000 × 280V
Tyre pressure	13kg/cm²	9.5kg/cm²
Turning angle of nose-wheel leg:		
– During taxiing		+/– 40°
– On take-off & landing		+/– 5°

Brake-parachute main technical details:

	Data
Type and quantity	PT-4952-58 [one chute with twin canopies – changed to an improved design on later variants]
Area of one canopy	52m² [560sq ft]
Permitted speed for deployment of brake-chute	Up to 350kph [189kts]

SPRD-63 rocket booster main technical details:

	Data
Maximum thrust	3,500–5,500kg [7,716–12,125lb]
Operating duration	13–17 seconds
Weight of charged booster	550kg [1,212lb]
Length of booster	1,710mm [66.70in]
Diameter	512mm [20.00in]

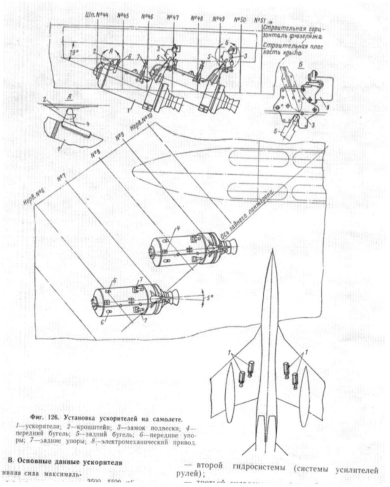

Фиг. 126. Установка ускорителей на самолете.
1—ускорители; *2*—кронштейн; *3*—замок подвески; *4*—передний бугель; *5*—задний бугель; *6*—передние упоры; *7*—задние упоры; *8*—электромеханический привод.

В. Основные данные ускорителя
ивная сила максималь-
                    3500–5500 кг

— второй   гидросистемы (системы усилителей рулей);
— третьей гидроси

Installation of the SP
63 rocket boosters.

The crew members were protected from behind by steel armour-plating, against penetration of the pressure cabin by 20mm cannon shells, and from below by duralumin armour, from shrapnel penetration by anti-aircraft artillery (AAA) shells. Behind the ejection seats of the pilot and navigator there were panels of AB-548 armour-plating, 15mm (0.59in) thick, which protected both the crew and the guide rails of their ejection seats and telescoping mechanisms. The radar operator was protected from armour-piercing shell fragments by a 12mm (0.47in) armoured panel of AB-548 steel, mounted at Frame 13 (the enclosing bulkhead of the pressure compartment).

The Tu-22 variants
Tu-22RD
Provision of an in-flight refuelling capability, incorporated in the basic design of the standard Tu-22R to increase the aircraft's range, resulted in the application of the new designation of Tu-22RD (*Razvedchik Dal'nyi* – literally Reconnaissance [Long] Range). Other changes introduced at this time were:

1. Improvements to the design of the fuselage Nose Section F-1
2. Design improvements to the pressure cabin Section F-2 and Section F-3
3. Modifications to the upper fuselage fairing and fin leading edge
4. Improvements to the aircraft's fuel system, which involved:
   - Removal of Fuel Tank 1
   - A change to the order in which fuel was consumed from the groups of tanks, in connection with which the TATs2-1V fuel-management controller was replaced by a TATs2-1B unit
   - Tank 2 was provided with four fuel pumps instead of the original two
   - The single-point pressure refuelling valve was relocated to the lower fuselage between Frames 13 and 14. Control of the refuelling process was carried out from a control panel mounted in front of the radar operator. The new system incorporated provision for purging fuel from the main supply line and filling it with CO_2 as a means of reducing a potential fire hazard in combat conditions. This procedure was carried out both on the ground and in the air, after refuelling
5. The fuel-tank drainage system was improved
6. The system of purging the tanks with neutral (CO_2) gas was improved
7. The fire-detection and suppression system was improved
8. The aircraft's high-altitude equipment was improved
9. Improvements were made to the electrical system and, in particular, OPS-57 formation (station-keeping) lighting and SPM-1 anti-collision beacons were installed
10. New aircraft and radio equipment was installed and older equipment was modified.

The powerplant underwent the most significant changes in the process of modification to the Tu-22RD standard, with more efficient RD-7M2 engines replacing the original VD-7Ms. The RD-7M2 was based on the VD-7M, but the newer engine's maximum thrust at altitude (11,000m/36,090ft), and at maximum speed, was 20% greater than the VD-7M in similar conditions. The RD-7M2's maximum thrust on the ground was 500kg (1,100lb) greater than the VD-7M. The increased thrust was achieved by means of:

- An increase in the maximum rpm of the engine at maximum dry thrust and in all reheat modes by 100rpm (i.e. increased to 7,500rpm)
- The introduction of a new first-stage compressor, permitting the inlet guide vanes to be set at –5° (instead of –10° to –13° on the VD-7M), permitting in turn a higher air mass flow through the compressor
- Increasing the temperature of the exhaust gas in the afterburner chamber to 1,950°C (instead of 1,775°C in the VD-7M)
- Introduction of an improved supersonic nozzle.

The main design differences between the RD-7M2 and the VD-7M were:

- A constant angle of –5° for the attachment of the inlet guide vane blades, with a simpler control system as a consequence of having no hydraulic mechanisms
- The first stage of the compressor rotor employed 20 blades (instead of 22 on the VD-7M), set at an angle changed by 2° at the pressure face, and with an additional change of angle to the upper section of the blades (by 5°) to reduce auto-oscillation. The rotor of the 9th stage of the compressor used blades whose chord was increased by 4mm (0.16in) in order to provide a greater anti-surge margin
- The nozzle, when operating in maximum reheat, with high pressure differentials (i.e. at high flight speeds) was divergent. In cruise reheat mode, and with low pressure differentials at the nozzle, it was convergent
- Ignition of the fuel mix in the afterburner chamber was achieved by means of an ignition chamber (the VD-7M used two igniters).

RD-7M2 operating parameters (in ISA conditions)

Parameter	Engine rpm	Thrust	SFC kg/kg thrust/hr	Maximum TGT
Take-off [max thrust on ground at V=0] for periods of not more than 5 minutes	7,500	16,500kg [36,375lb]	2.15	645°
Maximum non-reheat thrust, on ground [V=0]	7,500	11,000kg [24,250lb]	0.87	645°
Nominal, on ground [V=0]	6,900	8,600kg [18,960lb]	0.83	540°
Maximum high-altitude reheat mode at 11,000m [36,090ft] and 1,700kph [918kts]	Not more than 7,450	13,250kg [29,210lb]	2.35	675°
Cruise reheat at 11,000m [36,090ft] at 1,300 – 1,400kph [702 – 756kts]	Not more than 7,450	8,000kg [17,637lb]	1.9	650°
Cruise at 11,000m [36,090ft] at 1,000kph [540kts]	6,950	2,500kg [5,511lb]	1.05	510°
Ground idle	Not more than 3,250	Not more than 450kg [992lb]	Not applicable	410°

Tu-22U

Design differences between the Tu-22U (*Uchebnyi*/Trainer) conversion training variant and the Tu-22R principally involved the installation of an instructor's cockpit, which projected prominently above the fuselage behind the cockpit occupied by the pilot under instruction. The navigator's station was largely unchanged from that of the Tu-22R/RD and mainly involved changes relating to the transfer to the navigator of power supply controls and operation of the SRZO-2 IFF system, plus operation of the radio communications and the US-8 receiver. The position occupied by the pilot under instruction was also largely unchanged from that on the Tu-22R/RD, with the obvious exception of system changes relating to the aircraft's dual-control capability. The instructor's cockpit was installed in the location previously occupied by the radar operator and was equipped very much like the cockpit of the pilot under instruction, with minor changes in the location and number of flight instruments.

The following changes were made to the pressure cabin (Section F-2) of the aircraft on conversion to the Tu-22U variant:

- Installation of an instructor's cockpit in the area previously occupied by the radar operator, between Frames 9 and 13, above the trainee pilot's cockpit, so that the instructor had an improved view. Emergency exit hatches were provided in the left and right sides of the instructor's cockpit, identical to the starboard emergency exit of the trainee pilot. The emergency exit windows opened inwards, and an inwards-opening direct-vision panel was installed on the left-hand side of the canopy
- A separate floor was installed in the instructor's cockpit
- An entry hatch and ejection-seat guide rails were installed for the instructor's cockpit, the entry hatch being slightly further forward than the radar operator's entry hatch on the Tu-22R/RD. The hatch cover opened outwards and was hinged at its rear edge, like that of the trainee pilot. The instructor's ejection seat rails were inclined at the same angle as those of the trainee
- Frame 13 was changed and the steel armour-plating in the upper part of this frame on the Tu-22R was replaced by duralumin plate, attached at the same points

The cockpits of the Tu-22U, showing the displacement of the instructor's station above that of the trainee and the slightly different glazing of the canopies. It can also be appreciated from this perspective that the navigator had a very limited view, other than in an oblique downward direction. *S Burdin*

- The navigator and trainee pilot were provided with special window 'blinds' to protect them from the harmful effects of solar radiation and to simulate instrument flying conditions 'under the hood'. These comprised:
  1. Blinds on the inside of the windscreen glazing of the trainee pilot, which were of fan-shaped design, comprising six fan lobes
  2. Blinds on the inside of the direct-vision panel, also of fan-shaped design, consisting of six lobes
  3. Blinds on the upper windscreen panels made of rubberised fabric with a concertina-type action
  4. Blinds on the navigator's window panels made of rubberised fabric, sliding on a rail
  5. Blinds on the upper side (eyebrow) windows made of rubberised fabric and sliding on a rail. The trainee pilot had remote control of the blinds using one hand, which allowed him to close the central window blinds and the navigator's upper side window blinds simultaneously
  6. The blinds of the central window incorporating fixed 'shields' and a movable sun visor
  7. The AFA camera hatches were provided with visors.

The framework of Section F-2 was also changed, involving strengthening of the area around Frame 1 and with the upper panels from Frame 1 to 4 being increased in thickness from 1mm to 1.5mm (0.04 to 0.6in).

Changes to Fuselage Section F-3 of Tu-22U
Changes to the forward fuselage Section F-3 relating to the installation of the instructor's cockpit, resulted in an increase in height of the pressure cabin Section F-2. In order to achieve a smooth transition from F-2 to F-3, new panelling was used which was effectively an extension of the instructor's cockpit and in the region of Frame 18 the new fairing met up with the original fairing of the Tu-22R. The fairing of the front section of the aircraft was identical to that of the Tu-22R and differed only in the panelling used.

- As a result of the removal of Fuel Tank 1, the area freed up was used as an accessories compartment, and a water tank for the aircraft's air-conditioning system was positioned here. A hatch was placed at Frame 14 for access to the accessories compartment from Section F-2. The hatch was increased in size at Frame 18 (the rear wall of the accessories compartment), through which it was possible to install the water tank
- In the area between Frames 24 and 31 additional quick-release service panels were provided for access to equipment.

Following removal of the original tail-gun installation, the PRS-3 gun-laying radar (NATO codename *Fan Tail*) and the TP-1A television sighting system, the tail section of the Tu-22U terminated in a smoothly rounded fairing, attached by bolts to Frame 85.

The flight instruments and navigation equipment of the Tu-22U were broadly similar to those of the Tu-22R and differed mainly in the installation of new equipment for the instructor pilot. The navigator also had the following modified installations:

- A KPP-M2 unit from the RSBN-2S short-range navigation system
- An indicator showing the great circle course provided by the BTs-63A stellar navigation system
- Warning lights relating to the fuel system and electrical power supplies

The AGD-1 artificial horizon indicator was moved from a separate mounting to the main instrument panel, and because of the increased number of instruments the area of the instrument panel was increased, with some instruments being repositioned. The trainee pilot's instrument panel had more warning lights than on the Tu-22R, and in an attempt to reduce glare and reflections the panel was painted with a special black paint called 'Muar' ('Moiré' – literally 'watered silk'). The layout of the instructor's instrument panel was identical to that of the trainee, which simplified the issue of instructions from the instructor to the trainee. The instructor pilot's instrument panel was displaced by 200mm (7.8in) from Frame 11 and was mounted on the support for the rudder pedals. The panel had a rubber-edged coaming to reduce reflections from the instrument dials and warning lamps, while the panel was illuminated with ARUFOSh-45 (*Armatura Reguliruyemaya Ul'trafioletovovo Osvyeshcheniya Shturmanskaya-45*) ultra-violet lighting (developed in 1945), and additionally with white lighting in the instructor's cockpit.

The hydraulic system was modified to take account of the requirement for dual control of the braking system, as well as to improve the nose-wheel steering.

Changes to the aircraft's avionics system involved the removal of the PRS-3 (Argon-2) gun-laying radar, while modifications were introduced in the Rubin (Ruby) navigation and bombing radar. This radar was known by the NATO code name of *Short Horn*, and was one of the mostly widely used Russian navigation radars, being standard equipment on a variety of bombers, transports and even helicopters.

The emergency escape system of the Tu-22U differed from that of the Tu-22R in that all three crew members sat on forward-facing ejection seats, whereas in the Tu-22R the radar operator faced rearwards. The navigator's seat and the seat of the trainee pilot did not differ from the seats on the Tu-22R, while the instructor pilot's seat was the same as that of the navigator. In the event of an emergency, ejection took place in the following sequence: trainee pilot, followed by the navigator and then the instructor. When the aircraft was on a ferry flight, when the aircraft commander occupied the trainee pilot's seat, the ejection sequence was changed to the crew member occupying the instructor's seat ejecting first, followed by the navigator and then the 'second' pilot. Raising and lowering the seat for normal entry and exit was carried out by an EPV-1 (*EhlektroPri Vod-1*) electrical drive unit under the seat. This allowed each crew member to raise or lower the seat independently on the ground. In addition to the mechanical means of escaping from the aircraft, each crew member also had a rope ladder attached to the inside of the fuselage near the emergency exits. This could be used in the event of a 'wheels-up' landing, or after a normal landing away from base when there was no supporting personnel or equipment with which to perform a 'turn-round'. Other minor changes involved the installation of a single AFA-41/20 camera in the accessories compartment, but no provision was made for inclusion of APP-22 and KDS-16GM chaff dispensers, in view of the aircraft's non-combatant role. On the other hand, six KD3-105A and four KD4-105A bomb racks were included, since the aircraft was designed to be used for bombing training.

Tu-22U with dummy refuelling probe

Commencing with Tu-22U Construction No. 3105, an in-flight 'refuelling' system was installed, which allowed the aircraft to be used to train pilots in this technique. However, it was never planned that the system would be used for actual transfer of fuel from the modified Tu-22U, but rather it would be used as a 'live' procedural trainer. The additional work involved in modifying the Tu-22U as an in-flight refuelling procedural trainer included the following:

1. Nose section F-1
   - A dummy refuelling probe, fitted with a balance weight, was mounted ahead of the cockpit
   - New strengthened Fuselage Frames 4n, 6n and 9n were incorporated into the fuselage structure
   - A new radome made of a fibreglass honeycomb sandwich was used.
2. Modification of the powerplant
   - The RD-7M was installed in place of the VD-7M
   - Fuel Tank 1 was removed, along with three ETsN-T fuel pumps
   - Fuel Tank 2 was removed, along with two ETsN-315A fuel pumps
   - Fuel Tank 2 was re-installed with two ETsN-315A and two ETsN-T fuel pumps
   - Fuel Tank 7 was changed
   - The order of fuel consumption from the tanks was changed.
3. Modification of the aircraft's high-altitude equipment and oxygen system, involving the following changes:
   - Installation of a water tank and condenser, an air-to-air heat exchanger and turbo-cooler, etc. in the accessories compartment, in place of Fuel tank 1, and the volume of the water tank increased to 430 litres.
   - A heating pipe, with flattened delivery heads, was routed into the instructor's cockpit, both to heat the cockpit and to prevent misting and icing of the cockpit glazing
   - A windscreen wiper was installed on the upper left-hand section of the instructor's cockpit windscreen frame
   - A receptacle was provided in the region of Frame 13 for plugging in a ground air-conditioning unit.
4. A Pion-B (Peony) antenna feed system was installed, involving the following changes:
   - Removal of the standard antenna set of the RSBN-2S short-range navigation system
   - Removal of the SRZO-2 IFF antenna units of Ranges I, II and III, with the exception of the forward antenna of Range III.
5. BANO-57 navigation lights and an antenna unit of the Pion-B antenna feed system was mounted in a dielectric cover on the wingtip fairing
6. Fin. An A3-05M antenna unit of the Pion-B antenna feed system was mounted on the fin-tip fairing, and a blanking plate was installed over the cut-out for the removed RSBN-2S antenna.

Tu-22P

Design differences between the Tu-22P (*Postanovshchik Pomyekh*) ECM variant and the Tu-22R baseline reconnaissance version were characterised by the following changes to the airframe:

1. All photo-reconnaissance camera equipment and control systems were removed from the payload (weapons) bay
2. The SRS-6 electronic intelligence (Elint) equipment was removed

A dramatic shot of a Tu-22PD *Blinder-E* landing at Machulishchi. *S Burdin Archive*

3. The weapons-bay doors were replaced by access doors which could only be opened on the ground
4. All bombing equipment was removed, with the exception of the BD6-105A bomb rack, which was modified to carry the special equipment crates (*konteinery*) for the ECM equipment
5. The avionics suite was changed and modified to take account of the changed role of the new variant.

During subsequent work involved in modifying the Tu-22P ECM variant into the extended range Tu-22PD, the aircraft underwent the same changes as applied to the Tu-22R when it was modified to the Tu-22RD standard.

Tu-22K
The Tu-22K dedicated missile-carrying variant of the aircraft incorporated the following design changes:

1. Fuselage:
    • The weapons-bay doors were specially modified to allow the aircraft to be used as a conventional free-fall bomber, as well as being able to carry a single Kh-22 (AS-4 *Kitchen*) air-to-surface missile. The Kh-22 missile was longer than the weapons bay, so the missile had to be carried in a semi-recessed position, requiring specially profiled cut-outs to be made in the fuselage skin ahead of the weapons bay, between Frames 30 and 44. These cut-outs were provided with doors which covered the unpressurised compartment below the wing torsion box, isolated from the rest of the fuselage. The doors of the main weapons bay and the doors covering the nose section of the Kh-22 missile opened inwards for loading of the weapon. Control of

the operation of the doors was by an air-operated system via electrically signalled pneumatic valves, from a switch on the electrical services panel at the navigator's station. When the aircraft was used as a free-fall bomber the weapons-bay doors opened outwards
- The weapons bay itself was modified with equipment specially designed for the carriage of the missile.

2. Hydraulic system:
- A hydraulic ram was installed on the weapons rack on which the missile was suspended, with the main supply provided by the primary hydraulic system and the reserve supply from the secondary hydraulic system. The hydraulic ram was designed to permit the rack to be extended in 12 to 18 seconds.

3. Emergency escape system:
- A valve was installed to place the rudder pedals and the control column in the position for ejection from the normal working position
- In order to prevent the safety pins of the air-operated valves of the pilot's and navigator's escape hatch covers from vibrating loose and falling out, the pins were fitted with additional locking devices.

4. Fire-protection system: Additional warning lights were installed to warn of the presence of fire in the engine compartment of the missile and in the aircraft weapons bay. On aircraft from the 43rd production series onwards, these lights were mounted on the central warning panel.

5. Pneumatic system:
- A system for the control of the weapons bay doors was installed
- A system for priming the pressurisation of the missile's electronic equipment compartments was installed
- Instead of the system for priming the Rubin (NATO *Short Horn*) radar, a system for priming the pressurisation of the PN (NATO *Downbeat*) radar units was installed.

6. Navigation equipment:
- The layout and composition of the instrument panels of the pilot and the radar operator was partially changed
- A TsNVU-B1A (*Tsentral'noye Navigatsionnoye Vychyslityel'noye Ustroystvo-B1A*) central navigation computer was installed to provide a continuous read-out of the aircraft's position, plus programming of navigation waypoints and processing of various control signals from other aircraft systems.

7. High altitude equipment:
- The air-conditioning system controls were repositioned
- An air-conditioning system for the missile warhead was installed, with the system's controls being mounted in the navigator's cockpit.

The pilot's cockpit of a Tu-22K showing the airliner-style control wheel with the traditional Tupolev logo and aircraft marque in the centre.

8. Electrical system:
   - The ultra-violet lighting system was replaced by red back-lighting of the instrument panels
   - The nose-wheel steering interlock with flaps lowered was removed to provide better manoeuvrability on the ground.
9. Radio equipment:
   - The navigator's radio control panel was slightly modified, along with a change of location of the pilot's radio control panel
   - An RV-25A radio altimeter was installed in place of the RV-25TAU unit of the reconnaissance variants
   - The PN (NATO *Downbeat*) navigation-bombing radar was installed in place of the Rubin (NATO *Short Horn*) radar
   - The Kurs-N (Course-N) target-locating and designation system of the K-22P integrated missile-control system was installed. This system was designed to locate and facilitate destruction of enemy land-based and ship-based radars using the Kh-22MP variant of the AS-4 *Kitchen* air-launched cruise missile, equipped with a PGP-K passive seeker head
   - The Shtyr' A-5 (Pin) and Romb-4A (Rhombus) equipments were removed
   - The Sirena-3 (Siren) radar warning receiver was interconnected to the PN radar
   - An SRZ-10 Latun' (Brass) unit of the Kremniy-2 (Silicon) combined-arms radar identification system was installed. This system was designed to identify (friendly) detected radars and targets which were equipped with radar transponders.
10. Weapons system:
    - A BD-294 weapons rack was installed
    - The layout of the navigator's weapons-release control panel was changed and the panel was made to be removable
    - Control of the weapons bay doors was changed.
11. A PT-12024-69 brake-parachute was installed, with twin canopies, each of 52m² (560sq ft) area.

Tu-22RM

The Tu-22RM differed from the basic Tu-22R (i.e. the variant not equipped for in-flight refuelling) in the following details:

1. Fuel system:
   - Fuel Tank 1 was removed
   - Fuel Tank 2 was equipped with two additional fuel pumps intended to supply the engines with fuel on start-up
   - The TATs2-1D automatic fuel-management system was replaced with a TATs2-1B unit.
2. Electrical system:
   - In connection with the aircraft's reconnaissance equipment changes, the 115V 400Hz supply for certain user services was redistributed. The starboard SGS-30-8RS generator was now a 'working' generator, supplying power to the SPS-15/153 ECM units, while the port generator serviced not only the R-847 communications radios, but also the heating of the cockpit glazing. Switching off any generator led to all 28V three-phase AC electrical services being fed from the working generator.

3. A total of five different camera 'fits' could be installed on the Tu-22RM.
4. ECM equipment:
   - One SPS-151MD set in place of the DK-20 rear gun turret and the PRS-3 (NATO *Fantail*) gun-laying radar, the ECM equipment being housed in the first compartment of a new 'common' tail fairing
   - One SPS-153DA set (with the possibility of being replaced by an SPS-152DA) installed in the second compartment of the new tail fairing
   - One SPS-151ME and one SPS-153ER set (with the possibility of being replaced by an SPS-152ER), installed in place of the removed fuel tank 1 in the forward fuselage
   - A Beryoza-P (Silver Birch) radar warning receiver was installed in place of the original SPO-3
   - Three sets of ASO-2I (i.e. letter I), firing IPP-26 infra-red flares, were installed in the rear of the main undercarriage nacelles (one in each) and in the tail fairing.
5. Radio equipment – additional installations:
   - An R-847T-EP radio (transceiver) was installed in place of the original R-836
   - An R-876T-EP radio receiver was installed in place of the US-8 receiver unit
   - Two R-832M transceivers instead of two R-802V and one R-832
   - A T-817 encryption unit
   - An SO-69 ATC transponder with associated UVID-30-15 electro-mechanical altimeter.
6. Additional installations in the pilot's cockpit:
   - An SO-69 transponder control unit
   - A Beryoza-P radar warning receiver indicator unit
   - An UVID-30-15 altimeter
   - A control unit for the T-817 transmission encryption system
   - A fuel-management system failure warning lamp on the instrument panel.
7. Additional installations in the navigator's cockpit:
   - A paired control unit for the starboard and port AFA-42/100 oblique cameras and a switch for selection and control of the camera installation, on the right-hand side of the cockpit
   - Control units for the short-focal-length cameras mounted in the camera crate, on the left-hand side of the cockpit
   - A control unit for the AFA-42/100 vertical camera, low down on the left-hand side of the cockpit
   - A new bombing control panel with a control unit for the 'special device' (*Spetsizdeliye*). [*The term Spetsizdeliye is a Soviet-era euphemism for a nuclear weapon. AD*]
   - A control panel for the T-817 transmission encryption system.

Aero-elasticity and problems of control

The Tu-22, like all other early-generation supersonic aircraft with thin wings, exhibited a range of problems connected with flight at high subsonic and supersonic speeds. These were, specifically:

1. Flutter
2. Aileron reversal
3. Self-generated oscillation of the ailerons (aileron buzz) and rudder

4. Problems of stability and controllability
- The main type of flutter (i.e. undamped structural vibration of the wing), generic to the Tu-22, arose from the asymmetrical nature of the undercarriage/wing relationship. The main factors influencing the speed at which flutter was likely to occur were the mass and stiffness of the locus of the undercarriage attachment to the wing and the stiffness and mass distribution of the wing itself. On the basis of theoretical and flight test research into wing flutter on the Tu-22, it was decided initially to mount anti-flutter weights in streamlined fairings at the wing-tips. These weighed 90kg (198lb) and projected 1 metre (3.28ft) ahead of the wing-tip leading edge. Apart from this, the stiffness of the outer wing panels was increased in line with the results revealed by static fatigue testing. These measures ensured a certain protection from the onset of flutter in the Tu-22R up to dynamic pressures of 4,080kg/m² (95,000lb/sq ft) and speeds of 920kph (496kts). However, this limitation did not allow the full performance potential designed into the Tu-22R airframe and its powerplant to be realised. Therefore, in order to guarantee freedom from the effects of flutter up to dynamic pressure limits of 5,000kg/m² (118,650lb/sq ft) and speeds of 1,020kph (550kts), it was decided to introduce a so-called 'flexible undercarriage mounting' of the main undercarriage bogies. Using this expedient meant that the main wheel bogies could 'oscillate' within the nacelle in the retracted position, within limits defined by special hydraulic dampers and a sequence of eight disc springs. Use of the 'flexible undercarriage mounting' also eliminated the need for the wing-tip anti-flutter weights, since the modification effectively transformed the retracted undercarriage into an internal anti-flutter device in its own right.
- Lateral control of the Tu-22K at speeds of the order of Mach 0.9 was achieved by use of ordinary ailerons. However, at high speed the effectiveness of normal ailerons was significantly reduced as a consequence of deformation of the wing (bending and twisting) caused by deflection of the aileron itself. In sufficiently high dynamic pressure conditions, the bending and twisting of the wing with aileron deflection led to complete loss of effectiveness of the ailerons and even to the phenomenon of 'aileron reversal'. This was characterised by the fact that an upwards-deflected aileron, for example, would create an aerodynamic moment which rotated the aircraft about the longitudinal axis, not in the direction of movement of the pilot's control column, but in the opposite direction. Aileron reversal was always preceded by loss of effectiveness of the ailerons, or so-called 'wing heaviness'. During flight testing of the Tu-22, without incurring the risk of an accident, crews would routinely take the aircraft right up to the speed beyond which aileron reversal was likely to occur. Nevertheless, the aircraft's general designer took the decision to limit the indicated airspeed (IAS) of the Tu-22 for normal operations in Soviet Air Force bomber regiments, in the justified belief that even an experienced regimental pilot would be much less ready for 'surprises' from the aircraft than a test pilot! However, significantly reducing the operating speed of the aircraft had an adverse effect on its combat capability. Therefore, OKB-156 (the Tupolev Design Bureau) took the decision to modify the Tu-22 by equipping it with a combined lateral (roll) control system involving the use of ailerons and flaperons.

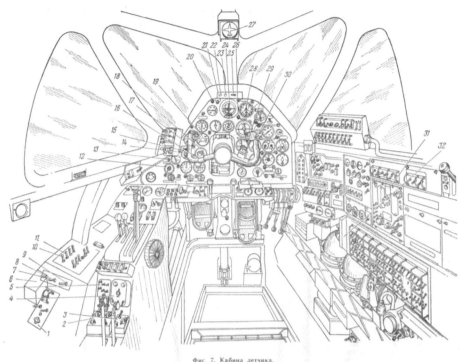

Фиг. 7. Кабина летчика.

1—пульт управления П-1 РСИУ-5В № 1; 2—щиток летчика РСБН-2С; 3—щиток управления М-50М СП-50; 4—абонентский аппарат СПУ-7; 5—пульт управления СПО-3; 6—пульт управления МС-61; 7—выключатель питания СПУ-7; 8—выключатель питания РСИУ-5В № 1; 9—выключатель питания РСИУ-5В № 2; 10—выключатель питания РВ-УМ; 11—выключатель ПО-500; 12—переключатель сигнализируемой высоты ПСВ-УМ РВ-УМ; 13—кнопка «Опознавание» РСБН-2С; 14—сигнальная лампа «Канал дальности неисправен» РСБН-2С; 15—пульт управления из комплекта «Путь-1»; 16—сигнальная лампа «Пролет зоны» РСБН-2С; 17—сигнальная лампа «Подлет к зоне» РСБН-2С; 18—прибор ППДА-П1 РСБН-2С; 19—указатель высоты УВ-57 РВ-УМ; 20—сигнальная лампа «Радиоглиссада включена» РСБН-2С; 21—сигнальная лампа «Опасная высота» РВ-УМ; 22—бленкер ГРП РСБН-2С; 23—бленкер КРП РСБН-2С; 24—прибор ППП-1П из комплекта «Путь-1»; 25—выключатель «Командные стрелки выкл.— вкл.» из комплекта «Путь-1»; 26—сигнальная лампа «Маркер» МРП-56П; 27—индикатор СПО-3 (блок ТД-410-7); 28—прибор НКП-1 из комплекта «Путь-1»; 29—кнопка «Рации» СПУ-7; 30—кнопка «СПУ» СПУ-7; 31—пульт управления АРК-11; 32—переключатель пультов АРК-11.

Diagram of the pilot's cockpit.

- The flaperons (broadly similar to what would be described in the Western literature as high-speed inboard ailerons) were, in essence, the Tu-22's outer flaps, located on the outer wing panels. Since the flaperons were mounted on the stiffest section of the wing (and close to the axis of the fuselage), the aileron reversal boundary (i.e. limiting speed) was shifted noticeably towards the high-speed operating regime and the aerodynamic limitation now became a problem of flutter. At take-off and during landing, and also at speeds up to around Mach 0.9, the aircraft was controlled by the normal ailerons, and the flaperons operated as normal flaps. Transfer of lateral control from normal ailerons to flaperons was performed automatically on take-off, after retraction of the main flaps and after reaching an indicated airspeed of 630kph (340kts). The normal ailerons were then locked in the neutral position and lateral control was taken over by the flaperons. The transition from normal aileron to flaperon was performed by means of a transfer unit which was mounted on the main spar. Switching back from flaperons to normal ailerons was also automatic, on lowering the main undercarriage or extending the flaps for landing, within the standard limiting speeds. On the first

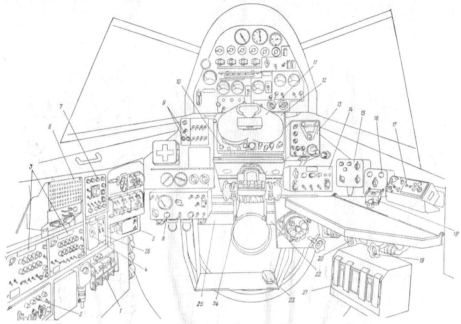

Фиг. 9. Кабина воздушного оператора.

Diagram of airborne operator's cockpit.

Diagram of navigator's cockpit of Tu-22R. (All taken from the servicing manual)

Фиг. 8. Кабина штурмана.

aircraft to be equipped with the flaperon system, the transition from one mode to the other was not automatic, but performed manually by the pilot. Transition from normal ailerons to flaperons was controlled by a switch on an electrical control panel mounted on the engine power lever quadrant. Using the manual system, transition was effected in horizontal flight with flaps retracted and at an indicated airspeed of 850kph (460kts), or Mach ≤ 0.9.

- During transition, the control column had to be held in the neutral position (or deflected in bank by no more than ±40° from neutral). This limitation was determined by the power of the flaperon electric drive motor. The time required for transition from normal aileron control to flaperon and back to normal aileron control was 23 ± 3.5 seconds. The control column had to be held steady and could not be moved during the transition. Control of the flaperons was performed through the control column, just as for the normal ailerons and all the control elements, including control rods located in the wing up to Ribs 19 and 20, remained unchanged when the aircraft was converted to the flaperon system. Introduction of the flaperon control system led to a significant increase in lateral control effectiveness at high indicated airspeeds and the raising of this effectiveness to the norms defined by the OTT of the Soviet Air Force (greater than 0.2 radians/sec). It also meant that the temporary operational speed restrictions set by the general designer (i.e. the Tupolev OKB) to minimise the effects of aileron reversal could also be lifted. In order to prevent flutter in the flaperons, which did not have mass balance weights, hydraulic dampers operating in parallel with the flaperon controls were introduced, which raised the critical limiting speed for the onset of the combined 'flap-wing' form of flutter.

- At high subsonic speeds, the shock wave which formed on the aerodynamic control surfaces shifted closer to the axis of rotation of that control. This led to the fact that given the aero-elasticity of the aircraft's structure, even a small displacement of the control surface would cause vibration and oscillation in the control surface. During the early flight test phase of the Tu-22's development, a significant increase in the amplitude of aileron and rudder oscillations was noted in specific speed ranges (for the ailerons at Mach numbers greater than M1.24, and for the rudder at Mach numbers of between M0.92 and M0.98). In order to eradicate these oscillations, dry friction dampers were installed on the ailerons and rudder, which, by effectively making the action of these controls 'heavy', prevented the onset of oscillation and vibration. Supersonic wind tunnel tests of a dynamically similar model, and the results of measurements of aileron and rudder vibration from flight tests, confirmed that the friction moment of the dampers installed on the ailerons and rudder was set at a sufficiently high level. A D2K-115 twin-channel damper was installed on the Tu-22 to counteract the oscillatory effects of vertical and lateral gusts. The operating elements of the system (RAU-107 aileron and rudder servos) were installed in the aileron and rudder control circuits. Gust oscillations were counteracted by automatic deflection of the rudder and ailerons (and flaperons) by an angle proportional to the angular rate of bank and yaw. Use of the dry friction dampers did not have an adverse effect on control of the aircraft since the friction action was easily overridden by the hydraulic actuators. Deflections of the rudder in flight at indicated airspeeds above 600kph (324kts) were not to exceed 7°, which was ensured by the use of a spring-assisted artificial feel system. Rudder deflection angles of from ±5° to ±25° resulted in the artificial feel system sharply increasing the force required on the pedals. Switching on and off of the flight artificial feel system was linked to retraction and extension of the nose-wheel and was performed automatically. In the event of loss of pressure in the hydraulic system below the permitted level, the flight artificial feel system (along with the main rudder and aileron artificial feel units) would be disconnected automatically from the flight control system.

- The main controls of the aircraft were an all-moving tailplane for control in pitch, a rudder for yaw control and ailerons and flaperons for roll control. The elevator was actuated via the control column (control yoke) through an RP-21AM non-reversible hydraulic actuator, which incorporated two rotary-action hydraulic motors, each of which was connected to an independent hydraulic supply. In the event of failure of one of the hydraulic systems (I or II), a third hydraulic system could be connected to the RP-21AM actuator to replace the failed system. In the event of failure of System I and II, tailplane control was effected solely by System III. If this system was also to become unserviceable, tailplane control could then be maintained by use of the MUS-5 electric drive unit, mounted on the RP-21AM actuator. Control of the rudder and ailerons involved the use of RP-22U and RP-23U twin-chamber non-reversible hydraulic actuators. The non-reversible hydraulic actuators fully absorbed the aerodynamic hinge moments generated as a function of the deflection of the control surfaces from the neutral position in flight. Therefore, in order to imitate the load on the control column, rudder pedals and aileron control yoke, spring-loaded artificial feel units were introduced into the tailplane, rudder and aileron (flaperon) control circuits. In case of necessity, an electrical trim system enabled the feel force to be reduced. In case of failure of the hydraulic systems, or the hydraulic actuators, the pilot could switch over to normal (non-boosted) manual control of the ailerons and rudder control via the normal rudder pedals. Because the Tu-22 was created in the 1950s, when little experience had been accumulated in the manufacture of heavy supersonic aircraft, the aircraft exhibited a number of peculiarities which had to be considered during its operation by Soviet Air Force bomber regiments.

1. It had a comparatively small longitudinal stability margin in terms of limiting load factor at subsonic speeds and an increased longitudinal stability margin at supersonic speeds
2. It exhibited increased longitudinal control effectiveness at high subsonic speeds as a result of the use of an all-moving tailplane
3. It exhibited the potential for creating large tailplane deflection angles with comparatively light force on the control column, connected with the fact that an artificial feel system had been adopted for the pitch control circuit
4. It exhibited a comparatively high degree of inertia in the longitudinal axis, leading to increased response delays to control inputs by the pilot, especially if these involved sharp, rapid movements of the column.

- These factors made control of the aircraft difficult in certain flight modes, since it required constant inputs from the pilot and also led to the possibility of over-stressing the aircraft, even with comparatively small displacements of the control column. Attempts by the pilot to bring the aircraft back under control and to a stable flight condition by rapid and over-enthusiastic control movements could lead to pilot-induced oscillations (PIO), with the attendant possibility of exceeding the permitted g-limits of the aircraft. Indeed, there were many tragic examples of this during the first years of operation of the Tu-22 by the Soviet Air Force (See chapter Nine). In order to provide an automatic system to counteract longitudinal (pitch) oscillations in all flight modes, the Tu-22 was fitted with a DT-105A twin-channel pitch damper and an AU-105A (*Avtomat Ustoichivosti*) automatic stability unit (autostabilizer), incorporating RAU-107M and RAU-107A actuators mounted in sequence in the tailplane control circuit. If, during stabilised flight, a vertical gust disturbed the aircraft's equilibrium, causing it to pitch up, then the aircraft would begin to rotate in the direction of the gust. The pitch damper would then deflect the tailplane so as to counteract the pitching moment, i.e. it would create a pitch-down moment. The control column itself would not move during this action. The roll and yaw dampers worked in an identical manner. The DT-105A operated constantly throughout flight, while the AU-105A autostabilizer only operated at subsonic speeds, switching on automatically following retraction of the nose-wheel and continuing to operate up to a speed of Mach 1. In this case, the pitch damper, deflecting the tailplane to counteract the angular rate of pitch-up, would effectively stop the pitch oscillations within 1.5 to 2.0 seconds. Installation of the AU-105A automatic stability unit (third channel of the pitch damper) improved the efficiency of Channels I and II of the DT-105A pitch damper and allowed a slight increase in the travel of the control column required to bring the aircraft within the permitted g-loading limit.

Flight with inoperative DT-105A and AU-105A units was characterised by low stability margins in terms of g-loading (i.e. the limiting g-loading was reached very quickly) at high indicated airspeeds, because of the effects of localised aero-elastic deformation of parts of the aircraft. In this case, the indicated airspeed could not exceed 750kph (405kts) up to an altitude of 8,000m (26,250ft). The pitch control circuit of the Tu-22 also incorporated an ADU-105 (*Avtomat Dopolnityel'nykh Usilii-105*) automatic control force limiter to limit the vertical loads and angle of attack by creating an additional load on the control column when it was pulled back. The SPN-105A, (*Sistema Privyedyeniya v Neitral'-105A*) was installed on the Tu-22 at the same time as the ADU-105A, and was intended to counteract automatically the failure of any of the pitch damper channels or automatic stability unit, which could have led to large undemanded tailplane settings at high speed. Apart from this, during the early stages of operation of the Tu-22 by Soviet Air Force regiments, the OS-1 (*Ogranichityel' Skorosti Peremyeshcheniya Kolonki Upravlyeniya-1*) control column movement rate limiter was introduced. The OS-1 was designed to prevent the control column being moved by the pilot at a speed/rate greater than the maximum rate of deflection of the tailplane (i.e. the maximum rate of actuation of the RP-21AM). The OS-1 was an additional unit of the ADU-105A and prevented the onset of loads greater than those permitted in the pitch control circuit. When moving the control column both back and forward at a rate of 250mm/sec (9.75in/sec), the OS-1 would create an additional force on the control column of not more than 7kg (15lb). When moving the control column at a greater speed, the additional force on the stick from the OS-1 increased sharply to 80kg (176lb) and more.

[Note: It should be remembered that the PN radar is installed in the Tu-22M3 Backfire-C bombers, which remain in service with both the Soviet Air Force and the Soviet Naval Air Force, along with the Kh-22 (AS-4 Kitchen) *missiles described above. All references to the radar and the missile in the past tense (relating to the Tu-22K* Blinder-B) *are, therefore, also applicable to the Backfire. AD]*

Self-protection systems of the Tu-22

Initially, all variants of the Tu-22 (i.e. Tu-22R, Tu-22P, Tu-22K, Tu-22RD and Tu-22PD) were equipped with a standardised self-protection suite (*kompleks oborony* – or integrated defence system). The self-protection suite consisted of:

1. A tail-gun installation armed with a 23mm R-23 cannon (Article 261P), aimed by PRS-3 or PRS-4 gun-laying radars, backed up by a TP-1A television sighting system, for rear-hemisphere protection of the aircraft within a 60° conical field of fire, measured from the longitudinal axis of the fuselage
2. SPO-3 Sirena-3 (Siren) or SPO-10 Sirena-3M radar warning systems
3. An SRZO-2M transponder unit
4. KDS-16GM and APP-22 chaff and flare dispensers.

The airborne operator (*vozdushnyi operator*) controlled the aircraft's self-protection systems and had all the relevant control panels and switches in his cockpit, apart from the control unit and indicator for the SPO radar warning systems, which were in the pilot's cockpit. When the aircraft was illuminated by a threat radar, the ensuing audio signal (buzzing) was passed to each crew member via the SPU-7 intercom and over the VHF radios.

It seems remarkable that sensitive electronic equipment such as the PRS-3/4 gun-laying radar (white radome) and the TP-1A TV camera (between the engine nozzles) could operate reliably, or at all, in such a noise-intensive area of the airframe. Clearly visible on the side of the DK-20/21 gun turret is the ejection tube for spent shell cases and links.

Ammunition belt for the 261P (R-23) cannon installed in the rear gun turret of the Tu-22.

Tail-gun installation

The aircraft's cannon armament comprised a single DK-20 (Article 9-A-242) trainable gun turret, armed with a 23mm 261P cannon. The cannon provided rear-hemisphere protection from attacks by fighters, including at night and when flying in cloud, and was also able to fire special chaff rounds to confuse intercepting fighter radars. The turret was powered by an electro-hydraulic drive system and was remotely controlled via the tail-warning radar. Ammunition feed was automatic, using a continuous belt feed system, the magazine being situated in the rear fuselage and linked to the turret by a special sleeve. Spent shell cases and links were ejected overboard. The cannon was directed onto the target by a PRS-3 (*Pritsel'naya Radiolokatsionnaya Stantsiya*) Argon, or PRS-4 Argon-2 gun-laying radar, known by the NATO codename *Fan Tail*. The radar, and an associated TP-1A television sighting system, was linked to the automatic control units of the turret to enable it to track incoming fighter and other targets. The PRS-3 (or PRS-4) radar provided independent search and lock-on to a target in the rear hemisphere, regardless of visibility conditions, and after lock-on it performed automatic tracking, producing angular coordinates, speeds and distance to target for the gun's computing unit. The TP-1A television guidance unit provided rear-hemisphere scanning and target detection in conditions of normal visibility and also calculated the relevant angular coordinates and range to the target. When fitted with the modified PRS-4 radar, the rear turret assembly was redesignated DK-21 (Article 9-A-243), but differed only in the construction of the radar antenna. The modified PRS-4 systems were installed on aircraft from Construction No. 4503 onwards.

Main data for the DK-20

Rotation angle	
Right, left, up, down	30° 30'
Ammunition load	500 rounds

The ECM transmitters of the Tu-22P were mounted inside a removable equipment crate (*konteinery*), with the spiral antennae of the SPS-44, SPS-55, SPS-77, SPS-22 and SPS-33 systems being mounted in a row along the centreline, covered by a 'flattened' dielectric fairing. The forward end of the fairing incorporated an air intake to cool the equipment crate. *S Burdin Archive*

The ECM equipment crates were designed to fit flush within the weapons (payload) bay, and to ease loading and unloading of the crate small access doors were provided at the front and rear. These doors also doubled as mounting plates for the hockey-stick antennae of the SPS-4M or SPS-5 (*Fasol'*-1) jammers. *Alfred Matusyevitch*

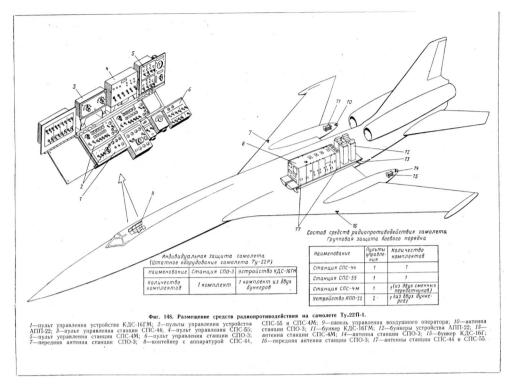

Индивидуальная защита самолета
(Штатное оборудование самолета Ту-22Р)

Наименование	Станция СПО-3	Устройство КДС-16ГМ
Количество комплектов	1 комплект	1 комплект из двух бункеров

Состав средств радиопротиводействия самолета.
Групповая защита боевого порядка.

Наименование	Пульты управления	Количество комплектов
Станция СПС-44	1	1
Станция СПС-55	1	1
Станция СПС-4м	1	1 (из двух сменных передатчиков)
Устройство АПП-22	2	1 (из двух бункеров)

Фиг. 148. Размещение средств радиопротиводействия на самолете Ту-22П-1.

1—пульт управления устройства КДС-16Г; 2—пульты управления устройства АПП-22; 3—блок-приставка к управлению станции СПС-44; 4—пульт управления СПС-55; 5—пульт управления станции СПС-4М; 6—пульт управления станции СПО-3; 7—передняя антенна станции СПО-3; 8—контейнер с аппаратурой СПС-44, СПС-55 и СПС-4М; 9—панель управления воздушного оператора; 10—антенна станции СПО-3; 11—бункер КДС-16ГМ; 12—бункеры устройства АПП-22; 13—антенна станции СПС-4М; 14—антенна станции СПО-3; 15—бункер КДС-16Г; 16—передняя антенна станции СПО-3; 17—антенны станции СПС-44 и СПС-55.

Diagram of equipment layout of Tu-22P1.

Diagram of equipment layout of Tu-22P2. (Taken from servicing manual)

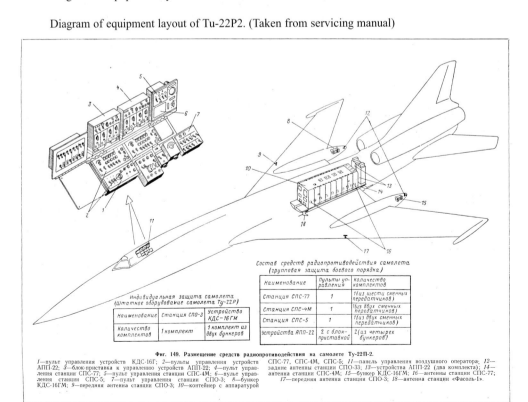

Индивидуальная защита самолета
(Штатное оборудование самолета Ту-22Р)

Наименование	Станция СПО-3	Устройство КДС-16ГМ
Количество комплектов	1 комплект	1 комплект из двух бункеров

Состав средств радиопротиводействия самолета
(групповая защита боевого порядка.)

Наименование	Пульты управления	Количество комплектов
Станция СПС-77	1	1 (из шести сменных передатчиков)
Станция СПС-4м	1	1 (из двух сменных передатчиков)
Станция СПС-5	1	1 (из двух сменных передатчиков)
Устройства АПП-22	2 с блок-приставкой	2 (из четырех бункеров)

Фиг. 149. Размещение средств радиопротиводействия на самолете Ту-22П-2.

1—пульт управления устройств КДС-16Г; 2—пульты управления устройств АПП-22; 3—блок-приставка к устройств АПП-22; 4—пульт управления станции СПС-77; 5—пульт управления станции СПС-4М; 6—пульт управления станции СПС-5; 7—пульт управления станции СПО-3; 8—бункер КДС-16ГМ; 9—передняя антенна станции СПО-3; 10—контейнер с аппаратурой СПС-77, СПС-4М, СПС-5; 11—панель управления воздушного оператора; 12—задние антенны станции СПО-33; 13—устройства АПП-22 (два комплекта); 14—антенна станции СПС-4М; 15—бункер КДС-16ГМ; 16—антенна станции СПС-77; 17—передняя антенна станции СПО-3; 18—антенна станции «Фасоль-1».

Main data for the 261P cannon

Rate of fire	2,000–2,500 rounds per minute
Muzzle velocity	850 ± 10m/sec (2,790ft/sec ± 33ft/sec
Weight of HE fragmentation shell	0.174kg (0.38lb)

Main data for PRS-3 (PRS-4) radar

Detection range against MiG-19-sized target with a closing speed of 100m/sec (19,685ft/min)	6,500m (21,325ft) 7,400m (24,280ft) for PRS-4
Lock-on range (MiG-19-sized target)	3,000m (9,842ft) 5,300m (17,390ft) for PRS-4
Scanning sector	Not less than 70°
Capability of shifting axis of scan zone in azimuth by an angle of	± 30°
Time to scan entire sector	Not more than 3 seconds
Minimum effective range	350m (1,150ft)

Main data for TP-1A television sight

Detection range against MiG-19 sized target	3,000m (9,842ft)
Targeting range	from 400 to 2,000m (1,312–6,562ft)
Scanning angles	
Horizontal	±70°
Vertical	Up 55° Down 45°

Radar warning systems

The SPO-3 (*Stantsiya opovyeshcheniya i Preduprezhdyeniya ob Obluchenii*) gave the crew all-round warning that the aircraft had been detected ('painted') by an enemy radar, the Russian term meaning literally 'station of notification and warning of [radar] illumination'. The SPO-3 (and later systems) provided an audible signal (a loud buzzing sound) to all crew members and a visual indication to the pilot, showing the direction from which a threat radar was illuminating the aircraft. It also triggered the release of chaff in the event that the threat was detected in the rear hemisphere. The four antennae of the SPO-3 were installed in the wing-root leading edges and at the rear of each main undercarriage nacelle, each antenna providing coverage in a 90° sector. In the vertical plane, the four antennae covered a sector of ±45° forward and to the rear, the system thereby providing effective all-round warning of the presence of threat radars. On aircraft of later production series, the SPO-3 was replaced by the lighter SPO-10 unit, although its performance was almost identical to the earlier system.

IFF systems

The Tu-22 was equipped with the SRZO-2M (*Samolyotnyi Radiolokatsionnyi Zaproschik-Otvyetchik*) 'aircraft radar interrogator-responder', i.e. an IFF transponder. Working in the response (*otvyetchik*) mode, it identified the Tu-22 as 'friendly' when interrogated by Russian (or former Warsaw Pact) ground-based, naval and fighter radars. It was also used to identify as either 'friendly' or 'hostile', ground, sea or airborne targets detected by the Rubin-1A, the PN radar (of the Tu-22K), or the PRS-3 (PRS-4) tail-gun control radars. The SRZO was fully automatic in operation and the eight antennae were mounted in fairings at the wing-fuselage junction, providing good all-round transmission and reception performance. The SRZO-2M had the following range capabilities:

- In the direction ground (ship) to aircraft – up to 300km (162nm)
- From aircraft to aircraft – up to 40km (22nm)
- From aircraft to ship – up to 70km (38nm)

Additionally, the Tu-22K *Blinder-B* was equipped with an SRZ-10M Latun' (Brass) radar interrogator (*Samolyotnyi Radiolokatsionnyi Zaproschik*), a long-range system designed to identify surface targets detected by the aircraft's PN (NATO *Downbeat*) radar at the greater distances of which this system was capable.

Passive jamming systems
The Tu-22 was equipped with passive jamming systems to augment and/or complement the aircraft's active jamming capability. It had two main systems, known as *Avtomat-2* (literally Automatic device or unit-2), comprising the KDS-16GM dispenser and *Avtomat-3*, consisting of the APP-22 system. The KDS-16GM (*Kassetnyi Dyerzhatyel' Spetsial'nyi*), or 'special cassette rack', was designed for installation in the undercarriage nacelles of the Tu-16 *Badger* bomber (hence the use of the alphanumeric 16G designation, meaning [Tu-]16 *Gondola*, or nacelle – 'M' indicating its modification for use on the Tu-22). It retained full commonality with the Tu-16 system when it was modified for use on the new aircraft. The KDS-16GM carried chaff in the form of dipole reflectors of metalised glass fibre (or aluminium foil), cut to specific wavelengths to jam a wide variety of enemy radar systems operating in the 0.6 to 12.5cm (2.4GHz to 50GHz) wavebands. Operation of the KDS-16GM was either automatic, linked to threat detection by the SPO-3 (SPO-10) radar warning receiver, or manually controlled by the airborne operator (*vozdushnyi operator*).

The KDS-16GM system consisted of two cassettes, each with 416 chaff bundles. There were ten different options for the release of chaff, and the overall time for continuous release, using the 'Series-Continuous' mode, with an interval of 0.3 seconds, was 4 minutes (i.e. 2 minutes per nacelle to release two bundles of 416 bundles). The chaff bundles were contained in boxes mounted in loops on transport belts (rather like a hunter's ammunition pouch), rotating on a drum mechanism, from where they were ejected into the airstream, dispersing into radar reflective 'clouds'.

The other passive jamming system of the Tu-22 was the APP-22 (*Avtomat Passivnykh Pomyekh dlya samolyota Tu-22*), or 'automatic system of passive interference for the Tu-22 aircraft'. The APP-22 was designed to release various types of chaff to jam enemy ground and naval radars, plus interceptor fighter radars, operating in the 0.8 to 4m waveband. The APP-22 was mounted in the payload (weapons) bay between Frames 58 and 60. The chaff-dispensing chute projected outside the airframe ahead of Frame 61. Two chaff hoppers made up the normal complement of the APP-22, and operation was controlled manually by the airborne operator. Compared with the KDS-16GM, the APP-

22 carried a significantly larger amount of chaff, although its operation was identical with that of the undercarriage nacelle-mounted system.

Variations in the self-protection systems of some Tu-22K aircraft
On a number of later-series Tu-22K aircraft, an automatic ECM system was installed in place of the rear gun turret and TP-1A television sighting system. The automatic ECM unit comprised the following units:

*An **SPS-100 Reseda-A** (Mignonette) active jammer*
Designed for the individual protection of the aircraft and capable of transmitting in the forward and rear hemispheres, operating against surface-to-air (SAM), air-to-air (AAM) and ground-based missile fire-control radars. SPS stands for *Stantsiya Pomyekhovaya Samolyotnaya*, meaning, literally, 'airborne interference station', i.e. airborne jamming set.

*An **SPS-5 Fasol'** (Haricot Bean) active jammer*
Providing barrage noise jamming against long-range early warning (EW) and guidance radars in the VHF spectrum. SPS-5 was used for collective protection of combat formations of Tu-22Ks, jamming enemy EW radars and preventing them from obtaining an accurate range resolution to the formation, or calculation of the number of aircraft in the formation.

Some Tu-22Ks were also equipped with SPS-151, SPS-152 or SPS-153 Siren' (Lilac) systems for individual aircraft protection. These jammers were mounted in the first accessories compartment (in the forward fuselage) so it was not necessary to remove the DK-20 (DK-21) rear gun turret when these jammers were installed.

Variations in the self-protection systems of some Tu-22P aircraft
At the end of the 1970s and beginning of the 1980s, a number of Tu-22P *Blinder-E* aircraft underwent a modification programme, in accordance with Bulletin No. 1295 (a joint Tupolev/Soviet Air Force document), to give them a new defensive ECM suite. This upgrade included the installation of SPS-151 (SPS-152, SPS-153) jammers and ASO-2I (i.e. the letter I) flare dispensers (*Avtomaticheskaya Sistema Otstrela*) for individual protection from attacking fighters in the rear hemisphere. The SPS-151 (SPS-152, SPS-153) units were mounted in the first accessories compartment in the forward fuselage and in a new 'standardised rear ECM equipment bay' (*Unifitsirovannyi Khvostovoy Otsek*), which was also used on the Tu-16 and Tu-95, hence the use of the term 'standardised'. The ASO-2I-E7R flare dispensers were also located in the rear ECM bay and in the undercarriage nacelles.

Variations in the self-protection systems of the Tu-22RM
This development of the Tu-22RD had an upgraded self-protection suite compared with that of the earlier aircraft, and included:

- One SPS-151MD jammer mounted in the 'first standardised rear ECM bay', replacing the DK-20 gun turret, the TP-1A television sighting system and the PRS-3 gun-laying radar
- One SPS-153DA jammer (with the possibility of replacement by an SPS-152DA), mounted in the 'second standardised rear ECM bay'

An excellent view of the large antenna fairing of the SRS-10 (Kub-3) electronic intelligence collection system of the Tu-22RDK. The Ukrainian Air Force crew posing for the photographer at Nezhin demonstrate the individual seating positions prior to being winched up into their respective cockpits. *Valery Romanenko*

- One SPS-151ME jammer and one SPS-153ER, (with the possibility of replacement by an SPS-152ER), mounted in the compartment previously occupied by Fuel Tank 1 in the forward fuselage (now the first, or forward, accessories compartment)
- A Beryoza-P (Birch) radar warning receiver in place of the earlier SPO-3 system
- Three sets of ASO-2I automatic flare dispensers, armed with IPP-26 (*Infrakrasnyi Pomyekhovyi Patron*) infra-red flares, mounted in the undercarriage nacelles and in the 'standardised ECM bay' (one set in each location)

The SPS-151 (SPS-152, SPS-153) systems were designed to provide individual protection of the Tu-22 from surface-to-air and air-to-air missile guidance radars operating in pulsed, continuous (CW) and quasi-simultaneous (quasi-CW) modes. The jammers were controlled from individual control panels (and a separate control panel for the SPS-151MD) located in the airborne operator's cockpit. The jammers had two main modes of operation, 'Receive' and 'Transmit' ('*Priyom*' and '*Pyeredacha*'). In 'receive' mode each set would perform only detection of threat radars, selecting and analysing relevant signals, while in 'transmit' mode, the system would generate appropriate responses in one of three different programmes. Jamming in 'Programme 1' was intended to provide individual protection from pulsed, CW and quasi-CW threat radars. 'Programme 2' jamming was intended to provide mutual protection of two or more aircraft, with two aircraft producing 'scintillation', or 'blink' jamming in turn, while 'Programme 3' jamming was intended to provide individual protection from pulsed radars.

The rear section of the undercarriage nacelle housed the KDS-16GM chaff dispenser, the square ejection chute for which is clearly visible in this view. Also visible on the undercarriage doors are the bulged fairings which provided clearance for the bogies to 'oscillate' within the nacelle without touching the airframe, as part of the 'flexible undercarriage mounting'. S Burdin

Particular features of the SPS-151MD installed in the 'standardised rear ECM bay'.

The SPS-151MD, unlike the basic SPS-151 mounted in the forward accessories bay, and the SPS-153 (SPS-152), had the following additional modes of operation:

1. Switching the direction of radiation of the standard jamming signal in the lower or general sector of the rear hemisphere, or in the lower sector of the forward hemisphere, at high altitudes

Some Tu-22K missile carriers were upgraded during service to carry the SPS-100 Reseda (Mignonette) active jamming system in a modified solid tail cone replacing the tail gun turret. Two of the system's teardrop-shaped antennae can be seen in this view, as well as the ejector slot for a chaff dispenser.

The modified rear fuselage fairing which replaced the original tail gun installation of the early *Blinders*, housing instead the aircraft's individual protection suite. Visible on this Tu-22RDM are the various small jamming antennae and cooling intakes mounted on the extended tail cone. *S Burdin*

2. An MV autonomous mode in the forward or rear hemispheres at low altitudes. Here MV probably means '*Malaya Vysota*', or 'low altitude'

Note: The suffix letters used in the designations of the above mentioned systems (SPS-151**MD**, SPS-153**DA** etc.) are not thought to have any specific meaning in themselves, but are covering letters for the frequency (frequencies) on which the system operates. As such, technicians and operators would know that part of the RF (radio frequency) spectrum within which each system operated, while keeping outsiders 'in the dark'.

Variations in the self-protection suite of the Tu-22U *Blinder-D*
Since the Tu-22U was not designed to have a combat role, and did not carry an airborne operator, the standard Tu-22 self-protection systems were not fitted on this training variant. It therefore lacked:

- The DK-20 rear gun turret
- The PRS-3 Argon gun-laying and tail warning radar
- The TP-1A television sight
- The SPO-3 radar warning receiver
- KDS-16GM chaff dispensers
- APP-22 chaff dispensers.

CHAPTER THREE

Tu-22 Weapons

Integrated weapons system of the Tu-22R (Tu-22RD) *Blinder-C*
The integrated weapons systems of the Tu-22R and Tu-22RD were identical, the difference between the two variants being the in-flight refuelling capability of the Tu-22RD (where the suffix letter D stands for *Dal'nii*, or 'long-range').

The weapons system comprised:

- A navigation bombing 'complex' (the Russian term '*kompleks*' usually means 'an integrated system', although 'complex' will be used when it is more convenient)
- A suite of bomb armament, including special bomb racks, etc.
- Equipment for the carriage and release of a 'special weapon' (i.e. a euphemism for a nuclear weapon).

The **navigation bombing complex** was designed to perform the following tasks:

1. Automatic and continuous calculation of the aircraft's position
2. Continuous read-out of the distance remaining to a waypoint (or the target) and the required heading
3. Automatic handling of the aircraft (through the autopilot), with inputs from the KS (*Kursovaya Sistema*) course and heading system, or from the NBA (*Navigatsionno-bombardirovochnyi Avtomat*) automatic electromechanical navigation-bombing computer in 'Navigation' mode and from the bombing radar in 'Targeting' mode
4. Radar-assisted bombing.

The 'Complex' included the following:

1. A Rubin-1A (NATO *Short Horn*) bombing radar (*radiolokatsionnyi bombardirovochnyi pritsel*)
2. An OPB-15 optical bomb-sight
3. An NBA automatic navigation-bombing computer – this was an electromechanical device
4. An AP-7MTs autopilot, designed to provide stabilisation of the aircraft about the three normal axes of flight, height stabilisation, execution of co-ordinated turns and spiral ascents and descents with an angle of bank of up to 40°, climbs and descents at an angle of up to 5° and rapid turns onto target heading according to signals from the OPB-15 bomb-sight

5. A KS-6A (*Kursovaya Sistema*) 'course system', providing magnetic, true and gyroscopically derived aircraft headings
6. A BTs-63A astro-tracking system (*Zvezdno-Solnechnyi Orientator* – ZSO) for calculation of the aircraft's position in relation to a selected star position.
7. A TsSV-1M central velocity and altitude unit, which provided the crew with read-outs of airspeed, barometric altitude, air density and outside air temperature, plus Mach number
8. A DISS-1 (*Dopplerovskii Izmerityel' putyevoy Skorosti i ugla Snosa*) Doppler navigation unit for calculation of ground speed and drift
9. An RV-25A high-altitude radar altimeter
10. An ARK-11 automatic radio compass.

The Rubin-1A navigation-bombing radar (the letter A indicating that it was designed originally for the Tu-22A), in conjunction with the OPB-15 bomb-sight, was designed for target search and radar-assisted bombing in horizontal flight against ground-based fixed targets and naval moving and stationary targets. Apart from this, the radar could be used to update position-fixing of the aircraft when flying autonomously using the NBA automatic bombing computer. In order to prevent frequency drift arising from the effects of enemy ECM directed at the aircraft, the Rubin-1A radar incorporated automatic retuning of the transceiver (transmitter-receiver).

Overall performance of the Rubin-1A radar
Target detection range from a height of 8,000m (26,250ft):

- Against large industrial complexes and cities   310km (167nm)
- For surface mapping   170km (92nm)

Maximum continuous uninterrupted work cycle 15 hours.

The OPB-15 bomb-sight
The OPB-15 was an optical asynchronous vectoring bomb-sight capable of semi-automatic target tracking. It was designed to permit bombing operations from horizontal flight against fixed and moving targets with conventional and nuclear ('special') bombs, set to explode above the target. It could also be used for high-altitude torpedo bombing and the sowing of mine barrages, with automatic calculation of targeting data from the manual input of speed and direction of movement of surface targets, from any approach direction. The OPB-15 could also perform offset targeting calculations.

In conditions of normal visibility (visual bombing), targeting was accomplished with the aid of a telescopic aiming and sighting system. The bomb-sight had a movable transverse aiming line to follow the trajectory of a guided bomb during its fall onto the target.

In the absence of visual aiming conditions, targeting was carried out with the aid of the Rubin-1A radar display, an electrical link between the OPB-15 and the Rubin-1A providing alignment of the optical sighting and radar sighting systems.

Six seconds before bomb release, the radar would signal the opening of the weapons-bay doors and simultaneously send a signal to the EhSBR-49 electrical bomb-release mechanism. The bomb-release mechanism could release bombs with a linear interval from 6.5m (21ft) to 5.6km (3nm) at ground speeds from 600kph (324kts) to 2,000kph (1,080kts). The OPB-15 was located in the navigator's compartment, between fuselage Frames 1 and 3.

Main performance details of the OPB-15
Altitude range for bombing – from 2,000m to 20,000m (6,560ft to 65,616ft)
True airspeed range for bombing – from 500kph to 2,000kph (270kts to 1,080kts)
Offset aiming point in any direction – from 0 to 25km (0 to 13.5nm)
Speed of moving target that could be tracked – from 0 to 100kph (0 to 54kts)

The **bomb armament of the Tu-22R** enabled the aircraft to be used both for long-range conventional bombing of strategic targets using a wide variety of bombs of different calibres, and for nuclear operations with a single nuclear weapon. The bomb armament (*bombardirovochnoye vooruzhenie*) comprised an integrated set of mutually linked electrical and mechanical devices and mechanisms, each of which was designed to perform a strictly defined task within the overall system. [*To some degree, this predated the notion of 'application specific' systems in modern computers, and is a feature of many Russian weapons systems.* AD] A common system of bomb-related equipment was installed on the Tu-22R to permit the carriage of both photo-flash bombs (flares) for when the aircraft was used as a night reconnaissance platform, and normal bomb racks for when the aircraft was to be used as a bomber. Bombs of all categories were carried in the weapons (payload) bay – no provision was made for external carriage of bombs. When the aircraft was to be used purely as a bomber, all camera-associated equipment and cameras were removed from the payload bay and this area would revert to being a bomb bay, with relevant bomb racks installed according to the actual type of bombing to be conducted. Bombs would either be carried on 'cassette-type' racks (*kassetniye dyerzhatyeli*), or on 'beam-type' racks (*balochniye dyerzhatyeli*) with sway braces, dependent upon the nature of the bombing task. [*The Russian definition of a 'cassette-type' rack is that of two vertically mounted beams to which sway braces are attached. Viewed from the side, it resembles a horizontal ladder with the bombs suspended directly from the sway brace.* AD] The Tu-22R could carry the following racks:

- KD3-22R cassette-type racks – four in total (two right-hand and two left-hand)
- KD3-22RS cassette-type racks – two in total (in middle of bay)
- KD3-105A – cassette-type racks – two (one left-hand and one right-hand)
- KD4-105A – cassette-type racks – four (two right-hand and two left-hand)
- BD6-105A – beam-type rack – one only

The BD6-105A rack was installed permanently in the weapons (payload) bay, between Fuselage Frames 48 and 51. (*The designations of the racks reflect their specific use on the Tu-22, with the use of the aircraft's type designation (22) being part of the nomenclature. The use of '105A' in some of the designations relates to the systems which were originally designed for the Aircraft '105A' prototype*)

When used as a bomber, the Tu-22R had two bomb-load conditions – normal and overload. The aircraft's normal bomb load was 3 tonnes (6,613lb) and in the overload condition it was up to 9 tonnes (19,841lb). A PU-105A electro-mechanical and

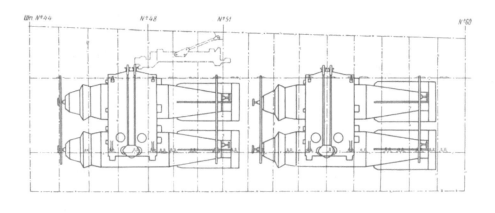

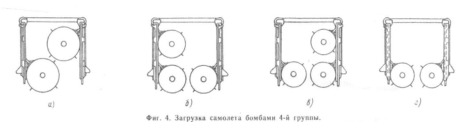

Фиг. 4. Загрузка самолёта бомбами 4-й группы.
Вверху—загрузка бомбами ФАБ-1500; *а*—загрузка бомбами ФАБ-3000, вариант № 4 (см. табл. 3); *б*—загрузка первого ряда держателей бомбами ФАБ-1500; *в*—загрузка второго ряда держателей бомбами ФАБ-1500; *г*—загрузка бомбами ФАБ-1500-2600ТС, вариант № 3А (см. табл. 3).

Bomb load variant for FAB-1500, FAB-1500-2600TS and FAB-3000 series of bombs.

mechanical fusing system was used to control the fusing of the aircraft's bombs. From aircraft of the 17th production series onwards, this was replaced by the PU-22R mechanism. The KD3-105A rack, with Der3-54 locks, was used for the carriage of bombs of calibre 50, 100, 250 and 500kg (110, 220, 550 and 1,100lb). The design and construction of the KD3-22R was identical with that of the KD3-105A and differed only in that in the upper part of the support beams there were assemblies for the attachment of transverse

Cassette bomb racks (*kassetniye dyerzhatyeli*) in the weapons bay of Tu-22R, showing the ladder-like structure. *S Burdin Archive*

beams when using the aircraft in the reconnaissance role. The KD4-105A, with Der4-49 locks, was designed to carry one of the following weapons: FAB-3000, FAB-1500-2600TS, FAB-1500.

The BD6-105A was used to carry heavy-calibre weapons, including any one of the following: FAB-9000, FAB-5000, FAB-3000, FAB-1500-2600TS and FAB-1500. Bombs of 1,500–3,000kg (3,300–6,613lb) calibre were carried on Der6-4 sway braces, and those of calibres from 5,000 to 9,000kg (11,022–19,841lb) were carried on the Der6-5D. The heavy FAB-9000 bomb was suspended from the outer support braces (distance between lugs 1,000mm/39.4in), while the FAB-5000 was carried on the central braces (480mm/18.90in between the lugs). A BL-52 electric winch was used to raise the bombs from the trolley up to the rack itself.

Bombing armament of the Tu-22R when used for night reconnaissance
The aircraft was loaded with FOTAB-250-215 photo-bombs (flares) in order to provide illumination for night reconnaissance operations. The standard load was 10 FOTABs (*Fotograficheskiye Aviatsionniye Bomby*) (four each on two KD3-22R racks and one each on two KD3-22R racks). An additional two KD3-22RS racks could be mounted along the central axis of the payload bay in order to carry the maximum number of FOTAB-25-215 flares. On each of the two KD3-22RS racks, three bombs could be carried, while four FOTABs could be carried on each of the four KD3-22R racks.

Bombs carried by the Tu-22R when used as conventional bomber

Calibre & Type	Maximum number	Max weight of one bomb	Overall bomb load
Night bombing			
FOTAB-250-215	22	216kg	4,752kg
(Normal load 10)			(10,476lb)
Standard free-fall			
Main Complement			
FAB-9000M-54	1	9,413kg	9,413kg
		(20,750lb)	(20,750lb)
FAB-5000M-54	1	5,249kg	5,249kg
		(11,570lb)	(11,570lb)
FAB-3000M-54	2	3,062kg	6,124kg
		(6,750lb)	(13,500lb)
FAB-1500M-54 + APP-22	4	1,500kg	6,000kg
		(3,306lb)	(13,227lb)
FAB-1500-2600TS	3	2,587kg	7,761kg
		(5,703lb)	(17,110lb)
KhAB-1500	6	1,552kg	9,312kg
		(3,421lb)	(20,529lb)
FAB-500M-54	18	475kg	8,550kg
		(1,047lb)	(18,850lb)
FAB-500M-62	12	500kg	6,000kg
		(1,102lb)	(13,227lb)

Calibre & Type	Maximum number	Max weight of one bomb	Overall bomb load
FAB-500M-62 + APP-22	6	500kg (1,102lb)	3,000kg (6,613lb)
FAB-500TS	18	508kg (1,120lb)	9,144kg (20,158lb)
FZAB-500	18	498kg (1,098lb)	8,964kg (19,762lb)
ZAB-500-400	18	407kg (897lb)	7,326kg (16,150lb)
FAB-250M-54	24	238kg (524lb)	5,712kg (12,593lb)
FAB-250TS	24	260kg (573lb)	6,240kg (13,757lb)
OFAB-250-270	24	274kg (604lb)	6,576kg (14,497lb)
ZAB-250-200	24	204kg (449lb)	4,896kg (10,794lb)
OKhAB-250-235P	24	231kg (509lb)	5,544kg (12,222lb)
Not in Main Complement			
FAB-3000M-46	2	3,091kg (6,814lb)	6,182kg (13,628lb)
FAB-1500M-46	6	1,526kg (3,364lb)	9,156kg (20,185lb)
FAB-500M-46	18	448kg (987lb)	8,064kg (17,777lb)
FAB-250M-46	24	243kg (535lb)	5,832kg (12,857lb)
KhAB-250-150SM-46	24	151kg (333lb)	3,624kg (7,992lb)
FOTAB-250-215	24	216kg (476lb)	5,184kg (11,428lb)
SAB-250-180MF	24	176kg (388lb)	4,224kg (9,312lb)
OFAB-100-NV	24	100kg (220lb)	2,400kg (5,291lb)
OFAB-100NV	16	100kg (220lb)	1,600kg (3,527lb)
OFAB-250-270 +APP-22	16	270kg (595lb)	4,320kg (9,524lb)
RBK-250-275AO-1sch	16	275kg (606lb)	4,400kg (9,700lb)
RBK-250-275AO-1sch + APP-22	8	275kg (606lb)	2,200kg (4,850lb)
P-50-75	24	75kg (165lb)	1,800kg (3,968lb)

Note: 'Main complement' was the list of bombs which the aircraft was originally designed to carry, while those not included in this list were bombs which were added to its capability during service.

Certain weapons load options involved the reduction in the number of bombs carried as a result of the inclusion of the APP-22 chaff dispenser unit for specific missions.

The special weapons complement of the Tu-22R
As previously mentioned, the Tu-22R, when configured for the bombing role, could also be used for the release of a 'special weapon', i.e. a nuclear bomb. The 'special weapons' equipment of the Tu-22R included:

• A control system for the automatic mechanisms of the special weapon (*Spetsizdeliye*), employed during delivery by the aircraft to the target
• A system for the carriage and release of the 'special weapon'
• A heating system for the weapons bay, designed to maintain a temperature of not less than +5°C throughout the flight to the release point.

The 'special weapon' was carried on the BD6-105A pylon with the aid of locks Der6-4 and Der6-5D. Regardless of the type of nuclear weapon used, only one such bomb could be carried, the choice being between either the Type '4' (7U-31), or the Type '6' (246N).

The weapons system of the Tu-22U *Blinder-D* training variant differed from that of the Tu-22R by the absence of a 'special weapons' capability, and by the absence of the KD3-22R and KD3-22RS weapons racks. Additionally, in view of the aircraft's pure training role, no provision was made to utilise the 'overload' bombing capability of the Tu-22R.

The Tu-22P *Blinder-E* dedicated ECM variant did not have a bombing capability, and all related equipment was removed on conversion to this highly specialised role.

With the Tu-22RM variant, the Tupolev Design Bureau had attempted to combine a nuclear weapon delivery capability on this aircraft with the daylight reconnaissance role of the original Tu-22R. However, the Tu-22RM variant did not see operational deployment with the Long-range Air Force Tu-22 regiments. The Tu-22RDM-2 variant, developed later (in the early 1980s), like the Tu-22P, had all bomb-related equipment removed and was a pure reconnaissance platform.

The bombing capability of the Tu-22K *Blinder-B* missile carrier
The Tu-22K *Blinder-B*, although designed primarily as the airborne launch platform for the Kh-22 AS-4 *Kitchen* air-to-surface cruise missile, retained the capability to conduct freefall bombing operations when necessary. Conversion from missile-carrier to freefall bomber was carried out by regimental engineering personnel. The aircraft's bomb armament comprised:

• The NBS (*Navigatsionno-bombardirovochnaya Sistema*) Navigation-Bombing System
• A system for the loading, carriage and release of bombs
• A comprehensive selection of bombs of various calibres.

The Navigation Bombing System comprised the following:

• The PN (NATO *Downbeat*) navigation-bombing radar. [*The Russian designation of this radar was a departure from the usual practice of employing a recognisable word to describe an aircraft's radar installation, PN meaning simply* Pritsel Nosityelya, *or literally '(radar) sight of the carrier', i.e. the Tu-22K itself. The word* 'pritsel', *meaning*

The 'king-sized' KMG (*Konteiner Melkikh Gruzov*) dispenser unit specially developed for the Tu-22K to enable it to carry out offensive operations from low altitude with small-calibre bombs. Shaped like a missile, the container was suspended from the aircraft's BD-294 weapons pylon, but there are no details of its use in service. *Alfred Matusyevitch*

'gun sight, or aiming sight', is often used interchangeably with 'radar', this being the case here. AD]
- An OPB-15 optical bomb-sight
- A TsNVU-B-1B (*Tsentral'noye Navigatsionnoye Vychislityel'noye Ustroystvo-B-1B*) central navigation computer
- A navigation and flight management system (incorporating a KS-6A course and heading unit, a TsSV-1M speed and altitude indicator, a BTs-63A astro-tracker, an AP-7MTs autopilot, the Put'-4K (Route) navigation system and a TsGV-5M central gyro-unit).

The Navigation Bombing System (NBS) of the Tu-22K provided radar targeting for the

The Tu-22 was often used to demonstrate its multi-role capability to high-ranking military and civil dignitaries. Here, a Tu-22R of 199 ODRAP at Nezhin is displayed with a typical range of cameras and bombs for its two principal roles. *Valery Romanenko*

An avionics technician seen carrying out ground checks on the antenna of the Rubin-1 navigation-bombing radar of a Tu-22R. The antenna is tilted around 45° from the horizontal, with the right-hand edge at the bottom of the compartment and the left side close to one of the support struts for the radome. Note the downward-pointing IFF antenna elements, tilted at an angle optimised for interrogation of ground/surface targets. *S Burdin Archive*

The angle of view of the OPB-15 optical bomb-sight window under the navigator's station is evident from this perspective. The triangular blade antenna serves the Parol' (Password) IFF system. *S Burdin*

aircraft when used for bombing in straight and level flight, in daylight or at night, in all weather conditions and at both subsonic and supersonic speeds (up to Mach 1.4). The NBS was capable of providing targeting solutions in the following conditions:

- On radar detected and visual targets at altitudes from 2,000m (6,560ft) to 20,000m (65,616ft)
- On targets not visible to radar at altitudes from 10,000m (32,808ft) to 13,500m (44,290ft).

The following actions were required to convert the Tu-22K from missile-carrier to pure bomber:

- Some units of the PN radar were changed
- Some units of the TsNVU-B-1B central navigation computer were changed
- The BD-294 weapon rack (for the Kh-22/AS-4 *Kitchen* missile) was removed, along with the electrical control panels specific to the carriage of the missile
- KD3 or KD4 cassette-type racks were installed (the type of rack depending upon the planned task)
- Electrical control panels for the bomb armament were installed
- If necessary, APP-22 chaff dispensers were installed.

In other respects, the bomb armament and associated systems of the Tu-22K *Blinder-B* were identical with those of the Tu-22R *Blinder-C*.

The missile armament of the Tu-22K *Blinder-B*
From the time of production of the first air-launched missiles in the former Soviet Union, it had become standard practice not to consider missiles and aircraft in isolation, but rather as an integrated system (i.e. a *kompleks*). Thus, for example, aircraft such as the MiG-25 *Foxbat* and Su-15 *Flagon* fighters were known internally as '*kompleks perekhvata*' (or 'integrated interception system') MiG-25-40 and Su-15-98, the -40 and -98 suffixes referring to the R-40 (AA-6 *Acrid*) and R-98 (AA-3 *Anab*) air-to-air missiles respectively. The tradition was well established for Tupolev designs, and the Tu-16 in particular, which was the designated carrier aircraft for a number of such 'integrated systems', a typical example being the Tu-16K-26 *Badger-G Mod*, designed to carry the Kh-26 (AS-6 *Kingfish*) ASM. The Tu-22 was no exception, and when it was decided to produce the missile-carrying variant, it was given the designation Tu-22K, where the letter 'K' stood for 'Kompleks', the actual 'Kompleks' being the aircraft, the missile and its associated guidance systems. Since the missile had the same series number as the carrier aircraft, the Kompleks was designated K-22, but the number was not added to the aircraft's designation. The K-22 system was designed for:

- Missile strikes against radar contrastive pinpoint and wide-area targets over land, plus strikes against radar contrastive stationary and moving targets (i.e. naval carrier groups) on the open ocean, as well as coastal targets, using the Kh-22PG (Kh-22M) radar-homing variant of the AS-4 *Kitchen* air-to-surface missile (ASM)
- Missile strikes against wide-area targets over land and at sea using the Kh-22PSI (Kh-22MA) variant of the AS-4 *Kitchen* ASM

The K-22 system comprised the following:

1. The Tu-22K *Blinder-B* missile-carrier
2. The Kh-22 (AS-4 *Kitchen*) air-to-surface missile
3. The K-22 radio command guidance system
4. Special test equipment and ground support systems.

The Tu-22K *Blinder-B* aircraft

A special BD-294 weapon rack was installed on the Tu-22K to facilitate carriage and launch of the AS-4 missile, the BD-294 being attached to a riveted framework. On the outside of the framework there were missile cooling and heating units, as well as electrical control units for the missile. Mating of the missile with the appropriate aircraft systems was via an electrical plug-and-socket assembly, a pneumatic valve, a hydro-pneumatic valve and an air-electric (*vozdushno-ehlektricheskii raz'yom*) plug mounted on the BD-294. The rack had two positions – lowered and raised. Retraction and lowering of the rack was performed by a hydraulic jack, controlled by the navigator. The lowered position was, self-evidently, the position in which the missile was attached to the BD-294 pylon on the ground and, of course, the position from which it was launched in flight. In the launch

The weapons bay of the Tu-22K, showing the substantial structure of the BD-294 pylon in the centre and the construction of the bay doors. Unlike those of the Tu-22R, each door was hinged along its length to allow the door to open inwards to accommodate the Kh-22 missile. The two vertically hinged doors served as airflow baffles when the aircraft was used in the pure bombing role, and the doors in the upper part of the photo were replaced by others closing around the nose contours of the missile when raised into the bay for flight. Note the two attachments for mounting the SPRD-63 rocket boosters on the right of the picture. *S Burdin*

Ground crew performing maintenance work on a Tu-22K. The main bay doors have been partially folded to accommodate the Kh-22 missile, and the BD-294 pylon has been lowered for missile attachment. Note also that the profiled doors to accommodate the missile's nose have been fitted and opened ready to receive the missile. *S Burdin Archive*

position, the BD-294 pylon assumed an angle of 1° down to assist separation of the missile from the pylon at launch. The raised position was the transit position, with the missile semi-recessed into the weapon bay and the BD-294 rack maintaining a parallel attitude to the longitudinal axis of the fuselage when retracted. Missile separation from all aircraft services at launch was automatic, control of the BD-294 pylon being the responsibility of the navigator, who had all the missile control panels in his cockpit.

The Kh-22 (AS-4 *Kitchen*) air-to-surface missile
The Kh-22 (AS-4 *Kitchen*) missile was designed to attack and destroy stationary and moving naval targets, as well as wide-area targets over land. When the Kh-22 was first introduced, there were two main variants of the missile – the Kh-22PG and the Kh-22PSI.

The Kh-22PG (Article 88) variant of the AS-4 *Kitchen* was equipped with an active radar seeker head, designated PG, hence the use of these letters in the missile designation. As with the PN radar of the Tu-22K itself, the letters PG represented a minimalist description of the radar, standing for *Pritsel Golovki*, meaning literally 'radar of the (seeker) head'. Both the PN and the PG radars were developed by the same design bureau (believed to be Leninets in present-day St Petersburg) and the use of these simple letter designations was perhaps an attempt to achieve a certain anonymity regarding their design origin at the time. The PG active radar seeker was designed to direct the AS-4 missile onto a target detected (and selected for attack) by the PN radar of the Tu-22K. Missile radar

A Kh-22MP anti-radiation variant of the AS-4 *Kitchen* air-to-surface missile under the fuselage of its Tu-22KP carrier. *Alfred Matusyevitch*

A Kh-22PSI variant of the Kh-22 missile (identifiable from the Doppler antenna under the nose cone) being offered up to its Tu-22K parent aircraft. The bay doors have been retracted inside the bay, whose internal profile now permits the raising of the missile from the AT-22 trolley, and all appropriate connections have been made to the BD-294 pylon.

lock-on to the target was achieved before launch, assisted by initial target parameters from the PN (*Downbeat*) radar.

The Kh-22PSI (Article 102) variant of the AS-4 was equipped with an autonomous Doppler-assisted guidance system, designated PSI in accordance with the procedure adopted for the Kh-22PG. In this case, PSI is thought to stand for *Pritsel so Schislityelyem puti s DISS*, a somewhat more elaborate designation meaning, literally, 'Aiming device with route calculation from DISS'. Here *Pritsel* has the more usual meaning of 'sight' or 'aiming device' and *DISS* is a Doppler navigator, or literally 'Doppler measuring device of ground speed and angle of drift'. The Doppler-driven PSI guidance system provided autonomous control of the Kh-22PSI missile throughout flight up to the point of impact. The Tu-22K's PN radar was used only to provide initial target detection and before launch the following data were entered into the PSI guidance unit:

- Initial range of the missile to the target
- Initial bearing to target
- The geographical latitude of the missile launch point.

After launch, the autonomous PSI system provided continuously updated range and course data to the missile's control mechanisms throughout the flight, permitting the Kh-22PSI to make a covert approach to the target.

During the course of operations with the Tu-22K, and following the design of the Tu-22M2 *Backfire-B* and Tu-22M3 *Backfire-C*, it was decided to produce a standardised variant of the Kh-22, designed to equip both the original Tu-22 *Blinder* and the new variable-geometry Tu-22M *Backfire*. Consequently, the K-22 weapons system was expanded to include the Kh-22M and Kh-22MA variants of the AS-4, the Kh-22M having exactly the same active radar guidance system and *modus operandi* of the Kh-22PG, while the Kh-22MA incorporated the autonomous PSI system of the Kh-22PSI, along with the APK-22A autopilot.

Burgeoning development of ground-based surveillance radars deployed against the former Soviet Union led Russian missile designers to consider development of countermeasures to neutralise this threat. The outcome of their studies was the design of yet another variant of the Kh-22, this time the Kh-22MP anti-radiation (ARM) version, which formed the missile component of the **K-22P system**.

The Kh-22MP (Article 103) was designed to attack and destroy ground-based and naval (ship-borne) pulsed radars, for which the Kurs-N (Course-N) passive target identification system was used to identify and select appropriate threat emitters. The Kurs-N receiving units were mounted inside the nose radome of the Tu-22K, the antennae being mounted below the antenna of the PN (NATO *Downbeat*) radar. (*During early trials of the Kurs-N system, the antenna was mounted externally on the side of the nose of the aircraft, but the external location had a deleterious effect on aircraft handling, particularly during in-flight refuelling, and was dropped in favour of internal installation.*) Operation of the Kurs-N processing equipment was the responsibility of the navigator. After modification, the aircraft was re-designated Tu-22KP, where the letter P stood for *Protivo-radiolokatsionnyi*, or literally 'anti-radar'. Externally, the Tu-22KP did not differ from the Tu-22K.

Main technical data for the Kh-22 missile

Length	11.67m (38.29ft)
Height	
(with lower fin folded)	1.81m (5.94ft)
(with lower fin in flight position)	2.44m (8.00ft)
Max diameter of fuselage	0.92m (3.02ft)
Wing span	3.00m (9.84ft)
Engine	One R201-300 twin-chamber liquid propellant rocket
Launch weight	5,665kg (12,489lb)
Launch altitude	10,000–14,000m (32,800–45,932ft)
Cruising altitude	22,500m (73,820ft)
Maximum launch range:	
against a cruiser-sized target	320km (173nm)
against a naval 'area' target	450km (243nm)
against an overland 'area' target	500–600km (270–324nm)
against an overland 'point' target	250–320km (135–173nm)
Maximum speed	3,600–4,000kph (1,944–2,160kts)
Probability of destruction of cruiser-type target	0.8 to 0.9

The Kh-22 missile employed a normal aerodynamic layout, comprising airframe, mid-set delta wings and horizontal tail unit, rocket motor, hydraulic systems, cooling systems, warhead and fusing system, plus an electrical system and flight controls. On operational missiles intended to be used for training purposes (i.e. practice launches), an RU-6M-SL self-destruct mechanism could be installed, along with a 'Vympyel' (Pennant) transponder unit. This guaranteed destruction of the missile in the event that it went astray, or out of control, during flight to the target area.

The maximum launch range of the AS-4 *Kitchen* missile depended on the aspect angle to the target and on the propagation characteristics of the atmosphere (including time of day and season of the year). The range was of the order of 270–310km (146–167nm) against a cruiser-sized target in ideal conditions, while the minimum permitted launch range was 200km (108nm). The entire system (aircraft and missile) was designed for the launch of the AS-4 from altitudes of 10,000–13,500km (32,808–44,290ft) and at speeds of 950–1,500kph (513–810kts).

The electronic control system of the K-22 Complex

The control system of the K-22 Complex incorporated the PN (*Downbeat*) navigation-bombing radar, working in conjunction with the TsNVU-B-1B central navigation computer and the radar and navigation systems of the Kh-22 missile.

The PN radar was designed to carry out the following tasks in all weather conditions, by day and at night:

1. Radar position fixing of target areas, search, detection and selection of radar contrastive ground (and naval surface) targets at ranges out to 500km (270nm) at altitudes from 1,000m (3,280ft) up to the aircraft's service ceiling. It was possible to use the PN radar at heights below 1,000m, but its performance was severely degraded by 'ground clutter'. The PN exhibited the following detection range performance:

- Up to 350km (189nm) against a cruiser-sized target
- Up to 500km (270nm) against area targets (covering an area of 10km x 10km (6.2 × 6.2 miles)
2. Input of essential data into the PG and PSI guidance units during launch preparation of the Kh-22 missile
3. Weapons aiming (targeting) at subsonic and supersonic speeds
4. Radar correction of the aircraft's current position, calculated by the TsNVU-B-1B computer and identification of 'unknown radar reference points' (i.e. by identification of possibly 'unknown', but nevertheless obvious geographical landmarks)
5. Identification of target nationality by use of IFF (Identification Friend or Foe)

Main technical data
1. Time to operating readiness after switching on – no more than 10 minutes
2. The radar was designed to be used for attacks on a single target by several aircraft at a time (without suffering mutual interference)
3. The angle of view in azimuth was:
   - In scanning mode – 180°, 60° and 20°
   - In tracking mode – 7°
4. The radar had the following operating modes:
   - Scanning
   - Auto-tracking in range
   - Control by the TsNVU-B-1B computer
   - Semi-automatic control of course and range
5. The antenna of the PN radar was gyro-stabilised in the longitudinal and pitch axes to minimise the effects of yaw
6. The PN was synchronised with either the SRZ-10M Latun' (Brass) long-range IFF interrogator, or the interrogation component of the SRZO-2M transponder unit in order to identify targets (namely surface vessels) detected by the radar. Apart from this, the radar could send blocking signals to the SPO-3 or SPO-10 radar warning receivers to prevent the PN's transmissions from triggering a 'false' response

CHAPTER FOUR

Reconnaissance and ECM Variants of the Tu-22

Tu-22R *Blinder-C* **and variants**

The reconnaissance equipment of the Tu-22R was designed to obtain data on the operational deployment of enemy weapons and military and defensive installations, as well as anti-aircraft radars, whose parameters would be recorded on special film. Analysis of the reconnaissance data was carried out after return to base. The reconnaissance equipment was divided into aerial camera systems and electronic intelligence (Elint) systems. The camera systems consisted of three daylight 'fits' and one night system, which were mounted in the weapons (payload) bay, and also included a FARM-2 (FARM-2A) radar screen camera (*FotoApparat dlya s'yomki Radiolokatsionnovo Izobrazheniya Mestnosti*) in the navigator's cockpit. The FARM camera captured radar images of the target from the Rubin-1A (Rubin-1L on the Tu-22RD) navigation-bombing radar for subsequent analysis on the ground. The camera control consoles were in the navigator's cockpit. The weapons-bay doors had optically corrected windows for the cameras, which allowed them to be used for daylight photography without the need for opening the bay. On early aircraft, the Elint equipment was the SRS-6 (*Stantsiya Radiotekhnicheskoy Razvyedki Samolyotnaya-6*) system and the entire equipment 'fit' allowed the aircraft to be used for target reconnaissance in all weathers, day or night and at high or low altitude.

A camera installation for daylight photo-recce operations by the Tu-22R, comprising two AFA-42/20, two AFA-42/75 and two AFA-42/100 (reading from front to rear). Just visible at the rear of the camera bay is the grey front panel of the APP-22 chaff dispenser. *Valery Romanenko*

Aerial photography options
Dependent upon the nature of the mission, the Tu-22R could be equipped in one of four
specific camera 'fits':

- Option 1 (*1-yi Variant*) – daylight photography from medium and high altitude
- Option 2 (*2-oy Variant*) – daylight photography from high altitude
- Option 3 (*3-ii Variant*) – aerial topography
- Option 4 (*4-yi Variant*) – night and twilight photography.

The **Option 1 (Variant 1)** 'fit' comprised the following:

- Four AFA-42/100 (or AFA-42/75) cameras mounted on a paired tilting framework.
  They were capable of operating from a height of 5,000m (16,400ft) to 20,000m
  (65,616ft), although the latter altitude was significantly beyond the capability of the
  aircraft itself. Each of the paired installations permitted either two or four overlapping
  strips of terrain to be photographed at the same time. Four-strip photography with two
  paired AFA-42/100 cameras covered an area with a width of one times the height
  (i.e.1H, where H is the height of the aircraft) and a distance of 23 times the height (i.e.
  23H). The second pair of AFA-42/200 cameras could be engaged after the film in the
  first pair had run out, or to duplicate the first pair. (When carrying out photography from
  an altitude of 13,000m (42,650ft), the width of the area using four-strip coverage and
  the above height/distance formula was, therefore, 13km (7nm), i.e. 1H, and the along-
  track distance covered was 600km (324nm), or 23H for each pair of 'strips'). The paired
  tilting frames for the cameras were mounted in the payload (weapons) bay, between
  Frames 48 and 49 and Frames 51 and 52. Additionally, there was a fixed installation
  holding two AFA-42/20 vertical cameras covering an area 3.2 times the height (3.2H)
  and an along-track distance of 220 times the height (220H)
- An AFA-41/20 camera for vertical photography of terrain with a width coverage of
  0.89H and along-track coverage of 380H. The AFA-41/20 was mounted on a framework
  between fuselage Frames 21 and 22, the frame itself being attached to the interior of the
  bay using quick-release pins. To reduce distortion during photography, the AFA-41/20
  vertical camera was mounted at an average pitch angle of 3° on aircraft from the first
  batch of the 15th production series
- One AFA-42/100 camera for oblique photography. The remote-controlled installation was
  mounted on the starboard side of the camera bay between fuselage Frames 20 and 21,
  allowing the camera to be tilted by an angle of 6° to 45° from the horizontal. Consequently,
  oblique photography could only be carried out from the starboard side of the aircraft.

Option 2 (Variant 2) used the following camera installations:

- Two paired AFA-40 cameras on two fixed mounts, capable of carrying out photography
  from 7,000m (22,965ft) to 20,000m (65,616ft) at speeds from 600kph (324kts) to
  1,500kph (810kts). During twin-strip photography, each AFA-40 camera covered a
  four-strip area of terrain measuring 0.92H x 24H (i.e. a width of 0.92 times the aircraft's
  height and an along-track distance of 24 times the height). Thus, for example, from an
  altitude of 13,000m (42,650ft) the width of the area covered would be 12km (6.5nm)
  and the along-track distance would be 310km (167nm).

The AFA-42/100 oblique camera, AFA-41/20 vertical camera and the single AFA-42/20 camera installations remained the same as for the **Option 1** 'fit'.

Option 3 (Variant 3) consisted of the following:

- A TAU-M topographical system using an AFA-41/20 camera installation. The TAU-M (*Topograficheskaya Aehrofotoustanovka*) supported topographical photography from altitudes up to 15,000m (49,212ft) and speeds up to 1,500kph (810kts), the AFA-41/20 camera covering an area of terrain with a width of 0.89H and an along-track coverage of 380H, (i.e. a width of 0.89 times the height and an along-track distance of 380 times the height)
- Two AFA-42/100 cameras on paired tilting supports, capable of photography from altitudes from 5,000m (16,400ft) up to 20,000m (65,616ft) and at speeds from 400kph (216kts) to 2,400kph (1,295kts). During two-strip photography each AFA-42/100 camera covered an area with a width of 1H and an along-track distance of 23H
- Two paired AFA-42/20 cameras covering an area with a width of 3.2H and an along-track distance of 440H. The film magazine was doubled in capacity compared with the installation in **Option 1**.

The AFA-41/20 vertical camera and the AFA-42/100 oblique cameras were unchanged from the **Option 1** 'fit'.

Option 4 (Variant 4) comprised:

- Two NAFA-MK-75 night cameras on paired mountings, enabling them to be tilted to the rear by an angle of from 0° to 30°. These cameras were capable of operating from heights of 375m (1,230ft) to 11,250m (36,910ft) and at speeds up to 1,500kph (810kts). Two NAFA-MK-75 cameras, illuminated by one FOTAB, provided coverage of an area with a width of 0.8H and an along-track distance of 0.4H. During twilight (or dawn) photography, without the use of FOTAB, the length of the along-track sector covered increased to 55H
- FOTAB-250-215 (*Fotograficheskiye Aviabomby*) photo-flares. Four modified KD3-22R flare cassette holders were mounted in a dedicated area of the camera (payload) bay along with a further two KD3-2RS medium flare cassette holders, on which up to 22 FOTAB-250-100 (lengthened), up to 22 FOTAB-250-215, or FOTAB-250 flares could be mounted.

The night cameras were installed in the camera bay in place of the daylight camera 'fit' if the aircraft was scheduled to undertake a night-time sortie. The NAFA-MK-75 was housed in a special container, comprising special panels and a screen to prevent the camera from being buffeted by the airstream when the payload-bay doors were opened for the release of FOTAB flares.

Following operation of the aircraft in the reconnaissance role, and with the agreement of the Tupolev Design Bureau (OKB-156), a fifth photo-reconnaissance Option appeared – the so-called 'Common' or 'Unified' system. This Option included:

- A fixed vertical camera set, comprising two AFA-42/20 providing area coverage with a width of 3.2H and an along-track distance of 220H

- Two NAFA-MK-75 night cameras on paired mountings
- FOTAB-250-215 photo-flares, mounted on two KD3-22R and KD3-22RS cassette holders in the payload bay.

With all reconnaissance equipment options, the FARM-2A (FARM-3 on the Tu-22RM) was permanently set up to record images of the target area and other potentially interesting terrain features from the radar screen of the Rubin-1A (*Short Horn*) navigation-bombing radar. Additionally, the navigator had a MIZ-9 voice recorder which he used to read visual reconnaissance data onto a special steel-wire data-recording medium, dictating onto the recorder anything of potential interest that he could see. The FARM-2A (FARM-3) recorded radar images automatically and was synchronised with the rotation of the antenna, along with the time of recording and the frame number, for ease of processing by ground intelligence analysts. Control of the oblique cameras was via a photographic sighting system directed onto any target area to be photographed.

Camera equipment installed in the Tu-22R *Blinder-C*

Number	Designation of installation	Reconnaissance option			
		Daylight			**Night**
		I	**II**	**III**	
1	Vertical AFA-41/20	1	1	1	–
2	Oblique AFA-42/100	1	1	1	–
3	Double AFA-42/20	2	2	2	–
4	AFA-42/100 in AKAFU cradle	4	–	2	–
5	Paired NAFA-MK-75	–	–	–	2
6	Paired AFA-40	–	2	–	–
7	AFA-41/20 with TAU-M	–	–	1	–
8	Photo-sight	1	1	1	–

Main data	Name of camera (AFA)				
	AFA-41/20	**AFA-42/20**	**AFA-42/100**	**AFA-40**	**NAFA-MK-75**
Lens type	Orion-20	Orion-1M	Telemar-7M	Telemar-12	Uran-16
Focal length in cm (in)	20 (7.9)	20 (7.9)	100 (39.4)	1800 (709)	75 (29.5)
Image format in cm (in)	18 x 18 (7x7)	30x30 (12x12)	30x30 (12x12)	50x50 (20x20)	30x30 (12x12)
Weight in kg (lb)	65 (143) with 120m (394ft) cassette.	62 (137)	98 (216)	Flight weight 385 (849) without support assembly	130 (286) without support assembly

Tu-22R *Blinder-C* electronic intelligence (Elint) systems
The initial Elint installation on the Tu-22R consisted of the SRS-6 Romb-4A (Rhombus-4A) system, which was designed to monitor and record, automatically on special film, pulsed radar transmissions from a specific range of emitters. In particular, the SRS-6 system performed the following:

- Simultaneous reception of pulsed transmissions within a defined frequency spectrum
- Automatic recording of detected signals on special photo-film
- A visual indication of the presence of radars illuminating ('painting') the aircraft on the port and starboard side
- After decoding of the signals recorded on the film, by ground intelligence analysts, it was possible to determine the wavelength and other parameters, plus the duration of the period of transmission.

Simultaneous with the recording of the radar parameters on the film, the aircraft's course and heading was also captured from the KS-6A heading indicator, along with the time of intercept, thereby allowing the position of the intercepted radar to be fixed. The SRS-6 system covered 34 frequency bands and the antenna pattern covered 50°–90° in the vertical and horizontal planes, its range performance being 125% of the distance to a ground-based emitter. It also had a mode of operation to prevent it being affected by the aircraft's own transmissions, blocking any processing during the transmission period of the PRS-3 tail warning radar, the DISS-1 Doppler navigation system, RV-25 (*Radio-vysotomyer-25* reading up to 25,000m/82,020ft) radar altimeter and the RSBN-2S short-range navigation system. The SRS-6 was fully automated and did not require the intervention of any crew member during flight, although the airborne operator (*vozdushnyi operator*) had access to the control panel and was able to check that it was working correctly.

The Tu-22RD had an additional Elint system in the form of the Shtyr'-5 (Pin-5), which operated in different modes and frequency ranges from that of the SRS-6, and augmented the capability of the latter.

Reconnaissance equipment of the Tu-22RM
The photo-reconnaissance equipment of the Tu-22RM was designed to create photographic images of the earth's surface and the surface of the sea, for both reconnaissance purposes and to record the results of its own bombing operations (bomb damage assessment, or BDA). The photo-reconnaissance equipment was installed in a special removable 'crate' (*Konteiner 1*), mounted in the payload bay, between Frames 33 and 44. The camera suite comprised the following:

- Two AFA-42/100 cameras, permitting oblique photography from the port side of the aircraft, with a camera tilt angle from 6° to 20° from the horizontal and from 6° to 40° from the starboard side of the aircraft
- An AFA-42/100 camera for twin-strip vertical photography in the 'Reconnaissance' (*Razvyedka*) mode and monitoring of the results of the aircraft's own bombing from medium and high level in the 'Check' (*'Kontrol'*), or BDA (bomb damage assessment mode)
- An AFA-42/20 camera for vertical, or oblique photography (with a forward angle of inclination of 52°)

A comparatively rare photograph of a 290 ODRAP Tu-22R with bomb doors open as it prepares to release its weapons during a bombing sortie at one of the ranges used by the Zyabrovka-based regiment. *Sergey Tsvetkov Collection*

- Two AFA-42/20 cameras, mounted with a tilt angle of 33° from the vertical on either side of the aircraft, for vertical/oblique photography with an overall width coverage of 3.49H (i.e. 3.49 times the height of the aircraft)
- An AFA-42/20 camera, mounted at an angle of 25° to the rear, for rear-hemisphere oblique photography for both reconnaissance and medium-level bomb damage assessment, as necessary.

Operation of the camera installations was performed via control panels in the navigator's cockpit – on the left-hand side of the cockpit he had controls for all the cameras in Crate 1 (*Konteiner 1*), plus the AFA-42/100 in the vertical mount (i.e. the BDA camera), and on the right-hand side he had paired controls for the AFA-42/100 oblique cameras.

The tilt angle of the oblique cameras was set using a special sighting system to fix the 'angle of look' for the right-hand (starboard) cameras between 6° and 40°, and between 6° and 20° for the left-hand (port) side cameras, with switches on the navigator's electrical control panel. Opening and closing of the blind over the sighting window of the AFA-42/100 vertical (BDA) camera was activated via a switch on the navigator's electrical control panel.

Five different camera Options (Variants) were available on the Tu-22RM:

1. the First Variant included:
   - Two AFA-42/100 oblique cameras (looking to the right and left), installed in the bay created by the removal of Fuel Tank 1
   - An AFA-42/100 for twin-strip BDA photography (camera mounted in the accessories compartment (*tekhnicheskii otsek*))
   - Four short-focal-length cameras in the removable crate, of which one AFA-41/20 was for vertical photography and photography in the forward hemisphere, two AFA-42/20 for vertical twin-strip photography and one AFA-42/20 for rear hemisphere photography and BDA.
2. the Second Variant comprised:
   - The First Variant suite of cameras
   - Two AFA-42/100 cameras additionally mounted in the payload bay, for four-strip photography.

3. the Third Variant comprised:
   - The First Variant suite of cameras
   - Two AFA-40 cameras additionally mounted in the payload bay, for four-strip photography
4. the Fourth Variant included:
   - The First Variant suite of cameras
   - Additionally, in the payload bay, a TAU-1M topographical unit and an associated AFA-41/20 camera (in this Variant, the AFA-42/20 installed in Crate 1 was not used)
5. the Fifth Variant comprised:
   - The First Variant suite of cameras
   - An additional installation of two NAFA-MK-75 cameras for night photography.

Reconnaissance equipment of the Tu-22RM-2
The Tu-22RM-2 carried the improved equipment Crate 2 (*Konteiner 2*), which incorporated the following systems:

- The 7R infra-red reconnaissance system, designed to perform day or night thermal terrain mapping in all weather conditions from heights of 200–4,000m (656–13,124ft) at a true airspeed of more than 600kph (324kts) and from heights above 4,000m at speeds greater than 770kph (415kts)
- An AP-402 camera for panoramic photography from heights of 100–1,000m (32–3,280ft) within the speed range 600–1,400kph (324kts–756kts)
- Two AFA-54-75 or AFA-54-100 cameras, mounted in AKAFU (*Aviatsionnaya Kachayushchayasya AehroFotoUstanovka*) tilting cradles, for vertical twin-strip or four-strip daylight photography from medium and high altitude. The altitude band for the use of the AFA-54-75 was from 2,250m (7,380ft) and 3,000m (9,842ft) for the AFA-54-100 up to the service ceiling of the aircraft. The AFA-54 was used for daylight photography
- A UA-47 camera system was installed in place of the AFA-54 for night vertical photography from 300m (984ft) up to 1,000m (3,280ft). Installation of this camera enabled photography to be carried out at a height of 300m (984ft) at a maximum speed up to 1,000kph (540kts), and at heights above 350m (1,148ft), at speeds up to 1,100kph (594kts)
- A total of 152 FP-100 photo-flash shells were loaded in the UA-47 installation (*Ustanovka Aerofotograficheskii-47*), the shells being fired from the UA-47 during a photo run to illuminate the target.

One of the most interesting installations on the Tu-22RM-2 was the Article 202 (*Izdeliye 202*) Shompol (Ramrod) sideways-looking airborne radar (SLAR), which was used to create a radar image (of near photographic quality) of a wide area of terrain and/or required targets. The system could be used day or night in all weather conditions within a height band from 500m to 3,000m (1,640ft to 9,842ft) at a true airspeed of more than 700kph (378kts) and at altitudes from 3,000m (9,842ft) to 14,000m (45,932ft) at speeds greater than 850kph (460kts).

An SRS-13 Elint system was also installed which was capable of intercepting and analysing a variety of pulsed emissions from enemy radars. Of greater interest, however, although not officially confirmed, is that it is believed that the Tu-22RM-2 carried equipment capable of detecting the presence of a nuclear weapon on board a ship at a considerable distance from the ship itself. Evidence suggests that this was a highly sensitive piece of apparatus capable of detecting neutron radiation 'leaking' from nuclear weapons carried by, or arming, an enemy vessel.

Reconnaissance equipment of the Tu-22RK (RDK)

Apart from the standard reconnaissance package of the Tu-22RD, the Tu-22RK (RDK) was equipped with the SRS-10 Kub-3 (Cube-3) Elint system. The SRS-10 was designed to perform detailed Elint intercepts of pulsed radars working in the centimetric waveband, as well as continuous wave (CW) radars. The system's direction-finding (DF) accuracy was to within 2–10km (1.25–6.2 miles), but one of the main advantages of the SRS-10 was that it incorporated a data-link between the aircraft and its operating base, by which intercepted data could be transmitted to the ground while the aircraft was still airborne. Preliminary analysis of intercepted signals could be performed before landing, general analysis on the ground taking about an hour, while detailed analysis took six hours. The antennae of the SRS-10 Kub-3 Elint system were mounted in canoe-shaped housings on either side of the crew compartment on the forward fuselage, although it could only use one set of antennae at a time. The width of terrain covered by each antenna was up to 450km (243nm), i.e. the receivers could 'look' at a swath of territory 450km wide. The data-link system had a stabilised operating range of up to 1,500km (810nm).

Reconnaissance systems of the Tu-22P *Blinder-E*

The means for conducting photo-reconnaissance with the Tu-22P were represented by the following systems:

- An AFA-41/20 vertical camera mounted on a framework between Fuselage Frames 21 and 22
- The FARM-2A PPI (radar) scope camera system, which was used to record radar images generated by the Rubin-1L navigation-bombing radar.

It was also possible to undertake a limited form of Elint collection with the Tu-22P, using the ECM receivers which would detect threat emitters, but the actual jamming components would not be switched on. In this case, it was not possible to fix the location of the emitters, but simply to note that certain radars were active in a given location.

Reconnaissance systems of the Tu-22K *Blinder-B* and Tu-22KP *Blinder-B Mod*

As with all long-range Air Force bombers, the Tu-22K and Tu-22KP were also capable of a limited form of reconnaissance in addition to their primary role. The reconnaissance assets of these two variants of the *Blinder-B* were the following:

- An AFA-34-0K vertical camera which was used for bomb damage assessment (BDA) when the aircraft was used in the pure bombing role, the camera being mounted in the first accessories compartment (*tekhnicheskii otsek*)
- Like all other Tu-22 variants, the Tu-22K and Tu-22KP had permanently fitted FARM-2A radar scope cameras. On the *Blinder-B* they were used to record terrain and target images from the PN (NATO *Downbeat*) navigation-bombing radar.

Additionally, on the Tu-22KP, it was possible to use this variant's Kurs-N (Course-N) target reconnaissance system as an *ad hoc* Elint receiver, in order to classify the parameters of any detected emitters. The primary function of Kurs-N was to detect active radars, against which the aircraft's Kh-22MP ARM version of the AS-4 *Kitchen* would be launched.

Reconnaissance systems of the Tu-22U *Blinder-D*
Although not designed to have a full combat role, the Tu-22U trainer carried the following equipment, giving it a limited reconnaissance capability:

- An AFA-41/20 vertical camera installation providing area coverage of 0.89H in width over an along-track distance of 380H (i.e. an across-track width of 0.89 times the aircraft's height and an along-track distance of 380 times the aircraft's height)
- As with all the combat variants of the Tu-22, the Tu-22U trainer also had a permanently fitted FARM-2A radar scope camera working synchronously with the Rubin-1A (*Short Horn*) navigation radar.

The specialised electronic warfare (ECM) equipment of the Tu-22P *Blinder-E*
The Tu-22P *Blinder-E* was developed as a specialised jamming platform to provide electronic protection (escort jamming) for groups of Tu-22K *Blinder-B* missile carriers and Tu-22R *Blinder-C* reconnaissance variants, using both active and passive jamming techniques against threat emitters in the metric, decimetric and centimetric wavebands. The threat emitters (i.e. enemy radars) were, primarily, surveillance radars, ground-controlled intercept (GCI) radars and anti-aircraft-missile target designation and guidance radars. There were five main sub-variants of the Tu-22P, each equipped with a different set of jamming transmitters, housed in special equipment crates and incorporating the following electronic countermeasures (ECM) systems:

The **Tu-22P1** had:

- A suite of SPS-44 (SPS-44-Yu), SPS-55 (SPS-55Yu) active jammers, plus a sub-set of one SPS-4M or SPS-5M Fasol'-1 (Haricot Bean) system (during the aircraft's initial operating period, the jamming suite consisted of two SPS-4M transmitters). These were all mounted inside Equipment Crate P1
- An APP-22 chaff dispensing system, mounted in the payload bay.

The ECM equipment of the Tu-22P1 was used for active jamming of a wide spectrum of threat emitter frequencies.

The **Tu-22P2** had:

- An SPS-77 active jammer and one subset of each of the SPS-4M and SPS-5M jammers (or a complete set of the SPS-5), mounted in Equipment Crate P2
- Two APP-22 chaff dispensers, mounted in the payload bay.

The Tu-22P2 was designed to suppress (jam) the most powerful threat emitters, whose operating parameters were already known and held in a 'threat library'.

The **Tu-22P4** had:

- A suite of SPS-22-70, SPS-33-70 jammers and a sub-set of the SPS-5 system, mounted in Equipment Crate P4
- An SPS-6 active jammer mounted inside the fuselage
- An APP-22 chaff dispenser, mounted in the payload bay.

The **Tu-22P6** had:

- A suite of SPS-22-70, SPS-44-70 jammers and two sub-sets of the SPS-5M system, mounted in Equipment Crate P6
- An APP-22 chaff dispenser, mounted inside the aircraft's fuselage
- An APP-22 chaff dispenser, mounted in the payload bay.

The **Tu-22P7** had:

- A suite of SPS-22-70, SPS-55-70 jammers and two sub-sets of the SPS-5M system, mounted in Equipment Crate P7
- An SPS-6 jammer, mounted inside the aircraft's fuselage
- An APP-22 chaff dispenser, mounted in the payload bay.

Equipment Crates P4, P6 and P7 were at the time of their introduction to service the most modern active jamming systems operated by the Soviet Air Force. These Equipment Crates were interchangeable on the Tu-22P4, Tu-22P6 and the Tu-22P7.

When fitted with Equipment Crates P6 and P7, the Tu-22P had to retain 2,000kg (4,410lb) of fuel in Tank 2 in order to keep the aircraft's rearwards centre of gravity within limits for landing (40%). When equipped with the P4 crate this fuel remainder in Tank 2 had to be increased to 2,600kg (5,732lb). This fuel could not used in the calculation of range performance, which, as a consequence, was reduced by 180–200km (100–110nm) for the Tu-22P when equipped with these crates. During operations involving the use of the APP-22 chaff dispenser, it was essential to install special filters in the Tu-22P's air-conditioning system. This was to minimise the effects of chaff particles which could enter the cockpit and affect the crew's vision and breathing if they had to fly through their own chaff 'clouds'.

Group ECM protection systems of the Tu-22P
The SPS-4M, SPS-5M and SPS-6 systems were all barrage noise jammers, and produced continuous noise jamming in the metric waveband. They had no receiving units and therefore transmitted noise continuously for the entire duration that they were switched on. They were not connected in any way with other equipment in the aircraft's ECM systems. They all had identical control panels, each of which provided control of the two transmitters of each system.

The SPS-22-70, SPS-33-70, SPS-44-70 (SPS-44-Yu) and SPS-55-70 (SPS-55-Yu) active jamming systems formed the Buket (Bouquet) suite and functioned in two modes – automatic and semi-automatic. In automatic mode they intercepted threat signals from an enemy radar system, selected the appropriate response mode and the sequencing of the jamming signals in the frequency range of the threat system, and then initiated the jamming process. Moreover, if the radiating frequency (RF) of threat radar was changed (re-tuned), the jamming transmitters would also automatically retune to the new RF. In semi-automatic mode the jammers only operated in fixed-frequency barrage mode, the selection of jamming frequency being the responsibility of the airborne operator (*vozdushnyi operator*).

The SPS-77 was an active jammer producing a continuous barrage of noise in the centimetric waveband, and therefore did not have any receiving elements, transmitting continuously for the duration that it was switched on. SPS-77 was capable of jamming enemy radars working in both surveillance and target tracking modes.

Jamming systems of Tu-22P

Name of equipment		Type of jamming
SPS-22-70, SPS-33-70, SPS-44-70 (SNS-44) and SPS-55-70 (SNS-55)	Automatic mode	Spot barrage, pulsed
	Semi-automatic mode	Spectral barrage, continuous transmission, non-directional 360-degree
SPS-77		Modulated noise, spectral barrage, continuous transmission, non-directional 360-degree
SPS-4M, SPS-5, SPS-6		Noise, spectral barrage, continuous transmission, non-directional 360-degree

The collective active jamming systems of any of the Tu-22P *Blinder-E* variants all produced the same effect on an adversary's surveillance, GCI and target-designation radar screens. This was the generation of a sector of interference on the screen emanating from the jammer aircraft, which made it difficult, or indeed impossible, for the operator to determine the range to the jammer and the group of aircraft that it was escorting. The interference also created azimuth and altitude errors in determining the location of the target group and prevented continuous accurate target tracking. The width of the sector of interference in azimuth depended upon the range from the jammer to the threat emitter. In order to augment the effect of the active jamming transmissions on an enemy radar, it was standard practice to dispense chaff from the APP-22 dispensers at the same time as the use of the active jammers. The APP-22 hoppers were loaded with chaff, cut to a number of different wavelengths, to provide maximum disruptive effect on enemy radar systems. Simultaneous sowing of chaff clouds as an integral element of the active jamming process increased significantly the interference on the PPIs (plan position indicators, or radar screens) of an enemy radar. This degraded the operators' radar-dependent situational awareness and made it difficult for him to determine the location of the Tu-22P in relation to the leading edge of the chaff cloud. Apart from this, a chaff cloud masked any escorted aircraft being protected by the Tu-22P in the event that they had fallen behind the jammer, for example, either on their planned flight route, or during a turn. The probability of a single Tu-22P providing effective ECM protection for a group of two or three other Tu-22s flying in formation with a longitudinal and lateral separation of 1.5 to 2km (0.8nm to 1.08nm) was:

- For the SPS-4M, SPS-5M and SPS-6 systems equal to 1.0 (i.e. 100%) at ranges of 100–130km (54–70nm) from the radar

- For the SPS-77 equal to 1.0 (i.e. 100%) at a range of 50km (27nm) and further
- For the SPS-22-70, SPS-33-70, SPS-44-70 (SPS-44) and SPS-55-70 (SPS-55) systems equal to 1.0 (i.e. 100%) at a distance of 150km (81nm) and further.

(As mentioned elsewhere in this book, the Tu-22P had been in operational service for around twenty years before NATO assigned it the separate designation of *Blinder-E* under the Air Standards Coordinating Committee (ASCC) codename system for Russian and Chinese weapons systems. Two sub-variants had been recognised before the aircraft was withdrawn from service – the *Blinder-E1* and *Blinder E2*, which it is likely equate to the Tu-22P1 and Tu-22P2. The practice had been discontinued by the time that information about the P4, P6 and P7 variants was available to intelligence analysts (if ever) and it is not thought that the P4, P6 and P7 ever became *Blinder-E3, E4 and E5*. The *Blinder-E1* had a centreline ram-air-intake, mounted directly onto the underside of the flush-fitting ECM crate in the equipment bay, plus four 'hockey-stick' antennae on each corner of the weapons-bay area, serving the SPS-4M and Fasol'-1 jamming systems. The *Blinder-E2* had a differently configured air-intake on the ECM crate centreline and a pair of forward-facing antennae mounted on each side of the fuselage around 3.5m (11.5ft) ahead of the wing/fuselage junction. On both aircraft, the air-intake fairing also doubled as the dielectric cover for the other antennae of the ECM suite, ranged along the centreline – see diagram on page 80).

CHAPTER FIVE

Introduction of the Tu-22

The first Soviet Air Force units to convert onto the Tu-22 were 203 ODRAP and 290 ODRAP (*Otdyel'nyi Dal'nyerazvyedyvatyel'nyi Aviatsionnyi Polk*), at Baranovichi and Zyabrovka respectively, in Byelorussia. (The contraction of these somewhat lengthy titles, meaning Independent Long-range Reconnaissance Air Regiment, recalls that of US Navy FAIRECONRON – 'fleet air reconnaissance squadron' – units.) The first Soviet Naval Aviation regiment to convert onto the *Blinder* was 15 ODRAP, subordinate to the Baltic Fleet Air Force and based at Chkalovsk in the Kaliningrad District. A brief historical digression is appropriate here to emphasise the huge technological leap represented by the introduction of the Tu-22 into Soviet Air Force service. One of the first regiments to convert, 290 ODRAP, had previously been a so-called 'heavy' bomber regiment (290 TBAP – *Tyazholo-bombardirovochnyi Polk*), albeit with a training commitment, and was involved in training crews on the Il-4 (*Bob*) throughout the Second World War. The regiment converted onto the North American B-25 Mitchell (ex-lend lease) in 1950 and began to receive the first Tu-4 *Bull* (a true 'heavy' bomber) in 1951, being re-designated (perhaps somewhat paradoxically) as 290 ODRAP in that year. In 1955, 290 ODRAP relocated to its permanent base at Zyabrovka and entered the jet era by converting onto the Tu-16 *Badger*, an event preceded by its sister regiment 203 ODRAP, which had converted onto the Tu-16R in 1954, and relocating to Baranovichi in 1955. (*203 ODRAP was later to be re-designated as 203 TBAP when its role changed after re-equipping with the Tu-22K* Blinder-B *missile-carrier in 1964*). By contrast with the Soviet Air Force, the Naval Air Force units which converted onto the Tu-22 had previously operated the Il-28R recce version of the *Beagle* twin-jet light bomber.

At the end of 1959, after operating the Tu-16R for five years, 203 ODRAP was ordered to send several pilots and engineers to Factory 22 at Kazan', to familiarise themselves with a new aircraft which they had been chosen to receive. The aircraft was, of course, the supersonic Tu-22, details of which had up to that time been a secret to all but the designers and a selected few in the military hierarchy. The pilots (all of First Class category – see Table), and ground engineers were shown the production line and underwent instruction on design aspects of the aircraft and its operation. Engine specialists were sent to the factory at Rybinsk to study the Tu-22's VD-7M engines, at the time the most complex powerplant planned for air force service. It was at this point that the pilots discovered that this large and complex aircraft was to have only one pilot and that a training variant had not been planned! Preparations for acceptance of the Tu-22 into service continued throughout 1960, and on 22 February 1961 the Soviet General Staff issued Directive 4/59209, which defined the measures that had to be adopted for this to occur. In accordance with this directive, 203 ODRAP was re-subordinated from 45 TBAD

(*Tyazholo-bombardirovochnaya Aviatsionnaya Diviziya*) Heavy Bomber Air Division, to 22 TBAD with HQ at Bobruisk.

Soviet Air Force pilot categories

Category	Minimum hours	Experience	Limitations
Basic	Training hours plus type conversion time	4 years	Day/Night – VMC only. Authorised above 500m (1,640ft) cloud base in daylight, with 5km (3 miles) visibility. Night – above 600m (1,970ft) cloud base, with 6km (3.75 miles) visibility.
Pilot 3rd Class	350 hours	5 years	Night VMC only. Authorised in daylight below 500m cloud base, with 5km visibility. Night – above 600m cloud base, with 6km visibility.
Pilot 2nd Class	450 hours	6 years	Authorised in daylight for 250m [820ft] cloud base, with 2.5km [1.5 miles] visibility. Night – below 600m cloud base, with 6km visibility.
Pilot 1st Class	550 hours	7 years	250m cloud base, with 2.5km visibility in daylight. Night – 300m [985ft] cloud base, with 3km [1.9 miles] visibility.
Sniper Pilot	1,000 hours	10 years	As for First Class, but categorised by competition.

At the same time, officers who had been selected for conversion onto the new aircraft had to report to the Flight Test Institute at Zhukovskii, where the first Tu-22As had been ferried. (At the time, a total of nineteen aircraft commanders, twenty navigators and fourteen airborne operators from 203 ODRAP had been trained on the new aircraft). The situation was complicated by the fact that the Soviet Air Force wanted to show off these aircraft to the Communist Party leadership at a special flypast in celebration of the October Revolution in November 1961. There was no alternative but to train these 'ordinary' regimental pilots on the Tu-22A, and so the 'new boys' had to make up the numbers in the nine-aircraft formation of *Blinders* for the planned flypast over Tushino airfield! Training for the flypast was conducted in parallel with routine test flying *as well as* converting the pilots from Byelorussia onto the aircraft! The lack of a dedicated trainer led to the adoption of a rather original method of instruction. Having studied the 'Temporary Instructions for Tu-22 Pilots', the trainees would climb into the cockpit of the Tu-22 and stand in the small space to the right of the aircraft commander. Thankfully this was big enough for the purpose, and with a test pilot occupying the aircraft commander's seat, the trainee would be talked through, step by step, all the actions which he would have to follow before being allowed to fly the aircraft himself!

Having successfully carried out several 'solo' flights on the Tu-22A, the 203 ODRAP pilots returned to their regiment by rail and continued to fly the Tu-16. (*At the time, the Tu-22K* Blinder-B *missile carrier, which 203 ODRAP had been slated to receive, was still undergoing factory trials and was a long way from service introduction*). In 1961, 290

One of the first Tu-22Rs delivered to 290 ODRAP at Zyabrovka, seen outside the second-line servicing area (TEhCh) in 1994. A feature of the early-series aircraft was the kinked join between the Rubin-1A radar antenna fairing and the fuselage, which on later aircraft became a purely vertical join. The nose-wheel is positioned in a special trolley which allowed the aircraft's nose to be raised to give the 8° angle required at take-off and was used as a ground training aid to accustom pilots to the cockpit view at unstick. *S Burdin*

ODRAP at Zyabrovka was also given the order to convert onto the Tu-22, and flight and ground crews attended the preliminary factory conversion courses at Kazan' and Rybinsk. The situation for the Soviet Naval Air Force was slightly more complicated by the fact that in 1961 the force had been reduced in personnel and equipment strength. This led to 15 ODRAP being re-formed as 306 ODRAEh (*Otdyel'naya Dal'nyaya Razvyedyvatyel'naya Ehskadril'ya*), or 306 Independent Long-range Reconnaissance Aviation Squadron. Consequently, the decision by the Naval Air Force GHQ to re-equip this squadron with the Tu-22R was rather unexpected, but conversion onto the new aircraft nevertheless commenced on 1 April 1961 (clearly with little concern about the choice of date!). Simultaneous with conversion onto the Tu-22R, a new base, was established at Chkalovsk, near Kaliningrad, with the runway lengthened to the required 3,000m (9,840ft) and taxiways improved to take this heavy aircraft. Towards the end of 1961, 306 ODRAEh moved into the new base and in November of that year the squadron was again re-formed as 15 ODRAP. (15 ODRAP had previously been based at Mamonovo (formerly Heiligenbal) since 1946, the year in which the Kaliningrad Region was ceded to Russia under the terms of the post-war Potsdam Conference.)

The first squadron of 203 ODRAP had the distinction of being the first unit to acquire the new bomber, and six crews were selected to ferry the first Tu-22As from the factory at Kazan'. Having each performed a single check flight at Kazan', these crews flew their new aircraft back to Baranovichi. Engineering support teams were also sent to Baranovichi from OKB-156, Kazan' and Rybinsk to assist in resolving any teething problems with the new aircraft. A rather unusual 'one-off' Tu-22 had also arrived at Baranovichi, along with the standard Tu-22As. This was an *ad hoc* attempt to produce a dual-control variant in the shortest possible time scale, devised by the engineers at Kazan', who modified one of the Tu-22As to incorporate an instructor's position in place of the navigator's seat. The emergency escape hatch cover above the navigator's seat was removed and a turret blister from a Tu-16 was put in its place. The instructor's seat in the newly configured cockpit could be raised higher than the normal position for the navigator, so that the instructor's head could reach into the blister and allow a degree of all-round vision. The design, not surprisingly, exhibited a number of shortcomings, although the aircraft was used with great success by 203 TBAP until the introduction of the dedicated Tu-22U trainer variant.

Conversion from the Tu-16 onto the Tu-22 brought with it changes in the personnel organisation of the regiments, occasioned by the need to reduce the six- to seven-man crew of the Tu-16R to only three on the *Blinder*, with supernumerary crew being posted to various other regiments. At this time, in 1962, Zyabrovka airfield was undergoing its second refurbishment, and during the runway-lengthening phase the air and ground crews of the first squadron of 290 ODRAP were sent to Baranovichi to convert onto the Tu-22 under the auspices of resident 203 ODRAP. The first 290 ODRAP pilot to convert onto the Tu-22A was the regiment commander, Colonel Plotnikov, followed by his deputies, Lt-Cols Popov and Aleksandrov, and the commander of the first squadron, Major Koval'chuk. After completing their training on the new aircraft in April 1962, the regiment commander and two other pilots flew three Tu-22As back to Zyabrovka. In the first months of operating the Tu-22A, there were frequent malfunctions and failures as a consequence of the aircraft having been insufficiently proved during the flight test phase. The main features which complicated the process of learning to handle the Tu-22 were:

1. The absence of a dedicated trainer and the fact that not every pilot was capable of converting onto a new type without demonstrated instruction. The navigator and airborne operator also had to be both bold and trusting to fly with a pilot who had never flown the aircraft before!
2. The aircraft demonstrated very sensitive response to control inputs, with instantaneous reaction to external airflow influences or control deflections, which could lead to 'pilot-induced oscillation' (PIO)
3. The impossibility of the crew members monitoring each other's actions, because of the isolated seating positions of the three-man crew
4. The aircraft's non-reversible control actuators required the pilot to develop very accurate motor reflexes to control inputs (see 2. above)
5. 'The opposite reaction to application of power' was difficult to get used to. On the Tu-16, for example, the pilot would chop power for the flare and slowly pull the control column back, as normal. On the Tu-22, however, the pilot had to chop power and then push the column *forward*, almost to the limits of its travel! This was psychologically difficult for a pilot, unused to pushing the control column of a large aircraft forward when just about to touch down. If this was not done, however, there was a danger of striking the runway hard with the tail bumper, or with the rear fuselage
6. Fuel consumption was unusually high with the Dobrynin VD-7M engines. The 'warm-up' runs and engine checks before take-off alone consumed around 2,000kg (4,410lb).

Pilots selected to fly the Tu-22 were Tu-16 commanders with at least 1,000 hours on type and holding the Pilot First Class category. The PTS (*Pilotazhnyi Trenazhor Samolyota*) fixed-base simulator was used in the early stage of conversion, one of the first of the new generation of Soviet flight simulators, but still only capable of demonstrating aircraft control in flight. It could not simulate take-off and landing, the two most dangerous phases of flight for the Tu-22. It was only some time later that the KTS-22 (*Kompleksnyi Trenazhor Samolyota 22*) procedural simulator was introduced, which could simulate take-off, route flying and landing of the Tu-22. The high landing speed of the Tu-22 compared with the Tu-16 was a major hurdle for the pilots to overcome, and there were many occurrences of aircraft running off the end of the runway in the early stages of operation. Regiment 'rationalisers' (*ratsionalizatory*), or 'methodology experts', suggested landing at high angles of attack, which led to the creation of the so-called '*ugol'shchiki* movement', '*ugol'shchik*' being a neologism translating roughly as 'angle (of attack) follower'. The objective of the 'movement' was to see who could achieve the highest angle of attack on landing, which resulted, of course, in many pilots undershooting the approach! The problem was resolved somewhat *more* rationally when test pilots were brought in to assist the pilots in developing a better landing technique, and then further improved following the introduction of the Tu-22U *Blinder-D* trainer. Mastery of the Tu-22A was an arduous process, and trainee pilots on the type continued to fly the Tu-16s, with which the second and third squadrons were still equipped, in order not to lose their flying categories. An example of the huge imbalance between Tu-22 and Tu-16 sortie generation was that in 1962, 203 ODRAP pilots flew a total of only 86 hours on the *Blinder*, while the Tu-16 total was 3,188 hours!

In parallel with conversion to the Tu-22 in the Soviet Air Force, 15 ODRAP of the Soviet Naval Air Force was also converting onto the type, with the crews of Majors Perevedentsev and Doroshenko being the first naval aviators to fly the Tu-22R, on 3 July 1962. (*Unlike the majority of the world's air arms, the Soviet Naval Air Force rank structure was the same as that for the Soviet Air Force*). Meanwhile, Soviet Air Force training on the Tu-22R was moving at such a slow pace that aircraft were being delivered to the third squadron of 290 ODRAP at Zyabrovka even though there were no trained pilots to fly them. To some extent this was hardly surprising since many of the pilots were Second World War veterans who had been flying the comparatively straightforward B-25 Mitchell up to less than ten years earlier. Many lacked formal education and found it difficult to convert onto the much more complex and quite revolutionary Tu-22 because of their age. These problems were brought into sharp focus in the case of the inspector pilots from the Corps Headquarters who were tasked with examining the flying abilities of the regimental pilots. These were highly experienced and respected pilots, but out of their depth in the supersonic jet age.

Major Ivashutin, a former 290 ODRAP senior crew chief on the Tu-22R, remembers the period: 'An HQ inspector pilot was in the cockpit and I, as '*startekh*' (*starshii tekhnik* – senior crew chief), was squatting alongside his seat, which was the normal procedure during engine starts at that time. The pilot pointed to one of the switches and asked, "Startekh, do I switch this on?", to which I replied, "Comrade commander, I'm not sure about that – I've switched on everything that I've been instructed to, but this one I don't know." The inspector then asked the navigator, "Navigator, tell me, do I switch this one on, or not?". The absence of a second pilot made the life of an inspector pilot very difficult (if not pointless), until the introduction of the Tu-22U. On another occasion, Ivashutin's Tu-22R returned from a night sortie with tree branches wrapped around the undercarriage bogies and he asked the inspector pilot from Corps HQ if there were any occurrences to report, to which the pilot replied, "Everything was normal." However, the navigator beckoned to Ivashutin and said: "You know, we almost suffered a major catastrophe – I told him that the heading should be such-and-such and that we should turn left, but he carried on regardless and lined up on the railway station. There was a train on the tracks and it was illuminating the rails with its headlight. The inspector pilot took the illuminated station to be the runway and descended, probably hitting the trees at that time." Since there were no other occurrences and everything seemed to work normally, the incident was not reported to HQ!' (*It is perhaps worth mentioning here that the touchdown area of Soviet military airfields was illuminated at the time by searchlights pointing down the runway, rather than using runway marker lights, making such confusion understandable, but not excusable*).

The last Tu-16s were handed over by 290 ODRAP to 200 TBAP at Bobruisk in 1963, and in the same year all the pilots of the first squadron of 203 ODRAP were authorised to fly 'solo' in daylight VMC and IMC conditions. Nevertheless, the accumulated flight time on the Tu-22 by 203 ODRAP in 1963 was still only 107 hours, while 3,688 were flown on the Tu-16. The year 1963 was also memorable for 121 ODRAP (later to become 121 TBAP) at Machulishchi, which had received the order to convert onto the Tu-22, once again following the established procedure of detaching personnel to the factories at Kazan' and Rybinsk before receiving its aircraft. After completing the theoretical studies phase at the factories, the crews commenced their conversion training on the Tu-22 itself at Baranovichi, where the first conversion centre had been set up. By early 1964, initial manufacturing problems with the Tu-22K had been resolved, and the first of this missile-carrying variant started to roll off the production line at Factory 22 at Kazan'. The introduction of the Tu-22K *Blinder-B* caused fewer headaches than with the Tu-22R, and most of the early teething problems had been eradicated by the time they commenced delivery to the first squadron of 203 TBAP at Baranovichi. (By this time 203 ODRAP had been redesignated 203 TBAP (*Tyazholo-bombardirovochnyi Aviatsionnyi Polk*) by the General Staff to reflect its offensive role as a heavy missile-carrying 'bomber' unit). The order to 'work up' on the Tu-22K was given in a directive from the General Staff dated 25 April 1964, the regiment receiving its first nine Tu-22K and one Tu-22U soon after, and by the end of the year it had a total of nineteen Tu-22K, nine Tu-22P and three Tu-22U trainers on strength.

As it continued its 'work-up' phase with the Tu-22R, 290 ODRAP was ordered to commence night-flying training on the aircraft, a task complicated by the fact that not even the test pilots had flown the aircraft at night at that time! Preparation for the first night flight occupied the aircrew and engineers for a whole month until that memorable moonlit July night in 1964, when 290 ODRAP commander, Colonel Plotnikov, accompanied by Lt-Col Zaitsev, an inspector pilot from the Corps HQ, completed their first night sortie in a Tu-22U. The flight lasted 40 minutes, and after landing, the two pilots signed the authorisation book granting each the right to act as night-flying instructors on the Tu-22. Plotnikov and Zaitsev then completed one more flight each on the Tu-22R, with night-flying training commencing in earnest soon after for the rest of the regiment. By now, conversion of the remaining regiments was gaining momentum, and all three squadrons of 290 ODRAP were equipped with the *Blinder*, with the regiment's third squadron operating the Tu-22P *Blinder-E* electronic countermeasures variant. In July 1964, 199 ODRAP at Nezhin in the Ukraine started to train on the aircraft, carrying out its first flights on the Tu-22U on 9 March 1965. Meanwhile, 30 ODRAP of the Soviet Naval Air Force, based at Saki on the Crimean Peninsula, commenced its training programme on the aircraft at Kul'bakino airfield near Nikolaev on Ukraine's Black Sea

A night take-off by a Tu-22PD *Blinder-E* of 203 TBAP at Baranovichi in 1993. *S Burdin*

coast. This base served as the Navy's main operational conversion centre. Also in that year, 203 TBAP was ordered to complete conversion onto the Tu-22 before 20 December 1965, its second squadron having commenced conversion at the beginning of the year, but the third squadron was still operating the Tu-16. Deliveries of the Tu-22K to 121 TBAP at Machulishchi and 341 TBAP at Ozyornoye had also commenced in 1965.

Intensive use of the Tu-22 really got under way in the mid-1960s, albeit sadly reflected in an increase in the number of accidents and tragedies experienced by the regiments, but without slowing the pace of training. In 1966, 203 TBAP achieved an annual total of 744 hours on the Tu-22 in daylight VMC conditions, compared with 144 hours on the remaining Tu-16s of the third squadron. The Tu-16 had been kept on to provide pilots with the IMC training necessary for retaining their flying categories. Deliveries of the in-flight-refuelling-capable Tu-22RD had also commenced in this period (mid-1960s), the first Tu-22RD (Bort No. 63) being delivered from the refurbishment plant at Ryazan' to the first squadron of 290 ODRAP at Zyabrovka. Whereas aircrew and ground crews had previously undergone pre-employment training at the aircraft and engine manufacturing plants at Kazan' and Rybinsk respectively, it was decided that from 1968 onwards this instruction should be carried out on military bases. Thus, all newly selected aircrew would undergo initial training at the 43rd Centre for Weapons Training and Aircrew Conversion at Ryazan', while ground crew would attend courses at Zyabrovka, hosted by 290 ODRAP. (*However, this was to change later when aircrew conversion training was carried out directly on the regiments.*) By the end of the 1960s, the bulk of the conversion programme was complete and most regiments were up to their established peacetime strength. The standard composition of Long-range Air Force (*Dal'nyaya Aviatsiya* – DA) Tu-22 heavy bomber and reconnaissance regiments comprised the following squadrons:

• The First Squadron – manned by the most highly trained crews
• The Second Squadron – manned by crews still gaining experience on type and completing their training
• The Third Squadron – the 'jamming', or '*shumovaya*' (noise generating) squadron, as it was known in the Soviet Air Force. The third squadron of any regiment in the Soviet Air Force was a training squadron, and in the case of DA Tu-22 regiments would have a minimum of two Tu-22U trainers, as against one on each of the other squadrons.

Take-off of a 121 TBAP Tu-22K *Blinder-B* at Machulishchi, in full afterburner, with the nozzles of the RD-7M2 engines fully open, 1993. *S Burdin*

A Tu-22K being towed to the TEhCh at Machulishchi in 1993.

Standard composition of an independent long-range reconnaissance regiment

Aircraft	Quantity
Tu-22P	4
Tu-22R	20
Tu-22U	5
Tu-124Sh, Tu-134Sh	1

Ground Training Equipment	Quantity
KTS-22 Procedural Simulator	1
'Strontsii' (Strontium) Simulator	1
SKT-53 Gunnery Simulator	3
PRS-3T Gunnery Simulator	2
UTB-3M Bombing Simulator	1

Standard composition of a heavy bomber air regiment

Aircraft	Quantity
Tu-22PD	6
Tu-22K	24
Tu-22U	5

Ground Training Equipment	Quantity
KTS-22 Procedural Simulator	I
Specialised Simulator	I
SKT-53 Gunnery Simulator	3
PRS-3T Gunnery Simulator	2
UTB-3M Bombing Simulator	I

Note: The 'Strontsii' simulator was used in the simulation of radar-assisted bombing with the Rubin-IA/IL navigation and bombing radar. The SKT-53 (Strel'kovyi Kinotrenazhor-53) gunnery simulator was used to train airborne operators to aim and fire the rear cannon.

The PRS-3T (Pritsel'naya Radiolokatsionnaya Stantsiya-3 – Trenazhor) provided simulation of the techniques associated with the PRS-3 Argon radar sighting system of the rear cannon installation.

The UTB-3M was used to simulate optical bomb aiming.

Selection and training of Soviet Air Force Tu-22 aircrew

During the course of Tu-22 operations, the location for training newly selected aircrew to fly the aircraft was changed from the 43rd Centre for Weapons Training and Aircrew Conversion at Dorokhovo, near Ryazan', to Central Officers' Courses held at Baranovichi, Zyabrovka and Machulishchi. This was entirely logical, since there were only three regiments equipped with the Tu-22K and two with the Tu-22R, all with an established strength of trained aircrew. They would only need to be 'topped up' in the event of an officer being withdrawn from flying duties, which would only be about one or two cases per year. There was little point, therefore, in maintaining an instructional cadre on the Tu-22 at Ryazan' to train only one or two replacements per year. Furthermore, the accumulated experience of the crews in the regiments was invaluable in the training process. In the early 1970s, the first wave of gradual 'rejuvenation' of the Long-range Air Force had commenced, and young pilots started to arrive in the Tu-22 regiments, if not directly from flying school, then at least after 'accelerated' experience on an operational type (e.g. the Tu-16). There were, for example, cases of newly graduated pilots spending a year as a co-pilot on the Tu-16, then going straight onto an aircraft commander's course, followed by a posting to a Tu-22 unit. The route followed by pilot and navigator candidates for the Tu-22 in the late 1970s and early 1980s was fairly typical of the standard procedure. In the first instance, Air Army HQ representatives would visit those regiments still flying the Tu-16, to brief the crews on the Tu-22 and seek volunteers who wished to fly the aircraft. Apart from a wish to fly the *Blinder*, candidates had to be qualified aircraft commanders of Pilot First or Second Class category and satisfy the medical criteria, particularly in terms of height. The latter was very important because the pilot's seat could only be adjusted over a 6cm (2.36in) range and the rudder pedals could not be adjusted at all. (Many of the older (shorter) pilots would place a cushion on the seat so that they could more comfortably reach the rudder pedals.)

After the briefing, the 'selection board' would make a note of the volunteers and return to HQ. Between six and eight weeks later, an order would be sent out inviting all those expressing a desire to fly 'the most formidable aircraft in the DA' to report to HQ 46th Air Army of the Supreme High Command in Smolensk. Apart from pilots who had voluntarily chosen to 'link their fate' with the Tu-22, there were those whose commanders had decided to rid themselves of 'awkward, free-spirited' pilots, and packed them off to Tu-22 regiments on a 'voluntary-compulsory basis', i.e. without the consent of the pilot! Usually, the deputy commander of the Air Army himself would select from the list of volunteers, and only rarely would a pilot get through the system who did not want to fly the Tu-22. Some pilots refused to be involved with the aircraft during the interview stage at Air Army HQ, typically saying things like: 'Comrade General, I have an aversion towards this aircraft.' After selection, the pilots would return to their regiments and continue to fly their normal training programme, in order to maintain their flying category, while waiting for their posting notice. After a further four to eight weeks, selected candidates would be sent to the Central Officers' Course (*Tsentral'nyi Ofitserskii Kurs* – TsOK) at either Baranovichi or Machulishchi, depending on whether they had been earmarked for the Tu-22K or the Tu-22R.

Theoretical instruction commenced in October of each year, and students spent two months studying the design of the Tu-22, equipment, aerodynamics, aircraft handling, navigation and tactics, etc. Since the trainees were all qualified aircraft commanders who had attended the aircraft commanders' course at the 43rd Centre for Weapons Training and Aircrew Conversion at Ryazan', much of their instruction was given by way of familiarisation briefings, and they only studied the particularities of the Tu-22 in depth. Actual flight training on the Tu-22U commenced in the following February, after the trainees had returned to their Central Officers' Course location at either Baranovichi or Machulishchi. The first flight in the Tu-22U was a familiarisation exercise, but by the fifth or sixth flight the students were exposed to a flight mode called 'limiting regime' (*predyel'nyi rezhim*), a flight at minimum and maximum airspeed. This involved climbing rapidly to the aircraft's service ceiling, where the pilot would chop the power before descending to low level at a rate of descent of 150m/sec (14,530ft/min) and an angle of 65–70°. The eleventh flight was a special pre-solo check flight, followed, if successful, by a first solo on the twelfth. Later in the course, a week was devoted to formation flying where the trainee would practise station keeping with other regimental aircraft. On completion of the TsOK phase in May, pilots were 'qualified' to join the third squadron to commence their mastery of the Tu-22 in earnest.

In the 1980s, the average age of a Tu-22 pilot was over 35, so it was decided to carry out an experiment with regard to bringing in 'new blood' to the regiments. As part of the experiment, 121 TBAP accepted four or five newly qualified pilots (lieutenants) straight from one of the military flight colleges, and although the practice was not continued, these young pilots, who did not conform to the usual stereotype, acquitted themselves very well. One of this group reached the position of deputy squadron commander and another became a Tu-22 squadron commander. On first acquaintance with the Tu-22, the aircraft inspired a variety of emotions, from abject fear to sheer delight. After the Tu-16, with its wide and capacious four-man cockpit, the Tu-22 pilot had to sit in a small, almost fighter-like cockpit and wear a 'bone dome' for head protection in the event of ejecting at supersonic speed and under high g-loadings. Difficulties in mastering the Tu-22 were largely the result of the rigid 'mind set' of the pilots assigned to fly the aircraft. The majority of Tu-22 pilots had graduated from the left-hand seat of other bomber types and had become accustomed to having a co-pilot to assist in cockpit management tasks.

Major Serikov, a former Tu-22 section commander, remembers the difficulty of adjusting to the single-pilot crew concept, saying that after around three years in the left-hand seat of the Tu-16 a pilot would become 'fat and lazy', relying on his co-pilot to do all the work. The aircraft commander would taxi the aircraft, release the brakes and perform the take-off, but the co-pilot would ensure that the aircraft was 'wings level' at lift-off, even though the commander still held the control wheel throughout the climb. The co-pilot would retract the undercarriage, landing lights and flaps and then at the top of climb the commander would give him full control of the aircraft. In addition to this, all radio communications were also handled by the co-pilot from the right-hand seat. For the descent and landing the responsibilities were similar, albeit in reverse, the commander performing the landing and then taxiing the aircraft back to the parking spot. Combat tasks were, however, the responsibility of the commander, working closely with the navigator. Then, as Major Serikov recalls, 'After this "lazy" life, you came to the Tu-22 and started darting around the cockpit – flaps, undercarriage, etc. – you had to do everything yourself from engine start-up to shut-down. Obviously, at first it was difficult, but then you got used to it, although after the first few flights you always landed drenched in perspiration.'

Not all pilots were able to cope with this 'independence', and in the mid-1980s a pilot was posted to 121 TBAP at Machulishchi, who, having qualified on the Tu-22, declared after a few flights that he could no longer handle the aircraft. He had flown for so long as commander of a Tu-16 that he found it impossible to break 'old habits', having to think, fly the aircraft and handle the radio, etc., with everything having to be done very rapidly, while cruising at 1,000kph (540kts) at medium and high altitude. Eventually, pilots were selected in groups of five, usually from the Tu-16 and M-3 *Bison* communities, only three of whom would normally get through the initial flight phase of conversion onto the Tu-22, and often some of these were then recommended to transfer to another type of aircraft. In flight the Tu-22 was as nimble as a fighter, but on the landing approach it was a laggard, and it was essential that the pilot's thought processes were always about 15–20m (50–60ft) 'ahead' of the aircraft, anticipating where a particular control input would place the aircraft. A pilot might fly the Tu-16 very well and yet not be able to handle the Tu-22 at all, and even instructor pilots on the Tu-134UBL from the training regiments were unable to master the aircraft. Most pilots would agree with the decision to 'chop' them from the course, realising that the lives of two other crew members would depend on their skill as the sole pilot on board, but some would ask for one more chance to prove that they 'had what it takes'. Some pilots, on the other hand, were ordered back to their units in a rather peremptory manner, being told to go back to an aircraft that they really did understand and forget about the Tu-22.

In the latter years of the Tu-22's service, pilots were even selected from the single-seat fighter community, although this was not an easy transition to make. One of these pilots, Captain Kovalyev, came to the Tu-22K on 203 TBAP at Baranovichi, after flying the Su-17M2 *Fitter-D* variable-geometry ground-attack fighter. The deputy commander of 203 TBAP, Lt-Col Ignatov, recalls that Captain Kovalyev completed the conversion programme without a problem, flew all his check flights perfectly and within a year had achieved Pilot First Class status. There were, however, those who were less successful; Lt-Col Ignatov had a young flyer, Captain Soldatkin, on the third squadron, who very

One of 121 TBAP's Tu-22U *Blinder-D* trainers at Machulishchi in 1993. *S Burdin*

much wanted to qualify on the Tu-22, but he just could not master this demanding aircraft. He had even written to the command staff in the Air Army HQ, asking that he should be kept on the programme, perhaps hoping that they might be swayed by the fact that it was a complex procedure to transfer to another aircraft type during training. They would usually not throw a pilot out of training, but would deliberate for a long time before taking such a decision, and this was the case with this particular officer. One instructor had already checked his readiness to go solo on the Tu-22 and refused to authorise him.

The usual procedure on 203 TBAP was to do two check flights on the Tu-22U, and if everything was OK, then the pilot would be cleared to carry out a solo flight on the Tu-22K. After two such flights on the Tu-22U, Captain Soldatkin was refused permission to fly solo on the combat variant, but the regimental command staff decided to give him one more chance. This time they used a different instructor, in order to make the check as objective as possible, but the result was the same – he was not authorised to fly solo on the Tu-22K. The regiment called in an HQ inspector pilot, who flew to Baranovichi to tell the unfortunate pilot that he would have to complete his training on a different aircraft. Pilots who did not complete type conversion on the Tu-22 were sent back to flight training school, probably to be 're-roled' on another type, and usually did not exhibit any

A Tu-22PD of 121 TBAP in the dispersal area at Machulishchi in 1993, surrounded by servicing vehicles and diagnostic equipment. *S Burdin*

particular problems in their flying ability. It was perhaps pilots like this, otherwise competent but unable to master the Tu-22, who inadvertently served as the source of the distorted rumours and adverse opinions about the aircraft, since most harboured a grievance that they had been unable to 'tame' this formidable aircraft. Their colleagues, knowing them to be capable pilots, simply chose to 'demonise' the Tu-22 as the most convenient explanation as to why a good pilot could not fly it.

Operating the Tu-22
From the pilot's point of view, the Tu-22 was a highly unusual aircraft for the Long-range Air Force, not only in the 1960s and '70s, but also in the latter years of its operation. Take-off was performed with the inner flaps set at 35° and the outer sections set at 20°, using medium reheat at low all-up weight (60–70 tonnes/132,275–154,320lb, dependent upon atmospheric conditions). At high all-up weights (up to 91 tonnes/200,620lb), maximum reheat was employed and, if necessary, additional rocket boosters could be attached to augment take-off thrust in high ambient temperatures, if runway length was a limiting factor. The take-off of the Tu-22, which demonstrated a very high thrust-to-weight ratio for an aircraft of its type at that time, consisted of two stages. The first stage was the ground roll up to the point of unstick, while the second stage involved a climb to 25 metres (82ft) with simultaneous acceleration along the take-off flight trajectory, the two stages combining to give the aircraft's take-off distance. At a take-off weight of 90 tonnes

(198,410lb), outside air temperature of 30°C, air pressure of 730mm Hg (973.3mb) and in zero wind conditions, the take-off distance was 3,400m (11,155ft). If the head wind component was 4m/sec (7.8kts) in these conditions, then the take-off distance increased to 3,600m (11,810ft). Before take-off, the pilot would set power in the following sequence:

- Moving both throttle levers forward together, he would set maximum dry (non-afterburner) thrust on both engines
- he would then engage afterburner on one engine, checking 'light up' by reference to his instruments and sensing the longitudinal jolt as it ignited
- next he would do the same on the other engine
- after stable ignition of afterburner on the second engine, he would set the required take-off power by moving both throttle levers forward on each engine.

Having warned the crew, the pilot would then release the parking brake and with sharp simultaneous movements with both feet he would ensure that both wheel (toe) brakes were fully released, so that the aircraft would not commence the take-off roll with brakes partially selected. The pilot maintained directional control on the take-off run using smooth, light rudder inputs, but in extreme cases he could also use differential braking on the main bogies. Since the engines were mounted high on the rear fuselage, the thrust axis operated at a considerable distance from the centre-of-gravity axis, which gave rise to a nose-down pitching moment. On the take-off run, therefore, the aircraft experienced a nose-down pitching moment due to its weight, not yet balanced by lift, a nose-down pitching moment caused by aerodynamic effects and a nose-down pitching moment due to the influence of the earth's surface. So, at a speed of 300kph (162kts), the pilot would pull the control column fully back (the all-moving tailplane angle being around 17–19°) and maintain it in that position until the nose-wheel started to lift off the runway. After the nose-wheel was raised, the speed would continue to build up and the effectiveness of the tailplane would increase, so the pilot could then gently push the column forward to a position allowing the aircraft to unstick at an angle of around 8–9°. (*It should be recalled that the control 'column' of the Tu-22 was actually a 'W-shaped' control wheel.*) The point at which raising the nose and nose-wheel unstick would occur was determined by reference to the changing view of the horizon relative to the cockpit glazing and the upper part of the aircraft's nose. Any reduction in the pitch angle on take-off would lead to an increase in the length of the take-off ground roll and the unstick speed, requiring the pilot to be particularly vigilant in this phase of flight. Such was the power of a lightly laden Tu-22 that during the take-off run at a weight of 70–72 tonnes (154,320–158,730lb) the aircraft would lift off the runway while the pilot was still setting the take-off pitch angle. In the initial operating period, when the RD-7M2 engines were still comparatively new, the Tu-22 could climb away from the runway with a rate of climb of 100–120m/sec (19,685–23,620ft/min) and at an angle of 70°.

At high take-off weights, the Tu-22 would lift off the runway after the pilot had set the normal take-off pitch angle of 8–9°, when the aircraft had reached the required unstick speed. The maximum permitted speed on the runway could not exceed 360kph (195kts) out of consideration for the rotational limit on the nose-wheel tyres, and at this speed the nose-wheel had to be either off the runway, or at least 'unloaded'. Usually the pilot did not always set the required angle of 8°, but would simply pull back on the stick, confirming that the nose-wheel was raised when he could no longer hear it thumping on the concrete slabs of the runway. This angle would then be maintained up to a speed 20kph (10kts) less than the unstick speed, this speed being necessary to establish the take-off angle of attack. It was impossible to demonstrate this on the Tu-22U, so much of the take-off technique was explained in theory. It was also not possible to demonstrate the take-off on the simulator, because this only provided simulation of the landing approach, the required distribution of attention during the landing and the landing itself – nothing more. [*Note: an earlier reference to the KTS-22 simulator suggests that it could simulate take-off, but possibly only in a broadly demonstrative sense. AD*] The pilot really had to cope with mastering the take-off technique on his own, without 'outside assistance'.

An exception to the foregoing were take-offs at maximum all-up weight (AUW), which was 85 tonnes (187,390lb) at the beginning of the Tu-22's operational life, established by the Tupolev OKB. Later, this was raised to 92 tonnes (202,820lb) after development trials, and in the 1980s the maximum AUW was again reduced, this time to 88 tonnes (194,000lb), albeit on this occasion because of engine thrust limitations. At this latter weight and with an outside air temperature of between 25°C and 30°C, using a 3,000m (9,840ft) runway, unstick would occur as the aircraft reached the last concrete slab of the runway! Consequently, take-offs at high AUW had to be performed at night or early in the morning, when it was not too hot. Apart from runway length, there was another limitation affecting take-off conditions – namely the maximum permitted rotational speed of the main wheel bogies, giving a maximum speed at unstick of 420kph (227kts). The undercarriage was retracted at a height of 25m (82ft), with a limiting speed of not more than 500kph (270kts), and flaps were retracted at a height of 10m (328ft).

Unstick speeds in relation to AUW in standard atmosphere conditions

Aircraft weight in tonnes	70	75	80	85	90	92
Unstick speed in kph (knots)	360 (195)	370 (200)	385 (208)	395 (213)	405 (219)	410 (221)

Piloting techniques during take-offs in weather-defined minima were the same as for normal conditions, although when taxiing in a crosswind the aircraft would try to turn into wind. Crosswind take-offs and landings were permitted if the wind speed was not greater than 12m/sec (23kts), but in exceptional circumstances, with the authorisation of the regiment commander, take-off and landing could be performed with a crosswind of 15m/sec (29kts). The maximum permitted tailwind component for landing on a concrete runway with a length of 3,000–3,300m (9,840–10,825ft), at a weight of 60 tonnes (132,275lb) had to be not more than 3m/sec (6kts).

The take-off distance for the Tu-22 could be reduced by using SPRD-63 (*Startovyi Porokhovoy Raketnyi Dvigatyel'* – developed in 1963) solid fuel booster rockets. The take-off technique when using the SPRD-63 rockets differed little from a normal take-off. In addition to his normal speed read-outs to the pilot (marking each 50kph/27kts increment, starting from 150kph/81kts), the navigator would warn the crew 20kph (10kts) before ignition of the boosters with the call: 'Attention! (*Vnimanie!*)', followed by 'Ignition (*Zapusk!*)' on reaching the required speed. The pilot would then press his 'Ignition' button (*Zapusk Uskorityelyey*) on the left-hand side of the control wheel, although an error of ±20kph (10kts) could lead to the boosters shutting down at lift-off, or an increase in the length of the take-off run. Take-off trials of the Tu-22 with the booster rockets were conducted at the 43rd Centre for Weapons Training and Aircrew Conversion at Ryazan'. The crew sensed the ignition of the boosters by their characteristic roar and the additional g-force. The pilot had to pull the stick back immediately after ignition, and with four SPRD-63 boosters, plus full afterburner, the take-off ground roll was around 1,000m (3,280ft) shorter than normal and achieved at a speed some 15–20kph (8–10kts) less than in the unboosted condition. The boosters could be jettisoned both in horizontal flight and during the climb, but the height had to be not less than 600m (1,970ft) and the speed no higher than 550kph (297kts), with undercarriage and flaps retracted. Research had revealed that the flames from the rocket motors caused significant scorching of the flaps, so the SPRD-63 was only used when operationally necessary and training flights were not authorised. No more than five rocket-boosted take-offs were permitted before the flaps had to be changed. Carriage of the Kh-22 (AS-4 *Kitchen*) missile had very little effect on the handling of the aircraft, albeit causing a marginal increase in drag.

After unstick, the Tu-22 was stable and handled well, although the hydraulic control booster system had not been perfected on early examples. The pilot could unload the control column using the trim mechanism, but this was not a particularly effective system, since the trim loads varied from aircraft to aircraft. As mentioned elsewhere in the book, all the early Tu-22s differed extensively from each other, in terms of equipment standards. Aircraft were delivered from the factory in a series of five aircraft at a time, but upgrades and improvements were being introduced on a continuous basis. Thus, one aircraft might have flexible undercarriage mountings, another would have flaperons (*ehlerony-zakrylki*), while some would have the original VD-7M engines and others would have the uprated RD-7M2, each with different automatic fuel-management systems. Even in the cockpit instrumentation it was impossible to find two aircraft that were identical. For this reason, the younger pilots always flew the same aircraft, so that they would be completely familiar with its particular layout of switches, push-buttons and instruments. Only the regiment's 'executives', plus the squadron and section commanders, were authorised to fly any aircraft without restriction, but even they would have problems from time to time, so to obviate potential confusion each Tu-22 had its own special 'flight reference card' (*Kartochka Osobyennostyey Samolyota*). This was signed by the regiment commander and was kept in a pouch on the left-hand side of the pilot's instrument panel, under the throttle quadrant. The card detailed all the particularities of the aircraft, such as the location of the nose-wheel steering selector button, the type of fuel flow meter and radio, etc. In spite of having this card, the pilot would, in the majority of cases, not use the trim mechanism and would have to haul back on the stick with a force of around 50kg (110lb) during the take-off run. As soon as the aircraft was airborne and gaining height, the pilot would unload the control column, but notwithstanding the trim difficulties, the Tu-22 exhibited better take-off behaviour than the Tu-16.

The Tu-22 also behaved very well at high angles of attack, and it was impossible to put it into a spin, even after exceeding the critical angle of attack. The aircraft would simply lose lift and begin to 'parachute', but would not drop a wing and flip over with 120°–160° angle of bank like the Tu-16. According to Lt-Col Chernyshev, a former squadron commander on 290 ODRAP, the Tu-22 exhibited a surprising degree of controllability, not only during take-off, but also in flight, where it could dive and climb with almost fighter-like agility. This is perhaps a convenient point to dismantle another myth with regard to the Tu-22's supersonic performance, perpetuated by several aviation historians over the years. Many have claimed that the aircraft had difficulty reaching supersonic speed and, having reached it, was unable to sustain this regime for long. It is, therefore, pleasing to be able to confirm that the Tu-22 could easily pass through the 'sound barrier' at altitudes starting from around 7,000m (around 23,000ft). During acceleration from around 9,000m (29,530ft) a Tu-22 pilot had to be careful not to go supersonic below 11,000m (36,090ft), since at altitudes above 9,000m it could even achieve supersonic speed in the climb. The maximum high-altitude afterburner regime (with nozzles fully divergent) was selected automatically when the pilot placed the throttle levers into the 'full afterburner' detent at a speed of around Mach 1.22–1.25.

Evidence for the ease with which the Tu-22 could break the sound barrier if the pilot did not monitor his speed in the climb comes from many reports of damage to the windows of buildings in the vicinity of airfields operating the aircraft. A Tu-22 of 290 ODRAP at Zyabrovka was responsible for causing extensive damage in a glass factory in the nearby city of Gomel', destroying a large amount of stock in the warehouse. In the 1970s a Tu-22 of 121 TBAP at Machulishchi broke all the glass in a café in the Byelorussian capital Minsk during a supersonic climb, and the roof of a house in the village next to Zyabrovka airfield was also destroyed by supersonic overpressure from a departing Tu-22. It must be emphasised that such supersonic 'excursions' were not in breach of the aircraft's operating limits set by the manufacturer and the Tupolev OKB – it was simply a 'feature' of Tu-22 performance in the early period of operations with the aircraft. However, in all cases of material damage caused by supersonic overflights, the regiments had to pay financial compensation to the occupants, and repetition of such occurrences was prevented by the decision to limit supersonic flight to altitudes above 11,000m (36,090ft). Flying the Tu-22 at speeds greater than Mach 1.4 above 9,000m (29,530ft) was made slightly difficult because of the tendency to wing heaviness and a fairly large negative banking reaction to rudder inputs. However, subsonic flight at high altitudes was easier than with the Tu-16, and wing heaviness in these conditions was counteracted by deflection of the flaperons and rudder in the direction of the 'heavy' wing until the sideslip was neutralised.

At high indicated airspeeds, using ailerons or flaperons for roll control, the Tu-22 was stable in the lateral plane throughout the speed range, right up to its limiting speeds, and 45-degree banked turns were permitted in these conditions. At high subsonic indicated airspeeds (greater than 650kph/350kts), the deflection required in the control column to produce a change in g-loading of one unit (1g) was considerably reduced. Consequently, movement of the column from the neutrally balanced position was not to exceed 40–60mm (1.58–2.36in). In the event of pilot-induced oscillation (*raskachka*) occurring, the pilot had to place the control column in the balanced (neutral) position, after which the automatic stabilisation system would suppress the pitch oscillations. The normal flight regime was the cruise, and a range-optimised profile was known as 'ceiling regime' (*po potolkam*). The most economical regime in terms of minimum fuel consumption versus range was flight at near-supersonic speed, after reaching about 8,500–9,500m (27,890–31,170ft). Here, the Tu-22 would fly in a continuous gentle climb as a function of weight change caused by burning off fuel. When flying an optimal profile (*po potolkam*) in non-reheat mode the aircraft would normally gain about 600m (1,970ft) in altitude after each hour of flight. The initial indicated airspeed in these conditions would be, for an altitude of 8,500m (27,890ft), 650kph (350kts); for an altitude of 9,000m

(29,530ft), 630kph (340kts), and for 9,500m (31,170ft), 610kph (330kts). These speeds corresponded to Mach 0.88, and after this speed was achieved it could be maintained throughout the flight. The cruising altitudes for such flights, dependent upon aircraft weight, were within the range 8,500m–12,000m (27,890–39,370ft). Apart from the foregoing, the Tu-22 was able to cruise within a wide range of supersonic speeds and at varying altitudes, although with the concomitant penalty of significant range reduction. The speed when flying an optimal (*po potolkam*) profile, using the cruising afterburner setting, was Mach 1.25, or 1,300kph (702kts). The range in this case, including the climb and descent segments, was three times less than that for flight in non-reheat mode. Turns during supersonic flight were recommended to be performed in full afterburner with a bank angle of 45–50°, consuming around 1,000–1,400kg (2,200–3,090lb) during the manoeuvre. Experienced pilots were able to perform turns with bank angles up to 70°, the Tu-22's fighter-like manoeuvrability saving both time and fuel if rapid directional changes were deemed operationally necessary.

As a large, heavy, swept-wing aircraft, the Tu-22 exhibited a number of peculiarities when flying in formation. In a typical formation flying exercise the leader would establish an indicated airspeed of 600kph (324kts) and report this to his wingman. At the assigned altitude for the exercise, the wingman would then begin to close on the leader, taking into consideration the fact that the Tu-22 generated two powerful wingtip vortices, with a diameter of around 2–3m (6.5–10ft). The power of these vortices persisted for a distance of around 7,000–8,000ft (around 23,000–27,000ft), trailing below the aircraft by about 25–40m (80–130ft), before gradually dispersing. If an aircraft entered the trailing vortex at a distance of up to 8,000m the crew would feel intense airframe buffeting, similar to that experienced in turbulence at high indicated airspeeds, and the aircraft would be ejected out of the turbulent flow. Often this would be accompanied by a loss of height of up to 50m (165ft) and an involuntary bank angle of up to about 50°, and in some circumstances could even lead to entry into a spiral dive unless the pilot could regain control in time.

According to the pilots, landing the Tu-22 revealed it to be an aircraft which handled well on the initial descent, but because of its highly swept wing and small wing area, the comparatively low landing speed meant that it was always on a 'knife edge' as it neared touchdown. If the pilot started to pull the stick back too early, the aircraft would commence the flare too high and could stall – if the flare was commenced low then it could result in a heavy landing at high speed. An extract from the chapter covering 'Landing the aircraft (Tu-22) at a weight of 60 tonnes (132,275lb) and less' eloquently describes the complexity of the landing process: 'After passing the BPRM (inner beacon), commence smooth reduction of rpm, so that the speed is 360–370kph (195–200kts) by the point of flare. Increasing engine rpm to adjust the aircraft's trajectory after passing the BPRM is undesirable since it complicates the landing. Maintaining the correct glide-slope trajectory, the point of flare should be planned to occur at a distance of 300–500m (984–1,640ft) from the threshold of the runway. Taking account of the actual landing weight, confirm once again that the speed is 360–370kph. An increase in landing speed above the designated speed will lead to an increase in the landing distance. A speed of less than 360kph is forbidden. Commence the flare at a height of 10–15m (30–50ft), with a smooth reduction in engine rpm down to flight idle. When throttling back, there is a tendency for the pitch angle to increase, which can lead to the flare being too high. The pilot must therefore counteract this. The flare should be completed at a height of 1–1.5m

(3.3–4.9ft). Hold the aircraft off, with a gradual descent so that a gentle touchdown is achieved on the main undercarriage bogies.'

The tendency for the aircraft to want to pitch up on throttling back the engines, which is called the opposite reaction to thrust variation (or 'Opposite reaction to application of power' in the aircraft operating manual), was an unpleasant characteristic of the Tu-22. This arose because the engines were mounted above the centre of gravity and produced a corresponding pitch-down moment. The aircraft possessed a low coefficient of lift as a consequence of using a highly swept wing, with little in the way of high-lift devices other than flaps, which had the same setting for both take-off and landing. The result of all this was that the Tu-22 had a high landing speed. This in turn led to the fact that an acceptable landing ground-roll could only be achieved with normal braking on a dry concrete runway with the aid of a brake parachute (actually a twin-canopy single 'chute). For example, the landing speed for a normal landing weight of 56.5 tonnes (124,560lb) was 305kph (165kts) where the ground-roll using the brake 'chute was 1,650m (5,410ft), but 2,175m (7,135ft) without. Landing the Tu-22 at a weight greater than 60 tonnes (132,275lb) was only allowed in exceptional circumstances at well-equipped airfields and in conditions of good visibility. Landing at a weight of between 65 tonnes and 75 tonnes (143,300–165,340lb) was only allowed in cases of extreme urgency, when all attempts to reduce the landing weight had been exhausted. Landing at a weight of greater than 75 tonnes was only authorised when it was impossible to eject from the aircraft in an emergency (for example if the nose-wheel could not be retracted). In these cases, pilots had to bear in mind that landing at a weight greater than 65 tonnes could result in damage to the main undercarriage bogies, which had a limiting speed of 330kph (178kts) for

A Tu-22U turns off the runway at Machulishchi to release the twin-unit brake-chute. *S Burdin*

A Tu-22U crew prepare for training sortie at Machulishchi in 1993. The crew member with his back to the camera has donned his white cotton helmet liner and his fellow crewman is already wearing the standard bone-dome helmet used in the Tu-22 fleet. *S Burdin*

touchdown. After each such a landing, the aircraft had to be carefully checked for any signs of structural deformation of the undercarriage, wing, nose and tail section of the fuselage, plus the engine nacelles, etc. During the period of the Soviet Air Force's operation of the Tu-22 up to 1990, 40% of all the accidents and write-offs occurred on landing and only 8% during take-off. Even experienced pilots considered that it was 'impossible to perfect the landing of the Tu-22 – it was really only possible to make its acquaintance'.

The former commander of the first squadron of 290 ODRAP, Lt-Col Chernyshev, claims that the landing phase was right on the limits of the pilot's reaction time: 'For example, the visual impulse from the eye to the brain travels at a speed of 60m/sec (197ft/sec) for the average person. Therefore, he can see, in real time, anything that is moving at a speed of 216kph (134mph/117kts). If the speed of motion is greater than this, then he actually sees what has already happened, i.e. it is an 'imaginary' representation of reality. On the Tu-22, this led to pilots of average and below average flying ability not always being able to fly the aircraft as well, or as successfully, as was necessary. The pilot had to learn that there was never sufficient time for the correction of errors during take-off, landing or in flight at low level and that it was always necessary to 'second guess' the aircraft's position in the next instant.'

The opinion was often aired that the flying qualities of the Tu-22 were so bad that it could not be compared with the excellent handling behaviour of the Tu-16 and that crews cursed the aircraft and even hated it. This opinion does not correspond with the truth. The author has met many pilots, navigators and engineers who served in the Tu-22 fleet and heard only one opinion of the aircraft: 'The Tu-22 was (like) a highly restive thoroughbred horse.' Uncomplimentary opinions about the aircraft were only expressed by one engineer – an engine specialist. His dislike of the Tu-22 was, to some extent, justified. The fact was that in the 1970s new RD-7M2 engines were no longer being manufactured, and aircraft were equipped with older engines which had undergone overhaul (*pyereborka*). By the 1980s some engines had undergone up to four or five overhauls. After this number of overhauls, the repair plant imposed its own operating limits on each engine, and, for example, the maximum afterburner time was eventually restricted to 1 minute 45 seconds, even though the take-off phase alone lasted 1 minute 30 seconds! This meant that the pilot had to use chronometer-like precision to be able to exploit the remaining 15 seconds of afterburner time during flight. Considering the fact that most experienced pilots would fly a variety of different aircraft in their regiment, they would be distracted not only by the stop-watch, but also by having to learn the individual limitations of each engine on each aircraft! A decision was taken, therefore, to compact all time-related restrictions on engine operation into a limitation on engine rpm instead. Consequently, in the mid-1980s, all operating restrictions remained as before and only the upper limit on rpm was lowered, resulting in this being fixed at 97% of the maximum power setting. As a result, afterburner was practically no longer used at an altitude of 13,000m (42,650ft). An illustration of the effect that age had on engine performance can be derived from the fact that on a new engine the fuel pressure entering the afterburner section was up to 65–75kg/cm² (925–1,065lb/sq in), whereas on an 'old' engine this would have fallen to 20–30kg/cm² (285–425lb/sq in), and a pressure of around 40kg/cm² (570lb/sq in) was considered good.

Overall, engine thrust dropped off significantly, and where previously (up to the mid-1980s) there was no difficulty in taking off, even in a temperature of 30°C, this could only be achieved later in high daytime temperatures by reducing the amount of fuel carried. Up to the early 1980s, Tu-22 engines were overhauled at Lutsk, in the Ukraine, a plant which provided a high-quality overhaul service. Eventually, however, it began to take on the maintenance of the Lyul'ka-Saturn AL-31F engines of the Su-27 *Flanker* interceptor, and it was decided to hand over the overhaul of the old Dobrynin RD-7M2 engines to a plant with a lesser workload. The facility chosen was located at Belaya Tserkov', near Kiev in the Ukraine, at the time both a repair plant dealing with the Kuznetsov NK-12 engines of the Tu-95 *Bear* and a Long-range Air Force Tu-16 base. However, the plant was unable to produce high-quality overhauls of the RD-7M2, the reasons for which could only be guessed at, although a number of possibilities had been suggested:

• Difficulties with the construction of the RD-7M2, which differed significantly from engines which the plant had previously handled and the fact that it was designed for supersonic cruising flight
• The need to set up more complicated production processes for the overhaul of this engine
• The need to install improved diagnostic facilities
• The absence of sufficient quantities of spare parts
• The lack of a highly trained cadre of technical personnel
• Insufficient financing for the plant to be able to master the overhaul of an engine new to these personnel (in fact, throughout its almost 20-year operating period, no significant sums of money had been invested in the overhaul programme for the RD-7M2).

Notwithstanding the foregoing, the Tu-22 regiments started to receive engines which had

RD-7M2 engines removed from a Tu-22. The main engine core is in the foreground, with the afterburner chamber and supersonic nozzle section behind. 290 ODRAP TEhCh at Zyabrovka in 1994. *S Burdin*

been overhauled at Belaya Tserkov', but because of the poor quality of repair, they also started to see a significant increase in the number of engine failures. Rarely a month went by without an unplanned engine shut-down being reported, caused by shedding of turbine blades, bearing failures, oil leaks and the like. In spite of the fact that the regiments always had a permanent representative from Belaya Tserkov' at the base, nothing could be done to improve the situation. Pilots became so used to landing on one engine that it seemed as though this was the natural order of things. The regiment second-line servicing unit (TEhCh) was always busy with repair and maintenance work, but the frequent engine failures added to the overall burden of their work. So, unserviceable engines were sent back to Belaya Tserkov', and the plant gradually began to get to grips with the scale of the problem and the work schedule required for the overhauls. Unfortunately, this also led to a deficit in the number of engines held by the Tu-22 regiments, and in order to resolve the problem the engineers started a campaign to equalise the overhaul life of the engines installed on the aircraft. This was done in the following way. One aircraft might have had one engine with only seven hours remaining before overhaul, while the other might still have had 100 hours left. Another aircraft might have had a similar imbalance in the overhaul life remaining on each engine, so the engines were swapped around so that one aircraft would have engines with similar amounts of operating life remaining. Although sounding straightforward enough, it was a laborious procedure, requiring first the engines to be swapped and then a test flight of the aircraft in accordance with a specially devised programme. Murphy's Law, recognising neither geographical nor political boundaries, had infiltrated the Soviet Union at this time, and sometimes other faults would show up during these *ad hoc* test flights and had to be dealt with! Additionally, of course, there was the need to maintain the combat-readiness state of the regiment, which required that 85–90% of the aircraft had to be available for combat at any given time. The workload of the regiment engineers at this time was, therefore, very high.

The problems caused by the low reliability of the overhauled RD-7M2 engines had obviously attracted the attention of Soviet Air Force HQ, which adopted a much simpler approach to resolution of the difficulties. The HQ Engineering Service created briefing material for the regiment ground engineers and technicians contained in an instruction entitled, 'The least reliable elements of the RD-7M2, methods of checking and their monitoring intervals". This required particular attention to be paid to the condition of inlet guide vane blades, lubrication pipes and fuel lines, the condition of the cooling system of the central and rear rotor bearing supports, elements of the afterburner chamber and the working blades of the second-stage of the turbine. The cause of the greatest number of engine failures was shedding of the second stage turbine blades, inlet guide vane blades and problems with fuel and lubrication system seals. Consequently, examination of these areas of the engine and checking for leaks in the fuel and oil systems had to be carried out with the highest frequency, covering preliminary, pre- and post-flight checks and the new SAF HQ-defined periodic checks. At this time, there was not a single Tu-22 pilot who had not had to land his aircraft on one engine at least once, but often as many as three or four times for some. Engine shut-down in flight had become such a commonplace occurrence that in post-flight briefings all that was discussed was whether the crew had taken all the correct actions, plus an expression of thanks for individual effort.

A senior pilot from 121 TBAP, Major Fut'yanov, describes one such occurrence on take-off in his Tu-22K, during an exercise: 'I had to carry out a simulated missile launch (*takticheskii pusk*) as part of a squadron formation. At the moment of take-off, immediately after unstick, one of the engines suffered a malfunction – throwing compressor blades. Luckily, the blades went straight up through the engine casing, without damaging the tailplane controls or the fuel system. There was also no fire. I immediately closed the fire shut-off valve, having shut down the engine to prevent any more fuel being pumped into it. I then continued the take-off on one engine. The speed started to drop off – 400kph (216kts) … 390kph (210kts)…. The height at that moment was 50m (165ft). I thought that if the speed continued to drop, then we would stall. It was impossible to eject – the height was too low. There was nowhere to divert to for an emergency landing. I started to push the control column forward smoothly to prevent (further) loss of speed. The airspeed indicator needle remained at 380kph (205kts). After reaching this figure, in a very flat climbing trajectory, the aircraft began to gain speed. If it had fallen another 20kph (11kts) that would have been it…. I was slowly beginning to climb and the rest of the group had set off *en route*. Having gained some height I started to burn off fuel. There was nothing else to do – I couldn't release the missile and couldn't jettison the fuel – this wasn't allowed. We circled for several hours in the airfield zone and then landed. After this flight I was awarded an engraved commemorative watch. Well, I've got four of these watches now….' [*I have translated Major Fut'yanov's description of this event literally, using his own sentence structure and length, to preserve the manner in which it was described to the author, Sergey Burdin. AD*]

Engine failures, of course, also occurred during the navigational stages of flight, and this happened to Lt-Col Epifantsev of 290 ODRAP, while flying a Tu-22R over the Black

Sea in December 1978. A fire broke out in one of the engines, which the crew was able to extinguish, and, displaying exceptional coolness, Lt-Col Epifantsev managed to land the aircraft without further incident at Kul'bakino airfield, near Nikolaev in southern Ukraine. Fire on board an aircraft in flight is perhaps the most feared emergency facing any aircrew, and a section commander on 121 TBAP, Major Serikov, had to contend with this in the most difficult of circumstances. He describes the event in his own words: 'On 11 August 1988, we were carrying out a night training flight as part of a group (of Tu-22s). With me in my crew was Captain Sitnikov, the navigator and Senior Lieutenant Myakota, the radar operator. One hour and 35 minutes had elapsed since take-off. Our altitude was 9,300m (30,510ft). I was the pathfinder (*informator*) for the group and was flying ahead of the main group with a 15-minute separation between us. Apart from normal weapons training, it was my task to inform the group leader about weather conditions along the route and in the vicinity of the target. Suddenly, in the vicinity of Ostashkov (in the Tver' District), I sensed burning in the cockpit. It has to be said that often we did not adjust the oxygen mask tightly to our face at those heights (it wasn't pleasant [*sic*] to breathe pure oxygen all the time from the masks). Within a few seconds smoke started to billow around the cockpit. I reported to the group leader, "Fire in the cockpit". According to standard instructions, in the event of fire on board, we had to switch over to emergency electrical power. The transfer switch was located on the lower part of the right-hand side of the instrument panel. The entire cockpit was filled with smoke and it had become impossible to see at all. However, the engines continued to operate normally. I managed to ventilate the cockpit slightly.

Then suddenly there was another unpleasant surprise – all the cockpit lighting went out. The electrical power supply had tripped off. Only two lamps were illuminated – one indicating "Damper Failure" and the other "Artificial Horizon Failure". We had no communication inside the aircraft, with the other aircraft or with the ground. It wasn't clear where we were flying over or where we were flying to. The artificial horizon wasn't working, so I didn't know what degree of bank angle the aircraft was in. Because it was dark, the natural horizon wasn't visible. I had to orient myself by the stars alone. They were clearly visible. Seeing the stars were above my head, I knew that we were not inverted. Then I unscrewed the light filter from one of the two serviceable warning lamps and used the palm of my hand as a reflector to illuminate the instruments. I was able to determine that we had lost about 2,500m (8,200ft) during this time. I climbed back up to 9,000m (29,530ft) and decided to head for Minsk and our base (Machulishchi). But how, and on what heading? The intercom wasn't working. I began to shout and stamp my feet to attract the navigator's attention. I was stamping them for about three minutes. Finally the navigator heard me. At this moment the radar operator managed to receive a radio broadcast. We could hear everything that was going on around us, but no one could hear us. Our group had lost contact with us and PVO Air Defence units had started to search for us. The PVO had detected us and we heard over the ether that we were actually 30km (about 19 miles) north of Orsha. This was something. Then we saw two towns alongside each other. It became clear that these were Polotsk and Novopolotsk (the latter identifiable by the flame from an oil refinery), near Vitebsk in north-east Byelorussia.

Here we hit another problem – it had started to get cloudy and it was beginning to be a little more difficult to hold a 'wings level' attitude (the stars were not very visible at this time). Fortunately, near Minsk, the cloud thickness wasn't too great and we came out of it at around 6,000m (19,700ft) with an angle of bank of around 15°. From the bad language that we could hear on the radio, we realised that we were in the control zone of the civil airport, Minsk-2. We were flying through the zone, out of radio contact, and were disrupting the normal civil air traffic flow to and from the airport. The military quickly explained that a 'missile carrier' was carrying out an emergency landing, and we continued on without incident to Machulishchi. By now, it had become quite difficult to control the aircraft. The aircraft was still trimmed for flight at 9,000m (29,530ft). During the descent it was essential to reduce the increasing load on the control column by use of the electromechanical trim mechanism, but in the absence of electrical power this wasn't working. I had to pull back on the control column so firmly that in the end I wrapped both arms around it and pulled back with my full body weight – my wrists were so tired that I could no longer hold the column normally. With two dampers out of three inoperative, the load on the control column reached 80–100kg (175–220lb). For this reason, I couldn't reduce the engine rpm to the normal setting for landing. I had to land at a higher speed of around 350kph (189kts). We arrived in the area of Machulishchi airfield and passed over the inner beacon, indicating that we were going to land. We approached for the landing using an abbreviated pattern, performing two 180-degree turns, rather than the usual four 90-degree turns of the standard pattern.

I made the final turn and suddenly the airfield went out of my field of view and I couldn't see it at all. I lowered the undercarriage on the emergency system, not knowing whether it had locked down or not. Control of the aircraft had become very heavy – the undercarriage had created an additional pitch-down moment. And then suddenly I saw the airfield a little off to one side. I turned towards the runway, using my full body weight to turn the control wheel. I passed over the outer beacon at 150m (492ft) – very low. The runway wasn't visible to me, since the controls were in such a non-standard position. Therefore, in order to direct the aircraft along the runway heading, I occasionally had to lower the nose. But after aligning the aircraft on heading I had to raise the nose gain to gain the height lost in that manoeuvre. So I flew the approach in a series of short dives and climbs. I passed over the inner beacon at only 40m (130ft), well below the glide path, but I didn't have the strength to pull it up any higher. There was about 50m (165ft) to go to the edge of the runway when the wheels touched the ground. We successfully managed to bounce onto the runway, but the brake 'chute did not deploy (we heard ATC reporting this on the radio). I started to use the wheel brakes and stopped at the far end of the runway. When we taxied off the runway the brake discs were glowing red, but (the wheels) did not explode.' [*Once again, in my translation, I have employed the same register and sentence length as Major Serikov when recounting this event to Sergey Burdin, in order to preserve his original style. AD*] For his heroic efforts, Major Serikov was later awarded the Order of the Red Star, while the other two crew members were given medals for their part in the incident.

There were less heroic incidents than this in almost identical circumstances. One of these involved Major Kovalyev of 203 TBAP (it will be recalled that Major Kovalyev came to the Tu-22K as a captain, after flying the Su-17M2 *Fitter-D* in the Soviet Tactical Air Force). Major Kovalyev's navigator detected a smell of burning in the cockpit and illuminated the likely source of the smell with a portable lamp, discovering this to be one of the transformers. The wafting smoke, illuminated under the ultra-violet lighting of the cockpit, looked orange, like flames. [*Note: According to earlier references in the book the cockpit lighting of the Tu-22K should have been changed from ultra-violet to red backlighting of the instruments. AD*] The navigator reported that there was a fire on board, and anticipating a command to abandon the aircraft and not fully understanding the situation, ejected at an altitude of 10,000m (32,800ft). Since the KAP-3 (*Kombinirovannyi Avtomat Parashutnyi*-3) combined barometric parachute opening device only operated at a height of 4,000m (13,120ft), the navigator was in free fall until reaching this level. Five minutes elapsed from the moment of ejection to the opening of the canopy, and the navigator suffered frost-bite during the free fall stage, but survived the ejection and eventually went back to flying duties.

Nevertheless, personnel assigned to the Tu-22 fleet were among the best in the Long-range Air Force, and during its almost thirty years of service a feeling of great affection for it grew up among the elite crews who had the privilege to fly it. In the next chapter we will take a more detailed look at how these Long-range Air Force crews conducted peace-time training on the Tu-22R, including reconnaissance, bombing and air-to-air refuelling.

CHAPTER SIX

Combat Application of the Tu-22R

As already mentioned in the opening chapter, the first variant of the Tu-22 to enter operational service was the Tu-22R, two independent reconnaissance regiments of the type being deployed to the central region of the European part of the former Soviet Union. These were 199 ODRAP at Nezhin in the Ukraine and 290 ODRAP at Zyabrovka, near Gomel' in the former Byelorussian Soviet Socialist Republic, now Belarus'. The Soviet General Staff was thus able to use these two regiments to monitor the entire territory of Western Europe (as far as the Greenwich Meridian), the Mediterranean Sea and North Africa. After the introduction of the Tu-22RD, with its air-to-air refuelling (AAR) capability, the operational range of the *Blinder-C* was increased to 3,500km (1,890nm), extending the 'zone of responsibility' as far as, and including, the Bay of Biscay. A total of fifty-four crews were assigned to cover these theatres of operation, twenty-seven crews for each regiment, and the Soviet General Staff assessed there to be a 0.82 probability that they would successfully complete any reconnaissance task assigned to them in time of war. Apart from these two Long-range Air Force regiments, there were also two independent naval reconnaissance regiments deployed in the European theatre of military operations, 15 OMRAP at Chkalovsk in the Kaliningrad District and 30 OMRAP at Saki on the Crimean peninsula.

The Tu-22Rs were delivered new from the factory at Kazan', configured as Reconnaissance Variant No. 1, and other photo-reconnaissance equipment standards were introduced for each aircraft later. Initially, there were two daylight photography variants and one night, but after a little while a third, and then a fourth daylight variant was offered. In later operation, yet another daylight option was developed by regimental specialists, a so-called 'universal' variant, designed for wartime use, which permitted the carriage of reconnaissance equipment *and* bombs.

The routes flown on reconnaissance sorties were quite diverse, embracing West Germany in the western sector, while the eastern routes went as far as Semipalatinsk in Kazakhstan, taking in Kandahar and its environs in Afghanistan in the south-east and reaching as far south as Turkey. Flights were also undertaken over Romania and Bulgaria, while there were almost constant flights into the Atlantic Ocean, and as far as the English Channel and the North Sea, plus the North Pole. A particular feature of flights over the Baltic Sea and the Atlantic Ocean was the constant presence of escorting NATO and other fighters. Typical tasks of the latter years of the aircraft's service were reconnaissance flights against the infrastructure of nuclear delivery systems (principally air bases), missile installations and surface ships and submarines in the naval theatres of military activity (*Morskie Teatry Voyennykh Dyeystvii*). A variety of tasks was included in the classified combat orders held in the HQ of the independent long-range reconnaissance regiments, to be put into action in the event of hostilities, but in the main these were to reconnoitre naval and military air bases. The profiles of the flights were also quite diverse, from extremely low altitude up to the aircraft's normal ceiling of 14,000m (45,932ft), flown in a variety of different formation groups. The minimum formation size and composition was the pair, offering both the guarantee of reducing tasking errors and acknowledging that 'two navigators were better than one'.

If flights were to be conducted along the western borders of the former Soviet Union, or over the sea, then it was obligatory to include Tu-22P *Blinder-E* electronic jamming aircraft in the formation. Usually the formation would comprise a pair of Tu-22R and a pair of Tu-22P, which would maintain their formation composition (close, open, or stream) to the target area, then split up to continue on to their respective targets. The tactic of employing the Tu-22R in a real combat situation was based on the premise that one crew would reconnoitre one target on one sortie, allowing a large target area to be covered in one flight. This tactic could only be employed as long as it was possible to 'punch a hole' (or corridor) in the enemy's air defence protection zone and keep this corridor 'open' for about two hours until the 'recce' *Blinders* had returned to their own territory. When preparing for a flight, the crew navigator would calculate the requirements for the aerial photography task (e.g. waypoints, entry and exit points, etc.), and would enter these in the navigation log, while data specifically relating to the target would be entered directly onto the navigation chart. Both of these documents were taken on the flight. Apart from the aircraft's standard camera equipment, crews also had to take hand-held still and movie cameras on board with them, which were used to take photographs and film clips of aircraft and ships which 'fell' outside the coverage of the normal on-board systems. Usually, this meant fighter aircraft which were escorting the Tu-22 at the same flight level. Crews were forbidden to carry any documents giving details of the targets (other than charts), the name of their squadron, operating base, information regarding 'electronic support' for their flight, notebooks, or Communist Party or Young Communist League documents. When flying in formation, a system of maintaining formation grouping was developed based on time-keeping. In order to earn the assessment of 'Excellent' (*Otlichno*), when flying with an along-track separation between aircraft of not less than two minutes, a deviation of not more than five seconds was allowed. However, when using the RSBN short-range tactical navigation system, a deviation of 20 seconds when turning onto the target heading would still earn the crew the assessment of 'Excellent'.

The recce regiments based at Nezhin and Zyabrovka regularly participated in operations with units of the Baltic, Northern and Black Sea Fleets, with 290 ODRAP from Zyabrovka frequently cooperating with the Northern Fleet and 199 ODRAP from Nezhin with the Black Sea Fleet. When working with the fleets, the crews would be subordinated to the appropriate HQ, on whose behalf they were operating, and the commander of the fleet's air force. The shortest route between the LRAF and SNAF areas of operation was to the Black Sea and usually involved passing over the naval range at Kherson. It was thus possible to combine in one flight bombing practice at Kherson and reconnaissance training. After working at the range, the route carried on south towards Turkey, the Tu-22Rs approaching to within 12.5–13 miles (20.1–21km) of the Turkish coastline, in order not to infringe Turkey's territorial waters, before continuing their recce flights along the coast. In enclosed waters like the Black Sea, a country's territorial rights extend to twelve miles (19.3km), whereas in open sea areas the territorial limits extend to thirty-one miles (50km). It was recommended when flying over international waters and crossing international airways to do this only during daylight hours. Permission to perform such flights at night was only given if there was no cloud and if visibility was good, with navigation lights switched on. When flying at a distance of 400km (216nm) from the coastline of the USSR, Tu-22R crews would switch off their identification systems (transponders), although in order to maintain formation in poor visibility it was permitted to switch on the transponder briefly in response to interrogation by a formation crew member.

Pilots loved to fly recce sorties looking for US Navy warships, and would periodically operate over the Black Sea whenever the US Navy was there. The Tu-22R would approach the target and photograph it from an altitude of 1,000–2,000m (3,280–6,560ft), but the ships would usually attempt to steam away from a 'meeting' with the Russian aircraft. The manoeuvrability of the Tu-22R was, of course, significantly greater than that of the ships, and the aircraft always managed to get their photographs of the target. Oblique photography was conducted from about 1,000m (3,280ft), and other photo-recce tasks were performed from around 2,000m (6,560ft). (Tu-22R crews would often also use the shipyards at Nikolaev in the Black Sea as a training target, photographing Soviet aircraft-carriers and other ships on the building ways.) When reconnoitring NATO and other targets in the Black Sea, the *Blinders* would set themselves up in a circular race-track pattern for about half an hour and carry out training photo runs. Sometimes they would operate a 'conveyor belt' system, where, as one pair departed the target area, another pair would arrive, and so on, until the entire regiment had had the chance to 'work' the targets. Photography from less than 1,000m was forbidden, although in fact, from around 200m (656ft), for example, this was not very effective anyway, and crews were forbidden from flying provocatively against foreign ships and aircraft. The normal magazine load of the tail gun was 500 shells, but these were necessary to assist in maintaining the centre of gravity (*sic*), and the ammunition belt of the aircraft was not actually linked up to the weapon. Loading the cannon (i.e. connecting the ammunition belt) only took about ten minutes, but could only be carried out on the ground. Long-range Air Force pilots recall at least one case where an airborne operator was punished for 'provoking' a foreign aircraft by letting off (firing) his empty cannon at it!

The longer range of the Tu-22RD allowed crews to reconnoitre targets in the North Sea and Arctic Oceans, and the flights, which took the aircraft around the Scandinavian peninsula, were described in the crews' jargon as 'going round the corner'. Flights 'round the corner' were flown from Zyabrovka, Sol'tsy, Olenyegorsk and Severomorsk. Reconnaissance flights over the North Atlantic Ocean required two in-flight-refuelling hook-ups, and Tu-22RDs of 290 ODRAP from Gomel' would depart their home base and carry out the first refuelling rendezvous between Petrozavodsk and Murmansk, before 'going round the corner' when abeam the Norwegian town of Trondheim. Refuelling on the return leg was performed over the Barents Sea, the Tu-22RD taking on 15 tonnes (33,070lb) of fuel in each direction, and the total flight duration being around 8hrs 45min. This was considered to be the absolute maximum duration for a sortie, since in spite of having an autopilot, the physical load placed on the pilot himself was extremely high, with no co-pilot to share the burden. Reconnaissance over the Baltic Sea involved flying a rather complex route, taking the aircraft over Poland, the former Czechoslovakia and East Germany. Flying along the inner German border, the Tu-22Rs would then enter the

Baltic Sea area, where they were usually immediately intercepted by Swedish SAAB Drakens (in the early years) and SAAB Viggens. The Swedes would then escort the Russian reconnaissance aircraft to try to determine where they would turn back towards Russian territory. If the Swedish fighters stayed with the Tu-22s longer than was reasonably tolerable, the Russian crews would call for assistance from the Soviet 4th Air Army fighter unit based at Kołobrzeg on the Polish coast. One such incident is recalled by a former navigator on 290 ODRAP, Major Labetik: 'The Swedes were alongside us and it was already time for us to make our turn, but they were in the way. We called the tower at *Kolobrzeg* (the airfield call sign was "*Svyaznoy*", meaning, appropriately enough, '*Communication*'), requesting help. The duty controller responded by saying that he would launch a pair of fighters (MiG-23s at the time), after which the 'escorting' Swedes disappeared.' (*The implication here is that the Swedish pilots, or their ground controllers, were probably monitoring the Soviet frequencies and understood enough Russian to know when they were no longer welcome!*).

Reconnaissance could be carried out on any sortie and almost always involved passing through two or three bomb range complexes. Additionally, so as not to lose their reconnaissance skills, crews would also carry out flights over real targets in the USSR, such as, for example, railway stations (to determine the composition of trains) and cities (to seek out particular types of factory). A potentially interesting episode in the history of the Tu-22 was the short-lived plan to use it to thwart the a mutiny which had occurred on 8 November 1975 on board a Baltic Fleet *Krivak 1* (Project 1135) guided-missile frigate, the *Storozhevoy* (Sentry). The frigate had been commandeered by the ship's political commissar, Captain Third Rank Valery Sablin, who had planned to sail the vessel from Riga to Leningrad and broadcast an appeal to the Soviet people to rise up against the 'gerontocracy' in Moscow. The incident occurred on 8 November 1975, the day after celebration of the 58th anniversary of the October Revolution, with a Tu-22R regiment being placed on alert to support two Tu-22K *Blinder-Bs* from 203 TBAP at Baranovichi and two more from 121 TBAP at Machulishchi, the recce crews changing into their flight clothing on board their aircraft (*sic*).

In the end, the sortie did not take place since the Tu-22 was not really suitable for such a task, although a total of sixty other combat aircraft were either placed on alert or actually scrambled, and the vessel *was* bombed by either Su-17s or Yak-28s. Although his actions were inspired by the purist of Marxist motives, Captain Sablin was found guilty of betrayal of the Motherland (*Rodina*) and later executed by firing squad. The Tu-22R was also used to test the alert and readiness status of the Air Defence (*Protivo-Vozdushnaya Oborona*) system of the former USSR, checking the air defences around Moscow, and large industrial and administrative centres in Russia, as well as those in Poland, Germany and Czechoslovakia. (*The nature of the flights was that the Tu-22R would act as a simulated aggressor, attempting to penetrate the defensive missile and fighter 'shield' surrounding these locations.*) Such flights were often combined with reconnaissance tasks along the borders between the NATO and Warsaw Pact countries, involving a route flown from southern Europe up to the north, passing over East Germany and descending over Poland. Then the entire group would continue in conditions of 'radio silence', with IFF switched off, and attempt to penetrate the Soviet Union's air defences as if they were a group of NATO bombers attacking from the West.

Elint collection flights along the borders between the Warsaw Pact and NATO countries were carried out at least once a month. These flights were described as 'special tasks' (*spetszadaniya*), and all crews were trained and qualified to undertake them. The objective was to search for radars of potential adversaries, to determine their operating parameters and performance. Gomel'-based 290 ODRAP was responsible for north and north-west Europe. (Interestingly, the most useful map for planning these flights turned out to be the Moscow–Berlin road map, at 1cm to 20km [1:200,000 or 3.16 miles to the inch] scale!). Nezhin-based 199 ODRAP in the Ukraine 'looked after' the southern regions. Sometimes, in order to provoke reaction from a ground radar site, Tu-22 navigators would switch on the aircraft's Rubin-1L navigation radar, steering the beam in manual mode and radiating an area close to the anticipated location of a threat radar. After such provocative action, the NATO radars would be switched from standby to active mode and the Elint equipment of the Tu-22R would then 'sweep up' the radiated signals. Another regular task for the Tu-22R was participation in exercises, often playing the part of the 'bad guys' (*plokhiye parni*). The largest-scale exercises were held in the far north of the USSR, with all the participating air units assembling at airfields on the Kola Peninsula. In these exercise scenarios, the Tu-22s would be escorted by Soviet Air Force tactical fighters, while PVO fighters and missile units would attempt to simulate shooting them down. When the Tu-22s tried to evade intercept, simulated air combat would ensue between the groups of fighters, adding an air of realism to these air defence exercises.

One of the squadron commanders of 290 ODRAP, Major Svezhov, took part in one of these exercises in 1975/6, the task for the Tu-22RD being to penetrate the defensive zone of a major military complex in the region. The area was being defended by a PVO fighter unit equipped with the Tu-128P *Fiddler-B* long-range patrol fighter, based near Archangel. As soon as the Tu-22RD had entered the fighter regiment's zone of responsibility, a pair of Tu-128s was scrambled to intercept it, directed straight onto Major Svezhov's aircraft, and a manoeuvring air battle quickly ensued. The Tu-128s were guided by GCI to obtain the best missile-firing solution against the *Blinder*, while the Tu-22 pilot attempted to evade. Svezhov was an experienced pilot and used the manoeuvrability of the Tu-22 to the full, exploiting its high speed, general agility and almost fighter-like rate of climb (up to 23,600ft/min) to prevent the *Fiddlers* from locking onto him. The result was that the Tu-22 managed to get away from the fighters and go on to carry out a simulated attack on the target, which was supposed to have been defended by the Tu-128s. The results of this realistic 'air battle' were studied very carefully by the PVO leadership, with many useful conclusions being drawn from it for application in future exercises and real-life scenarios. From the point of view of the Tu-22 fraternity, it had been a convincing demonstration of the general ability of the aircraft to evade shoot-down in similar circumstances. It was also concluded that if the crew (specifically the pilot and airborne operator) saw an approaching missile in good time, then an experienced pilot, knowing the capabilities of his aircraft, could out-manoeuvre it, or cause it to detonate harmlessly outside the lethal zone of the warhead. Such air combat scenarios (fighter affiliation exercises) were practised by both the reconnaissance and the heavy bomber (i.e. missile-carrying) Tu-22 regiments, and in 1968 alone, 203 TBAP conducted 174 practice air combat events.

One of the most frequently practised recce methods in the regiments was visual reconnaissance, which for successful results required a high degree of crew cooperation, particularly between the pilot and the navigator. It was imperative to have good mutual understanding between these two crew members (and even with selective composition of crews this was not always the case), in order to find targets and pass their coordinates to

The graceful lines of the Tu-22 are displayed here to perfection, confirming a paradox often encountered in military aircraft design that although often designed to destroy, they can often possess an almost artistic beauty. This Tu-22RD was operated by 290 ODRAP from Zyabrovka in the former Byelorussian Soviet Socialist Republic. Note the station-keeping marker lines on the fuselage and undercarriage nacelles. *Sergey Tsvetkov Collection*

other members of the formation, quickly, clearly and precisely. On the Tu-16, the pilot could observe the navigator when he was using the bomb-sight, as he peered through the visor (or 'boot' [*sapog*], as it was known in the squadrons) in front of his radar screen. He could also see the second navigator and even indicate with hand movements if he wanted something done urgently, but the Tu-22 had one significant disadvantage in this respect, and that was that none of the crew members could see each other inside the aircraft. Consequently, the skill of using the intercom was highly developed by Tu-22 crews, with the manner and urgency of expression determining the actions to be carried out by this or that individual. If they spoke quickly, a rapid response was required and if delivery was more laconic, then it meant that there was still time for reflection. Since crew members all possessed different temperaments and personalities, it was always possible for mistakes to be made because of mutual misunderstandings. Much attention, therefore, was devoted to the process of developing crew cooperation on the Tu-22 regiments; crews were 'grown' very much as if they were 'delicate plants' and it was a complex and painstaking procedure. Although it might sound paradoxical, it was for this reason that highly competent pilots and navigators often found it difficult to obtain promotion. A regiment commander would find it difficult (indeed would not *want*) to split up an experienced crew who worked well together, although compatibility, once developed, did not disappear completely, even if a crew had not flown together for some time. All the Tu-22 regiment and squadron commanders with whom the author had the good fortune to discuss the issue considered that the process of re-forming (or reconstituting) crews was somewhat 'painful'. However, the regiment commanders said that when forming crews to undertake 'special tasks', they would select the older and more experienced individuals from the entire regiment, saying that, 'We have First Class pilots and navigators and so-and-so will fly with so-and so.'

The Tu-22R was not the ideal platform for visual reconnaissance, since the pilot's limited view from his cockpit and almost total absence of view for the navigator meant that they were virtually blind to the 'outside world'. The Tu-22 pilot would see a target before any other crew member and they could not assist him, but unlike a fighter pilot, he would lose sight of it as he approached, since the aircraft's long nose would shield it.

Some 5–7 seconds would elapse, after the pilot had sighted a target, before the navigator would be able to see it, if the aircraft was at 600m (1,970ft). According to some Tu-22 crews, the person with the best view for visual reconnaissance was the airborne operator, but he, of course, was facing backwards in his seat, although he did have good sideways vision! All the experience of operating the Tu-22R showed that in spite of the wishes of the General Staff, it was physically impossible to conduct visual recce with the aircraft from heights as low as 400–600m (1,312–1,970ft). Nevertheless, in spite of its limitations, the Tu-22R was frequently used on maritime reconnaissance missions, photographing foreign naval vessels and submarines. On these flights, the aircraft would try to approach as close as possible, from a variety of angles, in order to obtain photography of a vessel's radar and communications antennae, missile launchers and guns, plus any signs of modifications or changes to the external appearance. The photographs would later be analysed by the reconnaissance services reporting directly to the General Staff. In the 1980s certain limitations were placed on the conduct of these flights. Penetrating cloud in the vicinity of surface targets was permitted down to a height of no lower than 600m (1,970ft), with the following minimum approach distances to foreign ships and aircraft being:

- 3km (1.6nm) from ships and commercial vessels – if the Tu-22R was flying at less than Mach 1, and 7km (3.78nm) if the speed was greater than Mach 1
- 5km (2.7nm) from aircraft carriers launching and recovering aircraft and 10km (5.4nm) when approaching from the bow or the stern
- 500m (1,640ft) from airborne aircraft if the Tu-22R's speed was less than Mach 1 and 1,000m (3,280ft) if it was greater than Mach 1
- the minimum permitted height for the overflight of an aircraft-carrier was 500m (1,640ft) and over other ships 300m (984ft).

Later, however, it was completely forbidden to overfly aircraft-carriers.

In the latter years of operation of the Tu-22R, a rather unusual task was added to the aircraft's list of capabilities – hunting submarines. From an altitude of 11,000m (36,090ft) a submarine cruising submerged at a depth of around 100m (55 fathoms) was easily detectable from its wake. Then, following the Chernobyl' disaster in April 1986, the Tu-22R was used to photograph the nuclear power station itself and the areas used for parking the special vehicles sent in to deal with radiation leakage and the sealing of the damaged reactor. However, in the mid-1980s much attention focused on a rather poorly thought-out policy of using the Tu-22R to hunt down Pershing-2 missiles which had then recently been deployed to Europe by the US Army. The task of searching for the launch positions of these missiles was assigned to every available means of reconnaissance, but the Tu-22R regiments soon became closely involved. The tactic developed for wartime application was to fly out to the predicted launch position of the Pershing battery, transmit its coordinates, turn onto the reciprocal heading, photograph the location and once more refine its position. The optimum height for searching for the missiles was 600m (1,970ft), the height being chosen in order to remain outside the lethal zone of the adversary's tactical surface-to-air missile systems. Every pilot had already been trained to fly the Tu-22 at extremely low level, this being one of the exercises in the Soviet Air Force's basic training requirements syllabus – *Kurs Boyevoy Podgotovki* – meaning literally 'Course of Combat Training'. Following successful completion of the low-level part of their training, pilots would receive an appropriate endorsement in their log book signed by the regiment commander. However, low-level flight training in the recce regiments was quite rare, although many pilots liked to fly the Tu-22 at extremely low altitude. The KZA (*Kontrol'no-Zapisyvayushchaya Apparatura*) automatic flight parameter monitoring and recording equipment installed on the Tu-22 could only 'fix' the height of the aircraft to an accuracy of ±300–400m (±984–1,312ft), this 'accuracy' being significantly less at heights below 1,000m (3,280ft). This effectively allowed the pilot to do virtually what he liked – almost to behave like a hooligan! However, regiment commanders considered that it was necessary to train and fly at such heights, since that is what would be required in wartime.

The minimum permitted heights for all variants of the Tu-22, with modified control systems and flexible undercarriage mounting, are given in the table:

Indicated airspeed	Height [Day]	Height [Night]
550–750kph	150	250
750–800kph	200	300
800–950kph	300	350
500–550kph	300	350

Prolonged flight at low and extremely low level was permitted in temperatures below +15°C at a speed of 650kph (350kts), while flights of no longer than 20 minutes were permitted within the entire speed range shown in the table in temperatures no higher than +25°C. In conditions of good visibility (6km and more, day or night), it was permitted to fly for short periods (not more than 20 minutes) at heights 50m (164ft) less than in the table if the datum height was less than 250m (820ft), and 100m (328ft) less if the datum height was more than 300m. The minimum permitted height in turbulence had to be not less than 250m (820ft), while the 'turbulence speed' had to be between 630 and 650kph (340–350kts). The maximum period of flight at extremely low level was 30 minutes, and after that the pilot had to climb to 100–150m (328–492ft). After around 5–7 minutes at the higher level, the pilot could again descend to extremely low level.

However, from a tactical viewpoint, flying at 100m (328ft) only made sense if the aircraft was attempting to evade enemy air defences, although, as already mentioned, the Tu-22R was not designed for carrying out reconnaissance at this height. It *was* possible to pick out missiles and vehicles from the Tu-22R at heights from 600m (1,970ft) to 1,000m (3,280ft), albeit only with some difficulty. After all, forward visibility for the pilot, was only approximately ten times the height at which the aircraft was flying. At low level, it was difficult for the navigator to assist the pilot, and turning onto the target was more a matter of chance than precise calculation. The fact of the matter was that the aircraft, both as a recce platform and as a missile-carrier, was designed for operation at altitudes not less than 2,000m (6,560ft). Everyone involved in employing the Tu-22R to search for missiles on the ground compared this task with 'searching for a black cat in a darkened room'. In the summer of 1987 (28 May) a crew from one of 290 ODRAP's squadrons at Nezhin was lost in a tragic accident while conducting such an operation. As previously mentioned, it was impossible to monitor the exact height at which a Tu-22 was flying using the aircraft's own built-in KZA system. Knowing this, it would be quite easy for a pilot to lose all sense of responsibility and get carried away by the adrenalin rush of flying a large aircraft at high speed close to the ground. It was quite likely, therefore, that the 290 ODRAP pilot simply over-estimated his ability and could not handle the Tu-22 in these circumstances, lost control and crashed. (*See Chapter Nine for details of this accident.*) The tragedy was compounded by the fact that at the very time when the Soviet Air Force was preoccupied with the search for the Tu-22 and its crew, a 19-year-old German pilot, Mathias Rust, managed to fly unhindered from Helsinki to Red Square in Moscow in a hired Cessna 172. After the loss of this crew, the Soviet Air Force leadership reassessed the value of 'missile hunting' with the Tu-22R, and all further training flights ceased.

Apart from reconnaissance tasks, Tu-22R crews also trained frequently in weapons delivery (bombing) at the many ranges at their disposal in the former Soviet Union. The main bomb ranges used by the *Blinder* recce regiments included Dubna and Polesskii in Byelorussia, Riika, near Tartu, in Estonia, as well as Kuz'minskoye, Gur'yanovo (38km/24 miles from Engel's), Studenka (26km/16 miles from Yoshkar-Ola) and Karanogaiskii in Russia itself, plus Lugovka and Kalinovka in the Ukraine. Each of the overland ranges covered an area of around 22km (14 miles) by 17km (11 miles) and had its own particular target arrangements, although the targets themselves were broadly standardised as to their type. The most densely 'populated' range in terms of targets was Riika, which had targets for summer and winter, day and night operations and targets for radar bomb scoring. The summer target complex was intended for bombing practice from high, medium, low and extremely low altitudes and consisted of a circle of 100m (328ft) radius in which a 100m × 100m cross was placed. The winter target was the same size, but was formed out of locally felled pine trees. The night target consisted of a circle of 100 metres radius, with 40 red lights disposed around its circumference and a cross in the middle comprising 21 red lights. Additionally, a column of five lorries and five tanks was arranged to represent a realistic-looking convoy of military vehicles. Also adding 'realism' were dummy 'Nike-Hercules' and 'Pershing' missile batteries located within the range complex, as well as a 'mock airfield' with a 940m (3,080ft) runway. Targets with angular corner reflectors were used for radar-assisted bombing. Only practice bombs (of 50kg calibre) were used against the night targets, so as to preserve the longevity of the target complex, while 500kg (1,100lb) bombs could be used against the other targets, but only with an overshoot aiming point (*perelyot*) of 300m (984ft). It was only permissible to use incendiary, smoke and night position-marking bombs if snow lay on the ground, and illuminating flares could only be used between November and March. The latter restrictions meant that night photography practice, using photo-flash bombs/flares, could only be carried out after snow, or for four months of the year.

In addition to overland bombing ranges, the recce *Blinders* could also use naval range complexes. One of the main water ranges was Range 700 (*700-yi Poligon*), situated in the Caspian Sea between the Tyulyen'i Islands and Cape Tiub-Karagan, north of Fort Shevchenko on the eastern shore. The target complex of this range consisted of several partially submerged barges and old decommissioned ships, which the Tu-22R could use for bombing practice. Bombing was carried out from medium altitude, resulting in fairly high fuel consumption rates for the Tu-22R. Consequently, flights to and from Range 700 involved a positioning flight from base to Engel's, where the aircraft would be refuelled and the armourers would load the aircraft with the appropriate bombs. Bombs were aimed directly at the ships, without using any 'ricochet' effect off the surface, the weapons themselves usually being FAB-250s high-explosive fragmentation bombs, albeit without any firing assembly. Only inert bombs were used on the water ranges, and it was also forbidden to use FOTAB and SAB illumination bombs, both to preserve the longevity of the targets and to avoid the harmful effects of the blast of explosions and chemical residues on marine flora and fauna.

Another naval bombing range frequently used by the Tu-22R was located in the Baltic Sea along an offshore stretch of coastline between Liepaja in Latvia and Klaipeda in Lithuania and controlled at the time by the Soviet Navy's Baltic Fleet. The target complex consisted of barges, with corner reflectors located alongside them for radar bomb scoring. Contrary to the practice of using an 'overshoot' aiming point at the overland bomb ranges, crews had to use a 250m (820ft) 'undershoot' (*nyedolyot*) of the barge targets on the Baltic water range, with the same objective of not inflicting too much destructive damage on the targets. A similar range to the Baltic complex was operated by the Northern Fleet just off the Kola Peninsula, not far from the entrance to the White Sea. Aircraft using the range approached it by flying along the coast, and in addition to standard target barges the complex also included decommissioned warships dating from the Second World War. Crews were permitted to bomb the ships directly. From an altitude of 6,000m (19,685ft) and 950kph (513kts), when carrying out radar-assisted bombing using the Rubin-1L navigation-bombing radar, the normal deviation of a bomb from the target was not to exceed 183.5m (602ft). When using the OPB-15 optical bomb-sight in the same conditions this figure was not to be greater than 155m (508ft), and all Tu-22 crews usually achieved good results for these exercises in the 'basic training requirements' standards (KBP) for the *Blinder* fleet.

In the mid-1970s, Iraq approached the Soviet Union with a request to purchase heavy-calibre bombs for its small force of Tu-22A *Blinder-A* bombers. By definition, these were bombs of 2,600kg (5,730lb) and more. At the time, the Soviet Air Force had a number of high-explosive bombs in its inventory, including the FAB-1500-2600TS, FAB-3000, FAB-5000 and FAB-9000, intended for use against heavily fortified targets, such as bunkers and underground storage facilities, as well as large naval vessels. FAB stands for *Fugasnaya Aviatsionnaya Bomba*, or High-explosive Aviation Bomb – the figures 3000, 5000 and 9000 referring to the calibre of the bomb in kilograms, as previously mentioned. (*By convention, the bomb's weight is always included in the designation, although the FAB-1500-2600TS departed slightly from this rule in that it is the* second *number which refers to the bomb's mass of 2,600kg*). Iraq had planned to use the heavy-calibre bombs in the mountainous northern region of the country, against the indigenous Kurdish population and in any potential hostilities with neighbouring Iran. Although the Soviet Air Force had carried out tests with FAB-1500-2600TS and FAB-3000 bombs in the 1960s, it had not conducted tests with heavier-calibre weapons on the Tu-22. Therefore, it was decided to conduct trials with such bombs, and two crews were selected from the two independent reconnaissance units at Nezhin in the Ukraine (199 ODRAP) and Gomel' in Byelorussia (290 ODRAP). The crew from 199 ODRAP was led by Major Vorob'yev, with Major Chernyshev leading the crew from 290 ODRAP. The airfield selected to host the trials aircraft and crews was Bobruisk in Byelorussia, evidently for security reasons, since it was not normally associated with Tu-22 operations, while the trials themselves were to be conducted at the Kherson bomb range on the Crimean Peninsula.

Initially, each crew dropped one FAB-5000, weighing 5,000kg (11,000lb), the Tu-22 'leaping' upwards quite 'energetically' by around 50m (165ft) when the weapon was released. There were no instructions in the flight operations manual to warn crews that this would happen, but the phenomenon was also witnessed by the second crew who were airborne to observe the behaviour of the other aircraft and the bomb after release. Paradoxically, the FAB-9000 had practically no adverse effect on the handling of the Tu-22, the aircraft's autopilot having been 'tuned' to the carriage of the heavy weapon and seemingly able to cope with the sudden change of mass when it was dropped. After release, the FAB-9000 descended in an almost horizontal attitude, giving a high probability of 'ricocheting' off the surface when it hit the ground. It was clearly visible as it fell away from the aircraft because of its physically large dimensions. In fact, although it was designated FAB-9000, the actual weight was 9,640kg (21,250lb), or very nearly 10 metric tonnes, and when it exploded it produced a mushroom cloud rather like a nuclear bomb, which rose to about 1,800–2,000m (5,900–6,560ft) in the air. The crater produced from a ground burst had a diameter of 122m (400ft), and in soft earth this would be even greater. The bombs dropped during the trials were fitted with four fuses – two nose fuses and two tail fuses, although the weapon was designed to have eight. The delay setting for the fuses was 0.2 seconds. During the trials flights each crew dropped three FAB-9000s from an altitude of 2,700m (8,560ft), and take-offs were performed at maximum weight.

The trials were held in July – the hottest month – in order to simulate the conditions likely to be encountered in the Middle East. The tests were designed not only to evaluate weapons delivery, but also to assess take-off methods, although landings with the FAB-5000 and FAB-9000 were strictly prohibited, except in an emergency. When carrying the FAB-9000 in particular, the aircraft's performance was very sluggish. If a landing *had* to be made with these bombs still on board then the Tu-22 would require a minimum runway length of 3,500m (11,500ft), and a higher touchdown speed, demanding exceptional skill from the pilot. These heavy bombs were so unusual that even loading them onto the aircraft was quite different from handling other bombs. At the moment of transferring them from the bomb trolley to the winch inside the bomb bay, the aircraft would 'sink' on its undercarriage by up to 21cm (8.25in) in the case of the FAB-5000, and 28cm (11in) with the FAB-9000! Consequently, if a vehicle was parked underneath the Tu-22 there was a risk of damaging the underside of the aircraft if there was insufficient clearance. Loading of the bombs was carried out on special servicing 'pans' provided with a deep pit filled with sawdust, so that if a bomb should fall off during the loading process it would not bounce and damage the aircraft. The tests were completed satisfactorily, but in the end the Soviet Union did not offer them for export to Iraq.

Since the Tu-22R had a nuclear weapons delivery capability and it was an integral component of the Soviet Union's 'nuclear triad', crews trained regularly for this role. As in all other Soviet Air Force units with a nuclear wartime role, the Tu-22R crews carried out monthly training exercises in loading, and operating with, dummy nuclear bombs. Before delivering the 'special weapon' (*spetsizdeliye*) to the aircraft, a purpose-designed heated tent was erected under the weapons bay. The weapon itself, either the Type '4' (7U-31), or the Type '6' (245N or 246N), also had a special trolley on which it was brought out to the arming 'pan', the tractor approaching the aircraft from the rear and stopping about 5 metres (16.5ft) from it. The trolley was then unhitched from the tractor and manoeuvred into position for loading, at which point the tent was opened up and the bomb was placed into the lowered position on the trolley. The bombs were very large and heavy, weighing around 6,300kg (13,890lb), so in view of the fact that the clearance between the bomb on the trolley and the fuselage was quite small, the trolley was manoeuvred under the weapons bay 'by hand'. If the air temperature was low, then the tent's heating system would be turned on.

Flights were also carried out with 'unarmed' bombs, while practice bombing with aerodynamic 'mock-ups' of nuclear bombs was also carried out at special ranges. The inert bombs were loaded with conventional explosives and had the same appearance and ballistic characteristics as the real weapon. If they were detonated at a normal bombing range, then all the bomb fragments had to be collected and destroyed because of their high security classification (i.e. top secret). Therefore, in spite of the fact that these 'training' bombs were filled with conventional high explosives, they were usually only dropped on specially guarded ranges. The main nuclear training range was situated in the northern part of the large island of Novaya Zemlya in the far north of Russia, inside the Arctic Circle. When using the range, the Tu-22Rs would perform a positioning flight from base to Severomorsk, where they would be refuelled and armed with the training bombs. After 'working' the range, the aircraft would always land at Vorkuta to refuel, before returning to Severomorsk via Novaya Zemlya. Such a strange route was chosen, evidently, to maintain an element of secrecy about the flights. Sometimes, bombing was conducted in the open sea area around the range complex, but in this case the bombs would always be inert. However, after signing the Strategic Arms Limitation Talks in 1976, all training in the delivery of nuclear bombs by the Tu-22 fleet ceased.

In the 1980s, a form of toss-bombing was developed for the Tu-22R, intended to reduce the height from which the aircraft would deliver its weapons load in wartime. This required the Tu-22 to descend to extremely low level and at the calculated moment commence a steep climb, with a rate of around 15–20m/sec (3,000–3,950ft/min), releasing the bomb or bombs at a predetermined point on the trajectory. In practice, this form of bombing was more the fanciful wish of military theorists than a real combat option for the Tu-22, since, as already mentioned, the task of finding targets at extremely low level was particularly difficult for both the pilot and the navigator. Added to this was the fact that the OPB-15 bomb-sight had not been designed for this kind of delivery profile, and the accuracy of 'toss-bombing' by the *Blinder* was very low.

Tu-22RDM-2

Also at the beginning of the 1980s, 290 ODRAP at Gomel' started to receive the first of a new variant of the Tu-22R – the Tu-22RDM – where, as usual, the additional letter M signified *Modifitsirovannyi*, or Modified. As is evident from the designation, it was developed from the Tu-22RD, and existing aircraft were modified to the new standard at the aircraft repair plant at Ryazan', long associated with supporting the *Blinder* in service. The basis of the modification was the installation of a new navigation system and computer, plus a new reconnaissance suite. The first Tu-22RDMs were delivered from the plant in Reconnaissance Crate 1 (*Konteiner 1*) configuration, although the reconnaissance equipment was not particularly well distributed within it and the crate itself, in the opinion of the crews, was also not very convenient to use. Access to the recce equipment was awkward and it was very difficult to carry out a role change, when required. Evidently in anticipation of teething problems, and on the understanding that Crate 1 was only a transitional standard, Soviet industry had already designed the more advanced Crate 2. When the No. 2 crates were delivered to the regiment, the aircraft received the new designation of Tu-22RDM-2. The crate itself was a 'container' in the true sense of the word, and marked 'Top Secret' because of the equipment it housed. It occupied virtually the entire volume of the payload bay and was raised and lowered on special built-in winches in the aircraft. Since it occupied all the available space in the bay, there was no room to carry bombs, although there was also no longer a requirement to carry flare bombs because a new illuminating shell had been developed to support night photography operations. However, since the candlepower of the illuminating shells was not as great as the original flares, night reconnaissance photography could only be carried out from heights no greater than 600m (1,970ft). In fact, the overall thrust of the development of the reconnaissance equipment of this variant was to reduce the altitude at which it could be used successfully against a potential adversary. Apart from improvements to the photo-recce equipment, the Elint capability of the Tu-22RDM-2 was also greatly improved, and permitted 360° electronic intelligence collection in the spectrum 1.8cm–22cm (1.3GHz–16.66GHz), or the entire frequency range of a potential adversary's electronic systems. Compared with the older Elint equipment, the new system offered increased sensitivity and better quality of recordings.

Crate 2 in the Tu-22RDM-2 was effectively divided into three sections – the Osyen' (Autumn) infra-red linescan system, a suite of standard aerial cameras and special apparatus for detecting the presence of nuclear weapons on territory or ships overflown by the aircraft. This equipment was designed to detect nuclear weapons on board a naval vessel at a range 20% greater than the range of the vessel's own air defence weapons, permitting the aircraft to approach close enough to guarantee confirmation that nuclear weapons were on board. Perhaps because of the greater effectiveness of the Tu-22RDM-2 in this maritime role, it was assigned to support the Tu-22K *Blinder-Bs* of 203 TBAP at Baranovichi and 121 TBAP at Machulishchi to direct the missile-carriers onto nuclear armed vessels at sea in time of war. These procedures were frequently exercised in peacetime, when a NATO carrier strike group (*avianosnaya udarnaya gruppa*) was in northern waters, providing realistic targets for both the recce *Blinders* and the missile-carriers.

As the internal situation in the Soviet Union worsened in 1989, in the build-up to its collapse two years later, the ongoing war in Nagorno-Karabakh in the Caucasus had become a worrying problem for the Soviet military. On 8 March 1989, 290 ODRAP was placed on standby to reconnoitre an area around the region's capital, Stepanakert, to try to locate eighteen Soviet Army tanks and four armoured personnel carriers which had been stolen from barracks near the city. The regiment was well qualified for this task since crews of the first squadron had been honing their skills in the use of their infra-red recce equipment, ideally suited for seeking out camouflaged vehicles and tanks. Although 8 March was International Women's Day and a traditional holiday for military units in the former Soviet Union and the 290 ODRAP crews had assembled in their briefing room to be told that four Tu-22RDM-2s were to be sent to the region, along with a Tu-22P *Blinder-E* electronic jammer. The Tu-22P and its specific configuration had been selected on the basis of the kind of radars which were expected to be in the hands of the rebel units in Nagorno-Karabakh. Inclusion of the *Blinder-E* was also a precondition of carrying out the operation. The four Tu-22RDM-2s departed Zyabrovka and headed for the region, passing over Georgia and Armenia, and had been given preliminary reports of where the rebels might have hidden the vehicles. After carrying out the recce sortie the crews were authorised to land at Mozdok, in North Ossetia, Russia's largest strategic air base in the Caucasus and the base of the Tu-95-equipped 182nd Heavy Bomber Regiment. Closer alternative airfields in Azerbaijan and Armenia were not available at the time because of the unstable political situation. Moscow was very eager to have the information collected by the Tu-22RDM-2 crews, and they were met on landing by a Ministry of Defence official at Mozdok. The photo-recce support unit at the base was unable to develop the film produced by the Osyen' infra-red linescan system, so the equipment was flown in from Zyabrovka on board an Il-76 *Candid* transport. The *Blinder's* infra-red recce equipment had located all twenty-two targets, and it turned out that the tanks and APCs had been parked under a rocky outcrop, part of which had been blown up, collapsing onto the vehicles. No other reconnaissance equipment could have located these vehicles, buried under piles of rock.

Another special feature of the Tu-22RDM-2 was the ability to undertake spectrozonal photography (see Chapter 1 for a brief explanation of this technique). Spectrozonal photography allowed crews to select a specific target from a complex spectral background, making it possible, for example, to locate a specific workshop inside a specific factory. The accuracy obtained using spectrozonal photography was to within 3 m (9.84ft) of the centre of the target area. Naturally, to obtain high-quality images, exceptional flying skill from the pilot was required. A navigator from the first squadron of 290 ODRAP, Major Anatolyi Labetik, characterised the crews' mood when undertaking this delicate task, saying that they had a little ritual which they would shout to each other on the aircraft:

Don't rock (*Nie kachai*)
Don't shout (*Nie krichee*)
Don't turn – Hold it (*Nie krutee, dyerzhee!*)

[*Clearly this has more impact in Russian, because of the brevity and 'melody' of the commands and the fact that the expressions rhyme more than they do in translation* AD.]

After a sortie, the data was processed in the regiment's reconnaissance intelligence cell, although the technique was not fully exploited by 290 ODRAP. It must be remembered that this was a period when the aircraft's on-board equipment was significantly more advanced than the supporting ground facilities. A new photo reconnaissance support building had been planned at Zyabrovka, with some work already started, and because the equipment and chemical process required standard atmosphere conditions, this was to have included pressure chambers. However, the work was not completed as a result of disbandment of the regiment.

The scope of the recce information gathered by Tu-22RDM-2 was very extensive, and at first glance it seemed expedient to re-equip the entire regiment, but the reconnaissance crates were very expensive and the Tu-22R and RD variants were still effective recce platforms in their own right. Night recce with the RDM-2 was extremely difficult, since it had to be conducted from very low altitude, usually from around 400–600m (1,312–1,970ft), although this was often reduced to 200m (656ft). Attempts to carry out night recce sorties from around 900–1,100m (2,950–3,610ft) were almost always unsuccessful. Pilots used to say about these flights that they were only useful for 'scaring dogs and horses'! The different capabilities of the regiment's aircraft was something of a headache in planning terms, since if night bombing had been planned, then the Tu-22RDM-2 could not be included in the programme, because the bombing would be carried out from at least 2,000m (6,560ft). The RDM-2 could not perform night recce from this height. Conversely, if night recce was planned for the RDM-2, then the rest of the regiment would have to fly without bombs, since they could not bomb accurately (or at all) from low level! Taking account of all of this, the first squadron of 290 ODRAP was equipped with the Tu-22RDM-2, the second squadron with Tu-22R and RDs and the third squadron had Tu-22P and PD dedicated jamming variants.

In the Soviet era, Russia had developed one of the most highly integrated defensive systems for the protection of its own borders and the forward line of own troops (FLOT) on the battlefield. The latter was divided into special sectors and protected by dedicated jamming helicopters (including numerous variants of the ubiquitous Mi-8/17, members of the *Hip* family and lesser numbers of the Mi-6 *Hook*). These were provided with top cover from fighters and augmented by ground-based jammers and Elint systems. On low-level sorties, uninterrupted communications were maintained between ground and aircraft by the use of radio relay aircraft (usually An-26RT versions of the twin-engined *Curl* transport and the four-engined An-12 *Cub*). In the 1980s, this integrated command, control, communications and intelligence (C^3I) system was further augmented by the inclusion of the Ilyushin-Beriev A-50 *Mainstay* Airborne Warning and Control System (AWACS), added to which appropriately equipped naval vessels could also be used to extend geographical coverage. In order to make full use of all of these facilities, Russia had developed a 'Control and Mutual Cooperation Plan' (*Plan Upravlyeniya i Vzaimodyeystviya*), which provided for the allocation of the frequencies to be used by all participants in any combat operation. This covered communications between aircraft in formation, radio relay aircraft and ships, regimental and divisional command posts and command posts of the Air Armies, the Soviet Naval Air Force and the central command post in Moscow. It also made provision for the allocation of search and rescue aircraft and ships to support combat operations.

The Tu-22 reconnaissance regiments had their own place in this broad operations plan, and, as already mentioned, no recce sortie would be authorised without the inclusion of a Tu-22P or Tu-22PD ECM variant, or *shumovik* (noise maker) as they were called in the regiments. The minimum size of combat formation for any task was the pair, but for over-water operations this was usually six aircraft, comprising two Tu-22RDM-2, two Tu-22R (RD) and two Tu-22P (PD). This composition would be perfectly justifiable over any sea area, but was absolutely essential in the North, where it was dark for around four to five months of the year. Recce flights along the borders and coastlines of target countries were always accompanied by 'escorting' fighters, most frequently Lockheed-Martin F-16 Fighting Falcons, which equipped several NATO countries, including Norway. The fighters would usually approach to take up a position under the Tu-22's payload bay, attempting to prevent the Russian aircraft from photographing ships on the surface. Pilots had to handle their aircraft with a certain 'virtuosity' to photograph their targets and avoid a collision with the fighters, and it must be remembered that the Soviet Air Force crews did not have any special survival suits for over-water flights in the far North. In the event of an emergency, they only had their integral life-jackets, and would have been unable to survive long in the icy waters of the North Atlantic or Arctic oceans.

The Tu-22s grew quite accustomed to the appearance of the escorting fighters, and generally knew which pilot had been sent up to intercept them. The commander of the first squadron of 290 ODRAP, Major Chernyshev, recalls some of these incidents: 'If the interceptor came in and stuck very close to you, then it was a Norwegian pilot. The Varangian (i.e. Viking – a possibly pejorative term used to describe the Norwegians) was very similar in temperament to the Slav. If he was told not to allow the Russian aircraft to photograph a ship, then he would be happy to 'bust a gut' to achieve his goal. If he behaved elegantly, like a gentleman, then it was an English pilot. They always did everything steadily and precisely. If it was a pilot who rather tediously wanted to show how an aircraft should be flown, then it was an American. His controllers would direct him onto a target and he would do everything by command. [*It is interesting to hear this comment from a Russian pilot, since it was the view that Western pilots usually held of Russian interceptor pilots!* AD] The Swedes were similar in style to the Americans. I remember the first time we flew over the North Sea in a Tu-22RDM-2 – the F-16s were swarming all around (us). [*Depending upon where the intercept took place, the F-16s, operated only by the Norwegians and the Danes in the region, would have been from either Norway, or Denmark, not Sweden.* AD] Externally, the Tu-22RDM-2 differed from the Tu-22RD and it was obvious that they were interested in recording the differences. We were approaching one of their ships and an F-16 slipped in under our payload bay, adopting a position from where they were usually able to block the camera hatches of the Tu-22R (RD). However, on the Tu-22RDM-2 the equipment crate contained a forward-looking oblique camera, and by the time the pilot had discovered where our camera hatches were it was too late – we'd already got our pictures. It was only after our third flight into the area that they had developed a new tactic. This involved one aircraft moving ahead of us to block the view with the oblique camera, while the second fighter acted as a spotter for the first.'

Experienced Tu-22 crews would often play their own games with intercepting NATO fighters. On one occasion, a Norwegian F-16 intercepted a Tu-22RDM-2 and formated on the Russian aircraft. The *Blinder* crew had been tasked to find out which airfield the F-16 had come from. The northern latitudes were divided into several zones, depending upon the state of the ice in the winter. The first zone consisted of detached icebergs, further north there was a zone of drifting ice floes and further north still there was the region of solid pack ice. The Norwegian fighters were only allowed to fly beyond the area of drifting ice if they had sufficient fuel. The experienced Tu-22RDM-2 crew exploited this knowledge and turned north. In order to remain with their target, the fighters were obliged to go in the same direction, rather pointlessly using up fuel, and after a short time they had to turn back towards their base. As soon as the airborne operator reported that the fighters had turned away, the *Blinder* turned in the same direction. The fighters could no longer cover their target, since they only had enough fuel to get back to base, so the F-16s virtually led the Tu-22 back towards their airfield, where the Russian aircraft was able to conduct its reconnaissance. (*Clearly this was from a stand-off location over the sea and not over the base itself.*)

Tu-22 reconnaissance regiment specialists from the aerial photography service (*Aerofotograficheskaya Sluzhba*), in conjunction with the Tupolev Design Bureau, had wanted to introduce the capability of even partially developing film from the short-focal-length cameras while the aircraft was still in flight. The justification for this would have been that in a typical one-and-a-half-hour transit flight back to base from a recce sortie it would have been possible to develop around 150 metres (almost 500ft) of film. However, it had not been possible to introduce the capability since the decision had already been taken to disband the Tu-22 recce regiments. Thus, after the rather short-sighted run-down of the Tu-22 regiments at the end of the 1980s, the General Staff of the Soviet Ministry of Defence was deprived of a supersonic reconnaissance aircraft equipped with the most advanced systems at the disposal of the Long-range Air Force. A belated, albeit welcome decision was then taken to install the reconnaissance crate from the Tu-22RDM-2 on a more modern platform. The aircraft chosen for this was, unsurprisingly, a modified variant of the Tu-22M3 *Backfire-C* swing-wing bomber, which received the designation Tu-22MR (R for *Razvyedchik*) after completion of the modification work.

Air-to-air refuelling with the Tu-22

Since the in-flight-refuelling-capable Tu-22RD was a reconnaissance asset, it was defined as a support aircraft in documents relating to arms reduction talks and was not included in any of the Strategic Arms Limitation agreements. Consequently, in-flight-refuelling training continued on the Tu-22 reconnaissance regiments right up to the time of their disbandment in the early 1990s. The Tu-22RD was equipped with the probe and drogue system, using the dedicated Tu-16N tanker, the Tu-22 itself receiving the following additional equipment:

- A cantilevered telescopic receiving probe, mounted on the nose
- A fuel-delivery pipe connecting the probe to the aircraft's fuel tanks
- A system for exhausting (purging) fuel from the delivery pipe.

A Tu-22KD takes on fuel from a Tu-16N tanker. The Tu-16N was built specially to serve the Tu-22 fleet as a tanker; the 'N' of its designation remaining unknown even today, albeit this was possibly an example of Soviet humour, intended to distract Western intelligence analysts. *S Burdin Archive*

The moving part of the probe was extended (shot forward) by compressed air at the moment of making contact with the basket (*konus*), the design of the system allowing for the action to be repeated several times if multiple refuelling contacts were required. The tanker's refuelling hose was always filled with fuel and pressurised to 5–5.5kg/cm² (71–78lb/sq ft) in order to maintain the circular cross-section of the hose and stabilise it behind the tanker when fully deployed. The hose was reeled out from within the bomb bay of the Tu-16N, and after it had been wound in at the end of a refuelling session, the bay doors were fully closed. The integrated hose and drum system on the Tu-16N had a system of red, green and yellow signal lights to inform the Tu-22 pilot of his distance behind the tanker. Each light indicated that a specific length of hose had been reeled out, or more specifically, the relative distance between the two aircraft. If the pilot saw a continuous green light, this signified that he was maintaining the correct distance. Simultaneous green and yellow lights indicated to the pilot of the receiving aircraft that the distance was small and that he had to reduce power. A single yellow light meant that he had to reduce speed rapidly. Simultaneous green and red lights told the Tu-22 pilot that he was dropping behind the tanker and that he should increase speed slightly, while a single red light warned him that the hose was fully extended and that he should increase speed in order to avoid disconnecting from the basket.

Main technical parameters of the Tu-16N Konus system

Aircraft speed during refuelling	830–890kph (450–480kts)
Refuelling altitude	5,000m (16,400ft)
Delivery rate	1,660litres/min (365 imp gal/min)
Duration of entire refuelling process (Formating, making contact, transfer maximum fuel load and disconnect)	25 minutes
Hose length	47 metres (154ft)

As already mentioned, not all aircraft in the regiments were equipped for in-flight refuelling, and the number of pilots authorised to conduct such flights was even smaller. Pilots selected to perform in-flight refuelling were the most qualified and experienced in the regiment. According to the orders of the General Staff of the Soviet Air Force, there were supposed to be eight qualified pilots in each long-range reconnaissance regiment, and initially these were to be the regiment commander, his two deputies and the three squadron commanders. The other two would be trained on an opportunity basis. However, this was not a hard and fast rule and could change as the regiment and squadron management structure changed. Air-to-air-refuelling training usually took place in the summer and was carried out in dedicated refuelling zones, which for the recce regiments were blocks of airspace near Sol'tsy airfield, near Petrozavodsk, with a large zone being allocated for AAR between Saratov (Engel's) and Kuibyshev, over the central Caspian Sea area. The Tu-22K *Blinder-B* regiments also had their own refuelling zones in an area around Ryazan' and another between Baranovichi and Machulishchi airfields in Byelorussia. According to the basic training requirements of the KBP, an AAR-qualified crew had to take on 50–70 metric tonnes of fuel per year to remain qualified, although in reality several crews received considerably higher levels than this. The KBP for the recce *Blinder* regiments required them to carry out AAR training twice a month: one day sortie and one at night, and the absolute minimum had to be not less than once per month.

There were two AAR methods employed by the Tu-22 fraternity – 'en route' (*poputnaya dozapravka*) and 'rendezvous' (*vstrechnaya dozapravka*). The simplest method was the 'en route' procedure, which involved the Tu-16N tanker getting airborne before the Tu-22, with the latter literally setting off in pursuit, to join up in the designated refuelling zone. The 'rendezvous' procedure was employed when a Tu-22 was returning to base after a 4–5 hour sortie, and as the name implies, required the *Blinder* crew to join up with the tanker from an opposing heading. This method, after a long and often exhausting recce flight, placed heavy demands on the crew, and usually only five or six crews in a regiment (out of twenty-seven) were qualified to perform 'rendezvous' refuelling. AAR was very much a team effort, with the main effort initially falling on the navigator, who was responsible for 'finding' the tanker using the RSBN-2SV short-range navigation system in the air-to-air 'Rendezvous' (*Vstrecha*) mode. Not only did he have to find the tanker, but also to identify the specific tanker for his aircraft, since more often than not several tankers would be refuelling several Tu-22s at the same time. In 'Rendezvous' mode the RSBN would give the navigator a heading to fly towards the tanker and he would then alert the other two crew members and the pilot would begin to close on the Tu-16N. The Tu-22 approached the Tu-16N from above and behind, and after establishing visual and radio contact, the tanker would deploy the hose from the 'bomb-bay'-mounted drum assembly. Initially, the hose trailed about 8–12m (26–39ft) below and 25–30m (80–100ft) behind the tanker.

After taking up position behind the Tu-16N, the crew of the Tu-22 would prepare to make contact, the navigator setting his stopwatch and the pilot and airborne operator preparing the fuel system, depending on whether it was to be a 'wet' or a 'dry' contact. If it was a live fuel uplift, the navigator monitored the duration of delivery and the aircraft's speed and geographical position, reporting this to the pilot on the intercom. Although the pilot had an airspeed indicator, he was too preoccupied with maintaining position behind the tanker to look down into the cockpit, and most navigators had become so used to sensing the aircraft's speed that they could tell the pilot to reduce or increase speed by as little as 5kph (2.7kts). The airborne operator also had the important task of monitoring whether the fuel-management system was distributing fuel correctly between the tanks. Clearly, however, the greatest burden was shouldered by the pilot, since if he could not make contact, then the efforts of his other two crew members were in vain. The correct position to initiate contact with the basket (*konus*) was from a distance of around 5m (16ft), at which point the pilot would reduce speed to stabilise behind it. As the aircraft then slowly approached the tanker and the refuelling probe was about 0.5m (1.6ft) from the edge of the basket, the pilot would 'shoot' the pneumatically powered telescopic tip of the probe into the locking mechanism inside the basket. It does not require much imagination to understand the skill required to place an 85-tonne (187,000lb) aircraft into a position where the probe can be fired into the middle of a 95cm (3ft) basket trailing behind a tanker only feet away from the nose. If turbulence and darkness are added to the scenario then it is no surprise to learn that pilots were always drenched in perspiration after any air-to-air refuelling sortie. All pilots were unanimous in their opinion that the Tu-16N was not the ideal aircraft to use as a tanker, since its own performance limitations required the AAR process to be carried out at speeds and heights which were too low for the Tu-22. The *Blinder* did not handle well behind the Tu-16N and the speed was scarcely sufficient to maintain normal horizontal flight.

A 290 ODRAP Tu-22RD takes on fuel from a Tu-16N tanker, conveniently showing off its 'coke bottle' area-ruled fuselage. *Sergey Tsvetkov Collection*

Instructions for pilots carrying out in-flight refuelling were that they should maintain a position where they were either in the green zone of the signal light system or in the red-green zone, close to the 'disconnect' position. In practice, the longer the length of hose reeled out, the faster fuel transfer took place. Sometimes, however, depending on the nature of a task requiring an AAR uplift, the refuelling time was so limited that crews would carry out the procedure in the red-green zone, or even completely in the red zone, in order to take on fuel as quickly as possible. This required very accurate handling of the aircraft and was usually only performed by highly experienced pilots. Pilots said that the most important thing to remember during AAR was not to get into the wake turbulence behind the tanker, otherwise the Tu-22 could be 'bounced' out of the trail formation with the Tu-16, possibly resulting in breaking the hose. The quantity of fuel transferred from the Tu-16N was 15.5 metric tonnes (34,170lb), of which 0.5 tonnes (1,100lb) was used during the refuelling process itself. Thus, after taking on fuel in the air, the weight of the aircraft could increase to 94–95 tonnes (207,230–209,440lb), and flying the Tu-22 at this weight, at the minimum control speed of 600–620kph (324–335kts) indicated airspeed, or 800kph (432kts) true airspeed, introduced additional difficulties for the pilot. The pitch dampers not only did not help the pilot during AAR, but actually hindered aircraft handling. During AAR the pilot would move the control column back and forth with small amplitude, but comparatively frequent inputs, which the control system took to be external disturbances of the control surfaces and would try to neutralise. Since the control column deflections were very small they seemed comparable with the movement of the actuating rods of the dampers, and the two would cancel each other out. Sometimes, this could lead to a delayed response by the aircraft to control inputs, where the pilot might have pulled the column back slightly, but the aircraft would not have reacted, and he might have already pushed the 'stick' forward again, with the aircraft only *then* reacting to the previous input. These actions would 'confuse' the pitch damper, which would feed in larger movements than required and then have to reverse the action.

Learning the technique of in-flight refuelling with a bomber-sized aircraft is difficult enough when the instructor and 'student' are sitting side-by-side, but it was imperative with a single-pilot aircraft like the Tu-22 to have a trainer variant capable of demonstrating it realistically. The value of the Tu-22U, equipped with a dummy refuelling probe, was that the instructor could actually show a trainee pilot how to approach the tanker, make contact with the basket and maintain contact in formation. However, what no one could demonstrate to a Tu-22 pilot learning this demanding procedure was the changing behaviour of the aircraft during a real transfer of fuel from the tanker. This deficiency in the Tu-22U as a training platform for teaching AAR procedures was described by Lt-Col Yerusenko, a squadron commander on 290 ODRAP: 'When transferring fuel from the tanker, a whole circus of activity starts – the aircraft's weight changes, the tanker's weight changes and the centre of gravity changes. All of this has to be taken into account. It is something that you have to experience for yourself – an instructor can only describe the process in words and brief you before flight, but everything else is up to the individual.'

In-flight refuelling was never easy, and Lt-Col Yerusenko recalls an occasion when he and Lt-Col Chernyshev were flying as a pair on a sortie from Zyabrovka which took them over the Aral Sea, a route which always required an outbound and an inbound AAR link-up. The first, 'en-route', uplift was made in the area of Mozdok airfield, over North Ossetia, from a pair of Tu-16N tankers out of Belaya Tserkov', their usual refuelling 'partners'. The 'rendezvous' link-up was made on the return leg, at night, over the Caspian Sea, and required the two *Blinders* to meet up with the *Badgers* in such a way that they would not turn in too far behind or ahead of the Tu-22s. There was little time for manoeuvre if either pair had miscalculated. Lt-Col Yerusenko remembers the ground controllers calling to tell them not to worry now that they had been refuelled, but a thunderstorm was raging on the ground and there would have been nowhere for them to divert if they had not met the tankers! Had they not been able to link up, they did not have enough fuel remaining to reach Astrakhan', Kapustin Yar or Vladimirovka, the nearest diversion airfields, although in fact these bases were never offered as diversion airfields anyway!

The missile-equipped Tu-22K *Blinder-B* regiments (341, 203 and 121 TBAP), like the recce *Blinder* regiments, each also had six to eight pilots qualified to carry out air-to-air refuelling. AAR training in these regiments started in the 1960s, with the first to become involved being 203 TBAP at Baranovichi. At this time the AAR instructors were all test pilots and the tankers were converted Myasishchev M-4 *Bison* four-jet bombers deployed to Baranovichi from one of the tanker squadrons at Engel's. By 1970, the method of in-flight refuelling of the Tu-22 had been fully developed and refined. Flights were always planned so that not less than half would be carried out at night. The AAR-capable Tu-22K *Blinder-B* and Tu-22M2 *Backfire-B* came within the ambit of strategic arms reduction agreements, although they were not strategic weapons by definition. However, the USSR decided anyway to prohibit air-to-air refuelling with the Tu-22K and Tu-22M2 (and eventually the Tu-22M3 *Backfire-C*), and AAR was removed from the KBP syllabus for the missile-carrying regiments following the official signing of the SALT agreement in 1981. Just before this, one of the pilots on 203 TBAP, Captain Fyodorov, unfortunately managed to receive a reprimand during one of the very last sorties involving AAR, which was flown against a NATO carrier attack group in the north. The regiment had deployed to Olen'ya airfield on the Kola Peninsula, from where six *Blinder-Bs* were tasked to depart from the base, routeing via the North Pole to attack the carrier group and carry out a simulated missile strike (*takticheskii pusk*) and return to Olen'ya. The aircraft had also been tasked to carry out an 'en route' refuelling link-up, led by the regiment commander.

The aircraft set themselves up to formate on the tanker, and the Tu-22Ks penetrated first one layer of cloud, then another, without sighting the tanker. The regiment commander gave the order: 'We'll penetrate one more layer of cloud – if the tanker is there we'll refuel – if not, we'll go.' The group penetrated one more layer, but there was no sign of the tanker. However, Captain Fyodorov found the tanker, directly alongside at 6,000m (19,685ft), made contact, refuelled and carried on with the mission! Since the rest of the group had not been able to refuel, the regiment commander turned the remaining aircraft round and returned to Olen'ya. Captain Fyodorov and his crew then found themselves in the strange situation of having taken on extra fuel and requiring to burn it all off again to get down to a safe landing weight, so he decided instead to carry on with the mission! They found the carrier group, carried out the simulated missile attack and returned to their deployment base at Olen'ya. However, in spite of successfully completing the assigned task, Captain Fyodorov was reprimanded by the regiment commander for leaving the combat formation, in contravention of orders. After signature of the arms limitation agreement the refuelling probes of the Tu-22U *Blinder-D* trainers assigned to the missile-carrying regiments were removed, but the process was soon halted when it was discovered that their removal altered the aircraft's centre of gravity. Therefore, the receiving element of the probe was simply blocked off on all remaining aircraft, and right up to the time of disbandment of the Tu-22K regiments, no further air-to-air refuelling took place, and crew training ceased.

CHAPTER SEVEN

Combat Application
of the Tu-22K

As already mentioned, three regiments of Tu-22K *Blinder-B* missile carriers were based at Ozyornoye (341 TBAP), Machulishchi (121 TBAP) and Baranovichi (203 TBAP), and were, for many years, the elite of the Long-range Air Force. Their wartime tasking would have seen them operating in regions where the adversary's air defence systems were most densely concentrated, with 121 and 203 TBAP being 'responsible' for targets in northern Europe (Holland, Luxembourg, etc.), while 341 TBAP would have been deployed against targets in central Europe. Apart from the main strategical-tactical axes of operation, all the regiments also trained to carry out strikes on naval targets in the Mediterranean, Black, Baltic, North and Barents Seas. Main and reserve targets were assigned to the regiments down to the level of individual crews, with the specific target details being presented in special documents, the so-called *pakyety* (*inter alia*, an official letter, or package). The *pakyet* was, in fact, a portfolio carrying the personal seal of the regiment commander, and all *pakyety* were kept in a secure area of the regimental HQ. Each *pakyet* or portfolio contained a full set of all the flight documents essential for a strike on a particular target, including charts, and details of the target and the type of warhead required to deal with it.

A 121 TBAP Tu-22K makes a sprightly departure from Machulishchi in the early 1990s, showing to good effect the 'coke bottle' area-ruled mid-fuselage. *S Burdin*

A 121 TBAP Tu-22K on the taxiway at Machulishchi. *S Burdin*

Each pilot in the regiment would be given two or three training and combat portfolios, a procedure not unlike that employed by RAF V-bomber crews. The type of warhead for the AS-4 *Kitchen* missiles would depend upon the nature of the target designated for a given crew. If the target was to be a carrier strike group, political and administrative centres, then the missile would be equipped with a nuclear warhead. If, on the other hand, the target was to be a chemical factory complex, so-called hydro-technical structures such as dams and locks, or a nuclear power station, or if the conflict had not yet deteriorated to the 'nuclear stage', then a conventional warhead would be employed.

The classic combat formation for a strike group was the 'pair' (more rarely a 'four-ship'), arranged in four echelons if part of a larger group. Formations based on a flight (of three aircraft), as described in the KBP (*Kurs Boyevoy Podgotovki*) basic training requirements manuals, were mainly used for training pilots to become wingmen. In this case a flight leader would train two wingmen at the same time. However, the pair was,

The twin-canopy brake 'chute of the Tu-22K can be seen in this photograph to be comparatively small, but effective, as the aircraft rolls down the runway after landing. *S Burdin*

nevertheless, the main formation element. The normal distance between a pair was 200m (656ft), with the wingman 500m (1,640ft) above the leader, although this usually only applied to training flights. In exercises, and when carrying out 'special tasks', the interval and distance could be reduced significantly. (Note: distance (*distantsiya*) is the longitudinal separation between aircraft, whereas interval (*interval*) is the wingtip to wingtip separation.) There were, of course, other formation types employed by the Tu-22K regiments, but regardless of the disposition of aircraft in a formation, it would always include at least one Tu-22P as an escort jammer and another configured for Elint collection. When they were first introduced to equip the third squadron of the missile-carrying regiments, the Tu-22P was configured with P-1 and P-2 ECM equipment crates. However, as radar systems and countermeasures improved over time, the more advanced P-4, P-6 and P-7 crates started to come into service, and the aircraft carrying these specific systems received the designations Tu-22P-4, Tu-22P-6 and Tu-22P-7. A combat formation of one squadron of Tu-22K *Blinder-Bs* would include four Tu-22P *Blinder-Es*, configured to any one of the above-mentioned standards, depending upon the task. The actual selection of the type of jamming system, and therefore the variant of Tu-22P required, was made at the task planning stage, taking into account the anticipated threat radars that might be encountered along the route.

The standard procedure was for a pair of Tu-22Ps to fly at the front of the main strike group, with the second pair at the rear, the lead pair of Tu-22Ps being 600–700m (1,970–2,300ft) above the missile carriers, and the rear pair maintaining the same level as the lead jammers. In between, the *Blinder-Bs* would be flying in trail formation at the same height as the lead missile carriers. This type of formation allowed the jammers to provide an ECM cone of protection for the entire squadron of missile carriers. All manoeuvres by the Tu-22Ps, if changing position in the formation, would be made with bank angles no greater than 15° in order not to disrupt the directionality of the ECM transmitters and thereby not interrupt their effect on target emitters on the ground. If the formation was attacked by fighters, protection of the forward and rear hemispheres would be achieved by the Tu-22Ps using the DK-20 gun turret, firing chaff shells to the rear, releasing chaff from the undercarriage nacelle-mounted KDS-16GM dispensers, or the SPS-151, SPS-152 and SPS-153 jammers and ASO-2I flare dispensers. However, using electronic jamming within the formation created problems for the *Blinders* themselves. No matter what ECM system was being used by the Tu-22P, it would affect both the Tu-22P and the Tu-22K alike, at a range of 4–5km (2.5–3 miles) from the jamming source. When they used the jamming systems, two-way VHF, HF and UHF radio communications would deteriorate significantly, and on some frequencies would even become impossible, and the ARK-11 automatic radio compass would also be seriously affected. On board the *Blinders*, the crew would hear permanent noise in their headphones, which would prevent two-way contact between the Tu-22P and the *Blinder-Bs* in the formation at a range of 5km (3 miles) from the jammer. The jamming signals would also affect the radar altimeters, leading to them over-reading by up to 70–120m (230–395ft) over water and shutting down completely over land. They would also affect the operation of the RSBN short-range navigation system and the PN (*Down Beat*) navigation-bombing radar.

In the latter case, when observing the rear sector with the PN radar, radial spikes would appear on the edge of the screen which would make it difficult to pick out a target. Consequently, jamming would not be used constantly throughout a sortie, but only at

A 121 TBAP Tu-22K in one of the earth-reinforced revetments (*obvalovanie*) at Machulishchi in 1993. Ground crew regarded the special engine access platforms as convenient and highly stable. *S Burdin*

points designated by the task. In the event of hostilities, the crews of the Tu-22P jammers would work out a special signals plan for the use of the collective protection jamming systems at their disposal. This plan would define sections of the route where the suite of systems could be tested in the air, and would designate the boundaries for switching on and off the systems to jam the enemy's threat radars, as well as including a contingency provision to cover systems malfunctions and failures. The Tu-22P airborne operator and navigator would work together on this plan to finalise the route that they would fly as escorts for the Tu-22K strike group, taking account of preliminary reconnaissance data concerning the locations of SAM radars near the front line and the target area. In planning the route, they would select a track which would take them round any radar site working in the frequency range of their jammers, at a distance sufficient for them to provide effective protection for the strike group. The boundary selected to be the point where jamming would commence would be the threat radar's calculated maximum detection range of the strike group at the planned altitude for attack.

The area where jamming would take place was a section of the route, about 200–250km (125–155 miles) long, where the enemy's air defence systems were expected to be particularly active. At about 20–30km (12–18 miles) before reaching the forward edge of the battle area (forward line of own troops), or naval attack group, the *Blinder* formation leader would contact the command posts controlling air, ground and naval forces in the region, warning them of the approach of the group. Around 5 to 7 minutes before reaching the 'boundary' line, the Tu-22P airborne operators would prepare their jammers for work. No more than five jamming transmitters could be switched on simultaneously by each Tu-22P, because of the high power consumption of the equipment. A 'pathfinder' group would have flown ahead of the strike formation, to reconnoitre the target, and if it was a naval attack group, the 'pathfinder' navigator would 'fix' the positions of vessels. An aircraft-carrier, because of its large size, produced a larger 'blip' on the screen than other ships, although decoy measures could be employed to make even a barge look like a capital vessel, using corner reflectors or other radar decoy systems. Consequently, in the 1980s, the General Staff issued a directive to the Tu-22K regiments that in time of war an attack on a carrier group would only be allowed if the 'pathfinder' group had established visual contact with the carrier and confirmed its geographical coordinates.

Exercise participation
Typical tasks developed for the heavy bomber regiments in training for war were bombing, missile launches, gunnery attacks on ground targets and reconnaissance, although the latter was not a major combat role for the Tu-22K units. However, as in all Soviet Air Force regiments, reconnaissance skills were practised frequently during most flights by all crews. The regiments did, of course, practise their main roles in all the major exercises held within the ambit of the Western theatre of military operations, one such exercise being the well-publicised Exercise *Zapad-84* (West-84) held in 1984. A major participant in this exercise was 121 TBAP. Responding to the exercise alert, the regiment's Tu-22Ks scrambled from Machulishchi in regimental strength and set course for the Riika bombing range, located 35km (22 miles) north-west of Tartu in Estonia. Having 'worked' the range in accordance with the exercise plan, the regimental formation descended to 100m (328ft) and continued their flight over the central part of the Baltic Sea at that level. Their flight continued undetected over the Baltic until the aircraft were abeam the former German Democratic Republic, the Warsaw Pact air defence systems in the area being unable to see the bombers, let alone take action against them. The formation then spilt into two columns, one skirting Berlin from the east and the other from the west.

One group landed at the Soviet Air Force base at Templin, north of Berlin, while the other landed at Falkenburg in the south, both groups touching down at around 23.00hrs. The presence of an entire regiment of *Blinder-B* missile carriers, 'armed' with training variants of the AS-4 *Kitchen* cruise missile, took not only NATO by surprise, but also senior officers at Group of Soviet Forces Germany (GSFG) HQ at Zossen-Wünsdorf. The following day was designated as a rest day, and at night the regiment departed East Germany and headed out over the Baltic Sea again, this time at an altitude of 9,000–10,000m (29,530–32,800ft), cruising at high speed and using ECM, successfully evading detection by 'red force' air defences. (*Note: the Russians did not follow the Western practice of designating exercise participants as 'red' and 'blue' forces, but it is likely that in this context, East German and Polish forces would have played the part of the 'bad guys'.*) On the return leg, the group carried out simulated missile launches

An early photo of a 121 TBAP Tu-22K taking off at Machulishchi, showing the fuselage angle at unstick and the characteristic downward-pointing forward bogies of the main undercarriage. *S Burdin Archive*

(*takticheskiye puski*) over 'B-46 Range' on the Kurshskaya Kosa (Kurshskaya Spit) near Kaliningrad, and then set course for base in Byelorussia. An identical exercise plan was practised by 203 TBAP from Baranovichi, but in this case the aircraft landed at Debrecen in Hungary.

   Flights at extremely low level were not only performed over the sea, but also over land, where both pilot and navigator had to demonstrate great skill and accuracy in handling the aircraft, and the timing of the waypoints at high speed close to the ground. At low altitude the RSBN short-range navigation system could not always pick up the beacons, and the time available to calculate route corrections was often extremely brief. Nevertheless, flight at extremely low level was an integral part of the training programme of the heavy bomber regiments equipped with the Tu-22K. Great attention was paid to these flights,

A Tu-22KP of the 2nd squadron of 121 TBAP at Machulishchi. This photo shows to good effect the specially treated (white-painted) panels of the fuselage, designed both to counteract corrosion and minimise the effect of thermal heating on the control runs passing under the fuselage skin. *S Burdin Archive*

After the nose-wheel lifts off, the aircraft continues to accelerate to the unstick speed. This is a Tu-22K of 121 TBAP at Machulishchi. *S Burdin*

unlike the procedure in the Tu-22 recce regiments, where extremely low altitude could not be exploited by the aircraft's reconnaissance equipment, and Tu-22K crews regularly practised flying at heights of 80–150m (260–492ft). Several factors were taken into consideration when planning these low-altitude flights, including the selection of periods outside the migration period for birds, since migratory activity was often quite intense at around 200m (650ft). Consequently the most favourable season so as not to interfere with migration patterns was from November to April. Additionally, it was essential to plan flights which did not conflict with civil air traffic, as well as to avoid natural and other obstacles *en route*. From the ground, these flights were quite staggering to watch and an unforgettable spectacle – first the aircraft would appear, then came the noise as the Tu-22 sped past at a height of around 100m (328ft) and 800kph (430kts)! According to Tu-22

All that remained of a 203 TBAP Tu-22K which suffered a major engine fire at Baranovichi in 1984 after a fuel-tank explosion during engine start-up for a night-flying sortie. Remarkably, the aircraft was rebuilt under the personal supervision of Lt-Col Nikolai Rachkov, 203 TBAP deputy commander for engineering services, using a low-hour fuselage from an ex-research Tu-22K at the repair plant at Ryazan'. After two years of repairs the aircraft was restored to flying condition, completing two successful test flights in July and August 1986. Although Lt-Col Rachkov had devised a test programme for the aircraft, including supersonic flights, the Main HQ of the Soviet Air Force refused to authorise its return to service and it was handed over instead to the Moscow Institute for Civil Aviation Engineers as a ground instructional airframe. Invited by the Tupolev OKB to submit the documentation relating to the repair as a doctoral thesis, Lt-Col Rachkov rather modestly declined. *Lt-Col Nikolai Rachkov*

pilots, the aircraft 'sat tightly' (*plotno sidyel*) in the air at this speed, was very stable and was easy to control. The standard formation grouping on these low-level flights was described as '30 × 30', i.e. with a wingtip to wingtip separation of 30m (98ft) and 30m separation longitudinally. However, they often also used to fly with a '15 × 15' structure. These dense formation groupings would be flown in pairs and as a four-ship (*otryad*), the latter giving a radar return identical to that from a pair of *Blinders*. The formation leader would fly a little lower and the others a little higher, in order to have room to manoeuvre rapidly should the combat situation require it. The entire regiment (up to thirty-four aircraft) would practise flying in these dense formations; it was not just the province of one or two 'excellent' crews.

It was, evidently, the aircraft's impressive low-altitude capabilities which led the General Staff to use the Tu-22K, along with the Tu-22R, to test the readiness capability of the Soviet Union's air defence system (PVO – *Protivo-Vozdushnaya Oborona*) to repel air attacks. These simulated aggressor missions were described as 'special flights' (*spetsial'niye polyoty*) and were usually assigned to the best pilots in the regiment. Major Fut'yanov recalls his involvement in this kind of training: 'Special flights were conducted in great secrecy. They were not even announced to the regiment's personnel. One Friday evening, after the regimental parade, the regiment commander called out – "Fut'yanov and Yesen'kin – stand up!" We left the rest of our crews to wait for us in the HQ building and we went off to the regiment commander's office. There, we were given a task for the

One of the ground crew of this Tu-22K of 203 TBAP at Baranovichi marks the wing-tip with a red-painted reference mark used to assist pilots in holding formation and maintaining the required distance and interval between aircraft. Note that reference lines have already been painted on the fuselage and across the undercarriage nacelles. *Sergey Tsvetkov Collection*

Saturday morning, when we were to take off as a pair, in complete radio silence, receiving start-up clearance from the tower with a green flare from a signal pistol. I had to join up with my flight leader Yesen'kin in the circuit and head north in tight formation, maintaining total radio silence. We flew up as far as Leningrad at high altitude, then followed a route via Belomorsk, Archangel and Plesetsk, before Yesen'kin descended to 80 metres (260ft), and I went down to 100m (328ft). We then turned back towards Moscow on an extremely low-level simulated attack approach, flying unhindered as far as the MKAD (*Moskovskaya Kol'tsevaya Avtomobil'naya Doroga*) ring road, turning west when PVO fighters were sent up to intercept us, the first reaction to our flight since we took off.' Often these air defence probing flights around Moscow were combined with weapons training at a bomb range *en route*, with the Tu-22Ks taking off from their own airfields and passing over Leningrad, Petrozavodsk and Kargopol', before flying through the range at Kuz'minskoye and heading back towards Moscow.

Wartime planning called for the employment of the Tu-22K force in divisional strength (i.e. using all three regiments at the same time) against particularly important targets. Regimental and divisional-sized formations would be given fighter top cover, the fighter units involved receiving special tasking orders in the event of the outbreak of hostilities. On the approach to the target, the regimental or divisional formation would perform a 'break', to the left and right, as two separate columns of individual aircraft. Then, on the command 'All together!', they would turn so that all twenty-five aircraft (of the regiment, or seventy-five aircraft of the division) would be directed at the target. Exercises which included this type of training would never be conducted in the vicinity of areas contiguous with other, non-communist, states so as to avoid the possibly alarming concentration of a large aerial 'armada' close to the border! Therefore, training flights in the vicinity of the border with the Federal Republic of Germany would involve a time displacement for the participating units so that the first wave of activity would involve, for example, ground attack units, then fighters and then the Tu-22s, etc. Sometimes, in order to provide realistic training for different (Warsaw Pact) HQ personnel, the flights would be carried out simultaneously, but in this case a regiment of Tu-22s would only be represented by a pair of aircraft. The so-called 'mirror' profile for regiment and divisional-strength attacks was also used to practise mass raids. The basis of these 'mirror' flights was that they would be flown not towards the west or the north as they would in wartime, but instead towards the east or the south. If a mirror was then held beside the routes it would show, literally, a mirror image of the flights leading to targets in Western Europe and the North Atlantic.

The heavy bomber regiments conducted bombing training at the same ranges as used by the reconnaissance *Blinder* units, but of course they specialised in their own main combat role – that of missile carriers. Live missile launch practice with the Tu-22K and the Kh-22 (AS-4 *Kitchen*) air-launched cruise missile commenced in 1965, albeit for a comparatively small number of crews. One of the first pilots to perform a live missile release, in 1968, was the commander of 203 TBAP, Colonel Volkov. By that year, all Tu-22K regiments were fully trained in the combat application of the K-22 system (i.e. the Tu-22K aircraft and the Kh-22 missile), and the first major exercise in which they participated was Exercise *Sever* (North) in the period 21–26 June 1970. During the course of this exercise each of the *Blinder-B* regiments carried out at least one AS-4 launch. There had been some problems with mutual interference between the guidance heads of the AS-4 when the aircraft were operating in a group, but by the mid-1970s these had been eradicated. Crews from 203 TBAP at Baranovichi were the first in the Tu-22K community to achieve a group launch of the AS-4, in a five-ship formation. Live missile firings were conducted at Range 700 (*700-yi Poligon*) in the Caspian Sea, using partially submerged decommissioned naval vessels as targets, and Range 600 (*600-yi Poligon*) situated in the wilderness of the Kazakhstan steppes. However, at the end of the 1980s/early 1990s, the Caspian Sea range was closed after protesters provided evidence that the region's ecology was being seriously damaged by constant military activity. In fact, after years of routine missile launches, the land-locked Caspian Sea had become seriously polluted by unspent fuel from the missiles and fragments of the exploded missile casings. Crews were, however, still able to carry out simulated launches, using real targets, such as ships, ports, oil refineries, etc., completing all pre-launch targeting activity, but without releasing the missile from the aircraft. Such simulated launches maintained crew combat proficiency at a very high level.

The live missile rounds (but not the warheads) held in the facilities of the special engineering service (SIS – *Spetsial'naya Inzhenyernaya Sluzhba*), underwent periodic checks and maintenance. As part of the maintenance procedures, the missiles would be loaded onto the aircraft for an airborne check of their serviceability status, after which they would be returned to storage. Every five years, the stored missiles would be sent back to the designated repair plant, where they would undergo any required maintenance and their airframe life would be extended, if appropriate. During this period, the regiment would receive a new batch of missiles, but before they too were placed in operational storage, they had to undergo batch quality-control tests (KSI – *Kontrol'no-seriiniye Ispytaniya*). These involved a series of KSI test launches of missiles that were to be held in operational storage in the regiment. This normally required around ten missiles to be launched, and on successful completion of these tests, with the reliability of the consignment confirmed, the new batch would then be placed in operational storage. The regiments usually tried to combine normal live missile firing practice with the KSI series of launches, and if in a normal year a regiment carried out only two or three practice launches, then during a period of KSI testing this figure could increase by a factor of three to four. This is perhaps a convenient point at which to dispel one of the many myths surrounding the claimed toxicity of the fuel and oxidising agent used in the Kh-22 missile and often published in books whenever this weapon is discussed. Before loading onto the aircraft, the missile was fuelled and the warhead armed, but this work was always carried out by the regiment's special engineering service (SIS), in a facility located outside the airfield perimeter, some distance from the aircraft dispersal area. After readying the Kh-22 for flight, the SIS would hand it over to squadron armourers, and although it was true that the SIS engineers performed their task in special protective clothing, the squadron personnel only needed to wear normal overalls to handle the weapon. In its armed and fuelled state the Kh-22 was no more dangerous than the aircraft itself, fully loaded with aviation kerosene.

The Kh-22 was towed out to the aircraft, mounted on a special AT-22 trolley (*Avtomobil'naya Telezhka* for the Kh-22) behind a tractor, which approached the Tu-22 from behind, either on the left or the right, parallel to the axis of the fuselage at a distance of no more than 13,500mm (44.3ft) from it. Having passed the wing of the aircraft, the tractor then had to turn towards the aircraft's fuselage at an angle of 45°, approaching to within about 2 metres (just under 7ft) before turning away from the aircraft and continuing to manoeuvre until the nose of the missile was in line with the nose of the aircraft. The AT-22 was then unhitched from the tractor and the rear of the missile was lowered on the trolley. The distance from the ground to the upper cut-out for the missile's fin, after lowering the tail section, had to be no more than 1,850mm (73in). Before positioning the missile under the fuselage, the forward and rear hinged sections of the weapons-bay doors were opened inwards and the clearance was measured at fuselage Frame 36. With an aircraft weight of 80 tonnes (176,370lb) and weapons-bay doors open, the clearance at Frame 36 had to be 1,910mm (75in) and 1,850mm (73in) at Frame 60. The missile was manoeuvred backwards under the Tu-22, pushed by a loading team of five technicians manhandling the trolley, until it was in the vicinity of Frame 36. Continuing to move backwards, and with the fin of the missile aligned with the axis of the fuselage, the missile was then offered up to the BD-294 weapons pylon. Red guide-lines were painted on the right- and left-hand sides of the fuselage at Frame 36, about 400mm (15.75in) from the fuselage centreline, to assist the loading team in guiding the tail section of the missile as they manoeuvred it into position. A crew of five men could load a Kh-22 onto the Tu-22K quite rapidly, the established 'norms' being 14 minutes to achieve a rating of 'Excellent' in operational evaluations, 15 minutes for a 'Good' assessment and 17 minutes for 'Satisfactory'.

It must be noted that the ground crew team involved in loading weapons onto the Tu-22K, including the Kh-22 missile, was made up of engineers and technicians from other specialisations (trades). At first sight, this perhaps might seem to be a rather strange practice, but there was a perfectly simple explanation for it. When the regiment was brought up to one of the wartime readiness states, the engineering personnel would have to load 25 missiles onto the aircraft. Simple mathematics suggests that this would require 125 men to load 25 missiles simultaneously, and this number of specialist armourers was just not available. Consequently, one armaments specialist would be designated to head each missile-loading team, who would direct and supervise the work of his non-specialist team members. The time spent on loading the missile depended very much on the skill of the team leader, who was also responsible for steering the AT-22 into position. An experienced team leader could place the missile and trolley under the BD-294 pylon on his first attempt, despite the fact that the combat-ready missile weighed around 5,700kg (12,570lb). Training in the loading of the Kh-22 was conducted both in daylight and more frequently at night, when the entire process was complicated by the reduced visibility in the dark. However, the benefits of night training were that frequent practice in these conditions led crews to be able to load the missile virtually 'with their eyes closed'. Nevertheless, it was essential to observe a regime of increased awareness when performing a night missile loading. However, during one such event in October 1988, tragedy struck when a 203 TBAP team was loading a Kh-22 at Baranovichi at night under exercise conditions.

It was normal procedure in exercise periods for specialists from the regiment's second-line servicing section (*Tekhniko-ehkspluatatsionnaya chast'* – TEhCh) to be seconded to the squadrons to assist in missile loading. One of the experienced specialists from 203TBAP's TEhCh had been designated team leader to load a Tu-22K from the regiment's first squadron. The loading of the missile had gone well. Part of the pre-flight checks was to open the tap on the small cylinder of ammonia mounted in the weapons bay, used in the missile air-conditioning system. The tap had to be opened by the aircraft's crew chief and the action checked by the senior crew chief, but in this case it was still closed. The aircrew came out to the aircraft, climbed aboard and started the engines. The navigator prepared to raise the missile from its lowered position into the transit position,

Схемы цели, порядок работы на боевом пути и инстр. контроля

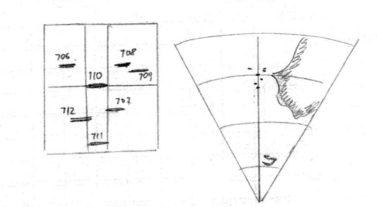

экипажу

A diagrammatic representation of the target layout at Range 700 in the Caspian Sea, located between Fort Shevchenko and the Tyulyen'i Islands (literally Seal Islands) in the upper centre of the map. The blue line defines part of the range boundary. The ship and barge targets, numbered in the 7xx series, are depicted as seen on the screen of the Tu-22K's PN radar, Target 710 being that used for missile attacks.

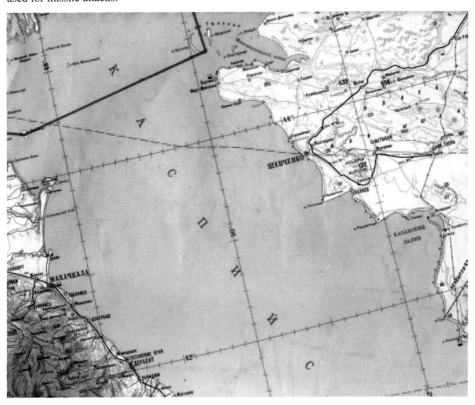

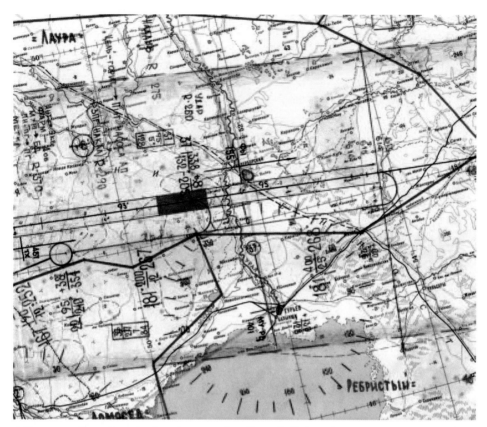

A fragment of a navigator's chart drawn up for a live missile launch at Range 600 in Kazakhstan. The yellow segment designates the guidance zone of the Kh-22, while the red sector overlaid on it designates the missile release zone and the black line inside the yellow area is the Tu-22K's flight (left to right) towards the target.

and just as the hydraulic pressure was reaching the normal value to start the process the missile team leader remembered the ammonia tank and gave a hand signal to wait. The team leader thought that the senior crew chief had understood the hand signal and had passed on his 'request' to the navigator. The team leader then jumped onto the wing of the missile and started to open the tap on the ammonia tank, but at that precise moment, suspecting nothing untoward, the navigator started to raise the pylon (and missile), with the team leader trapped between the fuselage and the missile... A particular feature of the system which raised and lowered the pylon was that it was not possible to lower it from an intermediate position – it could only be lowered after it had been locked in the upper position. It must be admitted that this tragic incident was the only one ever recorded during Tu-22K operations.

The navigator of the Tu-22K had two radar screens associated with targeting the Kh-22 missile – one showing the image produced by the aircraft's PN (NATO *Down Beat*) nav-attack radar, and the other showing the image derived from the PG seeker head of the missile itself. (It will be recalled that PN stands for *Pritsel Nosityelya* – literally '[radar] sight of the carrier' and PG for *Pritsel Golovki* – or [radar] sight of the [missile] head).

When selecting the target and preparing to launch, the navigator would check the coincident alignment of the PN and PG antennae in pitch, by aligning special markers on both screens. As soon as this occurred the PG seeker head would lock onto the target and the navigator would enter the aircraft's altitude into the missile's on-board computer. The detection range in normal search mode was 370km (200nm), while the launch 'boundary' was 260km (140nm). However, the PN radar had a mode known as 'Scan 180' (*Obzor 180*) in which the antenna performed a 180-degree scan of the forward hemisphere, which enabled the detection range to be extended to 420km (226nm). After missile seeker head lock-on, there was a lapse of 30 seconds for it to be reliably confirmed by illumination of the ASTs (*Avtomaticheskoye Soprovozhdyeniye Tseli*) warning light. This was then followed by preparation to launch the missile, although no further actions would be performed by the navigator if the launch was to be simulated (i.e. *takticheskii pusk*). If it was to be a live launch, the missile's batteries would be connected and the electrical supply would be switched to 'autonomous'. On some Tu-22Ks the BD-294 weapons pylon was lowered automatically, but on the remainder the navigator would perform this operation manually from a control panel in his cockpit. On completion of all preparatory activity, the navigator would report to the pilot: 'Ready to launch' and on the pilot's command the missile would be released.

In the event of malfunction of the PN radar on the approach to the target, the Kh-22 could be launched using the 'PG Scan' (*Obzor PG*) mode, where targeting was performed solely using the PG radar, albeit with the penalty of a reduction in detection range. After separation from the pylon, the missile would briefly maintain the same speed as the Tu-22K, until ignition of the liquid propellant rocket motor in initial acceleration mode about 3 seconds after release. At the same time, the ventral fin of the missile would be lowered into the flight position, the warhead would be primed and the autopilot programme switched on. Around 11 seconds after release, the missile's flight controls would be activated according to the required pre-programmed trajectory and it would commence a steep climb, although the missile would first sink about 500–700m

A pair of Tu-22Ks performs a low fly-by over Machulishchi at around 15–20m (50–70ft). Such low-level flights were often performed by Tu-22 crews, albeit at a slightly higher level (around 80–150m/260–500ft), but usually in manual mode, without the benefit of automatic flight control or terrain-following radar.

A 121 TBAP Tu-22KP departs from Machulishchi on a training flight, 'armed' with a Kh-22MP anti-radiation variant of the AS-4 Kitchen *missile*, identifiable from its full dielectric nose cone. *S Burdin Archive*

(1,640–2,300ft) before this occurred. Control of the missile's heading would be taken over by the PG guidance head electronics 25 seconds after release, while continuing to accelerate and climb. After reaching a velocity of Mach 3.44, the booster rocket motor would be shut down and the flight would continue on the cruise motor alone. The climb angle would be reduced and a flatter trajectory adopted, with simultaneous triggering of the altitude control channel. On reaching its assigned cruising altitude of 22,500m (73,820ft), the Kh-22 would make the transition to horizontal flight. When the sighting angle between the missile and the target was 30°, at a distance of 60km (32.4nm) from the target, course guidance of the missile would cease. At this point, the altitude channel would be shut down, along with the rocket motor, while a 'temporary programme mechanism' would be triggered to put the missile into a dive. After 20 seconds (counted

A 121 TBAP Tu-22K with a Kh-22PSI missile seen during one of the frequent (monthly) training sessions where the weapon was loaded onto the aircraft as part of the ground crew training programme.

by the temporary programme mechanism), pitch and heading guidance would be taken over again by the PG seeker head, and on reaching the target, the warhead would detonate at a pre-set distance. Emergency release (jettison) of the missile could be carried out from both the raised, transit position, as well as with the pylon in the lowered position. However, the releasing it in the transit position at a speed greater than Mach 0.9 and with sideslip angles greater than 2° could result in the missile hitting the fuselage.

It must be admitted that the reliability of the PN radar on the Tu-22K was not particularly high, and there were cases where missile launches had to be abandoned because of radar malfunctions. However, this was more a reflection of the poor level of professionalism of the navigator than the poor reliability of the radar. In fact, the navigator had a number of options for launching the missile, and if he was sufficiently well trained, then more often than not he would be able to overcome any such difficulties. The maximum number of live launches was achieved at the end of the 1980s, with 203 TBAP launching a total of 22 missiles in 1989. Only two years before this, Major Mikhailov and his crew from 203 TBAP achieved the first supersonic launch of a Kh-22 in the USSR. The *Blinder-B* regiments often used to carry out a task known as 'Flight through two ranges' (*Polyot cherez dva poligona*), using a training route to the Black Sea which passed through two of the region's bombing ranges – Kherson, and Kalinovka, situated 25km (15.5 miles) north east of Dzhankoi on the Crimean Peninsula. After working the ranges they would fly as far as the central area of the Black Sea, but taking care not to infringe Turkish airspace, approaching only to within about 40–50km (25–30 miles) of the Turkish coast. Whenever a NATO carrier-led force was in the North Sea, the *Blinder-B* regiments would take the opportunity to practise strikes against these naval formations. This would usually involve 121 TBAP from Machulishchi, which would deploy to Olenegorsk on the Kola Peninsula, or 203 TBAP from Baranovichi, deploying to the naval airfield at Severomorsk. From their deployment bases they would depart to the North Sea, going 'round the corner' just off northern Norway, where they would be 'met' and escorted by Norwegian fighters. Having carried out their simulated attacks on the carrier group, they would return via a standard waypoint off Spitzbergen, and then, when abeam Franz Josef Land, they would set course for Olenegorsk or Severomorsk, as appropriate. After rest and refuelling, they would return to their home bases in Byelorussia.

It appears that the success of the Tu-22 as a major weapon had turned the heads of military theorists in the upper echelons of Soviet Air Force HQ, and new formation groupings were often being dreamed up, but the biggest novelty was to consider using the Tu-22 as a ground attack aircraft! It was suggested that the aircraft's defensive tail cannon could be used to destroy ground targets, and crews started to train regularly in this role in 1976. Before this, of course, Tu-16 crews had also developed the technique of firing at ground targets, with their tail guns. One of the section commanders of 121 TBAP, Major Serikov, recalls the introduction of this rather surprising combat innovation for the Tu-22: 'The cannon was really essential for us to be able to fire anti-radiation and infra-red flare shells, to create a sort of defensive chaff or decoy flare barrier. And now suddenly we were expected to hit targets with it on the range. At a speed of 500kph (270kts) and from 100m (328ft) the airborne operator had to find the target, direct the cannon, fire off a burst of shells and, of course, hit the target.... Nevertheless, we'd been given the task and we had to carry it out. It was written into the training plan. At the time, there was still snow on the ground on our nearest range, so there was little danger of causing a forest fire with our cannon fire. In summer, we mostly used the range at Kherson, which was essentially

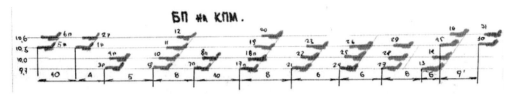

Various formation groupings were practised by Tu-22 crews and the diagram represents a 31-aircraft formation in which the Tu-22s were stacked between 9,700 and 10,600m (31,825–34,775ft). The strike groups (otryady, or sections) followed each other with a 6-10 minute interval. The number with a letter alongside the aircraft symbol indicates the number of the aircraft in the formation and the variant – K for Tu-22K, P for Tu-22P and R for Tu-22R. After passing the 'front line', or the enemy air defence identification zone, the formation could tighten up so that the distance between the aircraft could be reduced to around 30–50m (100–165ft).

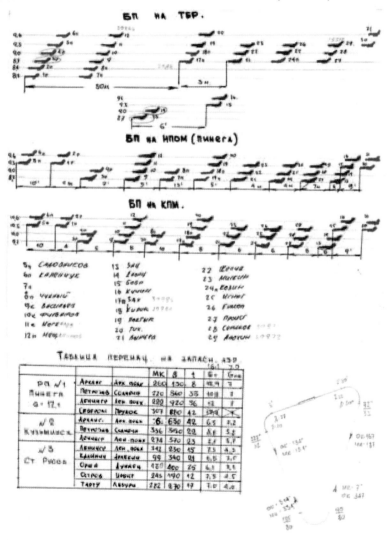

a sandy range. On the first occasion, we tried firing once, then twice, but did not destroy the target and wondered what we could do next. I approached the range and along with the navigator started to look for the target. We eventually found it, and when the target appeared below us I gave the command to the airborne operator (who controlled the cannon): "Permission to open fire." The cannon was in the correct position, with the barrels depressed, and he counted down "One, two, three" and then fired. The range controller called us and said: "I observe your fire." Basically, if you hit the range you got a score of "Excellent"!' The cannon firing practice only ceased in 1991, and the training had been very intensive up to then over a period of fifteen years. The maximum number of practice firings was carried out by 203 TBAP in 1989, with a total of forty-five sessions recorded.

Although optimised as a missile carrier, the Tu-22K could also used be used for freefall bombing, although most crews would affirm that it was not particularly well suited to the task. There were no problems when bombing visually identifiable targets, since the aircraft had the same OPB-15 bomb-sight as the Tu-22R, but when using the PN radar, it was quite a different story. The main problem resided in the fact that the PN radar was designed for long-range targeting of the Kh-22 missile, which was, itself, a long-range weapon, whereas bombing was carried out from a much shorter range and was much less accurate. Nevertheless, bombing was a regular feature of Tu-22K training and could be performed at both subsonic and supersonic speed, the first supersonic bomb release in ordinary squadron service being recorded in 1965. This was performed by Lt-Col Osadchii and his crew (Lt-Col Osadchii was the commander of the second squadron of Baranovichi-based 203 TBAP), using the range at Kuz'minskoye, 85km (53 miles) from Cherepovets in the Vologda region. Conversion of the Tu-22K from missile carrier to pure

Tu-22KD on ramp – A somewhat formal line-up of ground crew of 203 TBAP at Baranovichi in front of their Tu-22K, reporting the aircraft's serviceability state to the squadron engineering officer. Day-to-day operations were considerably less formal than this. *Sergey Tsvetkov Collection*

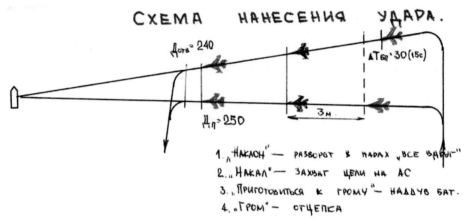

A navigational plot for a regimental strength attack by Tu-22Ks on a surface target, drawn up by navigator Captain Konyryev. On the command 'Slope' [NAKLON (HAKΛOH)], the regiment would make a turn in pairs 'All at once' [VSE VDRUG (BCEBΔPyΓ)] and target the ship. On the signal 'Prepare for Grom' [PRIGOTOVIT'SYA K GROMU (ΠPNΓOTOBNT6C& K ΓPOMY)], the codeword [meaning 'thunder'] for missile release, the navigators would set the *Kitchen* missiles' batteries to 'super charge' [nadduv] and on the command 'Grom' [ΓPOM] they would launch the Kh-22 missiles. Intervals between strike groups were 3 minutes and break-away from the target was carried out at around 240–250km (130–135nm)

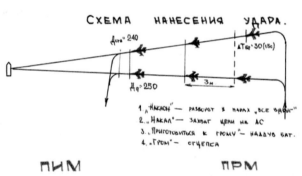

ПИМ

40ᴀ	100ᴀ	120ᴏ	120ᴏ	100ᴏ	40ᴏ
332	292	32	272	32	292	332

КАРСАВА - АЛУКСНЕ
V= 850 ß=30° S=76км t=6,50

ПРМ

60ᴀ	150ᴀ	180ᴏ	180ᴏ	150ᴏ	60ᴀ
282	342	192	12	192	342	282

БЫХМА - ХААПСАЛУ
V 1000км/ч ß=40° S 86.6 t= 8,12

ТАБЛИЦА ПЕРЕНАЦЕЛИВАНИЯ

РУБЕЖ	АЭРОДРОМ	ОК	S	t	G
СОВЕТСК	СОЛЬЦЫ	56	620	36	18.0
	ШЯУЛЯЙ	47	150	8	12,1
	КАЛИНИНГРАД	259	105	6	11.3
	ОСТРОВ	25	480	28	9.0
КПМ	БАРАНОВИЧИ	254	125	8	5,8
	БОБРУЙСК	124	130	8	5,8
	ОЗЕРНОЕ	164	410	24	7.8
	ОРША	86	190	13	6,3

bomber was a time-consuming and arduous task for the ground crew, so an 'interim fit' was developed, involving partial conversion so that small-calibre practice bombs could be dropped. This could be carried out in a few hours by squadron ground crew. Full conversion required the removal of the special BD-294 pylon for the Kh-22 missile, plus all other missile-associated equipment in the weapons bay, and required a whole day for completion. Conversion for bombing also required the bomb-sight to be installed in the navigator's cockpit, and the weapons-bay doors had to be made to open outwards, instead of inwards when armed with the Kh-22. For these reasons, one or two Tu-22Ks were usually maintained in the regiments as pure bombers, and 121 TBAP at Machulishchi had two such aircraft, one of which (Bort 16; c/n 1204) was among the oldest airframes in the division. These aircraft were used whenever pure bombing missions were planned, but still had to be converted back to missile carriers when the regiment was placed on operational alert.

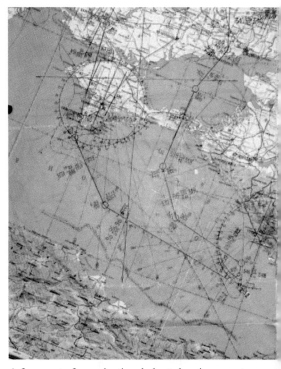

A fragment of a navigational chart showing a route flown by 290 ODRAP from Zyabrovka over the Black Sea. The small circles on the track lines are waypoints. Note the precisely defined line marking the boundary of Turkey's territorial waters.

The Tu-22KP and the Kh-22MP anti-radiation missile

After years of operation of the Kh-22 air-launched cruise missile (ALCM) on the Tu-22K *Blinder-B*, the missile was selected to be the basis for a long-range anti-radiation missile (ARM) for use against threat radar systems of potential adversaries. The development, designated Kh-22MP (*Protivo-radiolokatsionnaya* – for anti-radar), was put through service acceptance trials by Baranovichi-based 203 TBAP in 1982, with practice launches taking place at Range 600 (*600-yi Poligon*) in Kazakhstan. Since the Tu-22KP did not have the range to operate over Kazakhstan from Baranovichi, Poltava was chosen as the temporary operating base for the trials and also had personnel who were familiar with the Kh-22. Initially, three Tu-22KPs were involved in the tests, this figure later being increased to six aircraft. The senior navigator of 203 TBAP, Major Shatov, was appointed as chief engineer-navigator for the trials, which also included an engineer from the Red Banner State Scientific Research Institute of the Air Force named for Valery Chkalov and a representative from industry. Before carrying out a test launch, each missile was test flown under a Tu-22KP over Range 600 to carry out pre-launch checks. After two such pre-launch test flights the Kh-22MP was cleared for a live launch, and in the course of the test series a total of eleven missiles were launched. After each launch, the engineers and navigators would work long into the night, discussing ways of improving the missile's guidance system. During the trials, a curious incident occurred, involving Lt-Col Ignatov and Major Shatov after one of their routine launches.

The deputy commander of 203 TBAP was controller of flying at the range and he had authorised the launch of one of the Kh-22MP missiles. After launch, the missile followed an accurate course towards the target. However, after a short time, the range controller questioned the crew about the flight of the missile, since the ground radars had lost it on their screens. After each launch, the aircraft usually accompanied the missile for about 60km (33nm), but in this case the missile had initially disappeared below the aircraft, then, after motor ignition, started to climb from under the nose of the Tu-22KP, with a characteristic white smoke trail. After it had made the transition to horizontal flight it was lost to sight and the aircraft had turned away to return to Poltava. The missile recovery team reconnoitred the target area by helicopter and found metal fragments of the missile, including some with part of the factory construction batch number. The enquiry team concluded that it must have been an 'anomalous' launch, but as the missile had fallen back onto range territory, then everything was OK. However, on the following day, someone phoned the range HQ from a nearby village, asking that the 'pole which the military had forgotten' be taken away. A group of personnel was dispatched from the range, and when they got to an area about 4km (2.5 miles) from the village they could see the Kh-22MP, standing vertically with its nose buried in the soft sandy earth, like a telegraph pole.

The missile was completely intact and it was possible for engineers to determine what had gone wrong during the flight! It turned out that the missile's height corrector had failed, giving false data to the AP-22 autopilot. In normal operation, the missile would make the transition to horizontal flight at about 22,000–25,000m (72,180–82,020ft), and continue in horizontal flight until the autopilot tipped it into a dive onto the target at an angle of 52°. Since the height corrector on this missile had failed, the missile continued to climb and eventually reached an altitude of 80,000m (262,500ft), where, because the aerodynamics of the missile had not been designed for flight in such rarefied conditions, it stalled and fell back to earth. As it fell, the seeker head of the missile again locked onto the target, and the controlling 'automatics' initiated another climb as if attacking the target using the normal attack profile. The missile climbed once more to 80,000m and again stalled and fell 'out of the sky', only to have the whole sequence repeated when it again locked onto the target radar on the range. When it had climbed to 80,000m for the fourth time, the motor eventually ran out of fuel. The launch had been made at a range of 480km (260nm) from the target, but having already flown this distance, it did a further 124km (67nm) during the repeated ballistic climbs and descents. It landed empty, without suffering much damage, and buried itself almost vertically in the sand. All the other launches were normal and the Kh-22MP was cleared for service.

Introduction of the K-22P integrated missile system (i.e. the Tu-22KP aircraft, the target-detection system and the Kh-22MP missile) was an interesting innovation for the Tu-22-equipped heavy bomber regiments, adding another task to their normal operations. This task was to carry out electronic intelligence (Elint) gathering against potential adversaries, using the LO-17 (*Kurs-N*) targeting system of the Kh-22MP missile, not for its primary purpose, but as a wide-band Elint receiver. The Tu-22KP variant of the *Blinder-B*, which carried the LO-17 system, equipped each of the second squadrons of 121 TBAP (Machulishchi), 203 TBAP (Baranovichi) and 341 TBAP (Ozyornoye) and performed their 'radio-technical reconnaissance' (i.e. Elint) flights along the borders between the Warsaw Pact states and NATO and other European countries. The flights were called 'Catapult Flights' (*Polyoty na Katapul'tu*), '*Katapul'ta*' being the callsign of the Soviet Air Force air traffic controller for the northern sector of the former East Germany, and were usually conducted in pairs. The aircraft would take off from their home bases and head towards the Baltic Sea, turning left to fly along the coast until reaching Sassnitz on Rügen Island, just off the East German coast. Here, they would turn south and switch on their Elint-collection equipment, flying down the entire length of the East/West German border, continuing as far as the south of Yugoslavia and taking in part of northern Greece. The *Blinders* would then turn and head for home. The flights were conducted at 9,000m (29,530ft) and the crews would remain in radio silence throughout, although the controllers at base would perform a continuous 'flight watch' on the leader, monitoring any attempts by other ATC controllers to determine what type of aircraft they were flying. The objective of the flights was for the navigator to use the Kurs-N system to determine the operating parameters of all threat emitters (radars) of the potential adversary (i.e. NATO countries) along that route.

The pair of Tu-22KPs would turn onto an operating radar and fly towards it until the navigator of the lead aircraft had recorded all its parameters. The operator of the threat emitter would often try to change the RF (radio frequency) or pulse duration (about five or six parameters could change), and the navigator needed time to 'fix' all of these for a successful 'intercept'. According to the operating principles observed by the Soviet Union for flights close to State borders, all routes had to avoid sectors which took the aircraft to less than 50km (31 miles) from the border, and to avoid approach angles to a State border greater than 30°. (In the case of these '*Katapul'ta*' flights, the State border should also be taken to include the borders of the Warsaw Pact countries involved.) Apart from this, it was also stipulated that 90° turns within a zone 75km (47 miles) from the border were not permitted. However, when carrying out 'special flights' not much attention was paid to the 'rules'. Consequently, the special *Blinder-B* flights often penetrated West German airspace by as much as 50, 60, 70 and 80km (i.e. between about 30 and 50 miles). After the navigator had captured all essential parameters of a given threat system, the pilot of the Tu-22KP would engage full afterburner and return to his 'own' side of the border to continue his flight. As soon as the navigator picked up another threat emitter, he would take a DF (direction finding) bearing, the aircraft would turn onto the new target and the whole procedure would be repeated. Only the lead aircraft of the pair engaged in Elint collection, while the wingman looked after navigation for both crews, since it was imperative for them to know exactly where they were at any given time when dodging back and forth across the border.

The wingman would alert the lead crew about how far into foreign territory they had 'strayed', and it was hardly surprising that the Tu-22KP crews frequently encountered NATO fighters on these flights, trying to prevent the *Blinders* from penetrating their airspace. In classic 'cat and mouse' style, the closer the Tu-22KP approached the border, the closer would approach the fighter, and if the *Blinder* turned away from the border, so would the intercepting fighter. There were occasions when the wingman was followed by NATO fighters for about 250–300km (135–160nm). The Federal Republic of Germany took a special interest in these intelligence-collection flights, particularly after the US Army deployed its Pershing-2 missiles on its territory. The Pershing-2 launchers had been moved up to the border, and it was quite easy for the Tu-22KP crews to find them. It was hardly surprising that these missions were called 'special flights' in the regiments, since the crews were never told about the take-off times in advance and were never told of the results of the intelligence collection afterwards! Following an Elint sortie, officers from the Main Intelligence Directorate (*Glavnoye Razvyedyvatyel'noye Upravlyenie* – GRU) of the Soviet Ministry of Defence would take away all the intelligence material collected on the flight. No record of the flights would ever remain in the regiment – all flight recorder data, navigation charts and the navigator's flight log would be taken away by the GRU. (The GRU was, and still is, the foreign-intelligence-gathering organ of the Russian Ministry of Defence, with a much wider sphere of activity than, for example, the United States Defense Intelligence Agency, its nearest equivalent.) The flights were deemed so important that they would sometimes take place when the weather was otherwise totally unsuitable for flying. One such flight was carried out by a pair of Tu-22KPs on a snow-laden winter day when there was no time to clear the main runway properly, and a small snow-clearing machine was used simply to clear a path for the aircrafts' nose-wheels. The two Tu-22s took off in practically zero visibility and landed at Nezhin in the Ukraine after their mission, all Byelorussian airfields being closed because of heavy snow showers.

The Tu-22 in the Afghan campaign
Soviet Tu-22s did not participate in actual combat missions, but a small number of Tu-22P *Blinder-E* electronic jammers did play a small part in supporting offensive operations over Afghanistan during the final months of Soviet occupation of that country. This was in 1988, when the 'Limited Contingent of Soviet Forces in Afghanistan' was preparing to withdraw after almost ten years of bitter and inconclusive combat there. The Long-range Air Force had been given the task of covering the withdrawal, carrying out bombing raids along the withdrawal route, to clear the way and provide safe passage for Soviet troops heading back to Russia. The aircraft selected for the bombing missions were Tu-22M3 *Backfire-Cs* of 185 TBAP, based at Poltava and Tu-16 *Badgers* from Belaya Tserkov' in the Ukraine. The actual missions were carried out from Mary-2 airfield in the Turkmenistan Soviet Socialist Republic and were initially unsupported insofar as stand-off jamming was concerned. However, after a number of successful operations had been carried out, Pakistan began to take an interest in the missions, and Pakistan Air Force F-16 fighters became a potential threat to the Soviet bombers. Consequently, it was decided to provide stand-off jamming support with a small number of Tu-22PDs. The first group of four *Blinder-Es*, from 341 TBAP at Ozyornoye, arrived at Mary-2 in October 1988. Their task was to suppress Pakistani radio-technical and radar systems (i.e. ground-based Elint and guidance radars) which could aid Pakistani Air Force F-16 attacks on the Soviet bombers in the Afghani-Pakistan border region. The third squadron of 203 TBAP at Baranovichi was designated to be the next group to prepare for deployment to Mary-2. Both 341 TBAP and 203 TBAP were well versed in this procedure, having operated frequently from other bases in the north and the south of the Soviet Union. The regiment engineering personnel had already prepared special 'pack-ups' of spares and equipment for daily maintenance and emergency repairs 'in the field', which were known in the Air Force as 'technical first-aid kits' (*tekhnicheskaya aptechka*). The group from 203 TBAP had begun to prepare for deployment in November, but did not actually leave until December 1988, having been delayed by several changes to the operational plan. The delays lasted for a month and a half before the aircraft were finally cleared to depart Baranovichi for Mary-2, with a planned intermediate stop-over at Poltava because of the great distance involved.

The Tu-22PD aircrews themselves performed the turn-round servicing and refuelling of the aircraft, whereas previously it had always been necessary to fly-in support personnel on a transport aircraft to carry out these tasks whenever an aircraft diverted to a different airfield. However, over a period of time, it was decided to train the aircrew to service and refuel the aircraft themselves, if they had to operate out of another base, the procedure being known as 'autonomous servicing'. Regiment engineering personnel prepared special reference cards for this task called 'Instruction cards for the turn-round of the aircraft by aircrew' (*Kartochki podgotovki samolyota k povtornomu vylyetu silami lyotnovo ehkipazha*). The card was always kept in a pencil pouch on the right-hand panel of the pilot's cockpit, which also contained another instruction card dealing with refuelling the aircraft – the 'Aircraft Refuelling Table'. The table defined the quantity of fuel which had to be pumped into each tank, dependent upon the total fuel uplift for a given task. Crews practised these procedures as part of their normal training, usually on a Monday, which was also usually a designated non-flying day (*parkovyi dyen'*), the training being conducted by the regiment's engineering personnel. During an 'autonomous' turn-round, the airborne operator would connect up the APA to provide electrical power to start the engines, meet the refuelling bowser and check the fuel for the presence of sediment or contaminants, ensure that the aircraft was earthed and then carry out the refuelling. The navigator looked after the recharging of the oxygen system, checked the levels of hydraulic fluid and the fluids required in the air-conditioning system. The pilot was mainly occupied with supervising the work of the other two crew members, as well as the lowering and raising of the ejection seats. The crews were well trained in autonomous turn-round procedures, and the only procedure which required outside assistance was in the closing and locking of the pilot's entry hatch, a task usually performed by one of the base's technical personnel. These procedures were employed when the Tu-22PDs made their transit stop at Poltava in December 1988. When the transport aircraft with the engineering support team from Baranovichi landed at Poltava, the Tu-22PDs had already gone, having performed their 'autonomous' turn-round and continued on to Mary-2. [*Although not stated here, it seems surprising that the support team did not know that the Tu-22 aircrew were to perform their own turn-round at Poltava!* AD]

On arrival at Mary-2, the Tu-22PD group found themselves immediately on a war footing, even though they were some distance from the actual combat zone. The airfield had previously housed various marks of Su-17 *Fitter* swing-wing fighter-bombers, and the base was littered with containers used to transport these aircraft back to the USSR by rail, as well as hundreds of spent shell cases from their cannon. Mary-2 was the staging post for many of the Soviet Air Force units going to and returning from Afghanistan, and aircraft and helicopters were landing almost continuously, transporting personnel and equipment in both directions. The first operational sortie for the Tu-22PDs was planned for three or four hours after their arrival at Mary-2, the aircrew changing immediately into camouflaged flight overalls, which at that time were not normally issued to 46th Army units. (The 46th Air Army of the Supreme High Command, with its HQ in Smolensk, was the Soviet Air Force's controlling authority for the *Blinders* based at Baranovichi.) The remainder of the group, therefore, had to work in their standard blue-grey overalls. The aircrew were issued with a personal weapon (a sub-machine gun) and two grenades, carrying out some practice firings that same day to calibrate the sights. After this, they did not fly without their weapons on any operational task. During this same period, the bomber units had also undergone a hand-over, and Mary-2 now housed ten Tu-22M3

Backfire-C bombers of 840 TBAP from Sol'tsy and ten Tu-22M3s of 405 TBAP from Balbasovo, near Orsha in Byelorussia. With twenty *Backfires* available, the military planners were able to put on two sorties per day, the first being conducted between nightfall and early morning, and the second being carried out in daylight, using ten aircraft on each sortie. The greatest burden fell on the Tu-22PD crews, however, since with only four aircraft they had to cover both the night sorties and the day sorties. Rear services and technical support (i.e. vehicles, ground servicing equipment, power supplies, etc.) for the Long-range Air Force group (bombers and jammers) at Mary-2 was provided from the 'maintenance unit' at Balbasovo airfield in Byelorussia.

The system of pre-flight checks of the aircraft was 'simplified' by comparison with normal peace-time procedures in order to keep pace with the intensive use of the aircraft. Consequently, the preliminary checks established in the 'Unified operating regulations No. 22' were not used, and the following procedure was applied instead: after three days of intensive flying, the fourth day was given over to servicing and eliminating any 'snags', after which the cycle would be repeated. A more radical approach was adopted to speed up the procedure of getting the crew in and out of the aircraft. On the right-hand side of the pressure cabin of the Tu-22 there was a small 'passageway' linking the individual cockpits of the navigator, pilot and airborne operator. Rather than open all three entrance hatches, the crew chief would open only the pilot's hatch, and the other two crew members would get to their positions by crawling along this 'passageway', obviating the need to lower the other two seats. The small hard standings at Mary-2 were full of large bombers, and pilots found it very difficult to manoeuvre on the narrow taxiways, which occasionally led to 'traffic jams'. On one occasion, a Tu-22M3 suffered a nose-wheel steering malfunction and obstructed the taxiway, causing a 'traffic jam', and it took several hours before a tug could pull the unserviceable aircraft onto the other taxiway. All four Tu-22PDs were located in protected hard standings and taxied out under their own power, requiring the pilots to taxi slowly, carefully and accurately in order to avoid causing any hold-ups. All the *Blinder* pilots coped with these 'traffic' problems very well.

The first aircraft to take off on an operational sortie were the Tu-22PDs, which would head out to the target area, switch on their jammers and begin to release chaff, after which the bombers would arrive to carry out their bombing mission. The *Blinders* conducted almost the entire flight in full afterburner, at an altitude of 10,000m (32,800ft), giving a flight duration of one and a half hours with a fuel uplift of 30 tonnes (66,140lb). The main operational problem at Mary-2 was the long time required to refuel the aircraft because of the lack of bowsers, the normal procedure being to refuel the bombers first, followed by the jammers. A consequence of this was that the senior crew chief (an officer-rank engineer), responsible for refuelling his aircraft, virtually had to spend the night under the Tu-22PD. The engineers and technicians, who were accustomed to working in the rather sparse conditions of deployment bases, coped very well with the intensive work schedule at Mary-2. This was, typically, two to three hours' sleep, then a drive out to the airfield, followed by another two to three hours' sleep after seeing off the first sortie, and then more flights…. The ground crew and airborne operators of the Tu-22PD group lived on the airfield in buildings previously used as a training centre, and now converted into a small garrison. The *Backfire* aircrew of 405 TBAD lived alongside them in the same garrison; living conditions were bad, but no one paid much attention to this aspect of their involvement in the Afghanistan campaign. The Tu-22PD pilots and navigators lived in the garrison at nearby Mary-1 airfield, travelling between the two bases by bus or car.

Surprisingly, in view of the poor living conditions, there were no reported cases of sickness among the ground and air crew personnel during their stay at Mary; garlic was provided in their food rations as a prophylactic against stomach and intestinal problems. To some extent it was a blessing that the detachment took place in the winter months, when there were no flies or other insects on the airfield, thus obviating the possibility of intestinal problems caused by insect-borne ailments. The toilets were all outside, which gave rise to certain problems because of the difference between daytime and night-time temperatures! At night the temperature dropped to around –5°C, and it was impossible to wash in the morning because the tanks had frozen. It was only possible to wash and shave later in the day when the temperature had risen to around +15°C.

The commander of the Long-range Aviation bomber and ECM group at Mary-2 was the ill-fated future President of Chechnya, Colonel Dzhokar Dudayev. (*Dudayev was later [1993] believed to have been assassinated by his former Soviet Air Force colleagues in an audacious missile attack as he used a satellite phone while standing outside his field HQ in Chechnya.*) Every three days, on the day appointed for aircraft servicing, Col Dudayev would organise a general parade for all the bomber crews and support personnel, in which everyone was informed of the results of their collective efforts. This included the number of bombs dropped, how many targets had been destroyed and their type, etc. The Long-range Air Force group was subordinate to a combined HQ located at Tashkent in Uzbekistan, under the command of General Varennikov, who was later to take part in the notorious *putsch* of 1991, which led to the downfall of Mikhail Gorbachev. The HQ at Tashkent issued all the tasking orders for the group, and all data relating to the employment of the group's assets were also sent back to Tashkent. Col Dudayev personally selected the attack locations for each of the tasks assigned to each unit. A number of engineers from the divisional HQ worked alongside the Tu-22PD group personnel at Mary-2, and representatives from the 46th Air Army HQ at Smolensk would also visit the base periodically to 'keep an eye on its work'. At the end of 1988, intelligence reports indicated that Mujahideen groups were planning to infiltrate the air base at Mary-2. Since the airfield was only 150km (93 miles) from the Afghan border, it was decided to provide a defensive cordon around the base, with motor rifle troops carrying out patrols in armoured personnel carriers.

Tu-22PD operations over Afghanistan provided crews with another headache in that they had been given the task of carrying out bomb-damage assessment photography in addition to their primary task. Had they been permanently based at Mary there would have been no problem with this, since the crews were at least familiar with aerial photography as part of the syllabus in their 'Basic Training Requirements' exercises. However, because aerial photography was performed rather infrequently, the film which was already loaded in the cameras of the Tu-22PD was not really suitable for use at this time of year, operating in mountainous terrain, and had, moreover, reached the end of its 'shelf life'. Obviously, in preparing for this particular detachment, no one had foreseen the need to use the Tu-22PD for photo-recce, and the quality of the initial photographs taken in the first few days was rather poor. The quality of photography was also degraded further by a particular feature of operating out of Mary-2 airfield. The airfield was situated in a muddy, desert locality and designed primarily to handle lightweight, fighter-sized aircraft. Intensive use of the taxiways and runway by the Long-range Air Force *Backfires* and *Blinders* led to the mud under the concrete slabs oozing out in periods of heavy rainfall, producing a thick film of liquid mud over the entire operating surface of the airfield. Consequently, when the

Blinders were taxiing or rolling down the runway, their undersides were sprayed with mud from the nose-wheels, which also covered the optically clear windows of the cameras located in the first accessories compartment behind the nose-wheel compartment. As a result of this, the cameras were unable to function properly, but a comparatively simple solution was soon found, when engineers removed the windows. Since the camera lens was positioned some distance above the cut-out for the window, the absence of protective glazing was not a problem because the mud did not enter the compartment. Also, by this time, the necessary replacement film had been flown in from Baranovichi, and when the aircraft were equipped with the new film and operating with 'open' camera hatches, the quality of the images improved considerably.

Unfortunately, the Tu-22PD suffered a very high equipment malfunction rate during operations out of Mary-2. Unlike the other Tu-22 variants, the Tu-22P and PD had an entirely different electrical power supply system, with each generator supplying a specific group of ECM transmitters. In view of the intensive and virtually constant use of the transmitters during flight, the generators were subjected to very high loads and would frequently trip 'off line'. There was nothing really unusual about the Tu-22PD operations over Afghanistan, but this was the first time that they had been used on this scale, so intensively and for such long uninterrupted periods of time. For this reason, the electrical equipment specialists had a fairly heavy workload compared with other aircraft tradesmen, and in the periods between flights they could often be seen crawling over the engines of the Tu-22PD, changing the electrical brushes on the engine-mounted generators. The experience and knowledge accumulated by the ground crews when working out of deployment airfields, with limited base facilities, greatly assisted them in eliminating operational 'snags'. However, the 'technical first-aid kits' which the ground crew brought with them from Baranovichi were also a great help in this respect. If the need arose for a specific spare part (e.g. generators, ECM transmitters, etc.) then these were flown in on an An-12 or Il-76 transport from base. Field servicing and repairs were carried out with the highest level of competence within the group, but full maintenance was always carried out back at base. If this became necessary, as an aircraft approached a specific servicing check (e.g. a 100-hour check), then a change-over of aircraft was organised. A replacement aircraft would be flown in from Baranovichi and the same crew would fly the other aircraft back for servicing.

Another problem surfaced during the deployment to Mary-2, this time arising from the fact that the aircrew had to carry personal weapons with them in the cockpit. In view of the fact that the cockpit of the Tu-22 was narrow and that all three crew members used the pilot's entry hatch to speed-up entrance and egress in operational conditions, their personal weapons would often damage the cockpit lighting as they crawled in and out. There was no special place to hang up the weapons (sub-machine guns), and they were usually hung up wherever possible. Consequently, there were frequent occasions when a weapon would switch off a piece of equipment as it swung back and forth on its lanyard during flight. The former head of second-line servicing (i.e. the TEhCh) on 203 TBAP at the time, Major Igor' Kozlov, recalls these problems: 'I once spent a rest day (*parkovyi dyen'*) checking the lighting and warning lamps, and it turned out that many of them had been smashed. In spite of this, the pilots didn't pay much attention to it, saying that there was no time [to repair them].' In the initial period of the deployment, support struts for the undercarriage doors would also often get damaged during landing because the concrete runway panels had been loosened (causing excessive vibrations in the undercarriage) and replacements had to be made in the airfield workshops. Another trade group which experienced a heavy workload during the deployment were the ECM specialists, responsible for servicing, pre- and post-flight checks and repair of the Tu-22PD's jamming systems. The post-flight checks required the technicians to remove the large equipment crate and check the ECM transmitters, an arduous task as some of the individual equipment weighed around 20kg (44lb) and access was difficult. The armourers were responsible for servicing and reloading the APP-22 chaff and flare dispensers, and one of the protected hard standings was converted into a loading area for this purpose. The head of this reloading team was an armaments specialist, but the other technicians were from all other trades. The teams for this task had been established for many years and each member knew his particular responsibilities when working at a deployment base. All other available personnel were also seconded to help with unloading bombs for the *Backfire* units, from containers which were delivered to the airfield on a regular basis by military supply trains.

The first and largest group from 203 TBAP was deployed to Mary-2 for one and a half months, from December 1988 to January 1989, and the New Year was 'seen in' on the base, but was not celebrated as the special holiday it would have been at home. Personnel were able to make phone calls to loved ones at home and there was the opportunity of going into Mary town, but flying operations still remained at a fairly high level. Col Dudayev had decided that it might be an effective operational tactic to carry out a strike on Mujahideen positions during the night of 31 December/1 January. However, he had overlooked the fact that since they were Muslims, they would not be celebrating the New Year at the same time, and the 'holiday present' he had planned for them was, therefore, rather pointless! Consequently, it was decided instead to designate 31 December and 1 January as rest days for the *Backfire* and *Blinder* group. A second 203 TBAP group arrived in January 1989 and stayed there until the end of the occupation of Afghanistan. By this time the intensity of operations had abated and the objective of the bombings had shifted north, to the area around the Salang Pass, which did not require ECM support from the Tu-22PDs. So, for this reason, the last *Blinder-Es* were sent back to their base at Baranovichi in February 1989. All the support equipment and personnel were loaded onto Il-76 *Candid* transports and flown initially to Balbasovo in Byelorussia and then on to Baranovichi, bringing the *Blinder's* brief, but nevertheless valuable, contribution to the contentious Afghan campaign to an end.

An embarrassing error
We have already mentioned, in the chapter dealing with the Tu-22R, the importance of crew cooperation on the *Blinder* and the value of flying as part of a constituted crew over a long period of time. A no less important factor in crew cooperation was the matter of honesty and integrity between the three members of the *Blinder's* crew, each of whom had a specific role to play and on whom the fate of all three depended. This obviously applies to all military flight operations, but the Tu-22 was quite different in the sense that all three crew members sat in isolation from each other, whereas on the Tu-16, for example, all four flight-deck crew could see each other. If necessary, they could provide mutual assistance and advice and monitor one another's actions, particularly if an error had been committed. A particularly unfortunate example of the latter occurred in 1983 on 203 TBAP at Baranovichi, for many years one of the best units in the Long-range Air Force. In the summer of that year the regiment was taking part in a routine exercise, during which two crews were designated to carry out live missile firing at Range 600 in Kazakhstan, while the remainder of the regiment were involved in simulated launches. The targets for those carrying out simulated launches were, as usual, the offshore oil rigs

forming the artificial island complex of Neftyaniye Kamni in the Caspian Sea, some distance from the Azerbaijani capital, Baku. Since the oil rigs showed up on radar rather like the masts of naval vessels, the *Blinders* operated against them as if they were ships. Having taken off from Baranovichi and completed the first phase of the exercise, with live firings at Range 600 and simulated attacks on Neftyaniye Kamni, the regiment's Tu-22Ks landed at Mozdok in North Ossetia for rest and refuelling. After refuelling, the aircraft were to take off on the return leg to Baranovichi at 24.00hrs, with a planned landing time at base of 04.00hrs in the morning, which would mark the end of the exercise.

The pre-take-off orders were issued to the crews in accordance with instructions, and the take-off heading was given to the navigators. However, when the entire regiment started to taxi out for take-off, the controller of aircraft at Mozdok informed all crews via the regiment commander, Lt-Col Tatarchenko, that the take-off course had been changed to the reciprocal heading (i.e. 180° opposite). All the navigators then inserted the new heading in their navigation computers and the aircraft took off using the new data. However, one Tu-22K flown by Major Mikhail Chizhov and his crew took off and set course in the opposite direction to that which would take them back to Baranovichi. His navigator had failed to insert the new heading in the aircraft's TsNVU-B-1B navigation computer, which had then started to calculate the entire route based on an incorrect orthodromic (Great Circle) course. Somewhere around the half-way point on the route the navigator realised that they were flying in the wrong direction, but because of fear of embarrassment and his weak personal qualities he did not admit his error to the crew. One can scarcely imagine what this navigator hoped the outcome to be! The Tu-22K eventually commenced the descent for landing, assuming that they were approaching the town of Baranovichi. When the aircraft broke through the clouds, the radar operator saw mountains and was the first to inform the crew that they had made a navigation error. However, the aircraft commander had already noticed that the sun was beginning to rise on the opposite side from where he expected it to be! It should be mentioned at this point that all the regiments used to fly 'radio silent' during exercises, but on this occasion the radar operator broke the rules and started to call on all available channels, albeit in vain, since no one responded. Eventually, in response to countless calls, the crew heard a voice saying: 'This is Mary-2, who is calling?' The airfield had joint civil-military status and at the time housed a regiment of swing-wing Su-17 *Fitter* fighter bombers. The Tu-22 pilot informed Mary-2 that he was very low on fuel and had to make an immediate landing, the ATC controller authorising this without hesitation.

On landing, the *Blinder-B* slightly damaged the runway surface, which had not been designed to take heavy aircraft, and immediately after leaving the aircraft, Major Chizhov presented the ATC controller with his watch, as a mark of gratitude for permitting them to land there. [*An interesting reversal of the well-established Soviet tradition of the pilot receiving a watch for a successful outcome in an emergency landing!* AD] At the same time, the regiment commander and Major Chizhov's squadron commander at Baranovichi had noted the absence of one of their aircraft on the first squadron's parking area. It was already five o'clock in the morning (Moscow Time), that is, some five hours after take-off, and the commanders would have deduced that the aircraft must surely have run out of fuel by then, and having heard nothing on the radio, feared the worst. When the regiment commander entered his office, there was a call on the ZAS secure telephone (*Zasekrechennaya Apparatura Svyazi*). It was from the Air Army HQ, and the regiment commander was told to seal up his safe and all flight documents. The significance of this procedure for Lt-Col Tatarchenko was that there must have been a major accident (*katastrofa*) or some other emergency. The regiment commander sealed his safe, as ordered, and locked his office, handing his seal over to the regimental chief of staff, after which Lt-Col Tatarchenko was no longer allowed back into his office. Then, at 6 o'clock in the morning the Commander of the Long-range Air Force called the regiment HQ with the surprising news that the missing Tu-22K had landed at Mary! The regiment's senior officers could not believe what they had just heard – 'How did the aircraft turn up in Central Asia?' The regiment's senior navigator, Lt-Col Shatov, took a navigation chart and drew a line from Mozdok, representing the reciprocal of the heading from there to Baranovichi, which obviously ended up in the region of Mary. It was only then that it became obvious that Major Chizhov's navigator had put the incorrect heading into the navigation computer. A commission headed by the C-in-C of the Long-range Air Force was sent to Mary to interview the crew, and then on the same day, they flew back to Moscow, where they were joined by the C-in-C of the Soviet Air Force, Marshal of Aviation Yefimov.

The investigation continued at Baranovichi, with the crew presenting a somewhat sorry sight, only the radar operator being able to hold his head high, having discharged his normal duties without fault. The direct perpetrator of the incident, the navigator, gave the impression of not understanding what was going on, but it was the pilot, Major Chizhov, who carried the greatest burden of guilt since he was responsible for the entire crew. After the investigation, Major Chizhov was demoted from his position as deputy squadron commander for political affairs (on the first squadron) and made a section commander on the third squadron. However, because he felt his honour had been besmirched he felt he was no longer able to serve, and retired from the Air Force. He moved to Lukhovitsy, just outside Moscow, where he got a job in the aircraft factory involved in building MiG fighters at the time, and where he had worked in his youth before joining the Soviet Air Force. He only worked in his new job for a month and died soon after, from a heart attack brought on by stress, less than a year after the embarrassing incident. The radar operator continued to serve in 203 TBAP, while the navigator had been advised by his former comrades to seek another post. He ended up serving at Bobruisk airfield, and two years later he was a Major working in the HQ of the 22nd Heavy Bomber Division! (*Readers will, I hope, empathise with the injustice of this situation, which seems to be a universal phenomenon and not restricted purely to military life!*)

The correct action for the navigator to have taken after he had realised that they were flying the wrong route was to have acknowledged this and told the crew, so that they could burn off fuel, before landing back at Mozdok. In spite of the fairly authoritarian leadership of the Soviet Air Force at the time, the navigator would not have received a heavy punishment for his mistake. The biggest punishment that he could have been given would have been the loss of his incremental pay rise, paid at the end of the year to all aircrew according to their flying category and individual achievements. It must be admitted that the incident also involved an intriguing string of coincidences. Whenever a navigator used the radar to fix the aircraft's position, he also took a snapshot of the radar screen with the FARM (*FotoApparat dlya s'yomki Radiolokatsionnovo Izobrazheniya Mestnosti*) camera, which was later used in post-flight debriefings. The investigation commission examined the FARM images from this flight and compared them with those produced by crews who followed the correct route, and they were surprised to note that they were very similar to each other. On the correct route there was a lake which showed up in more or less the same place on the FARM image of the 'lost' aircraft and on another the map images looked similar to the correct route. Only one pair of FARM images revealed a significant difference between the two routes, there being no railway line on the erroneous route, whereas this showed up very distinctly on the correct route.

CHAPTER EIGHT

Emergency Escape and Life-support Systems

Coincidental with the development of jet aircraft in the former Soviet Union after the Second World War, the need arose to provide adequate survival and escape facilities for pilots and crews at the higher flight speeds and altitudes of which these new aircraft were capable. At that time, in every Soviet aircraft design bureau (OKB), there were special departments dealing with the development of aircraft high-altitude equipment and life-support systems (i.e. cabin pressurisation, oxygen supplies, etc.) and designing an ejection seat became a logical extension of their work. In the 1950s, Nikolai Vasil'yevich Kirsanov headed the Tupolev OKB department faced with the difficult task of designing and developing ejection seats for a planned new supersonic fighter (The Tu-28/128 *Fiddler*) and bomber (Tu-98 *Backfin*). The department had already acquired some useful experience in this field, having developed ejection seats for the Tu-16 *Badger*, although these exhibited a very low level of commonality between the five crew stations of this aircraft (four on flight deck, plus tail gunner). Only the pilots' seats of the Tu-16 could be said to be standardised; production quality, servicing and repair procedures were extremely poor and, in addition, reliability left a lot to be desired. In proposing an ejection seat suitable for supersonic aircraft, the OKB-156 design team therefore decided to provide a standardised seat for all crew members of any future aircraft.

The resulting seat was designated KT-1 (meaning *Kreslo Tupoleva* – No. 1, or Tupolev Seat No. 1) and other Soviet design bureaux used an identical designation system for their seats (e.g. KS-1 for the first Sukhoi-designed ejection seat and KM-1 for the first Mikoyan seat). The KT-1 was thus adopted for installation on the Tu-22, becoming the main component of the aircraft's emergency escape system, comprising the following:

- The KT-1 ejection seat
- A system for raising and lowering the seat for crew entry and exit on the ground
- An emergency jettison system for the external hatches
- (Alternative) emergency exits
- An LAS-5M-2 emergency life raft.

All three crew members of the Tu-22 could only eject downwards, the pilot and navigator facing forwards on ejection and the radar operator (*radist*) or airborne operator (*vozdushnyi operator*) facing backwards. The seats could be lowered to a convenient height above the ground to facilitate crew entry to their individual stations. Apart from their obvious emergency escape function, the seats were designed to provide a comfortable working position for the crew during flight. In the event of having to eject, the external entry hatch covers were first jettisoned by a pyrotechnic mechanism. The actual process of ejection was fully automatic and reduced to three simple manual operations by the crew – lowering of the tinted face visor on the 'bone dome' (helmet), placing the seat in the correct position for ejection and activating the ejection handle in the arm rest. All subsequent actions occurred automatically, up to the point of separation of the crew member from the seat.

On ejection, the crew exited the aircraft in the following sequence – radar operator (or airborne operator as appropriate), navigator, and then the pilot, the operators and the navigator ejecting on the command of the pilot. In the event that the emergency had precluded use of the SPU (*Samolyotnoye Peregovornoye Ustroystvo*) intercom system, illuminated warning signs located on the instrument panels of the operator and navigator displayed the legend 'Abandon aircraft!' ('*Pokin' Samolyot!*'). These warning panels illuminated when the pilot flicked the appropriate switch on his emergency egress panel, located on the right-hand side of the cockpit in the vicinity of fuselage Frame 8. Corresponding red warning lights were located on the pilot's instrument panel, informing him that the radar operator (or airborne operator) and navigator had ejected from the aircraft. As mentioned above, the KT-1 ejection seat had been designed for maximum commonality and standardisation between aircraft of the Tu-22 series. The seat was equipped with a variety of mechanisms to enable it to operate in the correct sequence after preparing for ejection and initiation of the ejection process itself. It also incorporated the following:

• A seat belt harness
• Arm restrainers with protective shields

The KT-1 ejection seats of a Tu-22U trainer, the proximity of each requiring a precise sequencing of departure from the aircraft in the event of an emergency. Although clearly not as complex as the escape capsule of the General Dynamics F-111 or its closer contemporary, the Convair B-58A Hustler, the Tu-22's emergency escape system was one of the most elaborate employing ejection seats. *S Burdin*

Lt-Col Eduard Kozinyets, deputy squadron commander of the third squadron of 121 TBAP, poses in front of his Tu-22PD at Machulishchi in 1993, wearing the typical flight clothing of the period. Note the throat microphone (*laringofon*) and that he also appears to be wearing a 'spetsnaz-type' T-shirt under his flying suit. *S Burdin*

A 121 TBAP Tu-22K on the pan at Machulishchi awaiting its crew. The sign hanging from the steps (*tribunki*) in front of the pilot's seat reads *Zapretnaya Zona* (Prohibited Zone), probably because the seats are armed for flight. It is clearly evident why ejection by the rearward-facing airborne operator was impossible if the undercarriage was extended! *S Burdin*

- Leg restrainers with protective shields
- Foot restrainers (in footrest)
- Facial protection in the form of the visor on the ZSh-3M protective helmet (ZSh-3 on earlier Tu-22 models), and the KM-32 oxygen mask (KM-30 on earlier Tu-22s)
- A headrest.

The seat-belt harness allowed the crew members to shift position in the seat during flight without the need to undo the shoulder and lap straps, using an inertia-reel system which provided 850–860mm (33.0–33.50in) of free play. The release and locking mechanism was mounted on the right-hand side of the seat frame. The navigator's lap straps could be slackened by 80–100mm (3–3.9in) on sliding the seat pan forward to make it easier to view the radar screen, the straps tightening automatically on sliding the seat back to the normal position. The KT-1 could be adjusted to the height of an individual crew member, with a range of adjustment of 150mm (5.85in) for the pilot and operator and 80mm (3.12in) for the navigator. Additionally, the design of the navigator's seat permitted a degree of posture change by means of sliding the seat pan forward by 197mm (7.7in) while simultaneously increasing the reclining angle of the backrest.

The seat pans could be adjusted in height and were designed to take the S-3 parachute (on the Tu-22R) and the S3-3I-Series 2 (on the Tu-22K). They had telescopic firing mechanisms (ejection guns) with an initial velocity of 7.5m/sec (24.6ft/sec), which permitted safe exit from the aircraft throughout the normal speed envelope of the aircraft. The seats were equipped with automatically activated stabilising fins near the headrest, the fins on the pilot's and navigator's seats being spring activated, assisted by airflow – and the radar operator's seat having fixed stabilising fins. The KM-32 oxygen mask and the ZSh-3M helmet visor protected the face from the initial airflow blast on ejection. Oxygen supply, seat separation and canopy inflation were all fully automated actions. In the event of ditching, the pilot would activate the aircraft's LAS-5M-2 life raft, which was located on the starboard side of the fuselage, by pulling on a lever to unlock the hatch jettison mechanism and trigger the CO_2 inflation bottle of the raft. As the life raft inflated it would force open the unlocked hatch cover and the raft would complete its inflation on the surface of the water. It was attached to the aircraft by a lanyard and could not float away before the crew were able to climb aboard after exiting the aircraft through their individual emergency exits.

The navigator's KT-1 ejection seat. *S Burdin*

The crew of a 121 TBAP (3rd squadron) Tu-22PD are assisted into their seats by ground crew, revealing the procedure to be quite manpower-intensive. *Lt-Col Eduard Kozinyets Archive*

Main technical data

	Tu-22R	Tu-22K
Number of ejection seats	3	3
Parachute type	S-3	S3-3I
Maximum g-loading on ejection	6g	≤8g
Duration of ejection process, including:	7 seconds (3+1; 5+0; 5+2)	
preparation to eject (i.e. the maximum time using mechanical method of jettisoning entry hatch covers)	3 seconds (established during flight trials)	3 seconds
ejection	practically instantaneous	
separation from the seat (the process of separation)	0.3 to 0.5 seconds	
start of separation	1.5 seconds after ejection	
deployment of parachute	2 seconds after separation from the seat	

Automatic mechanisms

Release of seat harness assembly, foot and leg restrainers and activation of separation process	AD3U (*Avtomat Dyeleniye 3 Unifitsirovannyi*) (Automatic Seat Separation Mechanism 3rd in series – Unified for common application)

	Tu-22R	Tu-22K
opening of parachute canopy	KAP-3 (*Kombinirovannyi Avtomat Parashutnyi-3*) (Combined Automatic Barometric Parachute Opening System-3rd in series)	
Ejection mechanisms		
Navigator	TSM-1700 telescopic firing mechanism	
Pilot and Operator	TSM-2300-28 telescopic firing mechanism	
Pyrotechnic cartridge	PK-5-2	
Maximum acceleration speed developed by the telescopic firing mechanism	Up to 10m/sec (32.8ft/sec)	
Minimum safe height for ejection		
in horizontal flight	230–245m (755–805ft)	350m (1,150ft)
in 'gliding' flight with engines off	340m (1,115ft)	*Not included in flight operations manual for Tu-22K*
Harness and support system	Separate – S3 parachute harness and seat harness	Separate – S3-31 parachute harness and seat harness
Individual emergency survival pack	NAZ-7	
Emergency radios		
Individual	Priboy (Surf)	
Collective (crew)	Kedr-C (Cedar)	
Life raft		
Individual	MLAS-1 (in parachute pack) (*Malaya Lodka Avariino-Spasatyel'naya-1*) (Small single-man dinghy)	
Crew	LAS-5M-2 (*Lodka Avariino-Spasatyel'naya-5M*) (Crew dinghy)	
Crew entry-hatch emergency opening system		
Air	Centralised, controlled by the pilot; Individual, operated by the ejection-seat handle	
Mechanical	Individual, controlled by emergency release handles	
Emergency jettison of crew entry-hatch covers	Pyrotechnic mechanism on each hatch cover	
Protective helmet and flight clothing (summer, winter)	ZSh-3M; standard flight clothing issued by Soviet Air Force for this category of aircraft	
Ejection sequence interlinked (synchronised) with hatch cover jettison	Cable interlock, preventing ejection in the event of a hatch cover not being jettisoned	

Pressurisation, cabin conditioning and oxygen supply of the Tu-22

The cabin pressurisation, air-conditioning and oxygen system of the Tu-22 was determined by the fact that the aircraft was designed to have a service ceiling in the vicinity of the target of 13,500–14,000m (44,290–45,932ft). The cabin-conditioning system provided a comfortable working environment for the crew throughout the entire flight, using air tapped from the compressor stages of both engines. In the event of one engine failing, the required cockpit environment could be maintained by one engine alone. An ARD-54 automatic pressure regulator maintained the correct pressure differential in all three crew compartments, giving normal atmospheric pressure up to 1,600–2,000m (5,250–6,560ft). At altitudes from 2,000–7,400m (6,560–24,280ft) the ARD-54 maintained a cabin pressure equivalent to that at an altitude of 1,600–2,000m (5,250–5,560ft), and at altitudes from 7,400m (24,280ft) up to the normal service ceiling it maintained a constant pressure differential of 0.4 atmospheres (405mb). It also had a combat mode of operation, giving a pressure differential of 0.2 atmospheres, in order to minimise the effects on the crew of rapid decompression of the cockpit in the event of sustaining damage from enemy action (e.g. fighter or missile attack). Cabin temperature was maintained automatically at +15/-5°C by a TRTVK-45M 'thermostatic temperature and cabin ventilation regulator', the pressure cabin being provided with both ventilation and heating. Air tapped from the engines' compressor stages for the ventilation system was cooled in an air-to-air evaporator, a VVR air-to-air radiator and a TKh turbo-cooler before being passed into the three cockpits at 10°C. Hot air was supplied from the TKh and VVR units via a special delivery pipe at a temperature of 80°C for cockpit heating, and a warm-air blowing system was provided to demist the inside of the cockpit windows.

Heating of the cockpits in winter and cooling in summer on the ground was provided by a ground air-conditioning unit plugged into the aircraft in the region of fuselage Frames 18 and 19. The Tu-22R, Tu-22RD, Tu-22RDK, Tu-22K and Tu-22KP had a weapons-bay heating system for when the aircraft was used to carry a 'special weapon' (i.e. a nuclear bomb). The crew were provided with oxygen for flights at altitudes up to the aircraft's normal service ceiling and endurance, from two SKG-15 liquid oxygen bottles, connected to independent, duplicated supply lines. Oxygen was supplied to each crew member via KP-24M demand-type oxygen regulators and KM-32M (or KM-30) oxygen masks. The two SKG-15 oxygen bottles were sufficient to support the three crew members on a maximum-endurance sortie in an unpressurised cockpit at an altitude of 12,000m (39,370ft). Apart from this, each crew member also had a separate KP-23 oxygen supply as part of the parachute pack, which provided 10–11 minutes of breathing time after ejection. Since the service ceiling of the Tu-22 was only planned to be around 13,500-14,000m (44,290–45,932ft), the use of special high-altitude equipment for the crew, such as pressure suits and helmets, was not considered necessary.

Using the KT-1 ejection seat

According to Tu-22 crew members, the method of entry to the three cockpits was fairly easy, albeit a little unusual. For ease of entry and exit on the ground the ejection seats were lowered on guide rails, with roller wheels following the shape (profile) of the individual entry hatch covers in the lowered position. These 'profiles' were like a continuation of the guide rails when the hatch cover was fully open for entry to the cockpit. Unlike on the Tu-16, the crew chief and mechanics assisted the crew of the Tu-22 to get into the aircraft and monitored the strapping-in procedure, after which the crew chief would raise the seat into the cockpit. (For a long time during the early operation of the Tu-22 this was an extremely long-winded and awkward procedure. A manual worm-drive winch was used to raise the seat, by means of a calibrated winding handle which was placed into a socket on the lower edge of the entry hatch, or by an electric drive mechanism which was part of the aircraft's ground equipment. However, from the first aircraft of the 46th production series, raising the seat was achieved by means of a winch with a permanently attached EhPV-1 electric drive unit.) Access to the seat in the lowered position was by a small step-ladder, which was referred to on the Tu-22 regiments as the 'tribunka', or 'little reviewing stand'. (This was a jocular diminutive of the Russian word for reviewing stand, or rostrum [tribuna], which was such an inseparable feature of Soviet-era military parades and 'set piece exercises' attended by senior officers and generals.) From a distance, a crew member standing on the steps would look as if he was 'reviewing his troops'.

It has to be said that this system of raising the seat, which at first glance seemed fairly simple, exhibited certain rather unpleasant peculiarities which were encountered during operation of the Tu-22. For example, there were cases of pilots and other crew members sliding back down the guide rails in the seat because of failures in the upper locking mechanism. Such an incident was described by Major Kostyetskii, a deputy squadron commander of the Air Force engineering service (Inzhenyernaya Aviatsionnaya Sluzhba – IAS): 'Ground crew were winching Major-General Nesterov, our Divisional Commander, into the cockpit of Tu-22U Bort No. 49, for a sortie in which he was to fly as instructor pilot. The Regimental Commander's deputies had assembled on the hard standing (aircraft dispersal) alongside the aircraft, since it was not every day that the Divisional Commander came to the airfield to fly. The ground crew had finally raised his seat up into the cockpit, which on the Tu-22U was rather high off the ground, when suddenly there was a crunching sound and the seat crashed back down on the rails. Fortunately the General had a sense of humour and treated the whole incident without reproaching any of the regiment's personnel. He released his straps, stood up on the 'tribunka' and said "Has the friction spring broken again?" ' There was a spring in the seat raising mechanism, which was wound tight during the raising process to maintain the seat in that position at the top of the rails. Sometimes, however, because of metal fatigue, after being fully wound up, the spring would break and it would not be able to hold the weight of the seat. The steps, therefore, were only removed from the aircraft after the entry hatches had been closed and locked, in order to prevent injury to crew members in the event of such failure.

The KT-1 ejection seat also had its drawbacks from the point of view of cockpit ergonomics, and the crew, particularly the pilot, would get very tired during long flights, in spite of the provision of inertia-reel seat belts which offered a degree of freedom to change position in the seat. The special cushions in the seat pans did not help much, either, and the majority of crew members had a somewhat sceptical view about the quality of the seats. There were odd cases involving the crewman/seat separation system, which employed an inflatable rubber chamber in the back of the seat. On ejection this was designed to inflate with compressed nitrogen gas as soon as the seat entered the airstream, forcing the occupant from the seat. However, there were occasional cases of spontaneous inflation of these cushions inside the aircraft during flight, throwing the pilot forwards onto the control column, and the navigator would be forced against his instrument panel to the extent that he could only move with great difficulty. The only method of dealing with the problem was to deflate the cushion with a sharp object, such as a pencil.

There were, however, even more serious deficiencies in the design of the seat, which affected crew safety. The main problem was the low trajectory speed of ejection. Ejection was usually extremely successful in straight and level flight, while climbing or descending and without any rotational movement, but if the aircraft was rotating about the longitudinal axis ejection was much more difficult. The significant g-loads (often changing in value during rotation) and the angular velocities to which the seat and its occupant were subjected in these circumstances prevented a normal exit (ejection) from the aircraft. The seat would simply become wedged on the guide rails and fail to leave the aircraft altogether, usually with tragic consequences.

The flight operations manual for the Tu-22R *Blinder-C* defined the minimum safe ejection height from the aircraft in horizontal flight as 230–245m (755–805ft). The trajectory of the navigator's and operator's (*radist* or *vozdushnyi operator*) seats had a straight downwards vector, with the vector of the pilot's seat arranged so as not to interfere with the other two seats. This requirement clearly affected the minimum safe height for ejection of all three crew members, and in the operations manual and regimental standing orders (*instruktsiya*) for the Tu-22K *Blinder-B* this was even increased to 350m (1,150ft). Tu-22 pilots recall that in the late 1960s and early 1970s a temporary standing order was brought into force in the regiments, ordering that the minimum safe ejection height was to be 2,000–3,000m (6,560–9,842ft). If the aircraft was descending, the height for ejection had to be not less than 3,000m (9,842ft), and if it was climbing the height had to be not less than 2,000m (6,560ft). The temporary standing order was later withdrawn, although experienced pilots claimed that the aircraft was extremely difficult to abandon from normal circuit height of 600–800m (1,970–2,625ft). By way of an example, pilots of 290 ODRAP at Zyabrovka quote an accident involving a Tu-22U on 5 September 1979. The aircraft's navigator, Lieutenant T, ejected at circuit height after the aircraft had suddenly flipped inverted, and in his own words said that everything had happened at great speed: ejection – parachute canopy opening – a few seconds' descent and then hitting the ground. The instructor-pilot, Major K, was less fortunate: he ejected, unstrapped himself from the seat and fell head first to the ground, being killed instantly. The aircraft commander, Captain L, managed to eject, but there was no time for the seat-separation process to begin and he flew into the ground still sitting in the seat. However, when crews went flying in the Tu-22 they all unanimously admitted that they did not think about these things – such was their dedication....

In order to prevent ejection through a locked entry hatch, an interlock system was provided in the seat-actuation system. This comprised a cotter pin inserted into the striker of the ejection gun, connected by a halyard to the hatch cover. On jettisoning the hatch (the first action in the ejection sequence) the halyard pulled the cotter pin out of the striker, removing this last locking element from the ejection gun, allowing it to fire. The halyard was attached to the hatch cover by a snap hook after the seat had been raised to the normal (upper) position. There were several cases where the ground crew had forgotten to attach the halyard to the hatch cover. One such incident, on 29 April 1984, which had tragic consequences, is described in the next chapter, covering the Tu-22's accident history. Frequently in these, and similar, incidents, hurried procedures are the main causes of such disasters, along with frequent changes to the planned tasking orders. The aircraft in this particular case had been refuelled for a long navigation exercise (navex), but the officer in charge of flying (*Rukovodityel' Polyotov* – RP), noting that the weather was now unsuitable for a navex, decided to change the task to a local-area flight (*polyot na rayon* – literally 'flight to the region'), near the airfield. This required the crew chief to reduce the fuel load of the aircraft, since it was too great for the short local-area flight and well above the aircraft's authorised maximum landing weight. However, in the meantime, the weather had improved and the RP ordered the crew chief to refuel the aircraft for a navex. This procedure happened a number of times before the aircraft actually took off, and as a result, the crew chief forgot that he had not attached the halyard!

After this incident, the Chief Engineer of the Soviet Air Force (*Glavnyi Inzhenyer Voyenno-vozdushnykh Sil* – GI-VVS) issued a special order requiring the crew chief to report on the aircraft's intercom (SPU) for recording on the MS-61 cockpit voice recorder the following action: 'Twelve blocking pins removed from the seats, interlock halyards connected.' This was done after the aircraft commander's hatch was closed (with all crew members in position and engines running), so that the procedure would not be overlooked in the inevitable bustle which preceded every flight. After introducing this procedure, no further incidents of this type occurred.

The aircraft had one other insidious feature! The radar operator/airborne operator (*radist* or *vozdushnyi operator*) could not eject unless the nose leg of the undercarriage was retracted! This was because the seat trajectory passed directly through the location of the extended nose leg! There was an incident involving a Tu-22 flown by a pilot by the name of Zavgorodnii, which suffered a failure of the aircraft's artificial feel system on take-off. This led to the aircraft becoming extremely heavy and difficult to control, and he gave the command to eject. However, the undercarriage was still extended and the operator could not eject. The undercarriage could not be retracted since, in the extended position, it assisted the pilot in maintaining control, by providing a pitch-down moment, so the pilot decided instead to burn off excess fuel and attempt a landing. For two hours the pilot held the control column with his legs (pressed up against his knees), and after burning off enough fuel to allow him to land, Zavgorodnii put the aircraft down safely. He was later awarded the Order of the Red Star for his expert handling of the situation.

It must be admitted honestly that many disasters could have been avoided, had the crews been more careful and observant in flight. A major part of the recorded accidents were the result of exceeding the precisely defined rearward centre-of-gravity limits of the Tu-22, a critical aspect of its aerodynamic layout and design. One reason for this was an increased rate of fuel consumption from the forward group of tanks, compared with that from the rear tanks. If the crew forgot to monitor any such difference, then an emergency situation could develop which would be too late to correct, and the aircraft would pitch up and become uncontrollable. Experienced Tu-22 pilots were of one mind in relation to flying the aircraft – it required expert knowledge of its foibles, great flying skills and considerable attention in all stages of flight. Not less than once a month, Tu-22 regiments would practise emergency egress procedures on the ground, using a simulator rig, so that crews would be ready for any emergency on the ground and in the air. This training also included the use of ejection seat rigs.

In concluding this chapter we would like to provide a brief analysis of the accidents and incidents involving the Tu-22, which will to some extent, perhaps, restore the reputation of the aircraft in Soviet Air Force service.

Accident rates of Long-range Air Force medium bombers

Type of aircraft	Number of incidents and accidents per 100,000 flight hours per year			
	1960–1969	1970–1979	1980–1989	1960–1989
Tu-16	2.48	1.5	1.75	2.0
Tu-22	20.17	6.1	5.93	8.59
Tu-22M	–	0	8.02	5.6
LRAF total	3.92	2.34	4.03	3.48

As can be seen from the table, the greatest number of accidents per 100,000 flight hours involving the Tu-22 occurred during the period of its pre-service trials (*Voiskoviye Ispytaniya*) and conversion training between 1960 and 1969. This aircraft demanded much from everyone involved in its operation, from the Long-range Air Force leadership right down to squadron-level air and ground crews, requiring them to re-examine seriously their approach to flight operations. When it entered service, the Tu-22 was well ahead of its time and had accelerated the introduction of supersonic bomber operations to the Soviet Air Force by at least two decades.

LRAF flight incidents by stage of flight and cause

	Take-off	Landing	Other stages of flight
Tu-16	27%	32%	41%
Tu-22	8%	40%	52%
Tu-22M	22%	56%	22%
Total	17%	37%	46%

A significant contributory factor in the accidents recorded for all three jet bomber types listed was aircrew error, this being particularly high for the Tu-16 and Tu-22M. In the case of the Tu-22, the causes were fairly equally divided between aircrew error, technical failure and [failures] in flight planning and control.

Effectiveness of the use of emergency escape systems by aircraft type in the period 1960 to 1989

Type of aircraft	Write-offs	Accidents	Number of aircraft lost	Number of aircrew lost	Number of aircrew involved in incidents	Number of ejections	Number who could have ejected	Average statistical probability of ejection/ survival
Tu-16	37	5	42	185	256	17	113	0.15/0.28
Tu-22	20	11	31	44	93	45	62	0.73/0.53
Tu-22M	4	7	11	14	44	19	28	0.68/0.68
Total	80	31	111	360	608	108	315	0.34/0.41

The data in the previous table show that the Tu-22 was not as dangerous for those who flew it as is commonly supposed, with the number of write-offs and crew fatalities for the Tu-16 being much greater than for the Tu-22. Moreover, according to the statistics, the probability of survival for a Tu-22 crew member in the event of a serious in-flight emergency was significantly higher than for the crew of the Tu-16. Disregarding the problems associated with the Tu-22's emergency escape system (*Sistema avariinovo pokidaniya samolyota* – SAPS), it should be remembered that the aircraft was designed in the late 1950s using the theoretical and technological knowledge base of that time. It was a very complex aircraft, but was, without doubt, a huge step forward compared with its predecessor, the Tu-16.

In the chapter which follows, we present details of incidents, accidents and write-offs sustained by the Tu-22 fleet in the three decades between 1960 and 1989. Although perhaps not as comprehensive as equivalent Western accident data, this information nevertheless provides a unique insight into Soviet Air Force operations in general and those of the Tu-22 in particular, and will be of considerable interest to a broad spectrum of readers, from the 'enthusiast' to the serious aviation historian.

CHAPTER NINE

Incidents and Write-offs Involving Long-range Air Force Tu-22s between 1960 and 1989

This chapter deals with the accounts of all recorded accidents involving the Tu-22 in the three decades of its operation by the Long-range Air Force regiments of the Soviet Air Force. It does not, however, cover accidents involving the aircraft operated by the two Soviet Naval Air Force (*Aviatsiya Voyenno-morskovo Flota*) independent reconnaissance regiments, nor accidents which only occurred on the ground. In the majority of cases, the author has chosen deliberately to remove all references to individual units, as well as the names of individual crew members, judging this to be the correct procedure from an ethical point of view. However, in preparing this section of the book, the author had the opportunity to interview Lt-Col (Rtd) Leonid Stepanovich Fedyaev, who ejected with his crew from a Tu-22K *Blinder-B* on 19 August 1970, the interview appearing immediately after the official account of the accident. The accident details have been drawn from an internal Soviet Air Force document entitled '*Analysis of accidents and write-offs involving Soviet Air Force aircraft in the USSR from 1960 to 1989*', published in 1990. Some material also comes from Sergey Burdin's own personal archive. Unlike the procedure adopted in Western military accident reports, the Russian practice is not to include details of accumulated flying experience of pilots or crew, or hours 'on type'. However, some idea of the levels of experience can be deduced from the categories of pilot involved, i.e. Sniper Pilot, Pilot First Class, Pilot Second Class and Pilot Third Class (*See Table in Chapter Five*). The accidents involved all four pilot categories, including one pilot with the highest skill level and most experience, i.e. a Sniper Pilot, and one inexperienced and comparatively recently qualified Pilot Third Class, with the majority of accidents involving broadly experienced pilots holding the First Class category. What follows are the first descriptive accounts of Soviet Air Force flying accidents to be published in English. They are of particular interest in that they describe accidents and human errors involving an aircraft which was regarded as a significant threat to the security of Western Europe throughout the latter stages of the Cold War. They thus provide a fascinating glimpse into Russian military flight safety and operating procedures in a period when the Soviet 'threat' and capabilities were perceived to be at their most menacing.

Explanatory Notes:
Russia employs a system to describe cloud cover in which the visible area from horizon to horizon is divided into tenths, whereas the Western practice is to divide it into eighths (oktas). This system is used in all the descriptions of weather conditions given in the accident reports which follow.

An 'otryad' (section) of a Soviet Air Force Tu-22 squadron sometimes comprised three, but usually four aircraft, dependent upon the requirements of a given period. It has no direct equivalent in Western squadron structure, but a 'flight' might be a relevant comparison. A *komandir otryada* (Section Commander), many of whom feature in the accidents, had 'full responsibility for the quality of training of crews in his *otryad* and was responsible for the training of his subordinates in all aspects of flight operations. These responsibilities were far-reaching and too numerous to list here, but embraced, *inter alia*, pre-flight organisation, flight safety and crew performance monitoring and post-flight debriefing and analysis.

Incidents occurring on take-off and climb-out
Write-off of Tu-22 1963 (no date)
Weather conditions: light cloud cover, visibility 10km (6.2 miles)

Circumstances
Major V and his crew had just taken off in good VFR conditions. After take-off, and settled into the climb, the aircraft suddenly began to pitch violently, caused by the pilot applying disproportionate elevator control inputs. During the violent pitching, the aircraft exceeded the maximum permitted g-loading and broke up. The crew perished in the accident.

Cause
The aircraft was subjected to destructive g-loading of the airframe as a result of the pilot applying excessive elevator control inputs because this early model of Tu-22 was not equipped with an artificial feel system.

Write-off of Tu-22 13.04.65
Weather conditions: 10/10ths cloud, cloud tops at 1,500m (4,920ft), visibility 10km (6.2 miles)

Circumstances
Section commander (*komandir otryada*) Major S, a Pilot First Class, and his crew were carrying out a daytime navigation exercise (navex). Some 37 minutes after take-off, while turning over the first waypoint at an altitude of 5,100m (16,730ft), the aircraft suddenly began to vibrate slightly. After two to three seconds the crew heard a loud bang, accompanied by an increase in the vibrations. At the same time, the navigator and airborne operator noticed clouds of smoke forming in their cockpits and the crew felt a distinct slowing of the aircraft. The aircraft commander switched off the autopilot, brought the aircraft out of the turn, reduced engine power and began to descend, the vibration and buffeting reducing at the same time. The aircraft commander gave the order to switch on the stand-by battery power supply for the instruments (because of the appearance of smoke in the cockpit). At this time the airborne operator saw that all the

ammeter readings were off the scale, switched off all the generators and transferred to battery power for the flight instruments.

After a rapid scan of the instruments, the aircraft commander saw nothing unusual in the operation of the engines and no signs of fire, or hydraulic system failure. Continuing to descend, he started to increase engine power, but the vibrations intensified, so he again selected the engines to flight idle. He then increased rpm on the port engine, with no increase in vibration, so he selected 50–52% on the UPRT (*Ukazatyel' Polozheniya Rychaga Topliva*) power lever, at an altitude of 2,500m (8,200ft), and put the aircraft into a gentle climb, turning left onto a new heading. During the turn and at an altitude of 3,500m (11,480ft) the crew heard a loud bang for the second time, smoke reappeared in the cockpit and the vibrations intensified.

The pilot gave the command to jettison the hatch covers. After jettisoning the hatch covers, the airborne operator could see flames at the rear of the aircraft and reported to the aircraft commander: 'Both engines are on fire!' The aircraft commander then gave the order to abandon the aircraft – he ejected first, followed by the navigator, the airborne operator ejecting last. (*This contradicted the standard procedure, where the operator was first to eject, followed by the navigator and then the pilot.*) After the crew had ejected, the aircraft continued to fly for a further 17km (10.5 miles) with its tail section on fire. It eventually struck the ground, in a slight bank, 30° nose up, exploded and burnt out. All three crew members escaped without injury.

Cause
Fire in the rear of the fuselage resulting from the failure of the starboard engine, accompanied by engine surge. It was established subsequently that a rotor bearing had failed, although it had not been possible to determine why the failure had occurred.

Findings
No blame could be apportioned for the failure.

Write-off of Tu-22 10.04.67
Weather conditions: 10/10ths cloud, cloud base 1,700m (5,560ft), visibility 10km (6.2 miles), head wind of 6m/sec (12kts).

Circumstances
Captain B, a Pilot First Class, and his crew were carrying out a training flight in the airfield zone involving aircraft handling at high subsonic (Mach 0.96–0.98) and supersonic speeds. The aircraft took off at 13.48hrs local time, with a take-off weight of 65 tonnes (143,300lb) and a normal take-off centre of gravity of 36% MAC (Mean Aerodynamic Chord), in full reheat.

The take-off roll, unstick, climb-out and undercarriage and flap retraction had all been normal. On reaching a speed of 450kph (243kts), established from the MS-61 cockpit voice recorder, vibration was felt which the crew assessed as 'strong'.

At an altitude of 1,400–1,600m (4,595–5,250ft) and 520kph (280kts), before penetrating cloud, the aircraft was levelled off, with the engines still in reheat. The climb was probably stopped because the pilot did not want to enter cloud when the aircraft was experiencing unusual vibrations and buffeting, the reason for which the crew did not understand. Levelling-off of the aircraft was accompanied by an increase in speed and a constant change of pitch trim.

Levelling-off in close proximity to the clouds, with constant trim changes and with the engines still in reheat mode, plus the strong vibrations and buffeting, all taken together, complicated the aircraft handling and distracted the pilot's attention from flying the aircraft. With all the distractions, the pilot did not notice that the aircraft had begun to descend rapidly with a pitch angle of minus 5° and a rate of descent of 35m/sec (6,890ft/min).

Having finally realised that the aircraft was descending, the pilot pulled back on the control column with considerable effort to bring it back to level flight. Unfortunately, this caused excessive g-loading and progressive longitudinal pitching (porpoising), leading to significant loss of height. On the third cycle of this pitching, at a height of 600–700m (1,970–2,300ft), the aircraft experienced excessive positive-g and broke up in flight. All three crew members perished in the accident.

Cause
Break-up of the aircraft following application of excessive g-loading. This in turn was caused by progressive longitudinal pitching when the pilot brought the aircraft out of an uncommanded descent, without using the correct power setting.

The pitching itself resulted from a negative feature of the Tu-22's longitudinal control system, where repeated energetic movements of the control column to attempt to stabilise the aircraft in pitch could lead to pilot-induced oscillations (PIO). It was not always possible to eliminate such oscillations by the usual piloting techniques.

Findings
The Ministry for Aircraft Production (*Ministerstvo Aviatsionnoy Promyshlennosti* – MAP) was held responsible for what was considered to be a manufacturing design defect (*Konstruktivno-proizvodstvyennyi nyedostatok* – KPN).

Write-off of Tu-22 15.05.69
Weather conditions: 10/10ths cloud, visibility 10km (6.2 miles)

Circumstances
Section Commander, Major D, a Pilot First Class, and his crew were scheduled to conduct a night navex, with a planned take-off time four minutes after the departure of another aircraft. The planned take-off weight was 76.6 tonnes (168,870lb), giving a calculated take-off run of 2,000m (6,560ft) lasting 36.5 seconds and a calculated unstick speed of 375kph (202kts). The pilot held the aircraft at the line-up point on the runway for about 3 minutes for final checks, and having tested the afterburners in maximum reheat, he commenced his take-off run. At a distance of 1,600m (5,250ft) from the threshold of the runway and at a speed of 312kph (168kts), 28 seconds after commencing the take-off run, the nose leg was raised off the runway. At a distance of 1,800m (5,905ft) from the start point and with 2–3° nose-up pitch, some 3 seconds after raising the nose leg, at a speed of 335kph (180kts), the afterburners of both engines suddenly shut down simultaneously. This was followed by the pitch angle increasing to 4–5° and subsequent rapid lowering of the nose at a distance of about 2,150m (7,050ft) down the runway and at a speed of 350kph (189kts), 35 seconds after commencing the take-off run. The aircraft commander brought the engines back to flight idle and released the brake parachutes, which were fully

deployed 350m (1,150ft) before the end of the runway, with the aircraft travelling at 320kph (173kts). The aircraft eventually rolled out onto the loose-earth emergency braking area (*kontsevaya gruntovaya polosa bezopasnosti*) at a speed of 250kph (135kts). The aircraft travelled along the emergency braking strip about 6m (20ft) to the left of the runway centreline, in a 1° left-wing-down attitude, with longitudinal pitching of the fuselage caused by the rough surface. At a distance of 397m (1,300ft) from the end of the runway, the nose-wheels became detached. As the aircraft continued to roll across the overrun area, the nose of the aircraft dropped and the nose leg dug into the earth, eventually detaching from the aircraft. With the nose of the aircraft now dug into the ground and still moving at an appreciable speed, the cockpit area was extensively damaged and a fire erupted in the forward fuselage. At a distance of 600m (1,970ft) from the end of the runway, the burning aircraft finally came to a stop.

As the aircraft was rolling over the loose earth surface, the airborne operator opened his emergency exit hatch, through which he escaped once the aircraft had come to a standstill. He tried to assist the pilot in getting out of the burning aircraft through the port-side window of the cockpit, but because of injuries sustained as the aircraft bounced along the emergency strip, the pilot was unable to use this emergency exit and he perished as fire engulfed the aircraft. The navigator also died from injuries sustained when his cockpit area ruptured and filled with earth.

Cause
Aborted take-off at a speed of 350kph (189kts), and 850m (2,780ft) from the far end of the runway, following the simultaneous failure of the reheat systems of both engines. The only reason which could be established for a simultaneous shut-down of reheat on both engines was the failure of the reheat maximum speed interlock system installed on Tu-22s powered by Dobrynin VD-7M engines. It was impossible to establish this as a definite cause, because the major parts of both engines were completely burnt out in the fire.

Findings
Blame could not be established for the cause of the reheat failure.

Write-off of Tu-22P 25.09.69
Weather conditions: 10/10ths cloud, cloud base 300m (984ft), cloud tops 1,500m (4,920ft), visibility 6km (3.75 miles).

Circumstances
Captain P, a Pilot Second Class, and his crew had taken off from Kubinka airfield near Moscow. Climb-out and entry into cloud went without incident. Some 57 seconds after take-off the pilot reported 'Cloud base 300 metres', after which no further communication was heard from the aircraft. The duty controller of flying noted that the aircraft had disappeared from the radar display at around 16–17km (10–10.5 miles) from the take-off point. The aircraft's crew did not respond to calls from the control tower. The aircraft had broken up and crashed in the vicinity of Zvenigorod.
Analysis of the flight data recorders showed that:

• The forward speed of the aircraft had increased to 735kph (397kts) 45 seconds after take-off

- After 1–2 seconds, g-loading had increased (showing 1.8–2.0) and the rate of descent had reached 60m/sec (11,810ft/min)
- After 63 seconds, the forward speed had reduced to 575kph (310kts), but the rate of descent had increased to 83m/sec (16,340ft/min).

Subsequently, the aircraft started to descend, with a rapid increase in speed, which by the 87th second of flight had reached 1,100kph (594kts), and the rate of descent was now 139m/sec (27,360ft/min). In the 82nd second of flight the g-loading had begun to increase, and 88 seconds into the flight had reached a value of 3.5g, reducing to 3.0g 90 seconds into the flight, increasing once again to 3.5. After 93 seconds of flight, the aircraft broke up.

The aircraft's reconstructed trajectory suggested that the emergency situation had occurred between 59–77 seconds after take-off, at a height of 500-600m (1,640–1,970ft) and a speed of 700–750kph (378–405kts).

The incident arose after the failure of tailplane trim-control system or the ADU, leading to unusual forces on the control column, making handling of the aircraft extremely difficult while climbing through cloud. The increased loads on the control column led the pilot to apply excessive force to control the aircraft, exacerbated by poor piloting technique. Lateral control of the aircraft was lost at a speed of more than 850kph (460kts) because of aileron reversal, and the pilot did not reduce engine power after beginning to descend and did not select 'flaperon' (*ehlerony-zakrylki*) control, which worsened the handling problem and allowed the speed to build up rapidly to 1,100kph (594kts).

Cause
The probable cause of the 'see-saw' flight trajectory was the failure of either the trimming system or the ADU (*Avtomat Doplnityel'nykh Usilii*), the automatic control force limiter in the tailplane control circuit.

Findings
The Ministry of Aircraft Production, Minaviaprom, was held responsible for the assumed cause of the accident.

Write-off of Tu-22P 02.10.69
Weather conditions: 10/10ths cloud, cloud base 2,000m (6,560ft), visibility 8km (5 miles), wind 90° from the left, 7m/sec (13.5kts).

Circumstances
Major G, a Pilot First Class, and his crew were scheduled to carry out a test flight of a Tu-22P after it had undergone a 100-hour maintenance check and minor upgrade. Take-off was performed in full reheat mode with a take-off weight of 72 tonnes (158,730lb). At the end of the take-off run, after the pilot had pulled back on the control column to rotate the aircraft to the normal take-off angle, the aircraft adopted a greater than normal pitch angle and rotated at 360kph (195kts). Attempting to reduce the pitch angle, the pilot pushed the column forward slightly, the aircraft responding with a rapid reduction of pitch angle, the undercarriage wheels settling back onto the runway. Applying a small backwards movement of the control column to avoid descending again, the aircraft once more responded with a sharp increase in pitch angle and started to climb. Repeating the slight

forward movement of the control column immediately led to another sharp reduction in pitch angle.

Recognising the 'symptoms' of pilot-induced oscillation (*Raskachka*), the pilot reported this to the ATC controllers. [*Note: there is no direct Russian equivalent of the Western term 'pilot-induced oscillation, but the actions described here for* Raskachka *are unequivocally pilot induced, and PIO probably best describes this characteristic of the Tu-22. AD.*]

During the cycle of oscillations, the aircraft had completed six full phugoid movements, and on the seventh steeply rising section of its trajectory reached an altitude of 1,000m (3,280ft) with a reduction of speed from 550kph (297kts) to 220kph (118kts). The crew ejected at this time and landed without injury. After the crew had ejected, the aircraft descended suddenly, coming out of the dive just above the ground and in an almost flat attitude with a bank angle of 45°, some 4,500m (14,770ft) from the end of the runway, crashed onto a cattle station and burst into flames. Significant damage was caused to the farm and its buildings.

Causes
1. Progressive longitudinal oscillations caused by reversed action of the pitch damper channels. When carrying out the maintenance and upgrade work on the aircraft, the factory specialist team (*Spetsialisty Zavodskoy Brigady*) made a mistake in the sequence of connecting the phases of the three-phase AC supply to the pitch dampers
2. The aircraft and the crew had been prepared for the test flight with flagrant breaches of the requirements laid down in the standing orders for technical and flight operation of the Tu-22P. The crew had carried out only a superficial check that maintenance work had been performed properly by the engineering technical service of the Soviet Air Force and were thus unable to assess the poor quality of this work
3. The aircraft commander had been cleared to fly the aircraft, without having the appropriate 'judicial authority' and with poor overall professional competence
4. The test flight was attempted without a preliminary taxiing check and high-speed taxiing checks on the runway, which prevented the crew from detecting any defects in control of the aircraft on the ground.

Findings
Held responsible were:

1. The specialist team from the Kazan' Aviation Plant, which had carried out the maintenance and upgrade work on the aircraft's control system
2. The squadron commander's deputies, who did not organise and monitor the training of the crew and ensure adequate preparation of the aircraft, releasing it for a test flight without preliminary taxiing checks
3. The aircraft commander, who breached the requirements of the Standing Orders for the crews of the Tu-22P and the method of conducting test flights of the aircraft
4. The Acting Regiment Commander, who authorised the crew to conduct the test flight.

Write-off of Tu-22P 24.05.74
Weather conditions: 7/10ths cloud cover, cloud base 2,200m (6,890ft), visibility 10km (6.2 miles), wind 40° from the right, 5–7m/sec (10–13.5kts).

Circumstances

Lt-Col M, a Pilot First Class, and his crew were scheduled to perform an inter-airfield flight between Baranovichi, in the former Byelorussian Soviet Socialist Republic and Ozyornoye in the Ukraine. The aircraft commenced its take-off run at 15.08.18 local time, but 23 seconds into the take-off, at a speed of 320kph (173kts) and 1,740m (5,700ft) down the runway, a fire broke out in the pressure cabin. On the navigator's read-off of the speed at 300kph (162kts), the pilot started to rotate the aircraft for take-off, and 2 seconds after confirming the speed, the pilot received another call from the navigator: 'We have a fire, commander, Fire!' The aircraft commander aborted the take-off at about 350kph (189kts). Chopping power on both engines and lowering the nose-wheel, the pilot started to brake, using the main wheel brakes, and reported to ATC: 'Aborted, cut the engines, request fire engine.' (In fact this was reported in the very abbreviated manner of Russian military reports as '*Prekratil, ubral, mashinu*', meaning, literally, 'Ceased [take-off], removed [power], machine [fire engine in this context].) Seeing that it would be inevitable that they would have to go onto the loose earth overrun area, the pilot shut the engines down and made the aircraft safe. After entering the overrun, the aircraft started to porpoise on the rough surface, and some 30m (100ft) from a railway embankment on the airfield boundary, the nose leg of the undercarriage collapsed and the aircraft's nose dug into the ground. At a speed of 200–220kph (108–120kts), the aircraft hit the embankment, which was located at a distance of around 408m (1,340ft) from the end of the runway, bounced over the railway line, exploded and caught fire. All three crew members were killed.

Cause

The likely causes of fire and smoke in the cockpit were:

- Ignition of AMG-10 hydraulic fluid which had leaked into the radio equipment units and the junction boxes located between the navigator and the pilot
- Leakage of AMG-10 fluid into the junction boxes and equipment units could have resulted from the loss of hermetic sealing of the drainage pipes serving the undercarriage braking system during taxiing and take-off. The pressure in these pipes was 1–3kg/cm² (14.22–42.6lb/sq in), and fluid could have leaked through a cracked pipe or damaged nipple connection
- Smoke could have come from the radio and other equipment (power transformers, etc.) located in the vicinity of the navigator's and pilot's seats. This equipment included, among other items, elements of the RSBN navigation system, the TATs2-1B fuel management system, the AP-7MTs autopilot and the BTs-63A star tracker unit
- A short circuit in the wiring of the electrical power supply junction boxes and circuit breaker panels located next to the navigator and pilot (including navigator's junction box, aircraft trim junction box, pilot's circuit breaker panel, navigator's circuit breaker panel).

Findings

It was not possible to establish the precise cause of the fire and subsequent loss of the aircraft, and no blame could be apportioned to any individual or group.

Write-off of Tu-22U 24.07.92 (Lt-Col Stepchenkov and crew)

Weather conditions: light cloud cover, visibility 8–10km (5–6.2 miles).

Circumstances

Lt-Col Stepchenkov, a Pilot First Class and squadron commander, had been scheduled to conduct a check flight after his return from a period of leave. The instructor was Lt-Col Os'kin, the Deputy Regiment Commander and also a Pilot First Class. The take-off was made in the direction of Gomel', with a subsequent turn towards Kazan. Up to the 70th second of flight everything was normal, and at a height of 930m (3,050ft) and flying at 510kph (275kts), the aircraft was levelled off. Then, 72 seconds into the flight, the rpm of the starboard engine dropped dramatically, the engine then flaming out after suffering damage to the rotor assembly of the first stage of the turbine. Turbine blades penetrated the core of the engine, also damaging the tail section of the fuselage and Fuel Tank 7, plus the left engine. Damage to the turbine blades had occurred in an area of fatigue cracks which had been welded during refurbishment and maintenance work carried out at an Aircraft Repair Plant dealing with the Tu-22. As a result of the dispersal pattern of the detached turbine blades from the right-hand engine, which penetrated the left engine, the fire warning lights for the left engine illuminated, with the legend 'Fire in left engine' on the annunciator panel. The 'Fire in right engine' warning panel did not illuminate, since the sensors on this engine had been destroyed. One second later, the 'Fire in the rear fuel tanks' warning panel illuminated.

The following is the chronological sequence of events after the initial fire warning occurred:

- 17.01.38 – the aircraft was overhead the outskirts of the city of Gomel', in the region of Novobyelits
- 17.02.16 – the crew, believing the fire warning indications to be true, shut down the 'good' left-hand engine. The right-hand engine continued to burn
- 17.02.44 – the instructor-pilot, Lt-Col Os'kin, started to turn away from the town
- 17.02.49 – the navigator began to read off height and speed for the pilots: 'Height 800, 700 – speed 400.'
- 17.03.05 – Lt-Col Os'kin reports to the crew: 'I think both engines have shut down.' The navigator confirmed that there was 'No output from both generators', after which the aircraft commander (Lt-Col Stepchenkov) gave the order to the crew, 'Eject!'. However, the instructor, Lt-Col Os'kin, gave a second order telling them to wait a moment
- 17.03.12 – the navigator continued to read off height and speed: 'Height 400, speed 500' and the instructor reported 'I will show you where to eject'
- 17.03.16 – the aircraft commander, Lt-Col Stepchenkov, shouts to the instructor, Lt-Col Os'kin, 'Eject, Semyonich, get out.' Semyonich! [Semyonich being the endearing, familiar form of Semyon]
- 17.03.23 – The instructor orders, 'Get out, get out, get out, eject!' The first to eject was the navigator, Major Ivanov, who left the aircraft at a height of 450m (1,475ft), followed by the aircraft commander who ejected at a height of 400m (1,312ft), his parachute only just opening above the tops of some trees. The instructor, Lt-Col Os'kin, ejected at 320m (1,050ft), outside the parameters for safe operation of the seat, and he was killed.

Cause

Rotor blade failure of the first turbine stage of the right-hand engine attributed to poor inspection procedures at the repair facility which had undertaken repair and maintenance work on the engines.

Incidents occurring in straight and level flight

Write-off of Tu-22K 19.08.70 (Captain Fedyaev and crew)
Weather conditions: light cloud cover, visibility 10km (6.2 miles).

Circumstances
Captain Leonid Fedyaev, a Pilot Second Class, and his crew had been scheduled to conduct a night navex in squadron strength (*v sostavye ehskadrl'yi*) involving a simulated missile launch *en route*. The planned flight duration was 4hrs 10min. The aircraft took off as number five in the group at 21.14hrs local time, with a take-off interval of one minute. The take-off weight was 91,950kg (202,710lb), centre of gravity was 36% MAC and the fuel load was 39,750kg (87,630lb). After 1 hour and 2 minutes of flight, at an altitude of 10,000m (32,800ft) and flying at 670kph (360kts) IAS, the pilot noticed a deflection of the control column to the right, with the aircraft on autopilot. He switched off the autopilot, and counteracting the bank to the left with a deflection of the column in the opposite direction, he continued to fly the aircraft manually.

Subsequently, it required a 60° deflection of the control column to the right to counteract the left bank, and the use of lots of trim to unload the controls. Trying to deal with the cause of the sudden banking of the aircraft, the crew checked the operation of the engines and the position of the undercarriage and flaps, but could find nothing wrong. However, when checking the contents of the fuel tanks they noticed a difference between the supply to the right and left engines, which later increased quite rapidly. The first reading gave 11.5 tonnes (25,350lb) for the right engine and 9 tonnes (19,840lb) for the left. The second reading gave 11 tonnes (24,250lb) for the right engine and 7 tonnes (15,430lb), while the third reading produced 11 tonnes for the right engine and 5 tonnes (11,020lb) for the left. The interval between readings was about 1.5–2 minutes.

On the command of the group leader, the pilot switched from flaperons (*ehlerony-zakrylki*) to normal ailerons for lateral control, but the banking tendency persisted. The pilot had also noticed that in order to maintain level flight he had to push the control column forward more and more, as a function of the increasing difference between the fuel supply to the left and right engines. He decided to abort the sortie, and commenced a descending turn to the left onto a reciprocal heading. With the tailplane set at 0° angle of incidence, the pilot reduced power on both engines and stabilised the rate of descent at 2m/sec (395ft/min). At that moment, in spite of the fact that the control column was held fully forward, the aircraft suddenly started to pitch up sharply, with a noticeable increase in g-loading, and the radar operator noticed a sheet of flame from the left engine. The aircraft commander ordered the crew to eject and, at 22.27hrs local time, all three crew members successfully abandoned the aircraft.

Cause
Loss of longitudinal control as a result of the leakage of 9–10 tonnes (19,840–22,045lb) of fuel over the last 11 minutes of flight in the main fuel supply line from the forward fuel tanks. This resulted in a rearward shift in the centre of gravity from 36% MAC to 57% MAC. The exact location of the fuel leak was not possible to determine because the aircraft was totally burnt out on impact with the ground. One of the possible locations of the leak was the fuel line in the vicinity of Tanks 3 and 4 at fuselage Frame 33.

Findings

Various enterprises contracted to the Ministry for Aircraft Production were considered responsible for the probable fuel line failure, but no specific blame was apportioned.

Personal account of the above-mentioned incident by Lt-Col Leonid Stepanovich Fedyaev, a former Tu-22 pilot on the 121st Heavy Bomber Aviation Regiment based at Machulishchi, near Minsk in the Byelorussian Soviet Socialist Republic (now the Republic of Belarus').

[Translator's note: *I have left the general style of Lt-Col Fedyaev's descriptions of the events surrounding the accident very much as he spoke them. The result is perhaps a little staccato on reading, but it retains the unadorned conversational flow of the pilot's recollection of his experience.* AD]

It was the second flying 'shift' of the day. In spite of the fact it had been Aviation Day the day before, everyone was sober. Generally speaking, we were always quite strict about this. Our task was to fly a normal navex, but we had a dummy missile (Kh-22/AS-4 *Kitchen*) under the fuselage. For this kind of flight we only put fuel in the fuselage tanks. The navex was to be flown in squadron strength. It had already started to get dark – it was around 22.00hrs. We were somewhere around Petrozavodsk and we were flying, as usual, on autopilot. Suddenly the autopilot disconnected and the aircraft quite rapidly started to bank to the left. I had to counteract this with large control inputs. I immediately wondered what could have caused the banking to occur. The wing tanks were empty – (in fact they had not been filled, of course), we checked the undercarriage lights – it was retracted. I decided to check the position of the flaps. It was already dark, so we had to engage the afterburners to illuminate the rear of the aircraft and the wing surfaces. The glow from the afterburners was sufficient for this, and the radar operator could see the flaps. He reported that the position of the flaps was normal. By now the angle of bank was so great that it was impossible to maintain heading. We were being pulled to the left. I reported to base that we had a problem with the controls. Then the navigator thought, could it not be the fuel system that was at fault? He looked at the difference in the groups of tanks for the left and right engine. This was 1.5 tonnes [3,300lb]. For an aircraft like the Tu-22, this difference was not out of the ordinary and was within normal parameters. Engines are, after all, different and can use fuel at different rates and for a 'gluttonous' engine like the RD-7M2, all the more so.

[*At this point it is, perhaps, relevant to interrupt Lt-Col Fedyaev's account and explain a little about the Tu-22 fuel system. Each engine was supplied from its own group of tanks. In order that the centre of gravity shifted as a function of fuel consumption within defined limits, the groups of tanks were installed in the fuselage on either side of the centre of gravity. The left engine was fed from the forward group of tanks and the right engine from the rear group.* SB]

I gave the order to my crew: "We'll head for a diversion airfield", telling the navigator to look for the closest base to us at that time. I then started to reduce engine rpm in order to begin the descent. I felt the aircraft's nose rise – the opposite effect to what I'd expected. Once again, I increased power. It was obvious that we had a big problem. I started to monitor the fuel consumption and from the forward group of tanks it seemed to be leaking as if from a bucket. I then reported over the intercom that the automatic fuel management system had failed. The radar operator also reported that the left engine was shooting out flames (because more fuel was going into the engine than being fully ignited).

The control column of the Tu-22 was not actually a column in the usual sense of the word, but more like a pair of handlebars, or control bars, sticking out of the instrument panel. The travel of the control bar from the neutral position was 20–25cm (7.9–9.85in). Now, when the fuel consumption was out of balance and the centre of gravity had shifted significantly to the rear, it was necessary to hold the control bar almost fully forward. The nose, however, continued to pitch up. Then I reported to the crew: 'Prepare yourselves! We're going to jump' (*Gotov'tyes'! Budyem prygat'*). When the control bar was right up against the instrument panel I gave the command: 'Abandon the aircraft!' The radar operator went out very quickly. I could hear the seat travelling down the rails behind me. For a long time the navigator did not seem to be getting ready to go and I thought, 'What's he doing, sharpening his pencils?' I was by this time in a semi-supine position when he finally ejected. I then went out straight after him and only just in time – the pitch angle was almost 90° and I was almost completely on my back when the seat finally worked. As I flew away from the aircraft in the ejection seat I was able to see that one of the engines was still shooting out flames (later, I wondered if leaking fuel from the forward tanks had got into the air-intakes).

After separating from the seat I found myself in a rather unpleasant position – I was in a spin. The angular rotational speed was so high that blood was coming out of my ears and nose and the blood vessels in the whites of my eyes had burst. It was only at an altitude of around 4,000m (13,125ft) that I was able to stop the rotation and operate the parachute manually. Almost at the same time, the KAP-3 (*Kombinirovannyi Avtomat Parashutnyi*) barostatic mechanism triggered, which was designed to open the parachute automatically. Now descending by parachute, I started to look around to see which direction to take after I'd landed. Below, I could see the burning wreckage of my aircraft. There was a river down there. I estimated that I'd have to head north where I could see lights in the distance. I thought that I'd probably have to get to the river and travel along it. Before reaching the ground I'd prepared myself for the landing … and then landed right on top of a pine tree. I was left hanging about 5 metres (16ft) above the ground, but I managed to use the branches to help me get down. Before doing anything else I sat down under the pine tree to gather my thoughts. To head towards the aircraft would not only be pointless, but also dangerous. The wood might well have been set on fire and I could end up in the middle of it. During my childhood I'd lived in the taiga and knew what could happen in these situations. So I left the area with the aircraft about two kilometres (one and a quarter miles) to my right and set off north, with the wind in my face. I had no survival equipment with me – no NAZ (*Nosimyi Avariinyi Zapas* – the standard individual survival pack for Russian aircrew) and no pistol. The aircraft was not equipped with them. Everything the same as usual….

After a little while, I came across a small plot of land, cut down a branch which I made into a walking stick with my parachute harness knife (*stroporez*), found a woodland path and set off along it. At about 6 o'clock in the morning I came to some habitation which turned out to be a sort of corrective labour establishment (rather like a prison). In this military region, the 'powers that be' had already been forewarned that airmen could 'turn up out of the blue' and that they must be afforded all possible assistance. They immediately poured me a glass of alcohol (*spirt*) and I drank it like water. I'd never drunk spirits before as a way of getting over some [bad] experience that I'd lived through. While I was there I finally looked in a mirror and saw that my face was caked with blood. I must have looked like a bandit in a den of bandits!

When dawn broke, they put me in a vehicle with a platoon of soldiers and we went out to the crash site. After all, there were secret IFF units on the aircraft. However, while we were on our way in the vehicle, the internal security officer (*ofitser vnutrennikh voysk*) who was travelling with me received a call on the radio telling him that the search and rescue services had already found the aircraft, the area had been cordoned off and there was no need to go there. We were directed to a helicopter alighting area, where we had to wait for a helicopter which was flying in from the crash site. It turned out that my radar operator had gone back to the aircraft after he'd landed and was found by a search and rescue team. Fortunately, the aircraft had landed in an area which had already been scorched by a previous fire and it had not started another.

We were flown in the helicopter to the airfield at Myedvyezh'ye. My navigator was found some time after 3 o'clock in the afternoon at a railway station which he'd reached after landing. We were taken by aircraft, for 24 hours, back to Machulishchi, and then they brought us back again (to the crash site). The accident investigation commission worked at the site for a week. Based on the results of their investigative work the commission expressed their gratitude to (me and my) crew for our competent actions. The commander of the Long-range Air Force promoted me to the post of section commander (*komandir otryada*), although at the time I hadn't quite achieved Pilot First Class status (I still needed two qualifying landings).

I was posted to 290 ODRAP at Zyabrovka (near Gomel') in my new capacity. There I served for a year and then went to the Monino Air Force Academy. Then, the aero-medical commission at Monino, which at that time had installed some modern medical diagnostic equipment from Germany, found a 'shadow' on one of my lungs, an area of about 3cm (1.20in). It was from a collapsed lung sustained during my spinning descent after ejection. After that, (after finishing at Monino) I was only allowed to fly on aircraft with dual controls. (After that) I parted company with the Tu-22.

Write-off of Tu-22K 22.05.73
Weather conditions: 4/10ths cloud cover, cloud base 1,500m (4,920ft), visibility 10km (6.2 miles).

Circumstances
Major P, a Pilot First Class and a Tu-22 section (*otryad*) commander, was carrying out a daylight navex in VMC conditions as part of a regimental strength formation at low and extremely low altitude. The aircraft were flying in a column of flights with 1,000m (3,280ft) longitudinal separation and 20m (65ft) height differential. The flights themselves were in wedge formation with a lateral separation of 50m (165ft) and longitudinal separation of 60m (197ft). Major P and his crew were in the left-hand 'wingman' position in the seventh flight. After 1hr 15min, in the final stages of the flight, at a height of 900m (2,950ft) and a speed of 650kph (350kts), still maintaining position as left wingman in the flight formation, the aircraft commander, Major P, noticed a difference of 2 tonnes (4,410lb) in the fuel consumption readings of the two engines,

between the forward and rear groups of tanks. The fuel remainder for the left engine was 5 tonnes (11,022lb) and 7 tonnes (15,430lb) for the right-hand engine. After 1hr 16min 40sec of flight, Major P reported to the leader of the regimental group: 'The automatic fuel management system has failed, we have yellow lights, I'm switching over to the second tank.' Some 77 seconds before the accident occurred, the aircraft pulled out of the formation so that the crew could deal with the problem.

On the command of the group leader, the pilot switched over to manual control of fuel management and continued to climb, reducing speed to 620–600kph (335–325kts). At a height of 900m (2,950ft) and at the assigned flight speed the aircraft suddenly pitched up sharply and rocked from wing to wing. The pilot pushed the control bar fully forward into the instrument panel, but the aircraft did not respond to his control inputs. Continuing to pitch up, the aircraft completed a half loop and with the port wing stalled went into an uncontrolled descent. Thirty seconds later, it crashed into a wood 59km (37 miles) south-west of the town of Baranovichi, exploded and burnt out. Two crew members ejected safely (pilot and operator), but the navigator perished with the aircraft. From eye-witness accounts of the way the aircraft disintegrated on impact and the way it sliced through the trees, it was established that it was rotating about the vertical axis as it fell. With practically zero forward airspeed and a pitch angle of 75–80°, it hit the ground with the left wing slightly down in a tail-first attitude.

Cause
Loss of control leading to nose-up pitching with a 4g loading on the airframe, followed by the aircraft stalling. The loss of control resulted from a rearward shift in the centre-of-gravity to a value of 51% MAC (when the permitted value should have been 40% MAC), caused by failure of the sequencing of fuel delivery by the automatic fuel-management system.

Findings
Held responsible were:

1. The Leningrad (now St Petersburg) enterprise, 'Tekhpribor', which had not taken effective measures to improve the reliability of the fuel-management system
2. The Tupolev Design Bureau, which had not taken appropriate action to prevent fuses burning out in the circuits of the BAS-52A system.

Write-off of Tu-22R 12.04.78
Weather conditions: Cloud cover 5–8/10ths, cloud base 1,500m (4,920ft), cloud tops 3,000m (9,942ft), visibility 10km (6.2 miles).

Circumstances
Captain M, a section commander and Pilot First Class, was scheduled to conduct an aerial reconnaissance sortie over the range at Povrusk. It was a daylight sortie in VMC conditions, flying in a pair with a time interval between aircraft of one minute and a 300m (984ft) height differential. The flight altitude was 4,800m (15,750ft) and the speed was 750kph (405kts). Flying as wingman, he was positioned to the left of the leader with a horizontal distance between the two aircraft of 5–8km (3–5 miles) and was visible to the lead aircraft's airborne operator, both with the naked eye and on his monitoring equipment

(*Radio-Tekhnicheskaya Sistema*). (The airborne operator of the Tu-22R was also referred to as the RTS Operator.) In order to ensure a correct approach to the target, the flight leader made two turns to the left by 10° and 20°, the operator maintaining 'eyeball' contact with the wingman throughout. After being airborne for 54 minutes, and passing 2km (1.25 miles) to the right of the target area, the leader commenced a turn to starboard. The wingman then moved into a position where he was visible to the lead pilot and his RTS operator, and also started his turn, but with a rapidly increasing bank to the right and descending. At an altitude of 3,000m (9,842ft), the wingman entered cloud and in a steep right-hand spiral descent, with the speed increasing to more than 800kph (430kts), crashed into boggy ground. In the rapidly evolving situation, the crew ejected from the aircraft, but the height and increasing speed of descent were outside the normal operating parameters of the KT-1 seat and all three crew members perished.

The flight leader called the range controller on the radio and was authorised to descend to 1,500m (4,920ft); he then carried out two passes over the range to try to locate the point of impact of the aircraft and search for any signs of the crew. Having failed to find the aircraft and crew, the flight leader called the regional air traffic control centre in L'vov and the base ATC tower. The regional air traffic control centre sent search and rescue helicopters and an aircraft to the scene of the crash.

The flight leader and Tu-22 squadron commander, Captain Davydov, said in his report: 'At a distance of 50–60km (31–37 miles) to the target area, I called Captain M on VHF, but did not receive a reply. There were no replies to my repeated calls. The range controllers reported that we were passing to the right of the target. On the navigator's command, I started the first turn. Turning my head to the left, I saw Captain M's aircraft off my left wing at a distance of about 3–4km (2–2.5 miles), banking to the right at an angle of 45–50°. He did not reply to my calls. Then, with an increasing angle of bank, the aircraft went straight towards the ground. I shouted to them on the radio to jump (*prygat'*). The aircraft then went into cloud and I did not see it again. I reported to the range what had happened, requested a descent to 1,500m (4,920ft) and made two approaches to look for the crew and the aircraft, but did not manage to find anything.'

Cause
The cause could not be established because it was impossible to extract the aircraft from the great depth to which it had penetrated the peat bog.

Write-off of Tu-22U 28.05.80
Weather conditions: no cloud, visibility 10km (6.2 miles).

Circumstances
Captain B, a Pilot First Class and instructor Lt-Col P, the squadron commander, were carrying out a daylight instrument check flight 'under the hood' (*v zakrytoy kabinye*) in the airfield circuit pattern. At a distance of 18km (11 miles) on the approach and at a speed of 500kph (270kts) the crew lowered the flaps to 20°. At 12km (7.5 miles), with a speed of 450kph (243kts) and at a height of 500m (1,640ft), after setting flaps to 35° (the landing position), the crew felt the aircraft bank sharply 30° to the right. The pilots countered the banking with full deflection of the ailerons and rudder. Attempts by the instructor and the aircraft commander to raise the flaps were unsuccessful. The crew reported the situation to ATC, and on the authority of the duty controller they climbed to

1,050m (3,445ft). Using considerable force to maintain 'wings level' flight, both pilots and the navigator prepared to eject. The navigator and the aircraft commander both ejected successfully, but the instructor, Lt-Col P, because of the considerable g-loading affecting the aircraft, left the aircraft at only 660m (2,165ft), with a very high rate of descent, which was outside the design limits for the KT-1 seat, and he was killed.

Cause
Failure of the flap control system because of damage to the flap transmission drive shaft and a manufacturing design defect (KPN) in this system on this series of aircraft.

Findings
The Ministry for Aircraft Production was held responsible for the failure.

Write-off of Tu-22U 29.01.81
Weather conditions: no cloud, visibility 10km (6.2 miles).

Circumstances
Senior Lieutenant V, a qualified aircraft commander, was carrying out a day navex in VMC conditions. Eight minutes after take-off, at an altitude of 4,800m (15,750ft) and doing 700kph (378kts), the instructor, Major K, the deputy squadron commander, drew attention to unusual pitch oscillations of the aircraft, assumed control and checked the fuel contents. He discovered that the total contents were only 15 tonnes (33,070lb) instead of 27 tonnes (59,525lb), and a significant excess amount (+5 tonnes/11,000lb) in the rear group of tanks. This had led to a rearward shift in C-of-G causing the aircraft to pitch up. Fifteen minutes into the flight, when the control column (control bar) had to be pushed fully forward to maintain level flight, the instructor gave the order to abandon the aircraft. At that point, the pitch angle started to increase sharply.

The first to jettison the escape hatches was the aircraft commander, at an altitude of 4,800m (15,750ft); the instructor, Major K, ejected while the aircraft was tumbling out of control. After stalling, the aircraft broke up. The aircraft commander, Senior Lieutenant V, initiated the ejection process and the seat fired, but he remained in the cockpit because his parachute harness had not been fastened. The navigator was unable to eject because of the high and constantly changing g-loads on the airframe. The aircraft hit the ground at an angle of 70–80° in the inverted position, exploded and was burnt out. Both the pilot (aircraft commander) and the navigator were killed – the instructor landed without injury.

Cause
Loss of control following a shift of C-of-G beyond the permitted limits, because of an intensive fuel leakage from Tank 2.

Findings
The Minaviaprom was held responsible for the accident.

Write-off of Tu-22 29.04.81
Weather conditions: 10/10ths cloud cover, cloud base 510m (1,675ft), cloud tops 3,000m (9,842ft), visibility 6km (3.75 miles).

Circumstances
Captain K, a Pilot First Class and his crew were carrying out a daylight flight in the airfield zone area. During the climb at an altitude of 3,000m (9,842ft), the crew felt a jolt in the aircraft. The aircraft commander, having checked the operation of the engines, reported to the crew that the engines were normal and continued the climb. At an altitude of 7,500m (24,600ft) the crew heard a bang and saw that the left engine had shut down and was on fire. The pilot commenced a descent. Thirty-two seconds after the engine failure, the aircraft banked sharply to the left at 90°, turning inverted, while rotating and falling. On the aircraft commander's order, the navigator and RTS operator ejected and subsequently landed safely. The pilot jettisoned his hatch cover and initiated the ejection sequence, but because the interlocking halyard had not been attached correctly, linking seat operation with the jettisoning of the hatch, he was unable to eject and was killed when the aircraft hit the ground.

The RTS operator, Lieutenant T, declared in his report:

After take-off and climb to 3,000m and sensing dynamic braking of the aircraft, I asked the commander, 'What's happened?' Somewhere around 7,300m [23,950ft] I noticed that the red failure warning lamp for the port engine's 28-volt generator had come on, which I reported to the commander. At the same time, he said, 'The port engine has shut down.' Once again I felt dynamic braking of the aircraft, and the aircraft started banking sharply to the left and turned over onto its back, under considerable g-force, which was changing constantly. At that moment, the aircraft commander ordered: 'Crew, abandon the aircraft!' At first, I couldn't use the ejection handle because of the considerable g-force, but at the precise moment when this was not so great I managed to eject. I was in free fall until reaching an altitude of 4,000m (13,125ft), and then the KAP-3 barostatic mechanism cut in and opened my parachute. As I was descending, I noticed the navigator's parachute, but could not see the aircraft. I landed safely and later met up with the navigator.

Cause
Detachment of the blades of the first stage of the turbine of the port engine and disintegration of the main engine casing, leading to an outbreak of fire, failure of the aircraft's control system and loss of control.

The reason for the tragic loss of the pilot was the failure of the ejection gun to fire because the seat locking pin, interlinked with the jettisoning of the entry hatch cover, was still in place. The interlinking halyard, connected to the hatch cover, which would normally extract the locking pin when the hatch cover was jettisoned, had not been connected, or had been incorrectly connected, by the aircraft's crew chief.

Findings
The aircraft's crew chief was held responsible for the death of the pilot because of his negligence in carrying out the ejection seat pre-flight checks.

Incident involving a Tu-22 on 29.05.84 – Lieutenant Akhmed Ali Al'bani of the Iraqi Air Force
Weather conditions: no cloud, visibility 10km (6.2 miles).

Circumstances
Lieutenant Akhmed Ali Al'bani of the Iraqi Air Force, undergoing conversion training at the Aviation Training Centre (*Uchebnyi Aviatsionnyi Tsentr*) specially established for Iraqi crew conversion at Zyabrovka (*See next chapter*), was performing a daylight sortie in the airfield zone, in VMC conditions. After take-off and climbing with the cruising afterburner setting, Lt Ali Al'bani, while checking the readings from the automatic fuel-management system, allowed his attention to be distracted from monitoring the climb. The aircraft then started to experience a significant increase in pitch angle and rate of climb. The operator and navigator had no idea of the cause of the aircraft's resulting behaviour. The operator jettisoned his escape hatch and ejected. Having noticed the considerable rate of climb, the aircraft commander pushed the control column (bar) fully forward, pulling -1g. The navigator, hearing the roaring noise in the cockpit, feeling the swirl of air (from the ejection of the operator) and confused by the effects of the negative g, also ejected. The operator, after the automatic ejection sequence had commenced, did not separate from the seat (maintaining a vice-like grip on the ejection seat handles throughout the descent), and flew straight into the ground, still sitting in the seat, and was killed on impact. The navigator sustained a fractured hip, but was otherwise unhurt. The aircraft commander, Lt Ali Al'bani, reported to local ATC the fact that his crew had ejected, performed two approaches and carried out a normal landing at his training base. Lt Ali Al'bani declared in his report:

> After take-off I retracted the undercarriage, flaps and landing lights. I used a take-off power setting of UPRT-84 (i.e. 84% power on the engine power lever setting). I set up the autopilot, selected the 'Bank' (*Kren*) switch on, 'Switch-on AP' (AP being *AvtoPilot*) but did not press the button. The angle of climb was normal. The navigator gave the command for the first turn onto a heading of 305°. At that moment, I noticed that the angle of attack had increased significantly (even the operator, Al'mari, had noticed this). At the same time, I looked at the fuel consumption indicator and at the yellow lamps, in order to make sure that the centre of gravity was within the normal range. Having confirmed that everything was normal, I started to push the control column forward and suddenly heard a sound, like an explosion. When I'd pushed the control column forward, and banking slightly to the right, I noticed that the red warning light was on, indicating that the operator had ejected. At that time the aircraft was descending vertically. When I set the power lever to 'Flight idle' (*Malyi gaz*), the navigator, Ashur, also ejected. I reported to the duty controller in the ATC tower that the operator and the navigator had ejected. Having carried out two approaches in accordance with the instructions of the RP (*Rukovodityel' Polyotov* – controller of flying), I made a normal landing off the third approach.

Cause
1. Gross error of handling by the pilot, allowing the aircraft to sustain g-loadings of -1 to +4.5g. (Believing that the pilot had lost control, both the airborne operator and navigator ejected without being commanded to do so)
2. Very poor crew resource management and coordination.

Findings
The aircraft commander, Lt Akhmed Ali Al'bani, was held responsible for the incident and its consequences.

Write-off of Tu-22R 28.05.87

Weather conditions: 10/10ths cloud, cloud base 450–500m (1,475–1,640ft), visibility 6–8km (3.75–5 miles). Snow squalls.

Circumstances

Section commander Major E, a Pilot First Class, and his crew were to carry out a daylight visual reconnaissance sortie at a true height of 450m (1,475ft) and at a speed of 600kph (324kts). On entry to the search zone, contrary to the tasked order, he descended to a height of only 200m (656ft). The wingman's crew stayed at 500m (1,640ft) on the order of the pairs leader. During the search of the tasked area, Major E allowed the aircraft to descend to 150m (492ft), witnessed by the triggering of the dangerous height warning on the altimeter. The crew, having completed the task in accordance with the set orders (*sic*), took the unfounded decision to perform additional approaches in the zone.

  Departing the designated search area, the crew flew into a snow squall. In the transition from visual flight to flight on instruments, the pilot allowed his attention to be distracted from handling the aircraft, since he was talking to the wingman's crew. The aircraft was now descending with around 40° of bank to the right and at a rate of descent of about 2,950ft/min. Three and a half seconds before the first impact with some trees, the pilot made an attempt to bring the aircraft's nose up and stop the descent, pulling back on the stick until the ADU (automatic control force limiter in the tailplane circuit) cut in, and deflected the ailerons up to 19°, to bring the wings level.

  The aircraft started to come out of the banked attitude at a height of around 70–80m (230–260ft) with an angular speed of up to 16° per second and from the descent, pulling up to 2.7g, at an indicated airspeed of 685kph (370kts). However, at a height of 10–12m (32–39ft) and descending at an angle of 2–3°, the aircraft struck the trees. Subsequently, at a height of only one metre (3.3ft) it stopped descending, and at a distance of 450m (1,475ft) from the first impact point, climbing slightly at about 2° angle of attack, the aircraft hit the main wooded area, broke up and caught fire. All three crew members were killed.

Cause

Gross breach of the assigned tasking order and conduct of the flight, along with a voluntary (self-authorised) descent to a less than safe height, accompanied by failure to monitor the height after the aircraft had entered a snow squall.

Findings

The aircraft commander was held responsible for the accident.

Incidents occurring during weapons training
Write-off of Tu-22R 02.04.76

Weather conditions: no cloud, visibility 10km (6.2 miles).

Circumstances

Captain Z, a Pilot Second Class, and his crew were carrying out a night navex including a reconnaissance training sortie over the range at Karanogaiskii, against Target 105, using four FOTAB-100-140 photo-flash bombs, equipped with thermo-resistant AT-EhA fuses. One hour and twenty-seven minutes into the flight, on the first approach to Karanogaiskii range, at an altitude 9,300m (30,500ft) and a true airspeed of 970kph (525kts), the crew carried out a preliminary marking drop of two FOTABs on the target, which they reported to the range controller. The range controller received the message, after which all communication with the aircraft ceased. After release of the two FOTABs, an explosion had occurred on board the aircraft. It caught fire, broke into two sections, which crashed to the ground, exploding on impact and completely burning out.

The RTS operator and the aircraft commander ejected successfully, opening their parachutes manually and landing without injury. The navigator had slid his seat forward to enable him to carry out the aiming of the FOTABs, and his belts were also undone, so he needed more time to prepare for ejection. He finally ejected at low altitude and his parachute did not have time to inflate fully before hitting the ground, and he was killed.

Cause
Detonation of the FOTABs in the weapons bay as a result of incorrect installation of the spherical plug on the cable of the fuse, and poor monitoring of the loading of the bombs by the armourers of the regimental engineering service (*Inzhenyernaya Tekhnicheskaya Sluzhba*). A contributing factor was the poor design feature of the weapons (bombing) equipment, which did not provide an interlock device that would have enabled the fuse to activate only after the bombs had been released from the suspension shackles.

Write-off of Tu-22R 18.05.77 (Major Kondratenko and crew)
Weather conditions: 4/10ths cloud, visibility 10km (6.2 miles).

Circumstances
Senior test-pilot Major V G Kondratenko and his crew were carrying out a test flight following the tragic mid-air explosion on 2 April 1976 of another Tu-22R (described above), to establish safe separation of FOTAB bombs from the aircraft using an improved fusing system. One hour and thirty-seven minutes into the flight, on the sixth approach at an altitude of 10,000m (32,800ft) and doing 610kph (330kts), an explosion occurred in the weapons bay after releasing a FOTAB-250T photo-flash bomb. The aircraft began to break up in the area of the weapons bay following the explosion, and the tail section, engulfed in flames, fell to the ground and exploded on impact. The forward section of the fuselage continued to fly on, with an increasing rate of angular velocity about the longitudinal axis in an increasingly steep dive, and eventually hit the ground and exploded. Fortunately, the crew were able to eject from the stricken aircraft soon after it had broken up at 10,000m, and all survived.

Cause
Detonation of a FOTAB-250T photo-flash bomb, armed with an ATK-EhA fuse, in the aircraft's weapons bay, which occurred after the FOTAB was released from the bomb shackle on the upper station of the KD3-22M bomb rack. The explosion occurred at the moment the bomb had descended from the rack by 49–55cm (19.5–21.7in), in the vicinity of the rack's second suspension station.

The most likely reason for the detonation of the FOTAB was the triggering of the fuse at the moment when the electrical pulse was delivered to the EhPU (*EhlektroPirotekhnicheskoye Ustroystvo*) electro-pyrotechnic unit, or with a very short time delay.

Findings
The factory where the fuses were produced was held responsible for the accident.

Accidents occurring during formation flying and in-flight refuelling
Write-off of Tu-22 26.06.69
Weather conditions: no cloud, visibility 10km (6.2 miles).

Circumstances
After carrying out a night formation flying in a pair, deputy squadron commander Major L, and Captain F, both Pilots First Class, set up on the landing course and overflew the main runway at a height of 2,000m (6,560ft). On the second approach, during the third and fourth turns at a height of 2,000m and a speed of 600kph (324kts), the right-hand wingman, Captain F, had fallen behind the leader, and when turning onto the final approach, trying to overfly the runway at the assigned lateral and longitudinal separation between the aircraft, increased speed and pursued the leader on a heading displaced less than 5° from that of the lead aircraft. During the 'pursuit', Captain F took the ATC controller's command for the group (i.e. pair) to break (*Razreshayu rospusk gruppy*) to mean 'Operate independently', and stopped observing the leader, believing that he was carrying out a left turn, and collided with him. Initially, the collision involved the upper part of the wingman's left-hand air-intake, which hit the lower part of the fuselage, and then the left side panel of the wingman's fin hit the side of the fuselage of the lead aircraft.

As a result of the collision, the wingman's fin was totally destroyed and separated from the aircraft in pieces. The aircraft flew on for a further 3km (2 miles), descending to around 1,500–1,300m (4,920–4,265ft), suddenly increasing its rate of descent with a sharply increasing angle of bank to the left and in the inverted position, at an angle of 60°, hit the ground and exploded. Captain F ejected from the stricken aircraft at a height of 1,300m (4,265ft) and landed safely about 1,600m (1 mile) away from the point of impact of the aircraft. Neither the operator nor the navigator was able to eject because of the high g-forces acting upon the aircraft, and both perished.

Major L, commander of the lead aircraft, having realised that his flying controls had failed, had also felt a strong vibration and strange noises. Having received a report from the operator that the starboard engine was on fire, he decided to abandon the aircraft and ordered the crew to eject. They did so at a height of 2,000m (6,560ft) at a speed of 600kph (324kts), and all landed safely. After the crew had ejected, the aircraft followed a right-hand spiral trajectory with a gradually increasing angle of bank and radius of turn, and 54 seconds after the crew had abandoned it, the aircraft hit the ground and exploded.

Cause
1. Unsatisfactory organisation and preparation by Captain F and his crew for carrying out a 'solo' [*sic*] formation flight at night as wingman in a pair. (In this context, 'solo' [*samostoyatyel'nyi*] probably means 'without having been fully checked out to fly in formation)
2. Captain F and his crew had been authorised to fly the sortie with insufficient practice in night formation flying
3. The leader and wingman in the pairs formation had breached the requirements laid down in NPP-63 (*Nastavlyeniye po Proizvodstvu Polyotov-63*) Flight Operations Manual (dated 1963) in their handling of the aircraft and general situation awareness

when carrying out a formation flight. Apart from this, the crew roster had been changed on the day of the flight and the leader of the pair was changed, which had not actually been essential for that particular task. No additional planning had been carried out to take into account the change in the formation structure in terms of crew experience.

Findings
The following were held responsible for the accident:

1. Captain F, the aircraft commander flying as wingman
2. Major L, the deputy squadron commander
3. The flight controllers
4. The Regiment Commander.

Write-off of Tu-22K 24.07.70
Weather conditions: 5/10ths to 6/10ths cloud cover, cloud base 2600–3,000m (8,530–9,840ft), visibility 8km (5 miles).

Circumstances
Section commander, Major K, a Pilot First Class, was carrying out his first solo daylight sortie to practise dry refuelling contacts and formation flying with a tanker.

The pilot made a normal contact with the tanker in the refuelling zone. While holding a normal position around 5–8m (16–26ft) below the tanker, the hose started to whip because of a momentary drop in pressure in the pipe. The pressure drop was caused by incorrect procedures adopted by the hose operator on the tanker, who maintained the pumps in the 'on' position and did not monitor the pressure. The windshield of the Tu-22 was sprayed with fuel, and the pilot took this to mean a 'self-disconnect' and slightly reduced power to drop back a little, at the same time commencing a turn to port. He did not confirm that it was a disconnect (either with the tanker operator, or by seeing the green 'Stsepka' light ['stsepka' meaning, literally tow bar or line and, in the context of in-flight refuelling, the fact that tanker and receiver were 'hooked up']). The Tu-22 drifted off to port, with the height differential between the two aircraft now reduced to 1–2m (3.3–6.5ft), and still connected to the tanker.

As a result of moving outside the permitted manoeuvring zone between the two aircraft, in terms of height and direction, the hose fractured at the weak link. The Tu-22's windshield was once again sprayed with fuel and the pilot lost sight of the tanker. Then, as result of fuel from the broken hose entering the air-intake of the Tu-22's starboard engine, it began to surge, followed by an explosion and flame-out. Being close to the vortex core of the wake turbulence from the tanker and with the starboard engine out of action, the Tu-22 suddenly began to bank steeply to the right. The pilot chopped power, but the bank to the right had occurred so rapidly that it was only by the time it had reached 60–70° that he was able to use left rudder and full left aileron to recover. The navigator ejected without being commanded to do so by the pilot, who was taken by surprise at his action. The rapidly developing situation was making it difficult for the aircraft commander to maintain control, and he was unable to bring the aircraft back to normal flight. At an altitude of 4,500m (14,760ft) the pilot ordered the radar operator to abandon the aircraft, and he himself ejected at 1,700m (5,575ft) and 600kph (324kts). The aircraft hit the ground soon after and exploded on impact.

Cause
The situation occurred as a result of a number of errors committed by the pilot, Major K, when flying the aircraft in formation with the tanker after the 'whipping' of the hose had occurred and the windscreen had been sprayed with fuel.

   The pilot's erroneous actions took the aircraft outside the permitted manoeuvring zone behind the tanker into the tanker's wake turbulence, fracturing the hose at the weak link and leading to the onset of an undemanded steep bank to the right. Fuel from the fractured hose then entered the starboard engine, causing it to surge, flame out and eventually catch fire. The whipping, or snaking, of the hose was the result of incorrect actions by the tanker's refuelling operator.

Findings
1. The Tu-22 pilot was deemed responsible for the accident
2. The tanker refuelling operator was held responsible for the hose being allowed to 'snake' during the refuelling practice.

Write-off of Tu-22K 21.05.73
Weather conditions: 3/10ths cloud, cloud base 1,500m (4,920ft), visibility 10km (6.2 miles)).

Circumstances
Section commander Major Sh, a Pilot Second Class, was carrying out a daylight formation training flight in a formation of nine aircraft. The nine aircraft were flying in a starboard echelon formation of flights, and the flights themselves were also in starboard echelon formation. The formation practice was being conducted at extremely low altitude in the vicinity of the airfield. Major Sh was flying as second wingman in the tail-end flight of the nine aircraft. After turning onto the third approach on finals, at a distance of 50km (27nm) from base, Major Sh lagged behind the leader of his section by 1.5–2km (0.8–1nm), then, having increased his closing speed to maintain formation, he overshot and ended up 50–70m (165–230ft) ahead of Major P, his flight leader.

   Realising that he was very close to the other aircraft in his formation section and worried that he might collide with them, Major Sh started to turn away to starboard in a 30° banked turn. At that moment, his radar operator, Junior Lieutenant S, shouted, 'Higher, commander!' He collided with the leader's aircraft, after which both aircraft separated. Major Sh, without checking the aircraft's control responses or checking the feasibility of continuing to fly the aircraft and without giving any kind of command, hastily ejected from the aircraft and landed safely. Twenty-one seconds later, at a height of 130–140m (425–460ft), the radar operator, Junior Lieutenant S, also ejected but was killed because the ejection height was too low for his parachute to open fully. The abandoned aircraft continued to descend at an angle of about 3–4°, the navigator, Captain P, remaining on board and perishing when the aircraft exploded on impact with the ground.

   The leader of the tail-end section of the nine-aircraft formation, Major P, having confirmed that his aircraft was responding normally after the collision, climbed to 900m (2,950ft) on the authority of the controller of flying. His approach for landing the damaged aircraft was performed 'flapless', and Major P demonstrated great skill in landing without further incident. As a result of the collision, the starboard section of the tailplane was extensively damaged from Rib 5 to Rib 15, the leading edge of the starboard wing was torn off and the aircraft had suffered other damage.

Cause
1. The mid-air collision was caused by gross breach of flight organisation and control on the regiment
2. Major Sh was authorised to fly the sortie without adequate training and the skills required to fly in formation and fill the second wingman slot in a starboard echelon section of three aircraft
3. Catastrophe followed the hasty and panicked reaction of Major Sh, who abandoned a still controllable aircraft without informing his crew of his intended actions.

Findings
The following conclusions were drawn from the commission of inquiry:

1. The person directly responsible for the accident and its tragic outcome for his crew was the formation section leader, Major Sh, who in the rapidly evolving train of events after the collision took no action to save either his crew or the aircraft and was the first to eject
2. The Regiment commander was held to be culpable for poor flight organisation and control.

Write-off of Tu-22U 05.09.79
Weather conditions: 4/10ths of alto-cumulus cloud, cloud base 3,600m (11,810ft), cloud tops 6,500m (21,325ft), visibility 10km (6.2 miles).

Circumstances
Captain L, a Pilot First Class, and his crew, were carrying out a night air-to-air refuelling check flight involving 'dry' contact with the tanker. Eight minutes into the flight, at 6,800m (22,310ft) and a speed of 820kph (443kts), or Mach 0.97, accelerating behind the tanker, the aircraft experienced severe vibration lasting for around 3 seconds. After the vibration ceased, the starboard wing dipped (side-slipped to the right). The pilots corrected this by retrimming the aircraft. The crew then performed two 'dry' contacts with the tanker as planned, after which they descended to circuit height (800m/2,625ft) and stabilised the speed at 500kph (270kts). On lowering the undercarriage when passing abeam the outer beacon (DPRM), a lateral g-shock of 0.79 was felt, and attempts by the pilots to maintain straight and level flight were unsuccessful. The instructor took the decision to abandon the aircraft and ordered the crew to eject. The navigator ejected and landed safely. Both pilots also ejected, but because the height was below the safe working parameters for the KT-1 seat, they were both killed.

The navigator, Senior Lieutenant T, stated in his report:

The take-off and climb were normal. After the first waypoint, Major K (instructor-pilot) picked up the tanker, off to the right and turning. Flying straight and level at 12km (6.5 miles) distance from the tanker, Major K gave the order to set an indicated airspeed of 800kph (432kts) and engage afterburners. The altitude at this time was 6,300m (20,670ft). After about 30–40 seconds, Major K told Captain L to keep an eye on the Mach number, which was approaching unity (Mach 1) at that time. I looked at the

KUS-2000 indicator (which provided a combined indication, with two needles, of indicated airspeed (IAS) and true airspeed (TAS)), and this showed an IAS of 800kph (432kts) and a TAS of 1,080kph (583kts). Almost immediately after this, the aircraft jolted and we felt severe vibration, which then ceased suddenly. At a speed of 780kph (420kts) IAS Major K said that the aircraft seemed to be pulling to the left, Captain L confirming this.

We carried out the third and fourth turns and started to formate on the tanker. The first contact and disconnect was normal. On the second disconnect, the aircraft jolted sharply again. Major K shouted to Captain L to maintain control, and he replied that he had control, but was unable to stabilise the aircraft and did not understand what was happening. Then we disconnected from the tanker, turned away to starboard, requested descent and on the controller's command we levelled off at 1,500m (4,920ft) over the DPRM. After this we descended further to circuit height at 800m (2,625ft) and 500kph (270kts). Major K asked Captain L if he had noticed that the ball of the EhUP was in the extreme right-hand sector of the indicator, and warned that they would have to be observant, because something was not quite right with the handling of the aircraft. (The EhUP is the *Ehlektricheskii Ukazatyel' Povorota*, or Electrical Turn and Slip Indicator.) Captain L then lowered the undercarriage and immediately after lowering it the aircraft banked sharply to the left and climbed. I saw that we were at 1,000m (3,280ft) and felt that I was being pushed strongly to the right. I decided to eject.

Cause
Loss of longitudinal stability and control because of damage to the vertical fin as a result of Mach-induced buffeting at an altitude of 6,800m (22,310ft) at Mach 0.97.

Findings
The aircraft repair plant (*Aviatsionnyi Remontnyi Zavod* – ARZ), which had carried out maintenance on the aircraft to an insufficiently high standard, was held responsible for the accident.

Incidents occurring during the descent, approach and landing
Damage to Tu-22R 15.10.65
Weather conditions: 10/10ths cloud, cloud base 600m (1,970ft), visibility 6km (3.75 miles), wind 6m/sec (11.65kts).

Circumstances
Captain P, a Pilot First Class, was making an approach to land after completion of a daylight navex. The landing was made at a speed of 330kph (178kts) and with a landing weight of 56.5 tonnes (124,560lb). Touch-down occurred on the starboard undercarriage bogie with a rate of descent of 5–6m/sec (984–1,180ft/min), and the aircraft bounced on initial contact with the runway, banking 7–10° to starboard. After the final touchdown, the aircraft again leaped into the air, and at that moment the left undercarriage leg started to fold. As a result of the rupturing of the retraction jack caused by the hard touchdown, flames began to appear in the left undercarriage nacelle. The pilot selected the brake parachutes and held the aircraft in a straight line down the runway. Having flown on for a further 190–200m (625–655ft), the aircraft settled smoothly onto the starboard bogie and the left wingtip. Having then received a command from the controller of flying, '*Na grunt*' (literally, 'onto the ground' i.e.

the grass strip alongside the runway), the pilot turned left off the runway some 1,000m (3,280ft) from the point of touchdown, swung round 90° to the axis of the runway and came to a standstill. The fire in the left undercarriage nacelle extinguished (automatically) after all the hydraulic fuel had been burned up. The aircraft sustained significant damage.

On 15 November 1966, almost a year later, the same pilot performed a heavy landing in the same conditions, in which the left undercarriage collapsed after a landing run of 350m (1,150ft). Damage to the aircraft was the same as in the first incident. Analysis of this pilot's landings, with the aid of the KZ-63 flight parameter recorder, showed that every third landing was made with 2g to 3.2g loading on the airframe.

Cause
Gross error of handling by the aircraft commander during the landing, leading to the onset of bouncing and pitching (*galopirovanie*). In a hard touchdown on one undercarriage bogie, with a rate of descent of 5m/sec (984ft/min), angular oscillations of the bogie can occur, with a frequency of around 10Hz, and the aircraft can start to depart from the runway and begin to bounce, which increases the amplitude of oscillation. This can then lead to the forward brake compensating strut hitting the torque links of the shock absorber and, in the reverse direction, of the bogie support beam hitting the shock-absorber strut. In this situation, the up-lock of the bogie can be accidentally released, with subsequent folding of the leg. [*From the context of the Russian account of this accident, it is not clear whether it describes a general set of conditions for such a sequence of events to occur, or the* actual *sequence involving Captain P's aircraft.* AD]

Findings
The aircraft commander, Captain P, and the executive staff of the regiment were held responsible for the accident.

Write-off of Tu-22 05.10.67
Weather conditions: 10/10ths cloud cover, cloud base 600m (1,970ft), visibility 6km (3.75 miles).

Circumstances
Captain D, a Pilot First Class, had been carrying out a daylight navex. On approach to land, after passing over the DPRM (outer beacon), the tailplane controls jammed. The pilot reported the incident to the controller of flying, plus the fact that he was unable to bring the aircraft out of the descent, in spite of all his efforts to do so. The aircraft crashed into the ground between the outer beacon (DPRM) and the inner beacon (BPRM), exploded and burned out, killing all three crew members.

Cause
The likely cause of the accident was a loose bolt jamming the moving parts of the RP-21 tailplane actuator, preventing the pilot from pulling the control column towards him.

Findings
The Minaviaprom was held responsible for the accident.

Write-off of Tu-22P 13.03.68

Weather conditions: 10/10ths cloud, cloud base 600m (1,970ft), visibility 10km (6.2 miles).

Circumstances

Captain V, a Pilot First Class, and his crew had been authorised for a daylight flight in the airfield zone. After the second turn, while approaching the point abeam the outer beacon (*traverz*), the pilot lowered the undercarriage, but did not get a green light to indicate that the right undercarriage leg was down and locked. He reported this to the tower. On the command of the controller of flying, the undercarriage was retracted and lowered again, with the same result. After this, the undercarriage was once again raised and lowered, using the primary and secondary hydraulic systems. The undercarriage light for the starboard leg still did not illuminate. The controller of flying then ordered the crew to perform a number of ILS approaches in order to burn off fuel and bring the aircraft down to minimum landing weight, overshooting at 150–200m (490–655ft) in each case. The controller of flying took the decision to get the pilot to land the aircraft on the left main undercarriage leg and the nose-wheel, and gave the crew the following instructions when the aircraft was on the fourth approach: 'Switch on inert gas, tighten seat belts' followed by 'After lowering flaps, make the aircraft safe, switch to battery supply for the instruments, shut down the engines after touch-down' and finally 'Land with a small amount of bank, on the left undercarriage bogie.'

After acknowledging the command to switch over to battery power, with a confirmatory 'Instrument power supply from batteries switched on' and the navigator's report, 'Speed 400kph, height 80m' (216kts and 262ft), communications between the aircraft and the tower ceased. After receiving permission to land, the aircraft's approach from the outer beacon to the point of flare over the runway was flown without any deviation. During the flare, at a height of around 3–4m (10–13ft), the aircraft ballooned upwards. The ballooning stopped at a height of about 10–12m (33–40ft), after which the aircraft began to descend, initially in a slightly nose down attitude and then with an increasing angle of nose-up pitch. Having descended to a height of 0.3–0.5m (1–1.6ft), the aircraft again ballooned upwards, and at a height of about 40–50m (130–165ft), the pitch angle increased to 70°. Losing speed, the aircraft stalled, and at a distance of 1,000m (3,280ft) from the threshold of the runway, crashed back onto the runway surface and exploded. All three crew members were killed.

Cause

The catastrophe occurred as a result of the aircraft experiencing uncontrollable pitch oscillations during the flare procedure, leading to loss of speed and an eventual stall.

The reason for the onset of the pitch oscillations was because both pitch dampers had been switched off when switching over to battery power for the flight instruments. The transfer to battery power was carried out by the crew on the command of the controller of flying and in compliance with the requirements laid down in the *Tu-22 Operating Instructions, Book 1, Edition 5 of 1964.*

The pilot, flying the aircraft on the approach with a rearward C-of-G of 40–42% MAC (because of the low fuel load), did not know that the pitch dampers had been switched off. This clearly made handling the aircraft on the approach very difficult. He had moved the control column with the same input rates as he would with fully serviceable pitch dampers, which had led to pilot-induced oscillation (*raskachka*), departure beyond the critical angle of attack and loss of speed, followed by a stall.

Write-off of Tu-22K 22.03.68
Weather conditions: 10/10ths cloud cover, cloud base 180–190m (590–625ft), cloud tops 470m (1,542ft), visibility 3km (less than 2 miles).

Circumstances
Major K, a Pilot First Class and section commander, was carrying out a daylight formation training sortie as section leader at an altitude of 3,000m (9,842ft). After the section had performed a formation break (*rospusk*), Major K entered cloud in the descent after the fourth turn in the circuit pattern, going down to 250m (820ft) over the outer beacon (DPRM) and, failing to see the ground, decided to overshoot. After completing the turn, the aircraft continued on the centreline with subsequent deviations of 100m, 200m and 300m, and at a distance of 4–5km (2.5–3 miles) from the runway, went outside the control sector of the RSP-6 airfield approach radar. After passing over the outer beacon at 12.49hrs local time, the controller of flying (RP) gave the order for the crew to climb to 10,000m (32,800ft) and head for Bobruisk, and then, after another minute, to head for Baranovichi. [*Although not stated as such in the report, the order 'to head for' these airfields can be taken to mean 'divert to'. AD*] At 12.53hrs, having asked for the aircraft's fuel remainder and being told that it was 6,300kg (13,890lb), the RP again commanded the pilot to divert to Bobruisk, on a heading of 003°. At a distance of 200km (108nm) from Bobruisk, Major K started his descent, having received landing conditions and the initial approach height of 1,200m (3,940ft) from the Bobruisk controller of flying, Lt-Col S.

At 13.08hrs Lt-Col S commanded the crew to head for (i.e. divert to) Zyabrovka. The crew turned back and at a distance of 70km (38nm) from Bobruisk took up course for Zyabrovka, which was 140km (76nm) away. Flying at 1,200m (3,940ft), the crew made contact with the controller of flying at Zyabrovka on VHF and received his airfield's approach and landing conditions. A little later, the RP informed the crew of their distance to the airfield, gave permission to descend to 600m (1,970ft) and then told the pilot to make a corrective turn to the right by 10°, because he was flying 40km (21.5nm) left of the required heading. This was followed by commands to make a corrective turn by 30° (*Dovyernitye vpravo 30 gradusov*), then 'Make a right turn' and then 'Set course 180°.' After transmitting the information that they were now 25km (13.5nm) from the airfield, the RP gave the order to orbit to the left.

In fact the tower was controlling a Tu-16 which was on the approach to Zyabrovka at the same time, at an altitude of 5,400m (17,720ft), but the ATC crew at that airfield did not see Major K's aircraft, which was flying at 600m (1,970ft) and 90km (48.5nm) from Zyabrovka.

At 13.19hrs, while approaching the airfield on a heading of 105° at 600m, about 45–50km (24–27nm) from the runway, the Tu-22's starboard engine flamed out after running out of fuel and the port engine started to operate unstably. The crew ejected from the aircraft at an altitude of 1,100m (3,610ft) and a speed of about 420–450kph (225–245kts) and landed safely in a wood 25km (15.5 miles) south-west of the city of Gomel'.

Cause
The crew abandoned the aircraft after the starboard engine had flamed out and the port engine had become unstable as a result of running out of fuel. The critical fuel situation was the consequence of:

- deficiencies in the organisation and control of flights by senior regimental officers at Ozyornoye airfield
- failure by Major K and his crew to maintain the most fuel-efficient power settings in the flight to the diversion airfield (*zapasnyi aehrodrom*), which led to an increase in fuel consumption
- uncoordinated actions by the Command Post (*Komandnyi Punkt*) of the Independent Heavy Bomber Aviation Corps (OTBAK) at Vinnitsa and Smolensk, in providing adequate support for an aircraft *en route* to a diversion airfield.

Findings
The following were all deemed culpable for the uncoordinated handling of the diversion of the Tu-22 and its subsequent loss:

1. The Regiment Commander
2. The Divisional Commander
3. The duty officer in the Command Post of the Independent Heavy Bomber Aviation Corps HQ in Smolensk
4. The Senior Navigating Officer in the Command Post in Vinnitsa
5. Section commander Major K and Section navigator Captain O
6. The controller of flying (RP) at Bobruisk airfield.

Write-off of Tu-22K 26.04.71
Weather conditions: 10/10ths cloud cover, cloud base 270–300m (885–984ft), cloud tops 1,500m (4,920ft), visibility 3km (less than 2 miles), wind 4m/sec (8kts).

Circumstances
Captain P, a Pilot First Class, was carrying out a training flight in the airfield zone to practise an approach to land from a calculated descent point in defined weather minima at night. Descent from the zone and following the landing course up to a distance of 11km (6nm) was handled without any noticeable deviation in height, heading or speed. From around 10km (5.4nm), however, the aircraft started to descend below the glide path, and at a distance of 7km (3.8nm) it was actually 60m (197ft) below the glide path. At that moment, the duty GCA (Ground Controlled Approach) controller reported, 'Distance 7, 20 below glide path, on heading.' The aircraft commander acknowledged by saying, 'Am correcting.' However, the descent was not corrected and the aircraft continued to descend below the glide slope. The increase in the angle of descent after the aircraft had passed the 10–9km (5.4–5nm) point was caused by the nose-down pitching moment when the pilot lowered the flaps from 20° to 35°. Thereafter, during the rest of the descent on finals, the aircraft commander did not fully re-trim the aircraft after selecting 35° of flap, and there was still considerable back pressure on the control column, particularly after setting flaps at 35°.

At this time, the pilot's attention was distracted from flying the aircraft when he was looking for the selector switch for the landing lights, which was located behind him and on the left side panel, and he did not notice the increase in rate of descent. He also did not react to the GCA controller's call, 'Distance 7, 20 below glide-path', although he had responded by saying that he was correcting. The navigator, occupied with monitoring the aircraft's heading and distance read-offs to the runway, also did not monitor the height.

As a result of the crew's errors, failure to carry out the requirements laid down in the aircraft's operating manual and imprecise and incorrect actions by the GCA controller, the aircraft had been allowed to descend prematurely, first to hit some trees and then fly into the ground. At a distance of 4,600m (2.5nm) and 208m (680ft) from the outer beacon, about 18m (60ft) left of the centreline, descending wings level on a 2.5° glide slope, the aircraft started to strike the tops of some trees with its left wing. It then hit the left mast of the outer beacon itself (DPRM), and with the bank angle to the left increasing to 23°, around 93m (305ft) from the DPRM, it struck a group of trees in ancient woodland and crashed into the ground, exploded and burst into flames, killing all three crew members.

Cause
Pilot error in the handling of the aircraft on final approach after reaching the 10km to 9km point in the descent, witnessed by the loss of height and descent below the glide path.
    The pilot error was a consequence of not having fully regained the skills of flying in reduced weather minima conditions at night, after a long break in flying in similar conditions.

Findings
The following were held responsible for the accident:

1. The aircraft commander, Captain P
2. The squadron commander and the regiment commander.

Damage to Tu-22P 12.03.73
Weather conditions: Cloudless sky, visibility 8km (5 miles), wind 20° from the left at 3–4m/sec (6–7.75kts), temperature 22°C.

Circumstances
Section commander Captain K, a Pilot Second Class, had been detailed to fly a daylight training sortie in the airfield zone. On the approach to land, after passing the inner beacon (BPRM), the pilot descended below the glide slope, then corrected his mistake and flared high, over the runway threshold. Touchdown occurred at a speed of 320kph (173kts), a g-loading of 1.6 and a touchdown point 500m (1,640ft) along the runway, without selecting flight idle on the engines (77.5% on the port engine and 87% on the starboard). Both brake 'chutes broke away after they had deployed. After being told by the tower that the brake 'chutes had detached from the aircraft, the crew became confused, apart from using the main wheel brakes on the runway, and did not take any emergency action after the aircraft had run onto the loose earth. With the engines still set at a high power rating, the aircraft ran 750m (2,460ft) off the end of the runway.
    Rolling over the emergency braking area, the aircraft hit the support post for the approach lights with its starboard wing, five concrete posts forming part of the airfield boundary fence and, turning right through 70°, slid into the house of a local inhabitant. The aircraft was substantially damaged, but the crew were unhurt. The assistant RP did not demonstrate much urgency in his instructions, and seeing the aircraft approaching at high speed, limited his commands to the crew to, 'Chop power' (*'Ubrat' gaz'*), an instruction which was not heeded by the pilot. The controller of flying (RP) himself did not set a particularly good example.

Cause
Pilot error, witnessed by the fact that the aircraft landed 'long', with a high power setting on both engines, resulting in the brake parachutes being torn off on deployment, causing the aircraft to enter the overrun at high speed and strike various airfield structures.

The poor landing approach was exacerbated by the negligent actions of the ground controllers in the ensuing emergency situation, who did little to assist the crew.

Findings
The aircraft commander, Captain K, was held responsible for the accident.

Accident involving Tu-22P 10.02.75
Weather conditions: 9/10ths cloud cover, cloud base 800m (2,625ft), visibility 8km (5 miles), wind 80° from the right, 4m/sec (7.8kts).

Circumstances
Senior Lieutenant M, a Pilot Third Class, was carrying out a daylight practice instrument training flight in a 'closed cockpit' (i.e. under the blind flying hood). At a distance of 7–8km (3.75–4.33nm) on the approach, the pilot mistook the packed-earth (or grass) landing strip (GVPP – *Gruntovaya Vzlyotno-Posadochnaya Polosa*) for the main concrete runway (*Betonnaya* VPP). His error was detected after passing over the inner beacon (BPRM) at a height of 30–40m (100–130ft), and he took the unfounded decision to overshoot, selecting undercarriage and flaps up. He selected full afterburner, but almost immediately made another decision, to land off that approach. Chopping power, he placed the undercarriage and flap selector levers to the 'Neutral' position. He landed with the undercarriage and flaps in the semi-retracted position, hitting the tail bumper on the runway and with one bogie on the earth strip and the other on the concrete, 1,650m (5,410ft) from the runway threshold and at an angle of 10° to it. On the landing run, the undercarriage collapsed completely, but the pilot tried to deploy the brake 'chutes. The aircraft slid along the concrete and the earth strip for a distance of 1,750m (5,740ft), hit a row of runway lights and the metal (iron) framework of the runway arrester barrier (ATU – *Avariinoye Tormoznoye Ustroystvo*) and came to a standstill.

Lieutenant M stated in his report:

'After passing the inner beacon I began to prepare for the landing, in spite of the fact that the navigator had told me, 'We're slightly left [of the centreline].' At a height of 30m [100ft] I realised that I was approaching the GVPP and attempted to go round again, selecting full power and placing the undercarriage and flap levers in the retracted position. At the point of flare, I realised that I could not go round again, chopped power and placed both levers (undercarriage and flaps) in the 'Neutral' position. I landed on the main undercarriage, but it started to collapse. I pressed the button to deploy the brake 'chutes, bounced over the runway and gave left rudder to direct the aircraft along the main runway. During the landing I acted upon the instructions of the controller of flying (RP).

Causes
1. The carelessness of the aircraft commander and his poor knowledge of the aircraft's aerodynamics

2. Insufficiently well inculcated piloting skills
3. Lack of timely assistance and advice from the ATC control group
4. Deficiencies in designating and marking out of the airfield.

Findings
The aircraft commander, Senior Lieutenant M, was held responsible for the accident.

Damage to Tu-22K 20.08.82
Weather conditions: Cloudless sky, visibility 10km (6.2 miles).

Circumstances
Captain N, a Pilot First Class, was carrying out a daylight training flight in the airfield zone. The approach to land, up to the point of passing over the DPRM beacon, was conducted without any deviations, but at a distance of 3km (just less than 2nm) the pilot was told that he was below the glide slope by 10m (33ft). At 2km (1nm) the navigator informed him that he was a little low and that the speed was 370kph (200kts). The aircraft passed over the inner beacon (BPRM) at 80m (262ft) at a speed of 360kph (194kts). About 600m (1,970ft) to the runway, the pilot selected flight idle on the throttles, commenced a rather high flare and passed over the threshold of the runway 'high'. Touchdown occurred at 270kph (146kts), 300m (984ft) into the runway, with a g-loading of 2.05 on the tail section of the aircraft. Inspection of the aircraft on the ground later showed that the tail-bumper jack and surrounding structure had been damaged, and the tips of both tailplane sections had been buckled, with deformation and cracks on the tailplane surface. The left edge of the cut-out for the tail bumper was buckled and part of the panelling had been torn away, and three areas of panelling around the brake 'chute housing had been damaged. The aircraft was repaired by the regiment's engineering personnel and was returned to service. The conclusions of the investigating commission were that the young crew had been trained in a rather 'formalistic' way, without taking account of individual capabilities and without inculcating the particular skills required in landing the Tu-22. The pilot was not experienced in landing the aircraft in different local airfield conditions.

Cause
Pilot error.

Findings
The pilot's section commander was held responsible, for having authorised the pilot for a 'solo' flight without sufficiently developed skills in the procedure of landing the Tu-22.

Damage to Tu-22 10.01.83
Weather conditions: 10/10ths strato-nimbus cloud cover, cloud base 350m (1,150ft), light rain, visibility 4km (2.5 miles), head wind 10–12m/sec (19.5–23kts).

Circumstances
Lt-Col ShCh, a Sniper Pilot, had been carrying out a night navex (his second flight in that particular flying detail). While approaching to land and flying over the railway track which passed across the airfield boundary 396m (1,300ft) from the runway threshold, the aircraft hit the air ventilation pipe of a refrigerated wagon of a passing train with its

starboard undercarriage bogie. The controller of flying, the runway controller and the duty GCA controller, who had seen the aircraft's descent below the glide slope, both visually and on radar, all gave several commands to the pilot not to descend below the glide path. After colliding with the train, the pilot landed on the main runway at a speed of 340kph (184kts), 250m (820ft) into the runway, 23m (75ft) left of the centreline, with a g-loading of 1.3. At a distance of 600m (1,970ft) from the runway threshold the starboard undercarriage leg touched down on the concrete. Seeing a trail of sparks from the starboard undercarriage leg, the RP gave the order to go onto the earth strip. At a distance of 800m, the starboard wing made contact with the runway surface and the aircraft turned right onto the strip at a distance of 1,750m (5,740ft). The aircraft came to rest 2,100m (6,890ft) from the threshold of the runway, 48m (157ft) from the edge, having swung round to the right, through 60°. On entering the earth strip, the pilot had shut down the engines and the RTS operator had jettisoned the escape hatch (*sic*), through which the crew exited the aircraft without any outside assistance after it had stopped.

Cause
Pilot error, as a result of distraction when close to the ground. Unsatisfactory flight organisation on the regiment, witnessed by the fact that the landing approach did not take into account the particular conditions of the approach corridor at that end of the runway (i.e. the presence of the railway line). There were also poor preventive measures in place to avoid striking obstacles on the approach, and a lax procedure for monitoring the actions of a highly qualified pilot, which was a causative factor in the poorly flown approach.
    A number of other factors contributed to the accident:

• The navigator had been posted in from another unit and had not flown in the local area with the crew in question, but had been authorised to fly a navex almost immediately after arrival
• The duration of the crew's first flight (a daylight navex) was not 2hrs 30min (as per the flight plan), but 2hrs 47min, so the crew could only have flown another sortie that day if it was in the airfield zone, or circuits. They should not have been authorised to fly another navex.

Findings
The aircraft commander was held responsible for the accident.
    The regiment commander was blamed for not taking measures to put in place adequate instructions for carrying out flights in the region of the airfield, and adopt approach methods which took into account the particular demands of the approach corridor to his airfield.

Heavy landing of Tu-22 29.03.85
Weather conditions: 8/10ths cloud cover, cloud base 800m (2,625ft), visibility 10km (6.2 miles), head wind 10m/sec (19.5kts).

Circumstances
Captain Ya, a Pilot First Class, had been carrying out a daylight training flight in the airfield zone in cloud. On the landing approach, after passing the inner beacon (BPRM), the pilot allowed the aircraft to descend sharply. The pilot also reacted quite sharply to the

RP's command to pick up the nose (*Poddyerzhi!*), and the aircraft ballooned upwards about 6–8m (20–25ft). As the speed dropped off and the angle of pitch increased, the pilot lost visual contact with the ground and made a hard landing 550m (1,800ft) down the runway at 230kph (124kts), exerting a 3.5g loading on the airframe. During touchdown, the tailskid struck the runway surface and the aircraft swerved off onto the earth strip. Having rolled for 450m (1,475ft) along the earth strip, the pilot managed to get the aircraft back onto the concrete, and stopped the aircraft within the confines of the runway.

Cause
Pilot error, in not correcting his poorly executed approach, using excessive force in pulling the control column back to slow the descent, coupled with ignorance of the use of the tailplane trim mechanism.

Findings
The aircraft commander and the squadron commander were both held responsible for the accident.

Accident to Tu-22U 30.08.85 (Captain V. F. Panin and crew)
Weather conditions: cloudless sky, visibility 10km (6.2 miles) no wind.

Circumstances
Captain V. F. Panin, a Pilot Second Class, with instructor Major V. S. Sadovnikov, the deputy squadron commander, was carrying out a night check flight with Panin flying the aircraft (*vyvoznoy polyot*) in the airfield zone. After completion of the flight in the zone, the crew made an approach, with a planned overshoot at 200m (656ft). The aircraft passed over the outer beacon without any deviation in height or speed, and the aircraft commander reported to the RP: '404, outer [beacon], overshoot' (404 being his individual call sign). Having received permission to overshoot, the pilot increased power to maximum dry thrust, selected undercarriage and flaps up and continued to descend on the glide slope to allow the speed to build up to 450–500kph (243–270kts) for the go-around. At a height of 140–130m (460–425ft) and flying at 380kph (205kts), the aircraft suddenly shook. The RP and his assistant noticed sparks coming from the one of the engines and informed the crew, also telling them to check the engine rpm.

The instructor, Major Sadovnikov, took control, and judged from the loss of rpm on the starboard engine that it had failed. Noting that the speed was not increasing and that they were losing height, he decided to lower the undercarriage and land. At the moment of engine failure, the undercarriage was in the mid-travel position, which created additional drag and hindered acceleration. The time for retraction and extension of the undercarriage with only one engine operative was 30 seconds, twice as long as normal. The aircraft overflew the inner beacon at 70m (230ft) and 370kph (200kts), with the flaps fully retracted. Delaying the descent in anticipation of the undercarriage extending fully and locking down, Major Sadovnikov turned to line up on the earth strip alongside the runway. The pitch angle had now reached 12–13° and the AUASP (*Avtomaticheskii Ukazatyel' Ugla Ataki s Signalizatsiyey i Peregruzki*) combined angle of attack and g-meter warning system had 'kicked' in. At 320kph (173kts), with a clean wing and at a weight of 61.2 tonnes (134,920lb) the aircraft 'sank' a little, since it was at minimum permitted flying speed in that condition, and it landed on the earth strip 25m (82ft) to the left of the concrete runway, 2,100m (6,890ft) from the threshold and about 4–5° off the centreline. After touchdown, Major Sadovnikov reduced power on the left engine to 'ground idle', and the aircraft, with partially extended undercarriage, careered along the earth strip for 250m (820ft), then back onto the concrete runway, subsequently running off the end into the overrun area on the extended centreline. At a distance of 600m (1,970ft) from the end of the main runway, the aircraft struck the support structure of the SP-68 ILS localizer mast, swung round to the right 20° and then hit the corner of the building housing the SP-68 transmitter units, seriously damaging the aircraft's nose in the process. After the aircraft had come to a standstill, the navigator made all systems safe and the aircraft commander shut off the fuel cocks, but it caught fire when leaking fuel ignited from the damaged tanks. The crew were able to evacuate the burning aircraft without injury.

Cause
The reason for the onset of surge in the starboard engine was fatigue damage to Blade 16 of the first stage of the compressor and subsequent damage to the gas-generator section of the engine.

The cause of the emergency on the approach was the starboard engine failing on the glide slope, at the point where the pilot was just about to go around again at a height below 150m (492ft), which prevented the crew from completing their planned task.

Accident to Tu-22U 12.08.86
Weather conditions: 5/10ths to 8/10ths cloud cover, high and medium, visibility 6-10km (3.75–6.2 miles), wind variable 2–5m/sec (4–10kts).

Circumstances
Section commander Major G and instructor (and deputy regiment commander) Lt-Col V (both Pilots First Class) had been carrying out a daylight check flight as part of a test programme following a 24-month refurbishment of the aircraft. On the approach to land, the undercarriage had not been fully extended because of a breach of approach procedures and failure to read the pre-landing checks. When the aircraft commander selected the undercarriage down, the crew did not confirm that they had three green lights indicating that all the wheels were down and locked. The aircraft commander selected the undercarriage lever to 'neutral', which led to the aircraft landing with a partially extended undercarriage, which subsequently collapsed during the 'roll-out' on the runway. The landing was made 350m (1,150ft) down the runway, at a speed of 310kph (167kts) and a g-loading of 1.3. At a distance of 1,450m (4,758ft) down the runway, the aircraft ran off to the left onto the earth strip and came to a stop 18m (60ft) from the edge of the main runway at an angle of 20° to the centreline. The crew evacuated the aircraft through the emergency escape hatches.

Lt-Col V, in correcting the errors committed by Major G on the approach, did not accentuate (i.e. positively ascertain) the fact that the undercarriage was (fully) down and did not monitor the actions of the aircraft commander. The aircraft commander did not report the position of the undercarriage to the RP when he asked for permission to land. The ATC crew were unable to determine the partial extension of the undercarriage because it was not fully visible to them in that position and a controller monitoring aircraft on the approach reported to them that the undercarriage was extended when the aircraft was 8km (5 miles) out. The pilot and instructor had not had any breaks in their flying activities.

Cause
The instructor and pilot had committed errors in the sequence of selecting the undercarriage down, which led to the aircraft landing with only a partially extended undercarriage.

Findings
The following were held responsible for the accident:

1. The instructor-pilot (who was also the deputy regiment commander), who did not monitor the actions of the crew, which had endangered the safety of the aircraft and led to it landing with a partially extended undercarriage
2. The aircraft commander, (and also a section commander), for his breach of procedures on the approach with regard to selecting the undercarriage down for landing.

Accident to Tu-22K 29.08.86
Weather conditions: cloudless sky, visibility 10km (6.2 miles), head wind 2m/sec (4kts).

Circumstances
Captain Zh, a Pilot First Class, had been carrying out night circuit practice in a closed cockpit (*zakrytaya kabina*), i.e. under the 'blind flying hood'. On his second approach, passing abeam the outer beacon (*traverz*), the pilot decided to lower the undercarriage after the third turn (contravening 'Instructions for pilots and crew of the Tu-22'), which he reported to his crew, although he did not lower it, did not read the check list and the crew did not remind him about it.

On the fourth turn (onto finals), the pilot reported to the RP: 'On the fourth turn, undercarriage down for landing, fuel remainder 6 tonnes', without having checked that he had three green lights indicating that the wheels were down. On passing over the outer beacon, he again reported undercarriage and flaps down, again without confirming that he had three greens. The aircraft touched down with its undercarriage retracted, 650m (2,130ft) down the runway, at a speed of 300kph (162kts) and a g-loading of 1.25, 10m (33ft) to the left of the centreline. It touched down on the rear fuselage, followed by the inner flap sections and then the undercarriage nacelles, before finally settling onto the main fuselage.

The landing weight was 56.5 tonnes (124,560lb) and the fuel remainder was 6 tonnes (13,230lb). The aircraft stopped 1,800m (5,900ft) from the initial point of contact with the runway. The crew had shut down the engines and made the aircraft 'safe' on the command of the RP during the landing 'roll', and evacuated the aircraft through the emergency escape hatches after it had come to a standstill and were not injured. The ATC crew had not been able to monitor the undercarriage's position because of the absence of external position lights. The aircraft suffered extensive damage to the underside of the fuselage, inner wing sections and undercarriage nacelles.

Cause
Lack of crew discipline, resulting in breach of 'Instructions for pilots and crew of the Tu-22', and failure to use the pre-landing check list (flight reference cards).

Findings
The aircraft commander and his crew were held responsible for the accident.
  This aircraft later became a 'gate guard' at the entrance to Ozyornoye air base.

Damage to Tu-22R 06.07.87
Weather conditions: light cloud cover, visibility 6–10km (3.75–6.2 miles), wind 20° from the left, 3m/sec (6kts).

Circumstances
Section commander Captain B, a Pilot First Class, was detailed to fly a daylight positioning flight from the operational deployment airfield at Borispol' (near Kiev, in the Ukraine) back to his base at Nezhin, also in the Ukraine. With the objective of burning off fuel to bring the aircraft down to normal landing weight, the crew carried out four approaches at base in closed cockpit conditions (i.e. practice instrument flight conditions 'under the hood'). On the penultimate approach, after opening the blind flying screens, at a height of 120m (394ft) and overshooting, in response to the navigator's check call: 'Undercarriage, flaps', the pilot briefly selected the retracted position, which was sufficient to unlock the gear from its extended position. Then, on the final circuit and approach to land, with the blind flying screens now folded away, the pilot reported three times to the RP and twice to the crew that the undercarriage was down and that he had green lights, without actually checking that this was the case. The aircraft touched down with a partially extended undercarriage, 400m (1,312ft) down the runway, at a speed of 320kph (173kts), with a g-loading of 1.3. During the roll-out on the runway, the starboard undercarriage bogie started to collapse more rapidly than the port side. The pilot realised this and used right rudder to pull off onto the earth strip. The aircraft, now with a fully retracted undercarriage, slid off onto the earth strip at an angle of 20° to the main runway, and came to a standstill at a distance of 1,450m (4,757ft) from the threshold and 110m (360ft) from the centreline. The crew evacuated the aircraft through the emergency escape hatches unaided.

Cause
Lack of discipline on the part of the aircraft commander, demonstrated by his failure to observe the requirements of the standard 'Instructions for the Tu-22 and the KBP' (Basic Training Manual), which led to poor cockpit management and landing with a partially retracted undercarriage.

Findings
The following were held responsible for the accident:

1. Captain B, a section commander (*komandir otryada*), for not carrying out the requirements laid down in the 'Instructions for the Tu-22 and the KBP' (*Kurs Boyevoy Podgotovki*)
2. The permanent controller of flying (*shtatnyi rukovodityel' polyotov*), for his inexpert commands to fly the circuit with undercarriage extended.

CHAPTER TEN

Training of Iraqi and Libyan Aircrews

As mentioned elsewhere in the book, the Tu-22 was exported to two Arab countries, namely Iraq (in 1973) and Libya (in 1975). After the decision had been taken to supply Iraq with the bomber version of the Tu-22 (Tu-22A Variant 'B'), it was also considered essential to set up a special training centre for both Iraqi aircrew and ground servicing personnel in the Soviet Union. For reasons of security the Soviet authorities did not want to use the existing 43rd Centre for Combat Application and Conversion Training at Ryazan', already involved in the training of Soviet aircrews on the recce and missile-carrying variants of the Tu-22. Consequently, in accordance with a directive from the General Staff of the Soviet Air Force, it was decided to set up a temporary, specialised aviation training centre, attached to 290 ODRAP at Zyabrovka in Byelorussia. The training centre (*Uchebnyi Aviatsionnyi Tsentr* – UATs) was designated 'temporary' since it had only been created to function for the duration required to train the Arab personnel, as defined by a special agreement signed between the USSR and Iraq, and was opened in December 1972. The Aviation Training Centre at Zyabrovka comprised the following departments:

1. Centre Administration
2. A flight training department (comprising twelve instructors)
3. A translation office
4. A secure facility (*sekretnaya chast'*, or secret unit, in Russian)
5. Two aviation Sections (*otryady*), with two Section commander-instructors, two Section navigator-instructors, two aircraft commander-instructors, two navigator-instructors and five radio-technical systems/airborne operator-instructors
6. Three Tu-22R and three Tu-22U aircraft
7. An engineering support unit.

Initially, the instructional teams were attached to the centre, with flight and technical training instructors coming from Nezhin in the Ukraine, as well as Baranovichi and Machulishchi in Byelorussia itself, while the aircraft were supplied from Soviet Air Force regiments for the duration of the training period. The centre was also supported by 1340 Aviation Technical Base and 980 Independent Communications Battalion, plus the airfield radar services already in place at Zyabrovka. Since the scope of the tasks handled by 290 ODRAP and the battalions had been widened as a result of needing to support the UATs, they were augmented by one or two specialists as necessary to train the Arab ground crews. The Aviation Technical Base at Zyabrovka also received some additional vehicles for the duration of the training period. These included an AKPM-3 aircraft washing bowser, a TZ-22 refuelling bowser, a ZSZh-66 for the replenishment of special fluids, an APA-50M electrical power generator, an aircraft tug and a UPG-300 unit for checking the hydraulic system. Two 'hotels' were also built on the base at Zyabrovka for the instructional staff and the Iraqi Air Force personnel.

There was a lot of fuss when the UATs was preparing to receive its first 'guests', with the Russian side being told the likes and dislikes of the Iraqi contingent and, particularly, what they liked to eat. They also had to consider what colours they should paint the walls of the rooms of their hotel, and the colours were changed twice before the Iraqis were satisfied. The first commander of the Aviation Training Centre was Lt-Col Shukshin, followed later by Lt-Cols Osyeev and Chernenko. The first group of Iraqis arrived at Zyabrovka in the middle of winter in 1973, having flown directly to Zyabrovka from Iraq, wearing only lightweight summer clothing, and many were accompanied by wives and children. At that time of year there was –20°C of frost on the ground, so the Iraqis were quickly wrapped in blankets and bundled onto buses to take them to their hotel on the base. This first group was the largest received during the existence of the centre, comprising a total of 300 personnel and families. Included in this number were ten crews selected for conversion onto the Tu-22, i.e. pilots, navigators, airborne operators, plus ground crew. A problem over the type of food provided for the Iraqi contingent arose in the first weeks of their presence at Zyabrovka. They used to eat with the Soviet air and ground crew personnel in the aircrew and ground crew mess halls, and one of the Soviet instructors, Lt-Col Yerusenko, recalls that he had noticed that his students would always seem hungry. What the Russians had not appreciated was the fact that the Arabs would only eat specially prepared (halal) meat, which had to be either mutton or veal, slaughtered according to Islamic tradition. Mutton and lamb was scarce and expensive in the area around Zyabrovka, so Lt-Col Yerusenko advised the Iraqis to purchase veal, rent two or three freezers in which to store it, and eat 'normal' meat. What they actually did was to dismember calves which they had purchased locally, skinning them behind the hotel with a special curved knife and observing the tradition of holding the head of the animal facing the East. Within a few days of being able to prepare their own meat, the problem of feeding their Iraqi guests appeared to have been resolved satisfactorily. The Iraqi aircrew lived on the second floor of the hotel, and no one from the non-officer ranks could visit without express permission, or unless they had been summoned specifically.

The training course at the UATs lasted nine months, and the pilots, navigators and airborne operators were only taught how to operate the aircraft in daylight conditions; night flying was not carried out by the Aviation Training Centre. Selection of pilots to fly the Tu-22 was carried out by a special commission in Iraq (and, later, in Libya), which included a number of Soviet pilots. The Arab side would propose a number of candidates, but the Soviet pilots would make the final selection. Selection was based on a number of factors, the main one being where the pilot had carried out his initial flight training, followed by the type of aircraft which he had flown, how well he flew and how many flying hours he had in his log book. Almost all the pilots, particularly among the Libyan group, were from wealthy families, and all (Iraqis and Libyans) had completed their flying training in Yugoslavia, Turkey and other Western countries. They had all been pilots for some time and were usually qualified on more than one type of aircraft. There were, of course, exceptions, and veterans of the Aviation Training Centre remember that in the first Iraqi group there was a very capable young pilot, Lieutenant Damin. He always used to boast that he was the youngest Tu-22 pilot in the world, and was, indeed, only 23 years old. He was equally proud of the fact that he came from the same district of Iraq as Saddam Hussein. At this time (early 1970s) the Tu-22 was considered to be very much a prestigious aircraft to fly and pilots were always very carefully selected. The Soviet instructors considered that their Arab students (both Iraqis and Libyans) were fairly competent pilots and had almost all previously flown fighters. In general, they were all well trained, but had little experience of flying in IMC conditions. All the Arab pilots had a fear of flying in cloud and whenever they were approaching cloud they would turn away, which always surprised their Soviet instructors. The Arab pilots would simply say that they did not have clouds in their countries, so there was no need to learn how to fly inside them!

During their conversion training, the Arab pilots would sometimes carry out their solo flights, not on the Tu-22R, but on the Tu-22U, in which case a Russian navigator would occupy the instructor's seat, to make sure that the Arab student did not make any errors. Occasionally, therefore, trainee pilots and navigators would be authorised to fly with comparatively limited experience on type. Students who had shown great aptitude during training would be allowed to fly 'solo' on the Tu-22R, and there were even rare occasions when the entire crew was Arab (*See Chapter Nine and the incident involving Lt Ali Akhmed Al'bani*). More often than not, however, crews were mixed Russian and Arab, with the Russian being any one of the Tu-22's three specialist aircrew members – pilot, navigator or airborne operator, as required. In 1975, the first contingent of Libyan students arrived in the USSR to begin their conversion training on the Tu-22, following the syllabus and procedures established in 1973 for the Iraqis, and like their Iraqi 'cousins', involved a small number of rear services support personnel. The latter were to be trained to support the aircraft's operation in Libya. Problems in training the aircrew and technical support crews of the Iraqi and Libyan Air Forces were similar, and it was particularly difficult for the Soviet instructors to become accustomed to the unusual Arab temperament.

Major Labetik remembers one curious incident illustrating this point rather graphically: 'I was the navigator on a sortie with Colonel Khayak of the Libyan Air Force. We had climbed to 11,000m (36,090ft) and were climbing further, up to the aircraft's ceiling (of around 14,000m (45,930ft)). Everything was normal. Then suddenly, he commanded, 'Landing' (*posdaka*). I said to him, 'Mustafa, what landing?', to which he replied, 'No, *posdaka*' (*sic*). We descended rapidly from 11,000m and the controller of aircraft at base did not understand what was happening, so I explained to him that the pilot had requested an immediate landing. The controller of flying queried this and asked 'What's happened?' The pilot would only say 'agzhet' (ostensibly oxygen in Arabic). ATC told him that he still had a lot of fuel on board and he could not land at that weight. Nevertheless, Col Khayak lowered the undercarriage at 600kph (324kts) and I shouted to him that the wheels would be ripped off – the speed was too high. We touched down at 380kph (205kts) and miraculously the parachutes were not torn off. We climbed out of the aircraft and were met by the head of the UATs, Lt-Col Shukshin. The Libyan pilot said to him, 'I need a car, I want to go home!' We asked him, 'What's wrong?' but he would only say, 'I'll tell you tomorrow what happened.' then he got into the car and rushed off….. Evidently he never *did* reveal the reason for his urgent need to land, but the incident did not have an adverse effect on his career, since he later went on to become Deputy Commander of the Libyan Air Force!

However, in spite of all the minor problems, the training which the Arab personnel received at the Aviation Training Centre at Zyabrovka was of a particularly high standard. The navigators who attended the training centre were taught not only navigation, but also the basic principles of aerial bombing. The initial phase of training was carried out using the Tu-124UShS navigation training variant of the *Cookpot* twin-turbofan airliner. For bombing training the aircraft was equipped with bomb racks on which it was possible to suspend P-50 50kg (110lb) practice bombs. The Tu-124UShS was on the strength of 290 ODRAP and was made available to the Aviation Training Centre when required. It was a particularly useful training aid for the Tu-22 units because between fifteen and twenty navigators could be trained in bomb aiming on a single sortie. Additionally, an instructor could more easily correct any mistakes which a student might make, or show certain exercises by example, if required. Sometimes, Tu-22 pilots (i.e. 290 ODRAP pilots) would fly out to the range on the Tu-124UShS, so that they could familiarise themselves with the approach and make a note of distinctive landmarks, etc. Trainee airborne operators destined for the Tu-22 had to complete not less than fifty hours of bomb-aiming procedures on the Tu-124UShS in order to qualify. The aircraft was in service with 290 ODRAP until the end of the 1980s, when it was replaced by a Tu-134UShS to perform the same task.

The second wave of Arab trainees arrived at Zyabrovka in 1982, and the temporary Aviation Training Centre was reactivated in compliance with Directive No. 315/5/1650 of the General Staff of the Ministry of Defence of the USSR, dated 5 May 1982 and Directive No. 314/5/825 of 24 November 1982. An additional Directive, 123/3/1298 of 4 December 1982 issued by the Main HQ of the Soviet Air Force, through the Commander

Iraqi pilots of the first intake at the Aviation Training Centre at Zyabrovka pose in front of the centre's HQ building in 1975.

A Libyan Air Force pilot (in the centre of the photo) and his navigator (on the right) after their first solo flight at Zyabrovka, holding bouquets of flowers with which this event was normally celebrated. *Aviation Training Centre.*

Another photo of an Arab crew after their first 'solo' on the Tu-22 at Zyabrovka. *S Burdin Archive.*

of the 46th Air Army of the Supreme High Command, completed the formalities for the reactivation of the temporary UATs. The total number of personnel on this occasion was 153 servicemen and thirty-six other employees and staff. The centre had been reopened to train eighteen Iraqi and seventy Libyan personnel, reopening on 6 December 1982. The first stream involved only the Iraqis, who completed their training at the end of 1983, followed in 1984 by crews from the Libyan Air Force. Since the Tu-22 had been participating in combat activity in both Iraq and Libya, the Soviet Union had decided that it was justified in training additional crews for the two countries. In order that Iraq and Libya could use the facilities of the Aviation Training Centre at any time, it was decided to place the running of the centre on a permanent footing. This decision was formalised by the signing of another Directive from the General Staff, 314/1 dated September 1986, and a Directive of the Main HQ of the Soviet Air Force, 123/3, dated 26 September 1986. After this, the UATs became a permanent training facility, although since there was no need to train large numbers of Arab personnel, it was possible to reduce the number of instructors and non-essential military personnel attached to the centre. The total number of personnel at this time was reduced to 127 servicemen of all ranks, and the Aviation Training Centre continued to function as a permanent facility until 1992. Then, with the cooling of relations between the USSR and Iraq and the USSR and Libya in the early 1990s, along with the preparations for the retirement of the Tu-22 from Soviet Air Force service, it was decided to close down the centre in 1993, a year before the disbandment of 290 ODRAP. In the two main phases of its existence, the Aviation Training Centre at Zyabrovka had prepared three groups of aircrew and ground crew to operate the Tu-22A *Blinder-As* of the Iraqi and Libyan Air Forces.

Operating the Tu-22 in Iraq and Libya
After signing the agreement for the supply of Tu-22s to the Iraqi Air Force, the Russian side had to find spare airframes which could be refurbished and brought up to a suitable standard for resale. The aircraft selected came from a batch of early Tu-22As which had been withdrawn from Soviet Air Force service, Tu-22Rs and Tu-22U trainers which had been languishing in various Scientific Research Institutes and air force regiments, as well as spare airframes from the Ministry for Aircraft Production. The aircraft were then transferred to the Kazan' manufacturing plant, where they were brought up to the *Ehtalon* standard described in Chapter One, and also underwent major overhaul. Additionally, they incorporated minor equipment changes compared with the Soviet Tu-22s, and the Russian IFF system was removed. All the combat variants (i.e. excluding the Tu-22U) were modified to the unified (*Ehtalonnyi*) standard as Tu-22A Variant B (*Bombardirovshchik*) freefall bombers. (*It is appropriate at this point to reiterate that there was no such variant as the Tu-22B, per se, this being an erroneous and perhaps 'lazy' contraction of Tu-22A Variant B*). As already mentioned, Iraq was the first export recipient of the Tu-22, in 1973, with the first ten crews being trained at the Aviation Training Centre at Zyabrovka in the same year. According to information at the disposal of the author, Iraq received ten Tu-22A *Blinder-As* and one or two Tu-22U *Blinder-Ds* under the agreement, which were all flown to Iraq by Soviet crews. The route took them over Turkey, which had authorised overflight of their territory, albeit with a certain measure of 'economy with the truth' on the part of the Russians. When questioned by the Turks about their nationality, aircraft type, and the number in the group, the Russians always replied 'Type N' (that is, a Tu-16), and that they were a flight (*zveno*) of three aircraft. There was always an English-speaking interpreter in the lead crew, who occupied the airborne operator's position and was there to communicate in English with *en route* ATC facilities.

Libya received its first Tu-22As in 1975, and the provenance of these aircraft was broadly similar to that of the Iraqi examples, comprising a mix of modification levels, all brought up to the *Ehtalonnyi* standard from a variety of sources. Libya took delivery of at least nine *Blinders*, including at least one Tu-22U, and were delivered in two batches, the first comprising five aircraft and the second four. All the Libyan *Blinders* were ferried from the USSR by crews from 290 ODRAP at Zyabrovka. The procedure was standard, with the aircrew being ferried by transport aircraft to the manufacturing plant at Kazan', where the refurbished Tu-22s were handed over to the 290 ODRAP personnel. The aircraft were then flown back to Zyabrovka, where they were refuelled before setting off for Libya, the route taking them via Chop in the Ukraine on the border with Hungary, Tököl, near Budapest, and then Dubrovnik in the former Yugoslavia. Thereafter, they flew down the Adriatic Sea between Albania and Italy, staying closer to Italy than Albania, because the Russians trusted the Italians more than the Albanians, with whom relations had deteriorated at that time. Once over the Mediterranean Sea, the *Blinders* headed for the Libyan coastal town of Misuratah, before turning to head for the capital, Tripoli, where they landed after their four-hour flight. (The delivery flight from the USSR to Iraq took about the same length of time.)

The flight was originally planned to be flown in pairs, with a two-minute interval between aircraft, but in the end they chose to remain within visible distance of each other during the transit. During the delivery, one of the Tu-22As, flown by Major Kolonchakov, suffered a hydraulic system malfunction, which resulted in AMG-10 fluid leaking into the pressure cabin. AMG-10 gives off pungent fumes, and this affected the crew's breathing and stung their eyes. The crew requested an emergency landing at Dubrovnik, but the officer controlling the ferry flight in the USSR refused the request, and also forbade them from returning to land at the Soviet diversion airfields at Stryj and Ozyornoye. The crew therefore had no choice other than to continue to their planned destination at Tripoli. When the aircraft rolled to a stop at Tripoli and the crew hatches were opened, several litres of AMG-10 fluid flooded out onto the runway (the aircraft perhaps stopping on the runway because of the hydraulic malfunction). During the handover of the Tu-22s to Iraq and Libya, the head of the Aviation Training Centre, Col Shukshin, would always be in attendance at the airfield, along with senior Soviet Air Force representatives, who would all return to the USSR on board an An-12 *Cub* transport after the ceremony.

The Tu-22s that were supplied to Iraq and Libya ended up being operated in almost identical conditions, both countries having approximately the same-sized population, with similar temperaments, character traits and social structures. Moreover, their geography was similar, with large desert areas and similar climatic conditions. The main operating base for the Iraqi Air Force Tu-22As was Habbaniyah, near the capital, Baghdad, and had two excellent main runways. The smaller fighter types based there were housed in hardened aircraft shelters (HAS), but the Tu-22s were kept in the open in sheltered hard standings, protected from the elements by special covers. The Libyan Air Force Tu-22As were based initially at Umm Aitiqah, close to the Mediterranean coast and near the capital, Tripoli, operating out of that airfield for a comparatively long time, until the middle of the 1980s. They were then transferred to a newly built airfield at Al Juffrah, some 600–700km (370–435 miles) south of the capital in the middle of the desert, which was also the base for a number of MiG-25 *Foxbats* (both interceptors and reconnaissance variants). The base was chosen because from here the Tu-22s (and the MiG-25s) could 'control' the entire territory of Libya, and it was also quite close to the border with Chad, with which Libya had had territorial disputes. Al Juffrah had been built by the Russians, and became operational in 1983 both as a military base and for civil airline services. On completion of the base, all the construction vehicles and machinery was dumped in a quarry on the edge of the airfield, because the Russians had been unable to sell the equipment to the Libyans and it would have been too expensive to return it to the USSR. The airfield had an excellent main runway, 3,000m (9,840ft) long, and both the runway and the taxiways were of cast concrete and were in excellent condition. The Tu-22s were parked in protected pens with high blast walls, while the MiG-25s were each housed in a HAS.

The group of Soviet advisers in Libya numbered from six to eight personnel, dependent upon the requirement of the time, and comprised a pilot, navigator and an airborne operator, plus technicians representing four engineering disciplines. (These were aircraft and engines, aircraft equipment, avionics and armaments.) A permanent interpreter was not attached to the group, but from time to time Russian students of Arabic from a military language institute in Russia would spend six months in Libya to improve their practical knowledge of the language. They would assist the group, but the absence of a permanent interpreter did not have an adverse effect on the work of the advisers, since many of the Libyan servicemen had a fairly good command of Russian, having completed some of their training in the Soviet Union. The advisory group worked six days a week in Libya, with Friday being observed as the Muslim holy day, each working day starting at 7 o'clock in the morning and finishing at 2 o'clock in the afternoon, in order to avoid the searing heat of the afternoon sun. The Soviet engineers worked mainly in the second-line servicing section (TEhCh), which occupied a large hangar capable of housing up to eight Tu-22s at any one time.

The hangar was erected at the same time as the airfield was being built, and was equipped with excellent diagnostic laboratories for checking aircraft systems, plus good lighting and air conditioning, not only of the laboratories, but also of the entire hangar space. Not a single Soviet Air Force regiment possessed such excellent engineering support facilities as this. However, all the equipment was gradually allowed to fall into disrepair: the electricity supply would periodically 'trip' off-line, the air conditioning would fail, water would leak from the pipes and rubbish and dirt was allowed to accumulate everywhere. The fact of the matter was that the Libyan servicemen did not like cleaning up and the women to whom such jobs would normally be given simply did not exist on the remote desert base. Outdoor servicing and maintenance was not performed at Al Juffrah, because of the heat, so if a malfunction occurred on one of the Tu-22s, it had to be towed to the TEhCh hangar, where personnel could work on it in more comfortable surroundings. The aircrew mess was also very well equipped and appeared quite unusual to the Soviet advisers: each room had an armchair and a bed and was also air-conditioned, and the colour of the background lighting could be switched between pink, red and green (!). There was also a bar where it was possible to purchase soft drinks.

The task of the Soviet instructor-pilot adviser was primarily to monitor the aircraft handling techniques of the Libyan pilots, using the Tu-22U *Blinder-D* trainer. Additionally, he would also be required to carry out flight tests on aircraft which had completed maintenance or repair work in the TEhCH unit on the base. The Soviet navigator-instructors assisted the Libyan navigators on the ground (in flight planning, etc.) and would occasionally fly with an Arab pilot, when required. The engineers mainly acted in the capacity of consultants, checking the work of the Arab personnel in preparing aircraft for flight, although in practice, they would perform the majority of the work themselves, particularly if it was a complex task. It was very difficult to get the Arab ground crew personnel to do any work or even teach them anything, and the Russian perception of them was that they were lazy. By the 1990s the Tu-22 had already gone beyond the guaranteed servicing period outlined by the Russians in the original contract, but the Iraqi and Libyan military always used to say, 'It's your equipment, you sold it to us. Now it's broken and you service it; you sort out the malfunction.' A typical example of their approach to work was described by one of the Soviet engineering advisers in Libya, Major Kostyetskii: 'I was working with a Libyan technician on the undercarriage control valve of one of their Tu-22s. I explained to him what had to be done and how to lock it. I asked him to bring me some locking wire and he went off and disappeared. I went looking for him and found him having a cup of tea. He told me that we should do it tomorrow!' The Arab officers had good technical knowledge, but only rarely put this knowledge into practice. In Iraq and Libya it was the senior non-commissioned officers (NCO) and other ranks who actually worked on the aircraft and in both countries it was considered more fitting for an officer to sit in a comfortable office, drinking coffee and smoking. In fact, the officers ordered their subordinates to do work, without actually checking what they were doing and how they were doing it, believing that working on aircraft was beneath their dignity – the task of the officer was to manage and supervise!

Unfortunately, the Arab junior ranks in both the Iraqi and the Libyan Air Force had very poor technical knowledge and skills, so the Soviet advisers tried at first to conduct themselves very much as pure consultants, passing on their knowledge and experience to the Arab ground crews. There were times, however, when things got out of hand and almost led to conflict! At the end of the 1980s, a Soviet engineer-adviser had decided to show some Arab technicians how to charge and service the accumulators used by the Tu-22. The Russian engineer suggested that the Libyan technicians should start the work, but they all refused, stubbornly claiming that everything should be done by the Russians on the base. An argument ensued and after a short time the Soviet engineer and the head of the Soviet advisory group were summoned to see the Libyan base commander. In the office with him were the chief engineering officer of the base and the head of base security. The Russian engineer was told that if any one of the Soviet advisory group did not wish to carry out any servicing tasks himself, then the Libyan authorities could have him sent back to the USSR within 24 hours. The rules were harsh. In the end, the head of the Soviet advisory group explained to his team that it would be better to do the work themselves so that they could continue to work in the country. Consequently, the Russian engineers started to change engines, perform engine checks on the ground, replace LRUs (line replaceable units) etc. The Arab 'specialists' would be present when this work was being done, but more in the capacity of 'waiters', carrying screwdrivers and spanners etc., a task with which the Arabs were quite happy.

There were other incidents, too. Again, in the 1980s one of the Libyan NCOs had begun to annoy a Russian engineer with his lazy attitude. The Russian ended up shouting at the Libyan because of his poor work, and he responded by stabbing the Russian in the thigh with a screwdriver! His injury was stitched and the Libyan was sent to work in one of the messes on secondary duties, and then later put on guard duty at the check-point controlling entry on and off the base. His duties were to stand on his own outside the guard hut, which in any case did not have air conditioning or electricity, raising and lowering the barrier for vehicles coming and going between the base and the local town.

However, he nursed a terrible grievance! A little while later, a group of Soviet advisers was passing through the check-point about 3-4 minutes before the official cease-work time. This same NCO opened the barrier, letting the Russian's vehicle pass through, then slipped his automatic weapon off his shoulder and fired off several rounds over the top of the vehicle. The Russians stopped and the Libyan NCO pointed to his watch and explained to them that they were leaving the base early! The vehicle reversed behind the barrier and precisely at 14.00 hours the NCO raised it again, allowing the Russians to drive on, warning them that next time he would fire straight at them, as per his instructions!

Indiscipline was not the sole province of the NCO and other ranks, and the officers would occasionally find themselves on the receiving end of harsh punishment. An established feature of Soviet Air Force operation of the Tu-22 was that after a long period of leave a pilot would carry out a number of check flights with an instructor on the Tu-22U as part of a specially organised refresher programme. In Libya, the fixed base KTS-22 (*Kompleksnyi Trenazhor Samolyota-22*) procedural simulator for the Tu-22, which would also be used in this programme, had been out of commission for some time. The Soviet advisory group did not include a KTS-22 specialist and the Libyan technicians were unable to repair it. As a consequence, the Tu-22 squadron commander, Colonel Khaled, told a pilot returning from a long period of leave (at the end of the 1980s) that he would have to carry out two check flights on the Tu-22U with a Soviet instructor and another check flight on one of the Tu-22As, before returning to normal squadron operations. However, after performing the two check flights, the Libyan pilot said that he was not yet ready to fly the Tu-22A and that he would still need a few more flights on the Tu-22U. Colonel Khaled was an officer with a fairly uncompromising attitude towards duty, and as a punishment for failing to carry out his order, he sentenced the pilot to two days in detention. The detention centre, or *talavush* as it was called, was located on the base, and the pilot, having sat out his punishment there, agreed immediately to fly the Tu-22A!

Such punishments were quite frequent in the Libyan Air Force, and engineering adviser Major Kostyetskii was witness to another example of the harshness of Libyan military discipline. He was working in the large TEhCh hangar at the base, and recalls an incident involving a sergeant engine fitter, who was a Palestinian immigrant. He was a very bad worker and after Major Kostyetskii had told him to adjust a control unit on one of the engines of a Tu-22 undergoing maintenance, the sergeant returned a little later saying that he had done it. He asked him if he had really finished the job, and received an affirmative reply, but the Russian engineer did not believe him. Major Kostyetskii climbed up onto the servicing platform, opened the engine cover and saw that the unit had not been touched. He asked the sergeant if he realised what he had done and that it could have led to an accident. This was the second time that this particular sergeant had deceived him, so he went straight to the man's superior officer, Captain Mohammed, and reported what had happened. The officer told the sergeant that he was under arrest, and drove him straight from the TEhCh to the base detention centre. When the adviser group was leaving the base after work that day they saw the sergeant standing outside in the exercise yard of the detention centre. He was stripped to the waist and on his knees, with his hands held behind his head while an armed guard stood alongside him under an awning, reading from the Koran. Detainees were held like this until they fainted, whereupon they would be taken inside, doused with water to bring them round and then taken outside again into the blazing sun. Their punishments were brutal.

However, even with the harshness of some of their punishment regimes, there were strange anomalies, such as the case of a Libyan pilot who had always had problems with landing the Tu-22, and on one occasion had landed with the brakes on, bursting all the tyres. The aircraft ran off the runway to the left and came to a halt about 100–200m (about 300–600ft) from the edge of the concrete surface, stuck in the sand. If this had happened in the USSR, the pilot would have had money taken out of his salary to pay for the damage, but senior Libyan Air Force officers decided that it was the fault of the Tu-22's design, in spite of the overwhelming evidence that it was pilot error. It took two days to haul the aircraft out of the sand and back onto the runway, after which it was checked for damage and deemed to be serviceable. It was even stranger to the Russian group that the squadron's senior officers had obviously approved the calling of a general parade at which the pilot was presented with a 1,000-dinar award by the Base Commander for having saved his valuable aircraft!

A point worthy of attention for the reader is the 'suspiciousness' with which the Arabs (both Iraqi and Libyan) would treat newly arrived Soviet advisers in their midst. As soon as a new contingent arrived on the base, the Arab officers would immediately start to test their knowledge and professional ability, albeit always somewhat surreptitiously. The Arab specialists would pose rather tricky questions and seek the answers to rather complex problems, just so that they might trip up the Russians, probably with the objective of causing embarrassment. The Russians however, were, prepared for this, having been briefed on the subject on special short courses in the Soviet Union. The courses were organised by the 10th Main Directorate of the Ministry of Defence for officers who had been appointed to so-called 'special assignments'. A 'special assignment' was generally understood to be service as an adviser in a foreign country 'friendly' to the USSR. The courses were intended to provide a background cultural briefing on the country, local customs, population, traditions and the rules of behaviour for foreigners, etc.

Arab engineers were very good at coping with 'standard' situations with regard to operating the Tu-22. They could successfully prepare an aircraft for flight, such as performing preliminary, pre-flight and post-flight checks, refuelling the aircraft, changing tyres, packing the brake parachutes and carrying out engine start-ups. Apart from this, they could also deal with a limited number of other 'standard' situations, but all Arab engineering personnel had one common failing – they could not deal with anything which was out of the ordinary. As soon as some kind of unusual malfunction occurred, however small, which required them to think, then they would disappear, afraid to do anything, and leave everything for the Soviet engineers to sort out. It was hardly surprising, therefore, that after the Soviet advisers left Iraq and Libya in 1992, Tu-22 operations in both countries' air forces also ceased at around the same time. Major Kostyetskii, one of the most experienced of the Soviet engineering advisers, was in Libya at the beginning of the 1990s, when the Libyans had been operating the Tu-22A for fifteen years, and worked with Lt (later Captain) Mohammed, the head of second-line maintenance in the TEhCh. Lt Mohammed had been involved with the Tu-22 since its delivery to Libya in 1975 and was therefore very experienced on the aircraft. A problem had arisen with the controls of one of the Tu-22s, and Major Kostyetskii and Lt Mohammed had to rebalance the rudder on the aircraft.

This was a very familiar task for Major Kostyetskii, and he started to carry out the work in his normal way. Lt Mohammed immediately told him that that was not the way it should be done, and no amount of explanation would convince him otherwise. He simply replied that he was not taught to do the job that way. Major Kostyetskii placed the aircraft operating manuals on the table. The manuals were written in Russian, Arabic and English, and Kostyetskii pointed out to Mohammed where there was a mistake in the Arabic version. The Libyan still did not believe him, and insisted once again that he had not been taught that way. The rudder was eventually balanced in the manner in which Kostyetskii had insisted was correct, and the Soviet adviser pilot carried out a successful test flight, reporting that the control problem had been eradicated. Major Kostyetskii later asked Lt Mohammed which one of them had been right about the rudder balancing procedure, adding, perhaps a little too smugly, that it looked as if it had been him (i.e. Kostyetskii)! At this, the Libyan officer exploded in anger, and with his hand, swept the manuals off the table onto the floor. He picked up a copy of the Koran and said, 'Only this Book is correct!' He was very a very resentful individual and did not speak to Major Kostyetskii for six weeks after this event!

The hot, dry climate of Iraq and Libya was perfect for maintaining the Tu-22's electrical and avionics equipment in a serviceable condition, but did, on the other hand, create problems for the engines and hydraulic system. The fuel system leaked because of delamination of the rubber seals in the high ambient temperatures on the ground, and hydraulic fluid would leak from the brake pipes and the reservoirs. The Soviet engineers also considered that the locally supplied aviation kerosene was more toxic than that available in the Soviet Union and was highly corrosive. However, regiment ground crews in the USSR would not pay a lot of attention to such small (sic) problems, and would continue to operate the aircraft. In the Arab air forces, as soon as there was the first sign of a drip, their engineers would turn to the Soviet advisers and say, 'This aircraft cannot fly. Sort it out – it's your equipment!'

During the 1991 Gulf War, the Libyan government decided to relocate all its aircraft to bases offering more protection from possible pre-emptive attacks by the United States and Coalition air forces, so the Tu-22s were flown to Al Kufrah, on the border with Sudan. (The Iraqi Air Force had also flown a number of MiG-23B *Flogger-H* fighter bombers to this base for the same reason.) The Soviet advisers were not sent to Al Kufrah, and languished for three months at the main base at Al Juffrah, until the *Blinders* returned at the end of the war. However, one of the Tu-22As developed an engine problem, requiring a fuel pump to be replaced in the RD-7M2's turbo-starter (auxiliary power unit), as well as dealing with a cabin pressurisation failure. Soviet specialists were 'invited' to carry out the repairs on the aircraft and were flown to Kufrah on a Libyan Air Force Il-76 *Candid* transport. The Russian team actually comprised one Russian Tu-22 airframe and engine specialist and a pilot and navigator, who would carry out the subsequent test flight. The Russian engineer worked for two days on the aircraft, replacing the pump and carrying out an engine run to check that it was serviceable, and also dealt with the pressurisation problem. It turned out that the technicians had not protected the pressurisation seal valve with its special cover, and sand had entered the mechanism during a sand storm, preventing it from operating correctly. The Russian engineer cleaned and greased the valve and the system was declared safe for flight, after which the pilot and navigator carried out a post-maintenance test flight and signed off the Tu-22 as serviceable. (Sand storms were a particular problem in Libya, and even more so in Iraq.)

Soviet advisers were detached to Iraq and Libya for a period of two to three years, and in each country, the Russian personnel lived in a small 'township' on the edge of the base.

At Al Juffrah, it was about 5–6km (about 3 or 4 miles) outside the base and was often referred to as the 'reservation'. It was surrounded by a fence, and entry was controlled by a military check-point, since the Arab officers and their families also lived there. The officers lived with their families in detached houses comprising a pair of two-roomed air-conditioned apartments, with two fridges, a shower and a bathroom. Living conditions were good. Initially, the Soviet officers were unaccompanied, but their families were able to join them after six months. The Russian advisers and their families could go into the local towns on Fridays, the Muslim holy day, to buy provisions at the market. There were two small towns about 18–20km (about 11 or 12 miles) from Al Juffrah – Khun and Uaddan, both of around 30,000 population, but the base was considered to be the worst place to be in Libya because of its distance from the sea. For the Libyan officers it was like a form of exile, since they all had apartments and houses in the bigger cities, so they were allowed to serve at Al Juffrah on a rotational basis. They would serve for six months at Al Juffrah, and then go on leave for three months, before returning for another six-month period, and so on. After two years of their stay in Libya, the Soviet advisers would be allowed to go to Sirt, on the Mediterranean coast, two or three times a year for two or three days at a time for 'recuperation and relaxation' (R&R). Sirt also housed a Soviet advisory group of PVO (*Protivo-Vozdushnaya Oborona*) specialists attached to the Libyan coastal air defence organisation, and the officers and families from Al Juffrah would stay with their PVO colleagues during their short seaside holiday.

Although the Tu-22 did not participate in actual offensive combat operations in Soviet service, both the Iraqi and Libyan Air Force *Blinders* were used in so-called local conflicts with contiguous states. In the late 1970s and early 1980s the political situation in Central and North Africa had become particularly tense, and Libya had been secretly supporting a group of militants in neighbouring Chad, opposed to the government there. Additionally, Libya had provided military assistance to Uganda, which at the time was involved in a long-drawn-out and unsuccessful conflict with Tanzania. This had subsequently drawn the Libyan Air Force into the fray with the decision to test its Tu-22s in the *Blinder's* first-ever offensive bombing operation. At the end of March 1979 a pair of Tu-22As carried out a bombing raid on the Tanzanian town of Mwanza, the country's second largest city, which lies on the southern shore of Lake Victoria. The city might have been selected as the target for this first offensive raid simply because it happened to be at the extreme limit of the range of the Tu-22A operating out of the main base for the Libyan Air Force *Blinders* at the time – namely Umm Aitiqah, near Tripoli. In the following year, Libya's attention was focused on Chad, where a civil war had broken out between forces led by President Goukouni Oueddei and the French-backed forces of Hissène Habré. Libya had openly declared its support for the insurgents in this conflict, and the Tu-22As carried out episodic bombing raids against concentrations of troops loyal to the government. It was also decided to relocate the Tu-22s to Kufrah, near the border with Sudan, in order to extend the radius of action of the *Blinder* against targets in Chad.

The Libyans' use of the Tu-22A in combat was not very effective, compounded by the fact that the Libyan aircrews had little or no experience of how to get the best out of the aircraft as a weapons system. At the Aviation Training Centre at Zyabrovka, they had been taught how to fly the aircraft, but not how 'to go to war' with it. The Soviet instructors had only had limited time to show the Arab pilots how to bomb with the Tu-22, and on their return to Libya, the crews virtually ceased to be involved in any kind of weapons training. The Libyan Air Force did not even operate a bombing range, where the Tu-22 crews could hone their professional abilities in weapons applications. The insurgents' campaign in Chad was a failure, and Libya signed a ceasefire agreement in 1981, although both sides realised that it would probably not hold for long, and Libya used this period to strengthen its influence in the border regions. This also led to the decision to construct the large base at Al Juffrah for Tu-22 operations, described elsewhere in this chapter. Having recovered from the losses of the previous year, the insurgent group rekindled the conflict in Chad with renewed vigour, and the war continued, with short breaks for negotiations, until the second half of 1983. Throughout this time the Libyan Tu-22s continued to carry out raids over the entire territory of Chad, albeit with limited success, until September 1983, when, under international pressure, yet another ceasefire was signed. Then, in 1984, a border conflict arose between Libya and Sudan after the latter had declared its support for Chad in these regional disputes, and in March of that year a Libyan Tu-22A bombed Sudan's second largest city, Omdurman, in reprisal. Epitomising the fickle nature of African regional politics, Libyan Air Force Tu-22s were then used on behalf of the new government which came to power in Sudan in 1985, carrying out attacks on targets in southern Sudan to suppress an anti-government revolt.

Meanwhile, on Libya's southern borders, peace only reigned in northern Chad until the beginning of 1986, and on 17 February of that year a single Tu-22A carried out a bombing raid on the airport serving the Chadian capital, N'djamena, hitting the main runway. The Tu-22A dropped three FAB-500 high-explosive bombs in what was a completely unexpected attack for the government troops. On this occasion, Libyan support for the rebels was so blatant that France decided to send a contingent of troops to support the government of Chad. However, the Tu-22As continued to participate in combat activity right up to the ceasefire in September 1987. In spite of intensive operations, the Libyan Air Force lost only two Tu-22As in combat, shot down by Crotale surface-to-air missiles, although this could be put down more to the comparative weakness of Chadian forces than any skill on the part of the Libyan pilots.

By contrast with the 'wartime' sortie rate, Libyan Air Force peacetime Tu-22 flight operations were not particularly intensive and were usually only conducted twice a week. Invariably this only involved one or two aircraft at a time, occasionally, albeit very rarely, three. Flights would only involve a single flying programme, or 'shift' (*smena*), and there was never any night flying, in spite of suggestions by the Soviet advisers and their

Two Libyan Air Force Tu-22As photographed over the central Mediterranean Sea in 1977 by a USN VF-111 F-4N Phantom from the carrier USS *Franklin D Roosevelt*. Wearing the Libyan Air Force's original national markings, it is likely that the Blinders were on delivery as part of the second batch of four aircraft acquired to augment the five delivered in 1975. *US Navy*

Photograph and signed expression of gratitude in Arabic on the reverse after the successful first solo on the Tu-22 by a Libyan Air Force Pilot in May 1975. *S Burdin Archive*

علیہ معقوظ بولغ

ربی اول طلعتہ فرادی پار ثالہ الدوشیتی

الا الطلعہ نو "ٹی ریورس"

یم ی

7/5/1975.

willingness to organise this. Flights were conducted in the early morning hours, when the ambient air temperature was not too high. By the 1990s, the Tu-22A was already a very old aircraft, and many pilots wanted to move on from this once prestigious bomber to something more modern. Many former Tu-22 pilots in the Libyan Air Force transferred to the Il-76 *Candid* transport fleet, which was considered by them to be an advancement! Once a year, the Iraqi and Libyan Air Force Tu-22s were flown to the USSR for repair and maintenance work at the Ryazan' Aviation Repair plant. Here they would undergo a major overhaul and be repainted in the relevant camouflage colours of the country of operation. In the case of the Libyan Tu-22A, this was a two-tone green scheme, with the large green Libyan Air Force roundel under the cockpit area and a smaller Libyan flag on the fin. On their return flight from Ryazan' the Libyan *Blinders* would make an intermediate landing at Benghazi on the Mediterranean coast, before flying on to their desert base at Al Juffrah.

The Iraqi Air Force Tu-22As had their main baptism of fire in the Iran–Iraq War of 1980–1988, by which time the Iraqi Tu-22 crews had accumulated seven years of operations with the Russian bomber. However, as with the Libyans, the Russian military advisers in Iraq did not feel that the Iraqis were capable of putting this knowledge to effective use. All the Iraqi *Blinder* pilots had an extremely high opinion of themselves, bolstered by the fact that aviation was always Saddam Hussein's favourite branch of service and the Tu-22 was regarded as Iraq's prestige weapon. The pilots were very proud of the fact that their exploits with the aircraft were always reported immediately to the leader. The Russian advisers felt that the Iraqi Tu-22 crews held the mistaken view that after graduating from the Aviation Training Centre at Zyabrovka, they no longer needed to improve their knowledge of the aircraft, or their handling skills. Clearly this was going to have a negative impact on the results of their combat activity. The range of the Tu-22A was sufficient to allow the aircraft to operate over the entire territory of Iran, so specially

An interesting study of a Libyan Air Force Tu-22A, demonstrating the elegant lines of the aircraft and the 'area ruling' of the mid and rear fuselage region. The underside was painted in pale duck-egg blue and the upper surfaces were thought to be finished in light and dark sand. *US Navy*

important targets were assigned to the *Blinder* squadron, and after the commencement of hostilities in September 1980, several raids were carried out on Teheran and Isfahan. These were probably intended to undermine the morale of the Iranian population rather than cause significant military damage.

Iran, however, turned out to be a very serious opponent, and it is possible that one of the Tu-22As was either damaged or destroyed as early in the conflict as 23 September 1980, although this remains unconfirmed. Iran's extensive and effective air defences quickly forced the Iraqis to reduce the intensity of operations with the Tu-22A. Nevertheless, attacks were still planned against the capital, Teheran, albeit with fighter escorts, and although the Russian advisers did not participate in combat operations they did try to offer suggestions about the best way to employ the Tu-22 in combat.

The Iraqi Air Force leadership paid scant attention to this advice. During combat operations, the Tu-22As also changed their main operating base, using Balad airfield, located around 70km (44miles) north of Baghdad, in addition to Habbaniyah. Western mass media also reported that Iraqi Tu-22As also used airfields in Saudi Arabia and Yemen between sorties. [*There is at least one reliable eye witness account of an Iraqi Tu-22 landing at Sana'a airport in Yemen during this period.* AD]. Another of the reasons for the reduced intensity of operations by the Tu-22A against Iran in 1982-83 was the reduction in the number of trained aircrew available to fly the aircraft. This was caused by promotions within the first batch of crews trained in 1973 and, according to Iranian sources, losses sustained by the Tu-22A squadron in combat. It was probably for these two reasons that a second group of Iraqi Tu-22 crews underwent training at Zyabrovka in 1983–84 and in the same period a number of *Blinders* were being cycled through the overhaul process at Ryazan'.

Since Iraq was still at war with Iran, the aircraft were flown back from Ryazan' in a different manner from normal, and this time it was decided that Iraqi pilots should collect the aircraft from the USSR. The handover took place at the end of 1984, with the last aircraft being handed over on 30 December. Crews from 290 ODRAP at Zyabrovka ferried the group of four aircraft from the repair plant at Ryazan' to Simferopol' airport on the Crimean Peninsula, a civilian airfield which had been selected as a 'neutral' location for the handover of the Tu-22s to the Iraqi Air Force crews. The entire airport was swarming with KGB agents, whose express purpose was to reduce to a minimum any contacts between the Iraqi and Russian pilots! Lt-Col Yerusenko, one of the squadron commanders of 290 ODRAP, recalls an event relating to the handover of the Iraqi Tu-22s at this time: "Security concerns had been taken to absurd lengths. Some time before the ferry flight to Simferopol' I had spoken to a representative from the special KGB department attached to 290 ODRAP, requesting permission to speak to the Iraqis when we handed the aircraft over. The KGB officer duly granted permission, and when I met up with one of the Iraqi pilots at Simferopol' Airport whom I had taught at Zyabrovka, we went up to the restaurant on the second floor of the terminal building, simply to sit and have a cup of coffee. I couldn't believe what an uproar I'd started! The KGB were thrown into a panic and started photographing us! When I returned to base, the rest of the regiment had already been told about my 'meeting', but since I had already requested permission in advance, this did not reflect badly on my future service.'

The Iraqi aircrews made a lasting impression on the Soviet instructors, and the pilots from 290 ODRAP who had been attached to the Aviation Training Centre to teach them how to fly the Tu-22 remember them for their odd character traits. They would always

All that remained of an Iraqi Air Force Tu-22U at Habbaniyah after an air raid during the first Gulf War in January 1991. It is not clear whether the damage was caused by Coalition forces, or whether the aircraft was destroyed by the Iraqis themselves. *Photo courtesy Aviation News*

Once the pride of the Iraqi Air Force during the time of Saddam Hussein, this Tu-22U presents a forlorn sight here in the sheltered revetment at Habbaniyah after an attack during the first Gulf War in 1991. Although fitted with a cut-down AAR probe, Iraq did not possess an in-flight refuelling capability for its *Blinder* fleet, this being a relic of its former Soviet service. *Photo courtesy Aviation News*

take everything very much to heart, like a child, and if they were criticised for their mistakes they would almost start to cry. There was also a very rigidly observed 'pecking order' in the Iraqi military, which was even evident in the way a crew would occupy the seats on the coach taking them to and from the airfield. The commander would always be in the first seat, followed by the next senior rank down and so on, until reaching the rearmost seats, which were occupied by the most junior-ranking person, on the coach. There was never an occasion when someone would sit in another's seat, even if it was

The sad end for the vast majority of the Tu-22s which were still in service after the demise of the Soviet Union – only six of the 104 aircraft sent to the 6213 Aircraft Disposal Base at Engel's for scrapping have been preserved as museum exhibits. *Aleksandr Ignatov Archive*

empty for the entire journey. Everyone knew that today he would be sitting in 'this particular seat', but tomorrow 'he might be promoted' and he could then move one place up in the bus! They also had a calmly fatalistic view about the death of a comrade in an accident, and always used the same explanatory phrase – 'Allah gives and Allah takes.'

From 1985, after a new batch of crews had been trained on the Tu-22A, the aircraft was once again sent into action against Iran. The *Blinders* were used mainly to carry out raids on key oil refineries and major military objectives in the Persian Gulf, but were also sometimes used to attack oil-laden Iranian tankers departing the Gulf. The static 'positional warfare' between Iran and Iraq had brought neither side any particular advantage in the five years of conflict, and it was perhaps for this reason that the Iraqi leadership decided to start bombing the Iranian capital, Teheran, along with Isfahan and Shiraz. From May of 1985, the Iraqi Air Force started to use the Tu-22A in raids on Teheran and other population centres – a phase of the war called 'The War of the Cities'. The tactic of total bombardment of the cities sometimes met with condemnation even among the Iraqi aircrews, and there is at least one recorded incident when a Tu-22A navigator, Captain Ismail, was summarily executed in front of his comrades for refusing to bomb an Iranian city. Raids by the Tu-22A on the major Iranian cities were always met with intensive anti-aircraft defensive activity, and a number of aircraft were damaged or destroyed, although precise and reliable figures are still not available. It has to be admitted, however, that the Arab pilot, unlike his Russian counterpart, did not think of his aircraft as though it were a 'living' being, considering, quite justifiably, that the 'life of a pilot is worth more than a machine'. Where a Soviet pilot in the majority of cases would

Many Tu-22 technicians did not care for the aircraft much and the legend on this Tu-22K perhaps sums up their feelings: 'Thank God they have gone! This was painted by the ground crew of 121 TBAP's second squadron (2 *Aviatsionnaya* **Ehskadril'ya**) before the aircraft was transferred to Engel's for scrapping. *S Burdin Archive*

struggle to the last second to save his aircraft, an Arab pilot would choose to save his own life.

The Tu-22As were flown on combat operations right up to the end of the war in 1988, but the tactics employed by the Iraqi Air Force, and the tasks assigned to their crews, did not allow the full potential of the aircraft to be realised. By the outbreak of the First Gulf War – Operation *Desert Storm* – in January 1991, the Tu-22A had virtually been withdrawn from the combat strength of the Iraqi Air Force, because of the lack of spares resulting from the UN embargo on Iraq and proper servicing by Iraqi ground crew. It has to be said that the Iraqi and Libyan Air Forces are not thought to have developed a soundly reasoned operational plan for their Tu-22 fleets, perhaps relying more on the aircraft's deterrent effect than using it as the offensive weapons delivery system it was designed to be. The modicum of success which the Tu-22 did have in Iraqi and Libyan service was disproportionately small compared to its acquisition and operating costs and similar results could probably have been achieved with equal effect using the many fighter bombers which both countries possessed. The inescapable conclusion is that the Tu-22 served the interests of the Iraqi and Libyan leadership more for prestige purposes than to prosecute a clear military policy for the offensive employment of a supersonic medium bomber force. Knowing now the destructive potential of the aircraft, the regional neighbours of Iraq and Libya have reason to be thankful that this was the case when they came under attack by the Tu-22 in the 1970s and 1980s.

Appendix

Main Technical Data for the Tu-22K *Blinder-B* with Dobrynin RD-7M2 engines and flexible undercarriage mounting –Data provided in the Technical Description of the aircraft published in 1966.

Description	Without Kh-22 missile	With Kh-22
Performance		
Maximum speed at a weight of 73.5 tonnes (162.040lb)		
in max dry thrust at 10,000m (32,800ft)	1,050kph	1,035kph
In maximum reheat at 10,000m (32,800ft)	1,480kph	1,380kph
In maximum high-altitude reheat at 11,000m (36,090ft)	1,610kph	1,550kph
Cruising speed:		
Subsonic		950–1,000kph
Supersonic		1,200–1,300kph
Range with Kh-22 missile and 5% fuel reserves for landing, cruising at 950–1,000kph (513–540kts) – for take-off weight of 92 tonnes (202,820lb)		4,400km
at supersonic speed 1,300kph (702kts) and take-off weight 92 tonnes		1,560km
with in-flight refuelling *en route* to target (subsonic)		6,150km
Missile launch range		400–500km
Radius of action of K-22 system at normal take-off weight of 92 tonnes:		
at subsonic cruising speed of 950–1,000kph		2,500–2,700km
at supersonic cruising speed of 1,300kph		1,100–1,300km
Maximum endurance carrying a Kh-22 missile at normal take-off weight of 92 tonnes		4.5–5 hours
Cruise altitude at supersonic cruising speed of 1,300kph – for take-off weight of 92 tonnes:		
at top of climb (horizontal flight)		10,100m
over target before missile launch		11,200m
after launch	12,200m	
at end of flight	13,300m	
Cruise altitude at subsonic speed of 950–1,000kph – for take-off weight of 92 tonnes:		
in horizontal flight		8,600m
over target before missile launch		10,000m

Description	Without Kh-22 missile	With Kh-22
after launch	10,800m	
at end of flight	11,800m	
Practical ceiling in region of target - for a weight of 73.5 tonnes:		
maximum dry thrust		10,600m
in maximum reheat	13,300m	12,950m
Time to climb to 8,000m (26,250ft) at maximum dry thrust for take-off weight 92 tonnes		13.5 mins
Time to climb to 9,000m (29,530ft) at take-off weight of 85 tonnes		10.5 mins
Radius of turn at 73.5 tonnes in region of target:		
at M0.9 at 10,000m		5.7m
at 1,300kph at 11,000m		10km
Maximum permitted angle of bank		50 degrees
Minimum permitted speed at sea level at take-off weight 92 tonnes		430kph
Minimum permitted speed at sea level at take-off weight 85 tonnes		407kph
Permitted wind gusts in subsonic cruise		10m/sec
Take-off run:		
at take-off weight 92 tonnes and unstick speed 412kph, flaps 25° in full reheat		2,700m
Take-off run in full reheat at 94 tonnes (207,230lb) using SPRD-63 rocket boosters (with flaps at 14°)		1,550–1,750m
Take-off run at 85 tonnes (187,390lb) with an unstick speed of 395kph (213kts) and flaps at 25° in full reheat		2.250m
With SPRD-63 rocket boosters at take-off weight of 85 tonnes and flaps at 14°		1,420m
Landing run at maximum landing weight of 65 tonnes (143,300lb) and touchdown speed of 330kph (178kts) using brakes and brake parachutes		1,900m
Maximum turn radius on ground:		
under tow		15m
under own power		13m

Description	Without Kh-22 missile	With Kh-22
Maximum indicated and limiting airspeeds established by the Design Bureau for operating the aircraft equipped with the flaperon control system:		
at heights from 0 to 8,000m (26,250ft)		960kph
at altitudes from 8,000m		1,060kph
limiting speed at all altitudes		Maximum speed at altitude plus 60kph
Maximum indicated and limiting speeds established by the Design Bureau for operating the aircraft, taking account of aileron reversal (using normal ailerons):		
at heights from 0 to 2,500m		850kph
at altitudes from 2,500m to 7,500m		800kph
at altitudes from 7,500m to 11,000m		850kph
at altitudes of 11,000m and higher the limiting Mach number was		1.4
Maximum indicated airspeed established by the Design Bureau for operating the aircraft on flaperon controls:		
at heights from 0 to 8,000m		960kph
at altitudes above 8,000m		1,060kph
Limiting airspeeds established by the Design Bureau for flight on flaperon controls:		
at heights from 0 to 8,000m		1,020kph
at altitudes above 8,000m		1,120kph
Maximum permitted g-loading		2
Maximum permitted g-loading on exit from steep spiral turn		2.5
Weight data, Centre of Gravity		
Normal take-off weight with SPRD-63 rocket boosters		94 tonnes
Normal take-off weight without SPRD-63 rocket boosters		92 tonnes
Weight of aircraft over target		73.5 tonnes
Maximum flight weight after in-flight refuelling		93.5 tonnes
Maximum fuel load (with fuel of 0.81 specific gravity)	42.9 tonnes	37.05 tonnes
Normal landing weight	56.5 tonnes	60 tonnes
Maximum permitted landing weight on concrete runway		65 tonnes
Weight of Kh-22 (AS-4 Kitchen) missile		5.7 tonnes
Permitted C-of-G limits with pitch damper engaged: FORWARD		
On take-off (undercarriage and flaps down)		35% MAC
In flight (undercarriage and flaps retracted)		30% MAC
On landing (undercarriage and flaps down)		30% MAC
REAR		
On take-off (undercarriage and flaps down)		39% MAC
In flight (undercarriage and flaps retracted)		40% MAC
On landing (undercarriage and flaps down)		40% MAC

Description	Without Kh-22 missile	With Kh-22

Engines

Type and number of engines — Two Dobrynin RD-7M2 turbojets

Take-off thrust at sea-level — 16,500kg

Specific fuel consumption — 2.05kg/kg thrust per hour

Thrust in maximum reheat at 11,000m and a True Airspeed (TAS) of 1,500kph Specific fuel consumption — 11,000kg / 2.25kg/kg thrust per hour

Airspeed limits in order to remain within permitted range of compressor blade self-oscillation at heights from 0 to 4,000m:

in ambient air temperature of +40°C and below — 1,020kph

in ambient air temperature of +40°C to +60°C — 910kph

Thrust to weight ratio at normal take-off weight — 0.3585kg/kg weight

Main Geometrical Data for Tu-22K *Blinder-B*

Overall dimensions

Wingspan — 23.646m (77.60ft)

Length of aircraft with IFR probe — 42.6m (139.76ft)

Height of aircraft on ground — 10.04m (32.94ft)

Fuselage

Length — 38.945m (127.77ft)

Maximum height of fuselage at Frame No. 33 — 2.689m (8.82ft)

Maximum width of fuselage at Frame No. 60 — 3.160m (10.37ft)

Maximum cross-sectional area of fuselage — 6.35m² (68.35sq ft)

Weapons bay door dimensions – length/width/height — 6.92/1.65/1.95m (22.7/5.41/6.4ft)

Wing

Wing area including leading-edge root extensions — 162.25m² (1,746.50sq ft)

Wing area without leading-edge root extensions — 151.25m2 (1,628sq ft)

Wing airfoil profile with 6% thickness/chord ratio:

at fuselage junction — P-60

at wing tip — SR-8

Root chord (theoretical) — 10.049m (32.97ft)

Chord at fuselage junction with leading-edge root extension — 11.067m (36.31ft)

Tip chord — 2.732m (8.96ft)

Aspect ratio (not including root extension) — 3.7

Taper — 3.68

Anhedral — −2.5 degrees

Wing sweep at quarter-chord line — 52 degrees 14 min 30 sec

Angle of incidence relative to the horizontal constructional
  axis of the fuselage (measured at fuselage junction)   + 1 degree

Ailerons

Overall area of ailerons   11.32m² (12.85sq ft)
Span of one aileron   4.160m (13.65ft)
Angles of deflection up/down   24/24 degrees

Flaps

Overall area of flaps   23.84m² (256.62sq ft)
Area of inboard flaps   14.04m² (151,13sq ft)
Area of flaperons   9.8m² (105.48sq ft)
Span of inboard flap   2.815m (9.24ft)
Span of flaperon   2.3m (7.55ft)
Maximum deflection angle of inboard flaps   35 degrees

Angle of deflection of flaperon:
Up   16°
Down   6°

Tailplane

Area   40m² (430.57sq ft)
Span   10m (32.80ft)
Airfoil profile (thickness/chord ratio 6%)   SR-7S-9
Dihedral of tailplane   5°
Angle of sweep at quarter chord line   55 degrees 8 min 22 sec

Angle of deflection:
Up   +1°
Down   −19°

Fin & Rudder

Area of fin   22.01m² (236.92sq ft)
Height of fin (from mounting point)   3.870m (12.7ft)
Airfoil profile (thickness/chord ratio 5%)   S11S-9
Angle of sweep at quarter chord line   50°

Undercarriage

Wheel base   14.465m (47.46ft)
Track   9.12m (29.92ft)
Angle of incidence of aircraft on parking area (measured
  between the horizontal construction line and the
  ground surface)   8 degrees 9 minutes

Main Technical Data for the Tu-22R *Blinder-C* with Dobrynin VD-7M engines – Data provided in the Technical Description of the aircraft published in 1966.

MAIN PERFORMANCE AND TECHNICAL DATA
Flight performance
1. Maximum speed over target at weight 69 tonnes:
   - In maximum dry thrust at an altitude of 10,000m 1,080kph
   - In maximum reheat at an altitude of 11,000m 1,410kph
   - In high-altitude maximum reheat (re-equipped with RD-7M2 engines) at an altitude of 11,000m, for aircraft with flaperons and flexible undercarriage mountings 1,640kph
2. Cruising speed:
   - subsonic 950–1,000kph
   - supersonic 1,300kph
3. Range (daylight variant) with 5% fuel reserves, plus 750kg for maintaining centre of gravity at less than or equal to 43% MAC (Mean Aerodynamic Chord) for landing:
   - at subsonic speed (950–1,000kph) at maximum take-off weight of 91 tonnes 5,650km
   at normal take-off weight of 85 tonnes 4,900km
   - at supersonic cruising speed
   at maximum take-off weight of 91 tonnes and 1,200kph 2,300–2,400km
   at normal take-off weight of 85 tonnes and 1,300kph 1,570km
   at maximum take-off weight of 91 tonnes and AAR *en route* to target 7,150km
   Range (night variant) with 10 FOTAB-250-216 flash bombs (2,160kg) and with 5% fuel reserves for landing, plus 750kg for maintaining centre of gravity at less than 43% MAC for landing:
   - at subsonic cruising speed (950–1,000kph):
   at maximum take-off weight of 91 tonnes 5,310km
   - at supersonic cruising speed:
   at maximum take-off weight of 91 tonnes and 1,200kph 2,100–2,200km
4. Maximum endurance (daylight variant) at speed of 950–1,000kph:
   at maximum take-off weight of 91 tonnes 6hrs 15min
   Maximum endurance (night variant) at 950–1,000kph:
   at maximum take-off weight of 91 tonnes 5hrs 50min
5. Cruising altitude at supersonic speed 1,200kph
   at maximum take-off weight of 91 tonnes:
   at beginning of flight 9,600m
   over target 11,000m
   at end of flight 12,800m
   Cruising altitude at subsonic speed of 950–1,000kph at maximum take-off weight of 91 tonnes:
   at beginning of flight 8,800m
   over target 10,500m
   at end of flight 12,000m
6. Practical ceiling in region of target at flight weight of 69 tonnes:
   in maximum dry thrust 11,100m
   in maximum reheat 13,500m
7. Time to climb to 9,000m in max dry thrust:
   at maximum take-off weight of 91 tonnes 19mins
   at normal take-off weight of 85 tonnes 15mins

8. Turn radius in region of target (at weight 69 tonnes):
    at subsonic speed (M0.9) at 10,500m   5.7km
    at supersonic speed (1,300kph) at 11,000m   10km
9. Maximum permitted angle of bank   50°
10. Permitted wind gust   10m/sec
11. Maximum permitted speed at sea-level:
    at maximum take-off weight of 91 tonnes   415kph
    at normal take-off weight of 85 tonnes   407kph
12. Take-off run at weight 91 tonnes and unstick speed 395kph:
    in maximum reheat (VD-7M engines)   2,830m
    with SPRD-63 boosters at weight of 93 tonnes   1,750m
13. landing run at landing weight of 55.4 tonnes
    landing speed of 290kph:
    using brakes   1,850
    using brakes and brake 'chute   1,300
14. Minimum turn radius on ground:
    under tow   15m
    under own power   13m
15. Maximum aileron reversal limiting speeds and Mach number:
    at heights from 0 to 2,500m (indicated)   850kph
    altitudes from 2,500m to 7,500m (indicated)   800kph
    altitudes from 7,500m to 11,000m (indicated) 850kph
    altitudes above 11,000m and more   Mach 1.4
16. Maximum permitted g-loading:
    at maximum take-off weight of 91 tonnes   2
    at normal take-off weight of 85 tonnes   2

Weight and Centre of Gravity Data
17. Weights:
    Maximum take-off weight without SPRD-63   91 tonnes
    Maximum take-off weight with SPRD-63   93 tonnes
    Normal take-off weight   85 tonnes
    Weight over target   69 tonnes
    Normal landing weight   55.4 tonnes
    Maximum landing weight for separate landings 65 tonnes
    Maximum fuel load (specific gravity 0.81) 48.5 tonnes
    FOTAB load in night variant:
      Normal 10 x FOTAB-250-216   2,160kg
      Maximum 22 x FOTAB-250-216   4,752kg
    Bomb load (as pure bomber):
      Normal   FAB-3000M-54   3,060kg
      Maximum FAB-9000M-54   9,413kg
18. Permitted C of G limits with pitch damper engaged:
    FORWARD
    On take-off (undercarriage and flaps down) 35% MAC
    In flight (undercarriage and flaps retracted) 30% MAC
    On landing (undercarriage and flaps down) 30% MAC
    REAR
    On take-off (undercarriage and flaps down) 39% MAC
    In flight (undercarriage and flaps retracted) 40% MAC
    On landing (undercarriage and flaps down) 40% MAC

Before fitting warning lights for the pitch damper system, aircraft had a limiting rearward centre of gravity on take-off of 37% MAC (Mean Aerodynamic Chord).

In certain cases, with increased awareness in handling the aircraft, it was permitted to land the aircraft with an operating pitch damper with a rearward centre of gravity of 43% MAC.

19. Engines – two VD-7M

20. Take-off thrust — 16,000kg
    SFC (specific fuel consumption) — 2kg/kg thrust/hr

21. Thrust in maximum reheat at altitude 11,000m
    at a speed of 1,500kph — 9,700kg
    specific fuel consumption (SFC) — 2.1kg/kg hr

22. Airspeed limits in order to remain within permitted range of compressor blade self-oscillation at heights from 0 to 4,000m:
    in ambient air temperatures up to +45°C — 850kph
    in ambient air temperatures from +45°C to +55°C — 750kph
    in ambient temperatures above +55°C — 700kph

Other characteristic values:

23. Wing loading:
    at maximum take-off weight of 91 tonnes — 602kg/m^2
    at normal take-off weight of 85 tonnes — 562kg/m^2
    with weight over target of 69 tonnes — 456kg/m^2

24. Thrust to weight ratio — 0.352kg thrust/kg mass

Index

Page numbers in *italics* refer to illustrations.